Growing and Propagating Wild Flowers

CAUTION

The National Park Service and the Blue Ridge Parkway supports and encourages the preservation of wildflowers. The methods in this book generally allow propagation without damage to the native stock. This is indeed a noble and pleasurable cause. However, except for edible fruits, nuts, and berries picked for personal consumption federal law prohibits the collection of any plant part, including seeds, in our national parks.

Gary Everhardt
Superintendent

Growing and Propagating Wild Flowers

by Harry R. Phillips

with contributions by Rob Gardner and
Charlotte A. Jones-Roe in collaboration
with the staff of the North Carolina
Botanical Garden

Edited by C. Ritchie Bell and Ken Moore

Illustrations by Dorothy S. Wilbur

The University of North Carolina Press
Chapel Hill and London

Library of Congress Cataloging in Publication Data

Phillips, Harry R.
  Growing and propagating wild flowers.

  Bibliography: p.
  Includes index.
  1. Wild flower gardening.   2. Plant propagation.
I. Moore, J. Kenneth.   II. Bell, C. Ritchie.   III. North
Carolina Botanical Garden.   IV. Title.
SB439.P48 1985   635.9′676   84-25734
ISBN 0-8078-1648-5
ISBN 0-8078-4131-5 (pbk.)

*To the Wednesday morning
propagation volunteers of
the North Carolina Botanical
Garden*

Contents

Foreword

For over three centuries the forests and woodlands of eastern North America provided much of the fuel, shelter, food, and medicine for the early colonial settlers and then for the needs and trade of a growing nation. The early trade cargos of plants and plant material from the New World were worth more than gold: lumber for buildings, boxes, chests, and cooperage; tall, straight, strong trees for the masts of sailing ships; fine woods, such as walnut and cherry, for furniture; a wide variety of herbs and drugs for medical use; and an array of showy native ornamentals for the gardens of Europe. Even today many millions of native plants are being dug each year to supply the growing demand for native species with horticultural, pharmaceutical, or homeopathic value. As the pressures of collection increase on the wild populations of these plants of commercial value, their conservation, and indeed their survival as part of the natural environment, becomes a valid concern, and it is this concern that fostered the highly successful native plant propagation program at the North Carolina Botanical Garden and, in turn, this book.

So long as the readily available supply lasts, the actual monetary cost of "foraged" roots, herbs, and wild flowers is minimal, and there is little fiscal incentive for commercial production. As the available populations of certain plants are "collected out" in one area after another, however, only commercial production can supply the market and, it can be hoped, allow the wild plant populations to reestablish in their native habitats to be enjoyed again by all.

Most of the more colorful, interesting, and commercially valuable wild flowers are our native perennials which, unfortunately, may take three to five years or more to reach maturity and flower. In addition, some species may have fairly simple, but nonetheless specific, soil, sun, and moisture requirements, and their seeds may have relatively complex dormancy systems which help insure reproduction and survival in nature but may pose some problems in horticultural material. It is not surprising, then, that these plants have, for the most part, remained "undomesticated."

However, over a decade of work with native species at the Botanical Garden has already shown that, as we suspected, the plants of a given native species are usually genetically, morphologically, and physiologically diverse. From this natural diversity comes the potential to "improve" the plants by selecting and breeding for those characteristics of greatest value in our gardens and in commercial propagation: more rapid germination of seed; faster maturity; larger flowers, or higher drug content in the pharmaceutical plants; and greater environmental tolerances. Although man first domesticated a few food plants over eleven thousand years ago, the scientific methodology developed over just the past century accounts for most of the greater yields in our agricultural plants and the greater beauty and utility of our horticultural plants. As grants and gifts become available for more research on native plants at such institutions as the Botanical Garden, the causes of both conservation and commerce can be realistically served.

By propagating native plants rather than "collecting" them, we become involved in "conservation through propagation," and because we still know so little about so many of our native plants, each gardener or grower can not only enjoy the beauty of native plants and the satisfaction that comes with participating in their conservation but also share in the pleasure of discovery.

C. Ritchie Bell

Acknowledgments

I am deeply grateful to the many people who helped in the preparation of this book and especially appreciative of the excellent contributions from my colleagues at the North Carolina Botanical Garden.

Much of the inspiration for this project comes from my long association with the members of the North Carolina Wild Flower Preservation Society; their keen interest in, and admiration for, North Carolina's native plants (and their truly wondrous potluck lunches and dinners) assisted in no small way with my introduction to the rich and varied flora of the Southeast. It was largely the work of Tom Shinn, past president of the society, and his wife, Bruce, and other members of the society that made possible the publication of the *North Carolina Native Plant Propagation Handbook*, which served as an excellent model for this book.

For specific sections that were contributed to the book, I extend thanks to these staff members of the North Carolina Botanical Garden: to Rob Gardner, Curator, for the outstanding section on carnivorous plants, for the section on planning and planting a perennial bed and the accompanying sample designs, for the chart of blooming dates, and for his many fine photographs that appear herein; to Charlotte Jones-Roe, Curator, for preparing the very informative section on ferns, for her helpful suggestions with the instructions for organizing a plant rescue, and for her fine photographs; and to Dot Wilbur, Program Coordinator, for all the illustrations that appear in these pages and for being so generous, supplying many of the specimen plants from her own lovely garden.

For their expert, thorough going-over of the final manuscript, I am indebted to C. Ritchie Bell, Director of the North Carolina Botanical Garden, especially for his clarification of my many muddled passages, his helpful suggestions in organizing the book's various elements, and his enduring support of the project, and to Ken Moore, Assistant Director of the North Carolina Botanical Garden and enthusiastic native plant gardener, for making this book possible in the first place through his patience and commitment to the "conservation through propagation" concept, for his helpful additions and correc-

tions in the text, for his fine photographs, and especially for his very fine recommendations regarding the uses in the garden for many of the plants under discussion here.

David Perry, my editor, has been enormously helpful and supportive of the project from its very beginning, providing a special patience and understanding and many timely comments regarding the book's organization and readability.

To these Botanical Garden staff members I am also most grateful: to Alan Johnson, Curator, for his knowledgeable recommendations and careful review of all phases of the propagation techniques described in part 2, and to Janie Leonard Bryan, Assistant Propagator, for providing recommendations, both valuable and innovative, regarding seed collection and cleaning techniques for many of the plants discussed and for her very competent work with our ongoing native plant propagation research program at the Garden.

I wish to express special thanks to Kendall Brown for her excellent renderings of perennial bed designs and for her advice with the section on pests and diseases; to John Shrader, wise beyond his years in the ways of raising wild flowers, for his help with the Gentians; to Patricia Gensel, Associate Professor of Biology at the University of North Carolina at Chapel Hill, for her thorough review of the section on ferns; to Larry Mellichamp, Professor of Biology at the University of North Carolina at Charlotte, for his review of the section on carnivorous plants; and to Paul Betz for helpful suggestions concerning style during the early going.

I wish to thank the Garden Club of North Carolina for their enthusiasm and ongoing efforts to promote the propagation of wild flowers by way of sponsoring the very successful Wild Flower of the Year Project in collaboration with the North Carolina Botanical Garden.

I am most thankful to Jori Hunken and David Longland of Garden in the Woods, Framingham, Massachusetts, both charged with fascination for the natural world, for answering with patience and sensitivity my endless stream of queries in the early days.

Finally, I express warmest thanks to Debbie Lawrence, Business Manager at the North Carolina Botanical Garden, for her friendship and unfailing support and abiding interest in the book, which were so important during its writing.

Growing and Propagating Wild Flowers

Introduction

On a seed-collecting trip several years ago we came to a halt above a wet mountain meadow. Below us lay the vivid red flowers of hundreds of Gray's Lilies bobbing above the meadow grasses. Once familiar in moist, sunny areas in the mountains, populations of Gray's Lily have been either completely eradicated or drastically reduced by development and agriculture. The area below us had remained intact only because the low area along the creek had been too wet to mow that season, and the plants had had an uninterrupted period of time in which to flower. After securing permission from the owner, we staked off a section of the meadow in which the plants were thickest to protect them from the mower. Returning later that summer, we were able to collect seeds from the plants in the staked area and begin propagation studies on *Lilium grayi*. That experience is typical of the many rewarding encounters with native plants that have become an important part of our program to develop practical alternatives to the "wild collection" of native plants for our gardens.

In the last few years the use of native plants in American gardens has increased dramatically. At the North Carolina Botanical Garden we receive an ever-increasing number of requests for information on growing and propagating a wide range of native species. Using native plants is no longer a rarified aspect of home gardening; gardeners everywhere are gaining an acceptance of and appreciation for the ornamental possibilities of their local flora. In addition, a growing number of professional landscapers are taking advantage of the possibilities offered by native plants in their designs. And, largely through the efforts of local garden clubs concerned with conservation, many civic beautification projects and public buildings now feature native plantings.

For far too long, however, we have relied on plants collected in the wild to furnish our gardens. Desirable but "difficult" species, such as the Trilliums, Bloodroot, and the Lilies, are typically acquired from commercial nursery concerns that offer "collected" stock. Indeed, the vast majority of commercially available wild flowers are removed from the wild, and fantastic numbers of plants are dug annually to satisfy the demand for wild species. We need not rely on collected material any longer, however, for most of the species collected from our natural areas are easily propagated in the backyard garden. All that is required of the gardener is an awareness of the usually modest propagation and cultivation requirements of the native species.

Many common wild flowers of roadside and field have been overlooked for use in our gardens, perhaps because they grow in such abundance, often in dry and barren soils. When given a chance, Yarrow and Blue-eyed Grass, for instance, make outstanding groundcovers in the garden and are especially attractive during the fall and winter months. Certain of our southeastern Goldenrods have long been admired by English gardeners for their usefulness in fall borders. Many plants that occur primarily in shaded areas in nature, such as Blue Star, Alumroot, Green-and-Gold, and *Coreopsis auriculata*, thrive in the garden when given a sunnier exposure. Clearly, there is still much to learn about the ornamental potential of our native plants; we just need to take a closer look.

This book is designed, first, to give you a thorough grounding in the fundamentals of gardening with native plant material and, second, to provide specific information on the propagation and cultivation of some one hundred genera of native plants. In the first section, "Cultivating Native Plants," we focus on the activities necessary to establish and maintain wild flowers in the garden. Special attention has been given to soil preparation, the vital first step, and to a general outline of the maintenance tasks involved in properly tending the wild flowers discussed here. Your understanding of their varied needs will be reflected in the vigor of the plants you are growing and in the overall quality of your garden. The advantages of distributing propagation activities over the course of the growing season are discussed in "Planting through the Seasons." From a practical horticultural standpoint, many wild flowers are best propagated during the summer and fall months and not just in spring, the season in which many of us concentrate our gardening energies. "Designing a Bed or

3

Border with Native Perennials" elaborates on a traditional method for displaying herbaceous perennials. The several examples, each in a different setting, show a few of the many possible combinations of wild flowers for your garden.

The second section, "Propagating Native Plants," is your "tool kit." In it you will learn how to equip yourself with procedures that will enable you to propagate and grow wild flowers at home. These include methods for collecting, cleaning, and storing wild flower seeds and pregermination techniques for "breaking" seed dormancy. In addition, step-by-step procedures for propagating native plants from seed and by asexual means are spelled out in this section. Finally, we give some general suggestions for controlling pests and diseases by maintaining a healthy and sanitary environment for your plants.

The third, fourth, and fifth sections, the heart of the book, provide specific propagation information for seventy-five selected wild flowers, a dozen or more of our native carnivorous plants belonging to four genera, and fifteen native ferns. We also treat numerous related species of the plants under discussion in less detail. The wild flower entries give particular attention to seed development and the appearance of both the fruit and seeds—information that will prove helpful when you are collecting mature seed, a necessary first step to propagating many native plants. Also included are clear-cut recommendations for propagating, caring for, and displaying your native plants. Most entries describe at least two methods for propagating the plant.

The appendixes include a guide to organizing your own "plant rescue," a production timetable for the species recommended here, a calendar of their blooming dates, and a recommended reading list.

Some of the propagation information found in the descriptions of particular wild flower species and in the production timetable is directed to nursery operators. This reflects our belief that increasing the general availability of propagated native plants is the critical step both in reducing the depredations of collectors and in increasing the horticultural use of native plants. By producing plants under efficient, controlled conditions, growers can introduce native plants into many different areas.

Much of the potential of the "conservation through propagation" movement rests with owners of nurseries and garden centers and their interest in producing quality plants of native species.

There is no mystery to setting up a large-scale production regime for most native species. In greenhouses and cold frames potted plants of salable size can be produced in just a few months. Many species which are field-grown require quart- and gallon-size containers six months from the time of sowing. Under the supervision of experienced propagators in a nursery setting, growing techniques for new species can easily be developed and refined.

Many botanical gardens, arboreta, and native plant societies have taken the lead in this kind of activity. Gardeners who want more information on working with native plants or want involvement with others engaged in the same activity should get in touch with their local organizations. Often these groups sponsor lectures and workshops to familiarize gardeners with the display potential of native plants and demonstrate helpful propagation techniques. Their newsletters sometimes feature native plants, discussing their merits and how to use them in the garden. While sources of propagated native plants remain scarce, some botanical organizations help fill the void by holding plant sales. The North Carolina Botanical Garden, for example, holds an annual wild flower sale and also provides seeds to its members and other interested gardeners. If your local garden or plant organization has no program on working with native plants, you could be instrumental in helping to start one.

Working with native plants invites experimentation. What *is* the best method for propagating *Penstemon smallii*? Seed, cuttings, or division? (Actually, all three are easy and reliable.) At what time of year should each procedure be performed? What are the plant's optimum growing conditions in the garden? Share your experiences with other gardeners. The sowing technique described for the Gentians, for example, was recommended by a local gardener who had tried it in his garden. The technique is now enthusiastically passed on to you, to be shared, we hope, with other gardeners.

Failures as well as successes are important in

determining appropriate techniques for handling a particular species. Experiment with plants in varied settings in the garden. Some of the best advice we have heard on this matter came from a noted Massachusetts wild flower gardener: "If a plant doesn't do well in one spot, try it somewhere else." She also urged us to "keep trying new things, because that's the fun of it." When we began our work with *Penstemon smallii* some years ago, we were impressed with its potential for use in the garden but puzzled by its tendency to rot just before flowering. In a conversation with a member of the American Penstemon Society our problem and its solution became clear. Most Penstemons require a soil with excellent drainage. We had planted *P. smallii* in a raised planting bed fortified with plenty of organic matter. Moisture retention is high in organic soils, a condition favorable to many plants but harmful to others, such as *P. smallii*. With this new information, we now add a shovelful of sand or coarse gravel to the planting soil when establishing new plants. We have also learned that *P. smallii* performs well in a gravel ditch with little or no maintenance!

There is a tremendous opportunity, and need, for original investigation in propagating certain native species. Although many wild flowers are readily increased by straightforward horticultural techniques, others require simple but specific treatment and present more of a challenge. For example, Columbine seeds germinate only when they are exposed to light in the seed flat, and the percentage of germination is higher after they have been given a moist chill for four weeks. Seeds of Butterfly Weed are quick to germinate—usually two or three weeks after sowing—but the plants often go into early dormancy or die during the next month. The fast-growing taproot can become pot-bound in as little as two to three weeks after the seedlings are transplanted. Root development needs to be checked weekly and seedlings stepped up to larger containers as needed. This kind of information, which can only be gained through experimentation, is crucial both for the home gardener and the nursery operator, whose concern is the large-scale production of plants by the most efficient techniques available.

Experiment with different combinations of wild flowers in your garden to create interest. Many native species are versatile in cultivation, and can be appropriate in naturalistic as well as formal settings: Boltonia, Joe-Pye-Weed, and Seashore Mallow are three good examples. Finally, try integrating native and exotic plants. The interesting possibilities are endless. In the garden all plants have their strong and weak points and winning features, and "native" and "exotic" are simply names.

Part 1. Cultivating Native Plants

Soil Preparation

The vigor and appearance of many wild flowers improve dramatically in cultivation, where they no longer have to compete for light, moisture and nutrients. Clumps of Green-and-Gold, for example, often exceed 18 inches in width and flower profusely in a sunny garden setting, while in their more shaded natural haunts plants are typically 6–8 inches across and produce many fewer flowers.

Among other factors, good soil must have a structure that insures proper air circulation, moisture retention, and drainage. Its texture should be friable, or crumbly to the touch. When a small amount is gently squeezed in the hand, it should neither compact into a ball nor break down entirely and become powdery. If your soil is naturally clayey or sandy, you will need to improve it by adding organic matter. Plan to prepare your beds two to three months before planting in them to allow the soil time to settle. To control weeds during the settling period, put down a mulch 4 to 6 inches deep.

Most wild flowers establish rapidly in a well-prepared soil. Although these general recommendations for soil preparation are sufficient for most of the species discussed here, some plants will benefit from specific alterations to the soil, as indicated in the instructions for cultivation in the descriptions of particular species.

For example, certain wild flowers of roadside and field, such as the Rudbeckias, Queen Anne's Lace, and the native Sunflowers, develop weak, rangy stems that tend to topple at flowering time when planted in rich soils high in organic content. These plants should be naturalized or established in poorer, mineral soils. If used as a border planting, they will need to be staked. Other wild flowers, such as the Mulleins, Butterfly Weed, and Bird-foot Violet, require well-drained soils. You may need to amend the prepared soil with additional sand, gravel, or other material that drains well to accommodate these species.

On the other hand, some woodland wild flowers, such as Umbrella Leaf, Jack-in-the-Pulpit, and Turtleheads, require constantly moist soil during the growing season. Add generous amounts of rotted leaves and peat moss to the soil to better retain moisture or plan to naturalize these plants in low, wet areas. Other shade-loving perennials, like Deciduous Wild Ginger, Toothwort, and the Phacelias, have rhizomes or roots running just below the surface of the soil and benefit from several applications of a leaf mulch during the year to help conserve moisture and enrich the soil.

The native soils in some areas of the country are especially clayey; that is, they are composed of soil particles tightly bonded, making drainage less than adequate for many herbaceous plants. Clayey soils retain excessive amounts of moisture during wet periods, and some plants may rot. In addition, these soils are often deficient in oxygen, which is necessary for healthy plants.

The best way to work with very clayey soils is to plant on them, not in them, by using raised beds instead. Turn over the clay soil with a spade or tiller and on top of it begin building up your bed with a prepared soil mix. The soil can be safely raised to a height of 2 feet without need for support. To stabilize the bed press a board or section of plywood against the sides and ends to form an angle sloping away from the bed. Next, use a garden rake to smooth the edges and round the corners. Over the next couple of months, your soil will settle at least 6 inches, further stabilizing the bed.

If you wish to raise the soil level more than 2 feet, the bed should be bordered for support. Railroad ties, landscape timbers, rocks, and treated boards are materials commonly used for this purpose. Because the soil in raised beds drains well, additional watering may be necessary during dry spells. Another advantage to raised beds—particularly those raised to 3 feet or higher—is that less stooping is required to maintain the bed.

Double digging is another technique for preparing planting beds. The deeper soil permits roots more room to travel—another safeguard against summer drought—and no supports are needed for the bed. The steps in double digging a bed or planting area are as follows:

1. With string and stakes, make an outline of your bed.
2. Scrape off the top 2 inches of vegetation using a garden spade with a flat blade.

9

3. Starting at one end, dig a trench the depth of a shovel blade, or about 1 foot, across the width of the bed.
4. Wheelbarrow the soil you just removed to the opposite end of the bed and park the wheelbarrow there.
5. Insert a spading fork into the bottom of the trench and rock the fork back and forth to loosen the subsoil for the entire length of the trench. It is a good idea to place a layer of rotted manure or compost in the trench and work it into the subsoil as you proceed.
6. Begin another trench next to the first. Deposit the soil you are removing from the second trench in the first one. Manure or compost can also be worked into this soil.
7. Again, rock the fork back and forth in the bottom of the trench. Continue digging, depositing the soil in the previous trench, and rocking the fork until you have reached the end of the bed.
8. Empty the soil from the wheelbarrow into the last trench.

Some gardeners will settle for nothing shallower than a bed that has been triple dug! To triple dig, make a trench the depth of a shovel blade as just described. Now, deepen the trench by removing another layer of soil with your shovel. The rest of the procedure is the same as for double digging.

Prepared soil may be added to your newly dug bed. If you were to add as much as 2 feet of soil, a double-dug bed would have a depth of 3 feet and a triple-dug bed would be 4 feet deep. The prepared soil that you put on top of the bed can consist of compost, rotted leaves, peat moss, topsoil, aged manure, and sand or horticultural-grade pine bark in various combinations. Sawdust may also be used, but during the first year it will rob nitrogen from the soil as it breaks down. Add nitrogen in the form of an all-purpose fertilizer (such as 8–8–8 or 10–10–10) to offset the requirements of the sawdust. As you mix your soil, remember to check its texture, or tilth, using the simple test described earlier. When squeezed in your hand, does the soil pack together and form a ball? If it does, add more

coarse sand or pine bark to improve the drainage. If it falls apart, add more organic matter to improve its structure.

If the soil in your area is naturally loamy, you are a step ahead of the game. As loamy soils drain better than clayey ones, raised beds and double digging are not as vital in the preparation of an adequate planting medium. Select a site in your yard that drains well and where the existing vegetation looks healthy. Stake out the dimensions of your bed and turn over the soil. Add 6 to 12 inches of prepared soil to the bed and, using a spade or rotary tiller, mix it thoroughly with the native soil.

Whether your finished bed is raised, double dug, or prepared as just described, you will want to have the pH of your soil analyzed so that you can properly adjust it to the needs of the plants. Unless otherwise noted, most of the species described in this book perform well in a soil with a pH of between 6.5 and 7.0.

Consult your county agricultural extension agent on the correct way to take a soil sample and where to send it to be analyzed. Include a note with your sample stating that you intend to grow perennials and would appreciate specific recommendations for soil improvement.

If your soil is acid, you will need to add ground limestone at the rate of five pounds per hundred square feet of bed space. This will raise the pH of your soil .5 to 1.0 unit on the pH scale. If your analysis indicates a more acid reading, increase the amount of limestone accordingly. To lower the pH of an alkaline soil, add iron sulfate at the rate of three pounds per hundred square feet or ground sulfur at the rate of one-half pound per hundred square feet. To make sure that your plants have optimum conditions, check and adjust the pH of your soil annually.

There are no short cuts to proper soil preparation. The extra time you spend preparing a deep, fertile, well-drained medium in your planting beds will pay dividends later in deep-rooted plants better able to withstand dry periods. Plants are also less likely to have problems with disease when they are raised in good soil.

Maintenance

For some gardeners the term "wild flowers" connotes hardiness and indicates that such plants should require little, if any, maintenance. Where native species are naturalized in an appropriate habitat this is indeed the case. However, to reach their full potential when planted in the garden, wild flowers should be regarded as cultivated plants and provided with the same care and attention as the other plants in the garden. Do not make the mistake of assuming that because they are native species, the Gentians and Turtleheads can fend for themselves even under adverse conditions. During dry periods they will dry out just as fast as the exotics in your garden and will need water to survive. Plants requiring constant attention or that are only marginally hardy in your area may not be worth your time. Aim for a low-maintenance garden.

Garden maintenance should begin just before, and end up just after, the growing season. Be fastidious in tending your garden—it will look better and be safer and you will enjoy it more. Begin in early spring with a general cleanup. Remove any winter cover that you may have put down the previous fall, prune back last year's stalks, and reposition plants that may have been heaved out of the soil over the winter. Before going any further, look for seedlings at the base of mature plants. Blue-eyed Grass, Green-and-Gold, the Lobelias, and Wild Bleeding Heart commonly produce crops of early-spring seedlings which can be carefully replanted or potted and grown on until large enough for permanent planting. Do not be afraid to eliminate the weaker specimens from your garden. After checking for new growth, use a cultivating tool to break up the crust that formed on the surface of the soil over the winter.

Fertilize around plants when new shoots appear in spring. Apply a 1-to-2-inch top dressing of manure and shavings and mix in superphosphate at the rate of one-quarter pound per square yard. Alternatively, apply a 5–10–5 fertilizer in granular form at the rate of one-half pound per square yard and scratch it into the soil. In mid-summer check the appearance of your plants. If the foliage of certain plants is lighter than usual or if some have a less than vigorous character about them, fertilize again at the same rate.

Proper mulching can save you considerable time in weeding and watering. Apply a 2-to-3-inch layer of mulch *between* plants. Rotting or shredded leaves, manures, wheat and pine straw, pea gravel, and locally available organic materials (peanut hulls, shredded tobacco stems, corn cobs, and so forth) are all suitable for use as mulches. To guard against the plants rotting, the mulching material should not touch the leaves of basal rosettes or flowering stems.

Mulching reduces the number of weeds, protects the soil (and roots) from the drying influence of the sun, and, as the mulch breaks down, improves the condition of the soil. Of the mulches mentioned above, leaves are the easiest to come by and also supply some nutrients to plants as they break down. By keeping the soil at more even temperatures, a mulch applied during the fall, especially in colder climates, can be effective at reducing damage caused by the alternating freezing and thawing of the soil (heaving) over the winter.

Interestingly, some wild flowers do not fare well, and eventually die, if the immediate area in which they grow is mulched. This is particularly true of species requiring soils that drain well and that contain only small amounts of organic matter. Butterfly Weed, *Penstemon smallii*, and the Mulleins fall into this category. The problem here is that an excessive amount of moisture is retained in the areas of the crown and root zone, and the plants rot. Care must be taken with some plants, such as the Lobelias, to remove fallen leaves that cover basal rosettes in October and November. The evergreen basal rosettes remain in active growth, taking advantage of the winter sun.

Correct watering techniques are among the least-understood aspects of garden maintenance. Initially, you can prepare both you and your garden for dry weather by double digging your planting beds. This will allow roots to grow deeper into the soil and be less dependent on surface water for moisture. Mulching keeps soil moist longer and further reduces the need for watering during the growing season.

During periods of drought, when additional watering is required to sustain plants, take the time to water deeply. Familiarity with the root system of each plant is helpful here. Bee-balm, Gaillardia, and the Rudbeckias, with relatively shallow root systems, will dry out sooner than plants with much deeper roots, such as Blue Star and the Mallows.

Ten minutes of hand watering is more effective than an hour of overhead watering from an automatic sprinkler. When watering by hand, position the hose at the base of the plant and leave it there until the soil is thoroughly saturated. A sprinkler system covers more area, but the water typically does not penetrate the soil as deeply, even when it is left running for several hours. A sprinkler also keeps foliage wet for extended periods and thus provides conditions favorable to fungal spores and other potentially harmful organisms.

Ideally, plants should be watered in the morning on sunny days. Avoid irrigating in the late afternoon and evening so as not to leave foliage wet overnight. Don't forget your plants after they flower; they will still need water during dry periods to produce seeds and to maintain a healthy condition as winter comes on. A dry fall can be disastrous for shallow-rooted perennials; when rainfall is below normal, additional watering is a must to insure robust plants the following spring.

"Pruning," declared an inveterate local gardener recently, "is the most important part of gardening." She was referring to the ability of some perennials to respond to a mid-season pruning with a second crop of flowers. "Sometimes," she confided, "I'll take a pair of hedge shears to entire areas of the garden!" The blooming period of certain native species can be extended by judicious pruning. Yarrow, the native Milkweeds, Ox-eye Daisy, and some of the Rudbeckias will flower a second time—a month or two beyond their normal flowering time—if their blooms are promptly removed when they begin to fade.

By removing blooms you are preventing the plant from producing seed, the final stage in its yearly cycle. With many species, seed production is directly linked to survival. The removal of spent flowers in effect "tricks" the plant into a second flowering and another chance at producing seed. This activity—known as deadheading—also gives the garden a cleaner look.

Pinching, another form of pruning, can be carried out earlier in the season, before flowering. Pinch off the tips of flowering stems to encourage a bushier habit and more blooms. The Goldenrods respond to pinching in June and July with more flowering stems and a tighter habit, which is very desirable in a border planting. Other fall-blooming composites, Bur-Marigold, Boltonia, and the Asters, for example, respond equally well to a midsummer pinch or two, taking on a more rounded appearance when in flower.

Grooming the plants in the garden, a chore for some, should really be looked upon as a reward for having done what was necessary to provide your plants with good growing conditions. Review your garden with a critical eye, and groom accordingly. For example, selective removal of a few stems can relieve the crowded condition that results when plants overlap. Division of course is another solution, but one best performed in the fall. This is also a way to rejuvenate older plants, whose centers grow more woody and less attractive with age; retain divisions from the edges of the clump and discard the old center.

Spreading plants, like Bee-balm, the Goldenrods, and Yarrow, will need to be curbed and pruned to a desired shape so they will not interfere with smaller plants. Deadheading, as mentioned above, is another way to tidy up your plants. Another advantage of this practice is that no seeds and seedlings are produced; this is desirable if you do not wish to increase your stand of a particular plant. Also, the plants are better able to conserve energy for the production of new shoots.

Staking, another aspect of grooming, is practical for plants with tall or weak stems likely to fall over during a summer wind or rainstorm. Effective staking should not be apparent; that is, staking material should support stems, yet be concealed, or essentially so, from view. In general, stake plants just prior to the onset of flowering so that you can accurately gauge the height of stems and the appropriate places to attach stakes. The problem of plants with long, arching stems, seemingly poised to flop, can often be traced to an exceptionally rich soil.

12

Staking Methods: wire hoop, shrub or tree prunings, a sturdy stake, continuous support system.

Many sun-loving species, especially those common to roadside and field, produce lush vegetative growth and abnormally long stems if grown in good garden soil. In a well-drained, mineral soil they will be more sturdy and probably require little if any staking.

Different species require different staking methods. A heavy-gauge wire hoop with two or three support legs is effective for bushy plants with many stems, like the Rudbeckias, Sundrops, and the taller Coreopsis; sink the legs a foot into the soil for stability. Shrub and tree prunings, especially pieces with many branches, are useful with tall plants with stems that have a tendency to spread apart; Bee-balm and Turtleheads are good exam-

ples. Remove the lower twigs and "plant" the branch in the ground in the center of the clump well before flowering. To support taller plants with one or several stems a single sturdy wooden, metal, or plastic stake, driven a foot or more into the ground, can be used. Stems can be attached to the stake with raffia, twine, or plant ties. Marsh Mallow, Blazing Star, and Cardinal Flower may benefit from this type of staking. Edging plants, like Blue-eyed Grass and Gaillardia, can be effectively staked with a continuous support system of stakes positioned every 3–4 feet at the base of the plants and connected with wire.

The time and energy you spend maintaining your garden will be reflected in its appearance. Make a schedule of maintenance activities and the best times to carry them out. Include in your schedule reminders to collect seeds of certain species. Blue Star, for example, flowers in the spring but several months elapse before seeds are mature and ready to collect. The capsules are essentially hidden by the leaves and easily forgotten unless you make a note to check on them in July. Although seeds mature over a shorter period of time with Trout Lily, Virginia Bluebells, and Fire Pink, capsules of these species typically fall to the ground while still attached to the stalk and can be overlooked. Further complicating the collection of seeds from these three species is their rapid decline after flowering—leaves yellow and are nowhere to be found within a month.

Perform maintenance chores at the right time during the growing season. We often do these tasks at a time convenient for us and not for the plants. For example, if you plan to fertilize, do so at the onset of the growing season when plants can best utilize supplementary nutrients. Get a headstart on weeding and remove weeds when they first appear and are easy to pull. Otherwise they can rob your plants of needed moisture, nutrients, and growing space. Above all, do your transplanting at the times least stressful for the plants, at either end of the growing season.

Planting through the Seasons

Many people associate wild flowers with spring, but wild flower gardening is practically a year-round activity. Learn to distribute your propagation activities over the course of the growing season. Take advantage of the warm months for sowing seeds outside. Carry out the bulk of your transplanting during the fall months, when the season favors the establishment of seedlings and divisions and promises healthy, well-rooted specimens the next spring.

Late Winter–Early Spring

This is the best time to divide many summer- and fall-blooming wild flowers. For example, New England Aster, Boltonia, the Goldenrods, Maryland Golden Aster, and the Lobelias produce basal rosettes of leaves during the late fall and winter months which may be safely divided at this time. These species make large, multiple rosettes in cultivation; they should be divided while they are still in their winter condition, before new shoots appear later in the spring. Certain bog species, like Grass-of-Parnassus, the Turtleheads, and Queen-of-the-Prairie, should be divided as soon as their leaves first appear. Some of the native mints, Bee-balm and Mountain Mint in particular, develop impressive mats of foliage over the winter; they may be divided now with minimal disturbance to the clumps.

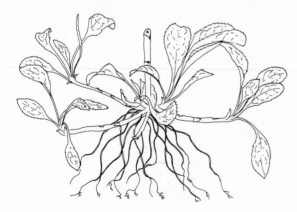

Basal rosettes of Rough-leaved Goldenrod.

"Irishman's Cuttings," a propagation technique in which a piece of the rhizome is included with the petiole when the cutting is taken, are appropriate during this season for some species. Such cuttings are made as leaves first emerge and are an effective production technique for Bleeding Heart, Deciduous Wild Ginger, Wild Geranium, and others.

Early spring, before plants "break," and the fall months, when plants go dormant, are good times to make root cuttings of some wild flowers, particularly Butterfly Weed, the Mulleins, and Stokes' Aster.

Seeds of some wild flowers should be sown now, indoors or in the cold frame. Gaillardia, Blue Curls, and Bur-Marigold, annual species, make spectacular late-summer and fall displays when potted seedlings are transplanted to the garden in spring. Plan to sow seeds of these wild flowers eight weeks before the last frost date. Slow-growing seedlings, like Foamflower, Alumroot, the Gentians, and Meadow-Beauty, benefit from having nearly the entire growing season to develop into specimens large enough for transplanting to the garden. Sow seeds of these species in late winter, carry them through the season in containers, where they can be tended regularly, and move them into the garden in the fall.

It is best to sow wild flowers that produce very small seeds now in flats or pots and watch them closely. Because tiny seeds can be easily washed or buried when sown outdoors, locate seed flats indoors or in the cold frame. The Lobelias, Sundrops, and the Mulleins are good examples. Germination percentages increase and seedling survival is greatly enhanced when seeds of these species are handled in this manner.

Late Spring–Summer

This is the optimum time to carry out most of your propagation from seed. After outdoor sowing in the warm months, the emerging plants will require little of your time because germination and seedling growth are so rapid. Young plants of numerous species started during the summer and transplanted to the garden a few months later will develop into well-rooted, flowering-sized specimens by the following year. A mid-summer sowing and fall planting strategy is also appropriate for biennial species, such as Queen Anne's Lace, Phacelia, and Sundrops (*Oenothera biennis*), which can be expected to flower the next year. Winter annuals like Calliopsis and *Phacelia fimbriata* can be sown directly in the garden; they will develop a basal rosette of leaves over the winter and then flower the following spring.

Some wild flowers that have an early dormancy are best divided while they are still visible. Blue Bells, the Toothworts, and Trilliums fall into this category.

Summer is also a good time to take cuttings of many wild flowers because warm temperatures encourage faster rooting. If you took cuttings in the spring, you would have to locate the rooting chamber indoors to maintain even temperatures. Although a good "take" could be expected from cuttings made in the spring, you would need to watch them closely to make sure they acclimated to new surroundings and did not dry out during the summer months. Fall, on the other hand, is a better time to transplant rooted cuttings because of cooler temperatures and less moisture stress. The native Mallows, the Beard-Tongues, Stonecrop, and Yellow Jessamine, a spring-flowering vine, are a few species that root readily when cuttings are taken during the summer months.

Fall

The months of October and November generally provide ideal conditions for dividing and transplanting herbaceous material in the garden. It is the least stressful time for plants to acclimate to new surroundings; shorter days, cooling temperatures, and relief from the drying effects of the summer sun favor transplants taking hold.

Spring, the season our thoughts most naturally turn to such chores, is in fact often a time when the climate is less conducive to plants establishing in the garden, especially in the southern states, where this season is often brief and moves abruptly into summer and the onset of hot weather. (In the

Northeast, where seasonal change is more gradual, spring planting is a workable alternative.) In the Mid-Atlantic and southern regions, at least, planting in the fall allows transplants several weeks to establish themselves during the dormant season, generally making for healthy, well-rooted specimens the next year. In addition, spring planting can require more maintenance: you need to provide a protective covering to shield plants from the sun until they are established, pay closer attention to watering, and watch for signs of diseases that can develop quickly with weakened or unestablished specimens.

Fall planting gets you into the garden at the end of the growing season, a time when many plants benefit from attention. Species that bloomed in the spring—Stokes' Aster, Fire Pink, Ox-eye Daisy, and Robin's Plantain—have developed rosettes with multiple crowns and can be divided. Deep-rooted plants, such as White Wild Indigo and Carolina Bush Pea, are also best handled now, as they go dormant.

As you work in the garden during the fall months, on the heels of the growing season, the habit, form, and color of your plants will be fresh in your mind. This is a good time to consider redesigning or renovating any areas that may need it. Although follow-up maintenance is usually less at this time of year, a dry fall can spell ruin for new

Basal rosettes of Ox-eye Daisy.

transplants. If rainfall is not regular during the fall, you will need to water often enough to keep the soil around plants evenly moist.

For some species, sowing seeds when they are harvested is advisable regardless of the season. The seeds of certain woodland wild flowers, such as Bloodroot and the Trilliums, germinate the next spring in dramatically higher percentages if they are sown immediately upon collection than they would if they were sown after being allowed to dry out in storage. Jack-in-the-Pulpit, Deciduous Wild Ginger, and the Toothworts are other spring-blooming perennials whose seeds should be sown upon collection in a moist, shaded, outdoor bed.

In general, plan ahead and carry out the particular activity at the time least stressful for the plants you are working with. Use these suggestions as a guide to charting your gardening year. For particular propagation and cultivation suggestions, handling techniques, and the best time to sow, divide, or take cuttings, refer to the information on species.

Designing a Border or Bed with Native Perennials

Begin your plan by preparing a list of plants you want to work with that are appropriate for the light or other conditions of the bed and then categorize them by height: low, medium, and tall. To achieve balance, consider such variables as season of bloom, flower and foliage color and texture, and habit of growth. When grown from seed, many perennials do not flower until their second year (refer to species descriptions for approximate size at maturity and length of time to flowering). Remember that many sun-loving wild flowers, such as Spiderwort, the Beard Tongues, Mountain Mint, and Blue Star, will grow to a larger size in cultivation than in their natural habitat.

If you intend the border to be a major focus in the yard—near a deck or patio, beside a path, or along a drive, for example—in your selection of plants give special consideration for when they flower since the best way to sustain interest in the border during the growing season is to plan for continuous bloom. In Great Britain, where perennial gardening has enjoyed popularity for many years, continuous bloom is easier to achieve, as flowers last longer in a cool, moist climate with few bright, sunny days. American gardeners, however, must generally contend with a hotter, drier climate and more bright days, conditions that cause plants to move in and out of flower more rapidly. If you keep a record of when the plants in your garden are in flower, you can fill in any seasonal gaps that appear with a few additions the next year.

On the other hand, you may wish to design a border with plants flowering at only certain times of the season, say, spring and fall, and thus shift the focus to other areas of the garden during the summer months. Or when you know you will be away at certain times during the season, you can choose plants that flower when you are at home to enjoy them. Select native perennials that bloom over a long period and plan to integrate them with some of the many attractive exotic perennials available commercially.

Perennial borders are often linear, or generally rectangular in shape and situated in front of a wall, fence, evergreen hedge, or collection of shrubs to highlight the flowers against a darker background. Island beds are another way to display perennials.

Typically they are loosely oval or randomly shaped beds set in an expanse of lawn or open area and provide opportunities to view the display from different angles.

Composing the perennial border—that is, deciding where to position the plants—is an entirely personal matter. There are, however, a number of general guidelines that you may find helpful. Wide borders and beds, those at least 8 feet deep, can accommodate bold groupings of one or more species which can, in turn, provide effective contrasts or backgrounds in the display. White Wild Indigo and Blue Star, for example, become dense, attractive foliage plants of medium height after they flower and make effective backdrops for lower, summer-blooming species, such as Butterfly Weed, Stokes' Aster, Sundrops, and Beard Tongue (*Penstemon smallii*). Think of the border in ranks: the first should include mostly plants shorter than 2 feet; the middle rank can contain plants that grow to 4 feet; and the back rank can be made up of taller specimens. Leave a narrow unplanted strip or path between the rear of the border and the background area to allow access for maintenance and to curb the spread of roots of nearby woody plants.

These are general suggestions only, and you need not adhere strictly to the short-medium-tall alignment; to create more interest in the border, vary the contour by bringing a few taller plants forward and allowing some mid-range plants room to spread toward the back. As you become familiar with the habit and appearance of a plant through the seasons, you will develop a critical sense for appropriate placement and for the most attractive combinations of plants.

Plants of low and medium height are typically planted in groups of three to seven, while taller, coarser plants are often planted individually. A sense of rhythm in the border may be achieved by repeating groups of a plant at intervals. Locate plants with complementary colors and bloom periods that overlap in close proximity—this is the challenge of creating an attractive border, a skill that you will continue to hone from one growing season to the next. A pleasing blend of colors in the border is a fitting reward for your efforts and will inspire you to try new combinations.

Some effective color combinations are:

Bee-balm and Queen Anne's Lace (red and white)
Blazing Star and Boltonia (purple and white)
Butterfly Weed and Stokes' Aster (orange and blue)
Fire Pink, Ox-eye Daisy, and Stokes' Aster (red, white, and blue)
Purple Cone-flower and Spiderwort (purple and blue)
Queen Anne's Lace and Chicory (white and blue)
Rough-leaved Goldenrod and New England Aster (yellow and purple)
Sunflower and Seashore Mallow (yellow and pink)

White is a desirable color in the border, as it naturally ties other colors together and also serves to tone down some of the more intense colors. The following native perennials all have white flowers:

Beard Tongue (*Penstemon digitalis*)
Boltonia
Foamflower
Ox-eye Daisy
White Wild· Indigo
Yarrow

Fill seasonal blank spaces in the border with annuals and biennials such as Blue Curls, Calliopsis, Gaillardia, Moth Mullein, and Queen Anne's Lace. Blue Curls, for example, is an excellent filler plant for the front of the border and makes a beautiful display of blue flowers in early fall. Queen Anne's Lace and Moth Mullein make good fillers for the middle and back layers, require minimal space, and provide attractive white flowers in late spring and early summer.

So that you are well prepared when it comes time to redesign, keep an ongoing record of your border and how you intend to alter the arrangement. Note the periods of bloom of your plants, good color combinations, and ideas you pick up from other gardens. Many of your best notions may be forgotten unless you commit them to paper. Photographing the border at various times during the growing season is also a way to focus on precisely the changes you want to make and to jog the memory.

The accompanying sample plans are provided as general guides for displaying native perennials. They can be used as models and should of course be altered in size and shape to accommodate your setting and to reflect your own design ideas.

Now a word of caution: be realistic when planning your perennial border. It is tempting to envision a sweeping, colorful display of flowers and forms and to begin on a large scale, but you may soon be overwhelmed, if not by the initial investment of time and energy needed to build the border, then certainly by the maintenance chores required if the plants are to become established and thrive.

If you are a beginning gardener or new to perennial gardening, plan to start small and observe carefully what is involved in properly caring for the plants through the growing season. Allow yourself a season or two to grow familiar with the responsibilities involved in tending a border. Then, if you are willing to commit more time to the project after that initial experience, expand your border to accommodate more plants and design possibilities.

Ferns are a good choice for the shade garden because of their natural tolerance for shady locations. In this plan almost one-quarter of the shade-garden planting is ferns. New York, Southern Lady, and Christmas ferns are used to provide a variety of foliage color and texture. Christmas ferns offer the added landscape value of being an evergreen. In spring a large part of this garden will be graced with a variety of delicate fiddleheads.

In nature many woodland wild flowers (the "spring ephemerals") bloom in early spring while adequate sunlight is still available, that is, before the deciduous trees are fully in leaf. So it is with the plants in this plan: the majority of plants will bloom in April and May with a display of pastel colors which show up especially well in the shade.

Summer will bring the cool greens of the ferns as well as the colorful flowers and fernlike foliage of Columbine and Bleeding Heart. Cardinal Flower, Great Lobelia, and Green Cone-flower, all of them scattered throughout this plan, will provide bold color accents in the fall.

Wild Flower Planting Plan for Full Sun

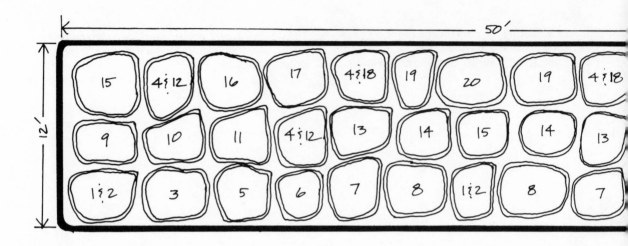

FRONT

※	SPECIES	COMMON NAME	HT.	COLOR
4	AQUILEGIA CANADENSIS	COLUMBINE	MEDIUM	RED
1	CHRYSOGONUM VIRGINIANUM	GREEN-AND-GOLD	LOW	YELLOW
13	BAPTISIA PENDULA	WHITE WILD INDIGO	MEDIUM	WHITE
10	TRADESCANTIA VIRGINIANA	SPIDERWORT	MEDIUM	PURPLE
7	BAPTISIA AUSTRALIS	BLUE WILD INDIGO	LOW	BLUE
6	OENOTHERA TETRAGONA	SUNDROPS	LOW	YELLOW
2	SILENE VIRGINICA	FIRE PINK	LOW	RED
5	ASCLEPIAS TUBEROSA	BUTTERFLY WEED	LOW	ORANGE
8	COREOPSIS VERTICILLATA	THREAD-LEAVED COREOPSIS	MEDIUM	YELLOW
3	STOKESIA LAEVIS	STOKES' ASTER	MEDIUM	BLUE
17	MONARDA DIDYMA	BEE-BALM	TALL	RED
11	ECHINACEA PURPUREA	PURPLE CONEFLOWER	MEDIUM	PURPLE
16	RUDBECKIA TRILOBA	BLACK-EYED SUSAN	TALL	YELLOW
14	LOBELIA CARDINALIS	CARDINAL FLOWER	MEDIUM	RED
18	PHLOX PANICULATA	GARDEN PHLOX	MEDIUM	PINK
19	BOLTONIA ASTEROIDES	BOLTONIA	TALL	WHITE
9	SOLIDAGO RUGOSA	ROUGH-LEAVED GOLDENROD	MEDIUM	YELLOW
12	LIATRIS SPICATA	BLAZING STAR	TALL	LAVENDER
15	ASTER NOVAE-ANGLIAE	NEW ENGLAND ASTER	TALL	PURPLE
20	SOLIDAGO SEMPERVIRENS	SEASIDE GOLDENROD	TALL	YELLOW

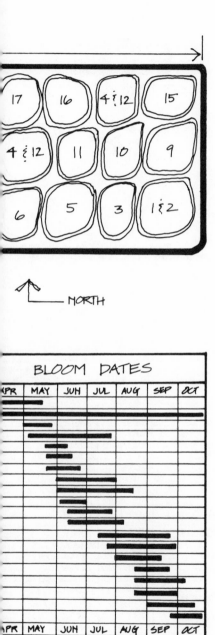

NORTH

BLOOM DATES

APR	MAY	JUN	JUL	AUG	SEP	OCT

This plan is designed for a completely open area which has no trees blocking the sun and which therefore receives eight to ten hours of direct sunlight per day. All of the plants used in this plan are most showy when they receive the benefit of full sun. Thirteen of the twenty species listed bloom at some time during the months of June and July, and thus the sun garden is at its peak during the mid-summer. In order to provide color in the garden throughout the growing season, however, additional species are included.

Because Columbine blooms early in the spring, grows rapidly, and produces a mass of showy flowers, it is scattered throughout the back and middle sections of this plan. To best take advantage of this quality of Columbine, it is interplanted with other species. Columbine can be closely interplanted with Blazing Star because these two plants will occupy different levels of the same space at different times of the year. Blazing Star, a tall, slender, fall-blooming plant, will grow up through the lower, mound-shaped Columbine. Thus one small planting area will provide two shows of color, one in the spring and one in the fall.

Soon after Columbine begins to bloom, White Wild Indigo and Spiderwort also begin to flower. Used in conjunction with Columbine, these two plants make pleasing color combinations maximized when all three are placed relatively close together. Bridging the period from spring to summer is the beautiful red and yellow combination of interplanted Fire Pink and Green-and-Gold placed in the center and at both ends of the front of the bed.

The most striking color patterns begin in the sun garden during June and continue through July, when Stokes' Aster and Butterfly Weed are blooming in the front, Purple Cone-flower and Spiderwort in the middle, and Bee-balm and Black-eyed Susan (*Rudbeckia triloba*) in the back.

In the fall Blazing Star offers tall spikes of lavender flowers which are especially attractive in combination with the sturdy dark purple New England Aster, the open delicate yellow sprays of Rough-leaved Goldenrod, and the white mounds of Boltonia.

21

Wild Flower Planting Plan for Partial Sun

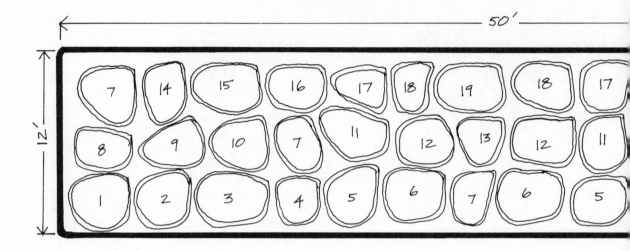

FRONT

※	SPECIES	COMMON NAME	HT.	COLOR
5	DENTARIA DIPHYLLA	TOOTHWORT	LOW	WHITE
7	AQUILEGIA CANADENSIS	COLUMBINE	MEDIUM	RED
9	DICENTRA EXIMIA	BLEEDING HEART	MEDIUM	PINK
8	AMSONIA TABERNAEMONTANA	BLUE STAR	MEDIUM	BLUE
6	ARISAEMA TRIPHYLLUM	JACK-IN-THE-PULPIT	LOW	GREEN/PURPLE
4	COREOPSIS AURICULATA	COREOPSIS	LOW	YELLOW
15	PENSTEMON DIGITALIS	BEARD TONGUE	MEDIUM	WHITE
11	TRADESCANTIA VIRGINIANA	SPIDERWORT	MEDIUM	PURPLE
1	PENSTEMON SMALLII	BEARD TONGUE	MEDIUM	PINK
2	SILENE VIRGINICA	FIRE PINK	LOW	RED
17	MONARDA DIDYMA	BEE-BALM	TALL	RED
19	FILIPENDULA RUBRA	QUEEN-OF-THE-PRAIRIE	TALL	PINK
10	RUELLIA CAROLINIENSIS	RUELLIA	MEDIUM	PURPLE
3	RUDBECKIA FULGIDA	BLACK-EYED SUSAN	MEDIUM	YELLOW
12	LOBELIA CARDINALIS	CARDINAL FLOWER	MEDIUM	RED
18	CHELONE LYONII	TURTLEHEADS	TALL	PURPLE
13	LOBELIA SIPHILITICA	GREAT LOBELIA	MEDIUM	BLUE
16	RUDBECKIA LACINIATA	GREEN CONEFLOWER	TALL	YELLOW
14	SOLIDAGO RUGOSA	ROUGH-LEAVED GOLDENROD	MEDIUM	YELLOW

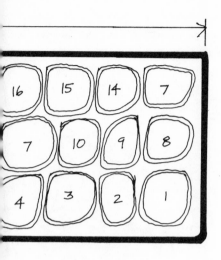

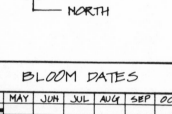

BLOOM DATES

PR	MAY	JUN	JUL	AUG	SEP	OCT

This plan is designed for a garden area that receives a total of five to six hours of direct sunlight per day. The plants in this plan are either adapted to or tolerant of a certain amount of shade, and they will provide interest and color from early April until the end of September.

Columbine, Toothwort, and Bleeding Heart highlight the month of April with a bright combination of red, white, and pink. Shortly after these plants reach full bloom, the beautiful sky blue of Blue Star and the golden yellow of Coreopsis join them. When these plants are carefully spaced, the mass of colors will carry the observer's eye for the entire length of the bed.

The delicate shades of the April garden turn slightly bolder in May. Coreopsis and Bleeding Heart continue to bloom and are joined by purple Spiderwort, Beard Tongues (pink *Penstemon smallii* and white *P. digitalis*), and red Fire Pink. Low clumps of Jack-in-the-Pulpit also add interest. The suggested plantings for May occupy at least part of all sections of the bed, the front, middle, and back. In the early part of the growing season none of the relatively tall plants located primarily at the back of the garden have had sufficient growing time to reach their maximum height and thus do not yet block their medium-sized plant neighbors which bloom earlier in the season.

The continuing bloom of Spiderwort, Beard Tongue, and Fire Pink provides color into June. July is primarily a time for Bee-balm, which has a unique crown-shaped head of brilliant scarlet flowers. Indeed, a tall clump of Bee-balm is a show in itself and is especially attractive to hummingbirds.

During August and September the blue Great Lobelia and bright crimson Cardinal Flower accent the middle of the flower bed. Yellow accents are provided in the front of the bed by Black-eyed Susans (*Rudbeckia fulgida*) and in the back by Rough-leaved Goldenrod and Green Cone-flower which have now grown to full size and thus tend to hide the spent foliage of the white Beard Tongue. The scarlet fruits of Jack-in-the-Pulpit are very prominent during this period.

Wild Flower Planting Plan for Full Shade

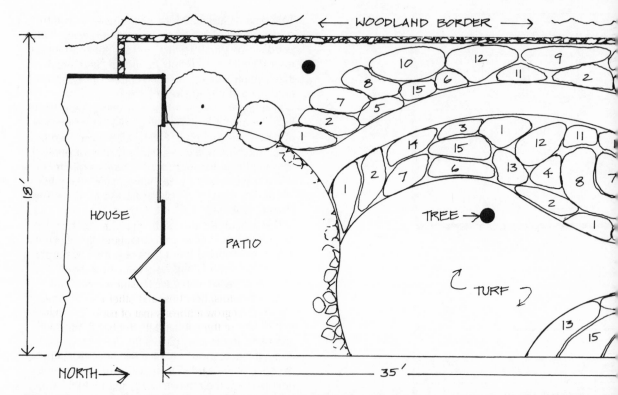

#	SPECIES	COMMON NAME	HT.	COLOR
3	SANGUINARIA CANADENSIS	BLOODROOT	LOW	WHITE
6	DENTARIA DIPHYLLA	TOOTHWORT	LOW	WHITE
7	AQUILEGIA CANADENSIS	COLUMBINE	MEDIUM	RED
2	TIARELLA CORDIFOLIA	FOAMFLOWER	LOW	WHITE
1	DICENTRA EXIMIA	BLEEDING HEART	MEDIUM	PINK
5	ASARUM CANADENSE	DECIDUOUS WILD GINGER	LOW	MAROON *
4	ARISAEMA TRIPHYLLUM	JACK-IN-THE-PULPIT	LOW	PURPLE/GREEN
10	GERANIUM MACULATUM	WILD GERANIUM	MEDIUM	PINK
11	HEUCHERA AMERICANA	ALUMROOT	LOW	BROWN *
8	LOBELIA CARDINALIS	CARDINAL FLOWER	TALL	RED
9	LOBELIA SIPHILITICA	GREAT LOBELIA	TALL	PURPLE
12	RUDBECKIA LACINIATA	GREEN CONEFLOWER	TALL	YELLOW
13	POLYSTICHUM ACROSTICHOIDES	CHRISTMAS FERN	MEDIUM	
14	THELYPTERIS NOVEBORACENSIS	NEW YORK FERN	MEDIUM	
15	ATHYRIUM ASPLENIOIDES	SOUTHERN LADY FERN	MEDIUM	
	* FLOWERS RELATIVELY INSIGNIFICANT, PLANT BEST USED FOR FOLIAGE			

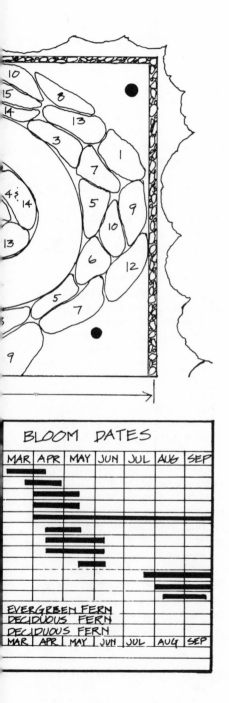

BLOOM DATES

MAR	APR	MAY	JUN	JUL	AUG	SEP

EVERGREEN FERN
DECIDUOUS FERN
DECIDUOUS FERN

MAR	APR	MAY	JUN	JUL	AUG	SEP

Because not all shade is the same, it is important first of all to determine the kind of shade you have. Is it the heavy shade cast by a building or group of evergreens, or is it the more desirable broken seasonal shade cast by large, well spaced, deciduous trees? Remember that even in nature very few plants grow well in dense shade; some direct or indirect sunlight is a critical factor in the health and survival of every green plant. Many plants do very well in the high shade or dappled sunlight created by a few well-spaced deciduous trees, but few plants tolerate well the heavy year-long shade beneath dense evergreens such as Rhododendron or Hemlock. To provide enough sunlight to grow woodland wild flowers it is usually necessary to select the better trees in your woodland garden area and then remove the smaller ones. Also, consider cutting off some of the lower branches of larger trees to increase both air circulation and light.

Maples, elms, beeches, and other trees have a tendency to grow a fibrous mat of roots just below the surface of the soil, and the roots are especially invasive in nearby beds that have been prepared for wild flowers. These tree roots will usually win out over your wild flowers in the competition for moisture and nutrients. Another important consideration is that continuous cultivation (i.e., frequently disturbing or digging the soil) underneath trees can damage or even kill the very trees in whose shade you are trying to garden. If you plant directly beneath established trees, it is best to prepare the planting area during the dormant fall and winter months. Do not subject the tree roots to repeated cultivation during successive years, especially during the growing season. Sometimes preserving fine specimen trees is more important than planting a flower bed. Keep all this in mind when selecting trees in whose shade you plan to grow wild flowers and in planning your shade garden design.

There are a few points worth noting about this particular plan. First of all, the homeowner selected 4 deciduous trees that were conveniently located and provide the proper amount of shade. Notice that few if any plants were located directly around the base of the trees since this is the most difficult place to grow herbaceous plants due to the heavy shade and tree root competition.

Diseases and Pests

The best strategy for combatting potential disease and pest problems is to provide the proper growing conditions for your plants. Also, sanitation and regular inspection of plants should have a high priority on your schedule of gardening activities, for those plants that are well tended and strong can better withstand an infestation. When a problem does arise, chemical sprays and drenches are not your only solution. Considerable information is available on the use of safe, efficient nonchemical remedies to insect problems (see the suggested reading list). Adopt a preventive approach to curbing disease in propagation and display areas.

Provide a healthy environment for your plants. As damp, shady areas can provide habitat for harmful organisms and insects, you should select a site with the proper light for the plants to be grown there. Plants receiving too much or too little light become weaker and more susceptible to attack.

Healthy soil is fertile and well drained. A medium lacking in nutrients or one that retains excessive amounts of moisture will stress most plants and increase the likelihood of disease. Improve the structure of your soil by adding organic matter and drainage material. (See section on soil preparation.)

Be careful to fertilize properly. Plants that are underfed or overfed are less resistant. Particularly when growing seedlings indoors, lush growth from overfertilization can be a problem. Fertilizing container plants can also result in a buildup of soluble salts. Make sure to water plants thoroughly between applications of fertilizer to flush out harmful salts.

Indoors or out, choose or create an environment with good air circulation. Crowded plants inhibit proper air flow.

Finally, irrigate properly. Water deeply and allow the soil to dry slightly between waterings. Water early in the day so that plants do not remain wet overnight, thus reducing the chance of fungal infections.

To maintain a sanitary garden begin by ensuring that your propagating area, including the surfaces on which you work, soil, containers, and tools, remains clean. This cannot be overemphasized. If you bring your plants, seeds, cuttings, and other plant parts into a dirty area, you increase the risk that they will be contaminated. New plants brought into the growing area or garden should be checked for disease and insects and isolated for a time before mixing them in with healthy plants.

Weeds and dead or discolored leaves may attract pests; keep your growing and display areas clean and groomed. You can reduce the risk of spreading insects and disease by removing all infected plant material when you first notice it. Keep a separate closed container for diseased material and dispose of it by burning. Do not put diseased plants or plant parts in the compost pile. Wash your hands after handling an infected plant.

Monitor your plants for damage. Frequent close inspection of plants, such as each time you water, will allow you to catch problems early on and begin appropriate treatment. Examine succulent new growth closely. Check the undersides and upper surfaces of leaves, flowers, buds, and stems. Watch plants for signs of damage, such as leaf discoloration, curling, puckering, spotting, plant wilting and collapse, webs, raised bumps, cottony masses, holes, and ragged edges.

Learn the common harmful insects, their life cycles, and the stages when the various methods to control them are effective. State and federal publications are available to aid with insect identification, and in most areas of the country county agricultural extension agents will help you determine the problem. Encourage beneficial insects (ladybugs, assassin bugs, praying mantises) and other natural predators (birds, toads, lizards) by protecting their habitat in the garden and by reducing the use of insecticides.

When you have correctly diagnosed an insect or disease problem and determined that action is necessary, consider your choices carefully before acting. Traditionally, the use of chemical sprays and drenches has been the most common method of pest control indoors and in the garden. Chemical pesticides affect more than the immediate area in which they are used; humans, pets, and beneficial predators are all susceptible to the potentially harmful effects of chemicals. There is still much to be learned concerning the short- and long-term effects of chemical sprays. We should, however, note the precautionary statements on the labels of some commercially available sprays concerning the hazards of the product to humans, domestic animals, and the environment.

Biological control and pesticides prepared with organic materials are safe, realistic alternatives to chemical methods. As a last resort, when alternatives to chemicals prove ineffective, commercially available chemical sprays may be your best tack in eradicating a persistent pest. Rotate within the selection of appropriate chemical sprays for the specific pest; that is, do not use the same spray on successive applications. Use three or four different sprays, and then repeat the sequence. (In many cases a single application of a chemical spray will be sufficient to remove the insect.) This helps retard the insects' ability to build resistance to one pesticide. Rely on target-specific sprays, not broad spectrum compounds which can kill beneficials like ladybugs, spiders, and bees.

The message here is to maintain a clean growing environment for your plants and reduce the possibility of disease by planning ahead.

Part 2. Propagating Native Plants

Collection of Native Plant Seed

Collecting native plant seed can be an interesting challenge for the wild flower gardener. More important, it is an opportunity to tap into a plentiful natural resource. For many wild flower hobbyists, seed harvest is the first step in establishing a new species in the garden. Where a sizable established population of a species is found, selective collection of seeds from a small to moderate percentage of the stand will have little or no effect on the reproductive potential of the population. The quality of the seed collected is more important than great numbers; in most cases a small quantity of mature seed will be sufficient for your needs. As your native plantings mature in the garden, you will soon have a reliable seed source to use and share with other wild flower gardeners.

With some species, such as the spring-blooming Trout Lily and Bloodroot, seed is ready for collection as early as April in our area. At the other end of the growing season, the seeds of such fall-blooming plants as Blazing Star, Bur-Marigold, and the Goldenrods can be collected in October. In between, many dozens of species mature and shed their seeds. Collecting seeds for an array of spring-, summer-, and fall-blooming native plants is almost a week-by-week procedure.

A herbaceous plant can change radically in appearance between flowering and fruiting. For example, Fire Pink (*Silene virginica*), strikingly obvious when in flower, declines rapidly thereafter. The upright stalks begin to lean and by the time the seeds are mature have usually found their way to the ground. Lower leaves fade to yellow and disappear; surrounding vegetation can easily hide the stalks and seed capsules.

Particularly with such species as the Fire Pink, you may find it helpful to record the precise location of a plant population in a field notebook when the plant is in flower. This will help you to return to that location when the plants are in fruit. Also, it would be wise to mark any especially desirable plants with a small piece of colored yarn, flagging, or stick labels to aid in finding them later. Standard paper "marking tags" often rot, or are eaten, before seeds are ripe and are thus not a reliable method for tagging plants in the field. In some cases several return visits may be necessary for the collec-

tion of mature seeds, as local weather trends may delay their ripening. In different years, seed of Fire Pink has been collected as early as June and as late as August from plants on the same road bank in the mountains of western North Carolina.

Confidence in recognizing a mature seed comes with experience. First, look for indications in the fruiting structures that hold the seeds. In general, capsules, pods, and berries will expand in size and turn from a lighter to a darker color as seeds approach maturity. For example, capsules of Cardinal Flower change from light green to brown. (Inside the Cardinal Flower capsule, seeds change from white to progressively darker shades of brown.) The inflated, drooping legumes of White Wild Indigo turn from pale green to blackish gray. The paired follicles of Blue Star, shiny green when formed, mature to a dull tan color.

Next, examine the seeds themselves. Seeds of different species mature at different rates, and it is important during the seed production period to pay attention to the special characteristics of seed maturation for the particular species you are interested in. Jack-in-the-Pulpit, for example, reveals its tight cluster of shiny green berries in early June. Not until late August and September, however, are seeds mature and ready for collection. During the grow-

31 August 1978
Kosteletskya virginica (in flower) Large population (150 ft) along roadside on NC #24, just north of Swansboro; on west side of road across from Swansboro Yacht Basin.

6 August 1979
Rudbeckia hirta · Extensive population w/ lg flowers at junction of NC #88 and Ashe Co. Rd. #1585.

Field notebook entries for seed collection.

ing season, the fruit cluster steadily expands and changes to orange and finally to red at maturity. Foamflower, on the other hand, produces ripe seed very rapidly—during the same month in which it flowers.

Most seeds turn darker in color as they mature, but a few, such as Jack-in-the-Pulpit, which has a fleshy covering over the seed itself, remain white or very light in color. Thus, the best way to determine whether a seed is mature is to break it open and look for a moist, white embryo inside. With many species, such as Blazing Star (*Liatris spicata*) and other members of the Aster family, some seeds may appear mature but contain no embryos. Another example is Fire Pink, whose inflated capsules are often empty. A close inspection for viable seed is a must before collection.

The Aster family, which numbers hundreds of attractive species (as well as some noxious weeds) in the Southeast alone, deserves special mention here. Each of the many small individual ray or disk flowers that is fertile produces a single fruit, called a nutlet, that contains a single seed. Many species flower toward the end of the growing season. The conspicuous tufts of hairs (the often silky pappus bristles) attached to the nutlets account for the dense, fuzzy appearance of the seed heads in such species as Maryland Golden Aster and the Goldenrods. Seeds of these and other fall-blooming species of the Aster family are best collected after the first frost, in October. Members of other genera in this family, such as the Purple Cone-flowers and Black-eyed Susans, lack a pappus. When in flower, these plants exhibit a tight head, or "eye," of disk flowers from which the ray flowers radiate. As the flowers fade, the disk expands and seeds begin to mature. Seed heads are best left on the stalk for at least a month after flowering. This will allow the seeds ample time to ripen and the heads to expand fully and begin splitting apart, making seed removal somewhat easier. Because most species of the Aster family produce only a small percentage of viable seed in a given population of plants, care is necessary when estimating the number of seed heads to collect.

Some wild flowers mature and disperse their seeds quickly and must be checked frequently. The seed capsule of Bloodroot, for example, can split and spill its seeds in just a few hours. A piece of netting or a fold of brown paper over the capsule held in place with a paper clip or tied with string will prevent the seeds from falling to the ground when the capsule opens. The intriguing fruiting structure of the Wild Geranium also requires a watchful eye. The fruit consists of five seeds, each separately enclosed in a locule. The locules are attached at a central point, and at the time of seed dispersal they recoil backward. Once the locules have recoiled, the seeds are gone. Since the seeds mature shortly after flowering, daily inspection is recommended.

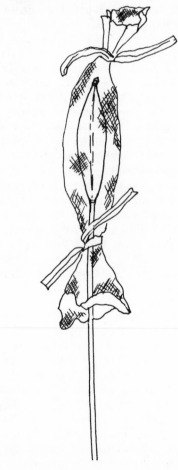

Netting around Bloodroot capsule to "catch" seeds.

Still other species, such as Butterfly Weed and Carolina Bush Pea, mature their seeds gradually, over a longer period. In central North Carolina, for example, both species flower in June and produce mature seed in August. The familiar pods, or follicles, of Butterfly Weed are usually still green when the seeds inside are dark brown and mature. The sign to look for is a split along one side of the pod. This is the time to collect the pods. Once the seeds are mature and ripe, the fruiting stalks can be cut and the pods allowed to dry slowly and split open to shed the seed. However, either in the field or indoors, it is easier to tie a short piece of yarn around the drying pod to keep it from opening after it splits. The seeds are much easier to harvest from ripe but unopened pods than after they have been shed. The flat legume of the Carolina Bush Pea appears shortly after the flowers. The structure is densely fuzzy and over the summer turns from gray green to dull black. When the seeds are ready, the legume has a tattered look and has usually begun to split. Although most wild flowers do not require the close scrutiny of Bloodroot to get a harvest of seed, they nonetheless mature their seeds at regular and often usually predictable times and should be monitored regularly.

Although the seeds of some species (especially in the Aster family) will continue to ripen after they are collected, it is important not to be too hasty when collecting wild flower seeds. Allowing seeds to develop fully and mature before collection will make cleaning simpler. Harvesting seeds that are not fully ripe should be considered only as a last resort when a return trip to the collection site is not possible before the seeds are dispersed. Seeds of Columbine and Foamflower turn from white to light green and finally to black as they mature. If collected when they are light green, the seeds will ripen and turn a shiny black a day or two after collection. Seeds of Butterfly Weed harvested when they are a light shade of brown will turn dark brown within a week after collection.

Finally, you can save considerable time and effort when collecting seed by keeping adequate notes of when and where to collect. By recording collection dates over a number of seasons, you can begin to construct a calendar or timetable for seed harvest. Such a reference is especially useful for the many spring-blooming species that mature their seeds rapidly and then die down—often without a trace, unless, as mentioned earlier, the stalks of choice plants were marked when the plants were in bloom with a length of brightly colored yarn.

As collectors of wild flower seed, we are practicing conservation through propagation. We are also giving ourselves an opportunity to glimpse the wide variety of their fruiting structures—their shapes, colors, and textures—to learn something of their interesting mechanisms of seed dispersal, and to appreciate the great diversity of wild flowers occurring in eastern North America.

Seed Cleaning

Wild flower seeds should be attended to as soon as possible after collection. With many plants, especially those that produce dry fruits, a period of air-drying will be necessary. Because the fruits, stems, and leaves that often make up the bulk of a field collection of "seeds" usually have a significant moisture content, seeds that are stacked or left in the collection bag too long will begin to heat up in just a few hours. Heat and the decay that accompanies it can seriously impair the germination potential of the seeds.

Upon returning to the house after a seed-collecting trip, always remove the collected material from the collection bag and spread it out on clean, dry newspaper. This is best done in a well-ventilated room with low humidity. Allow the fruits and other plant materials to dry for a few days prior to cleaning. During this slow-drying period the fruits of many species will split or open and either shed the seeds or at least make them easier to remove.

You should also be alert to the possibility of insect infestation in field-collected seeds. Careful observation at the time of collection of both fruits and seeds is a must. In some cases the invading insects are tiny and can easily be overlooked by the casual observer. Still other insects are similar in appearance to the seeds in size, shape, and color, making them even more difficult to spot. Despite careful planning to arrive at the right time to collect mature seeds, you may discover that plants have already been visited by insects whose larval stage feeds on the developing seeds of specific plants. The native Mallows, for instance, are in the same family as cotton and are host to the weevil. When collecting Mallow seeds, be sure to examine the interior of the capsule closely for evidence of weevils. Some seed coats will probably show a round hole bored in them by the weevils, but not all the seeds will be damaged. Weevils and other insects or their larvae can be effectively eliminated by fumigation, but damaged seeds will likely remain inviable.

To fumigate seeds put them in a paper or plastic bag with one or two 3-inch-long sections of No-Pest Strip. Close the bag tightly and store it in a cool, dry place for ten days to two weeks. At the end of this period the insects should have been elimi-

nated and the seeds can then be cleaned. This procedure has proven safe and reliable. Care should be taken, however, to wash your hands after handling the No-Pest Strips. Some gardeners and commercial seed dealers choose to fumigate all new seeds as a wholesale preventive measure. This should not be necessary for the home gardener, however, as long as seeds are thoroughly inspected at the time of collection.

The best method for cleaning dry seeds can usually be determined by examining the condition of the capsules or pods after a few days of drying. When the capsules or pods have begun to split or dry out or otherwise show signs of decomposing, place them in a paper bag and shake vigorously for a minute or two. The agitation should free most of the seeds from the fruits. Wild flowers appropriate for this method include Columbine, Foamflower, and the native Mints. Another practical method for removing dry seeds is threshing. This involves loosening the seeds from the fruiting structure, generally by moderate beating or crushing. The seeds of both the Bur-Marigold and Coreopsis, among several others, can be cleaned by beating. When collecting seeds of these species, cut the fruiting stalks a foot or two below the seed heads. After the plants have air-dried for a few days, grasp the ends of the stalks and beat the seed heads into an open container, such as a large paper or plastic bag, bucket, box, or wheelbarrow. Seeds of both the Penstemons and the Mulleins are easy to remove by the crushing method. Simply remove the capsules from the stalk and mash them with a rolling pin, jar, or mallet. If you spread the capsules in a thin layer in a large plastic bag and then crush them, the job may be a bit neater.

The seed heads of other species producing dry seeds, such as Stokes' Aster, Purple Cone-flower, and the popular Black-eyed Susans, must be handled individually. To remove the seeds effectively the seed heads, or cones, must be split open. If collected too soon after flowering, the seed heads will be hard and nearly impregnable. Waiting until the heads expand and soften, often a month or more after the flowers fade, makes seed cleaning much easier. It is not difficult to separate out nutlets of Stokes' Aster and the Cone-flowers during cleaning, but Black-eyed Susan seeds are surrounded by considerable chaff and are not so readily identified. They are very small, charcoal gray, and quadrangular in shape. A sieve or some blowing method will be necessary to remove the chaff.

After the seeds have been extracted from the capsules, additional cleaning will likely be necessary to remove chaff and litter. A small amount of litter stored with seeds will not pose a problem. When you sow the seeds, however, the operation can be carried out more efficiently with a clean seed lot. Spacing seeds in a flat or seedbed is easier with clean seeds, and that attention to proper spacing is important in obtaining healthy seedlings, not beset by crowding and the accompanying stunting.

The most convenient way to clean the seeds is with sieves. You will need to acquire or construct at least three or four sieves, each with a different-sized opening in the screening material. Many horticultural supply houses offer such sieves at reasonable prices. Perhaps the best, the U.S.A. standard sieve series, includes screen openings of many different sizes, fitted with brass rims. You can also fashion a set of sieves yourself with a minimum of effort and expense from window screens and hardware cloth of different sizes cut and fastened to wood frames.

The seeds of Evening Primroses and Sundrops, for example, are held in small, ridged capsules. To remove the seeds most efficiently, you must crush the hard capsule, and, in so doing, you will unavoidably mix some debris with the seeds. This debris will consist of particles both larger and smaller than the seeds, and at least two sieves will be necessary to separate out the seeds.

Even with the best sieving technique, however, some litter—that similar in size to the seed—will be held back. There are three techniques that can be employed to further separate the seeds if you want really clean seeds (although, again, for most purposes a small amount of litter mixed in with the seeds is not harmful). The first, the flotation method, involves pouring the mixture of seeds and litter into a container of water and leaving it undisturbed for a period of about fifteen minutes. The

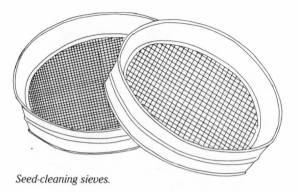

Seed-cleaning sieves.

lighter litter and undeveloped seeds will remain on the surface of the water, while the heavier, viable seeds will sink. The litter and bad seeds can simply be skimmed from the surface of the water and discarded. Good seeds should be spread out and allowed to air-dry for two days prior to storage. The second technique, blowing, uses a hair dryer (but watch the heat) or small fan to direct a stream of air across a pile of unseparated material to blow away the litter and leave the heavier seeds. Seeds and litter should be thinly spread on a flat surface and the moderate air current applied. For small seed lots a regular sheet of paper and a few puffs of breath will do quite an adequate job. The third technique is the ancient process of winnowing, or repeatedly pouring the seeds and litter from one container to another with a fan or a light breeze to blow the litter away.

Cleaning seeds that are produced in a moist, fleshy or pulpy fruiting structure, such as that found in Jack-in-the-Pulpit or Prickly Pear Cactus, requires a different strategy and appropriate cleaning techniques. When mature, the fruit of Jack-in-the-Pulpit is a tight cluster of red berries. Each berry holds from one to three small white seeds. If left unattended after collection, berries will begin to mold and the seeds inside will eventually be destroyed. The seeds should therefore be removed from the berries as soon as possible. Separate the berries from the cluster and soak them in water overnight. Next, place the softened berries in a sieve and hold them under a faucet, regulating the flow of water to separate the red pulp from the seeds. Further manipulation and some gentle mashing with a wooden spoon may be required to isolate the seeds.

The berry, or "pear," of the Prickly Pear Cactus poses a different problem. (When collecting these berries, beware of the tiny, hairlike spines—called glochids—covering the plant. They are picked up with the slightest skin contact and cause an immediate irritation. It is best to wear gloves when collecting the berries and later to rinse the fruit in water to remove as many of the spines as possible.) The numerous, hard seeds inside the sweet-smelling berry are bound together by a very sticky purple substance that demands enormous patience to remove. First, split open the berry and scoop out the cluster of seeds inside. Next, spread the seeds out on a sieve and with a strong household cleaner scrub the seeds and rinse. Usually three or four such washings are required to clean the seeds thoroughly.

Many seeds with a hard seed coat that are borne in a fleshy fruit or are surrounded by a fleshy layer (for example, Dogwood and Magnolia, respectively) can be easily separated from the softer fruit material by soaking them for a few hours (or overnight), draining them, and spreading them out in a thin layer between several sheets of newspaper placed on a smooth, firm (and washable!) floor. Wearing soft-soled shoes, walk slowly over the newspaper several times, then open the paper, scrape up the seeds and pulp, and rinse thoroughly in a sieve under running water. Much of the larger pulpy material can be removed by the flotation method. Spread the cleaned seeds thinly on clean newspaper for a day or so to dry.

Seed Storage

Under optimum moisture and temperature conditions, which vary from species to species, the seeds of some plants may remain alive and viable for many years. Some seeds of the Arctic Lupine, discovered in an ancient lemming burrow in a melting glacier, were still viable after "cold storage" for ten thousand years! Many weed seeds remain viable for ten to one hundred years, but other seeds, presumably more highly specialized for specific ecological situations or dispersal methods, may remain viable for only a few years. Generally speaking, the seeds of most plants native to the eastern United States lose viability in direct response to increased moisture or temperature, or both. Conversely, viability is extended when the seeds are stored dry and cold.

You may of course plant freshly collected seed immediately, and let nature take its course. However, germination is usually higher and more uniform with wild flower seeds stored in the refrigerator immediately after cleaning. The potential for germination of seeds left unattended or not properly stored is greatly reduced, if not lost entirely. On the other hand, seed that is stored properly should remain viable for a much longer time, in many cases for years. The seeds of Blazing Star (*Liatris spicata*), for example, remain viable in cold storage for at least six years. This can be a great advantage, for it means that you do not have to find new sources of seed for a particular species each year. A supply of stored seeds will prove especially valuable in years when seed harvest is below normal due to adverse weather conditions, insect problems, or difficulty in collecting seeds as they ripen.

Refrigerator storage is important because to keep seeds fresh for sowing, you must reduce the rate at which they respire, or "breathe," and normal refrigerator temperatures (34–41°F) are sufficient for this purpose. Small amounts of dry seed can be stored in envelopes, vials, or small plastic film canisters which are then placed in plastic bags and sealed. Larger quantities of dry seed can be stored in plastic freezer containers or clean jars with screw-on lids. Be sure to label each lot of seed (both inside and outside the package is a good idea) with the species name, date and place of collection, and when refrigerated. Use a permanent marker.

It is important when storing dry seeds, such as those of plants in the Aster family or those produced in dry pods, to keep the moisture level as low as possible in the storage container since moisture levels that are too high can support detrimental fungal growth and may even cause (or permit) germination. Therefore, make sure that "dry" seeds are allowed to air-dry further for a day or two before and after cleaning. As a further safeguard against moisture buildup, put a small amount of powdered milk or silica gel in a porous wrapper such as cheesecloth or a piece of nylon stocking and place it in the bottom of the envelope or container. These materials will draw moisture from the air and away from the seeds.

Seeds produced in moist, fleshy fruits, however, require a different strategy: they must be stored in a moist environment immediately after cleaning; otherwise they may enter an extended period of dormancy, in which they may take as long as two years to germinate after sowing, or may actually become inviable. In general, moist seeds should be stratified, or layered, in a damp medium in airtight containers and refrigerated until the following

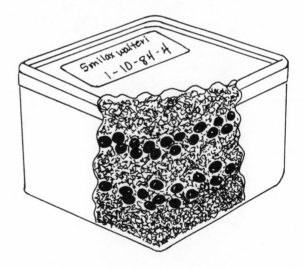

Seeds stratified in damp, whole-fiber sphagnum moss.

spring. Whole-fiber sphagnum moss, moistened and then wrung free of excess water, is an excellent material in which to stratify seeds because it remains uniformly damp for at least six months in cold storage and also inhibits fungal growth. Peat moss and sand may also be used but tend to dry out quicker and must be checked monthly during the storage period. Germination inside the container can be a problem with seeds of some wild flower species if they remain in damp storage for more than six months. Also, once germination begins in the storage container, mold is more likely.

Seeds of some species, such as Bloodroot, Toothwort, and Trillium should be sown immediately upon collection. Bloodroot and Toothwort seeds should be sown in an outdoor seedbed and kept moist during the growing season; germination is likely the following spring. If seeds are allowed to dry out, it will take two years for germination. If you want to exchange these seeds with other gardeners or hold them for later sowing, stratify them in the refrigerator, but do not be surprised if seeds so stored do not germinate in the same season

they are sown. The alternating freezing and thawing of the soil over the winter months may also be crucial for germination in seeds of some species. Trilliums must be handled only outdoors because dormancy factors in both seed and the buds of mature plants require freeze and thaw periods to "break" in the spring.

With many wild flowers, it is possible to simulate the natural influences on their seeds through proper storage and pregermination techniques. With seeds of other species, such as the Trilliums, more experimentation is needed to find techniques to induce germination artificially.

In general, dry seeds produced in dry fruiting structures should be stored dry and seeds surrounded by a moist, fleshy covering or fleshy arils should be stratified. Whenever possible, sow seeds in a prepared seedbed outdoors upon collection. However, very small seeds are easier to sow indoors in a more controlled setting. There are, of course, exceptions to these rules. Refer to the species descriptions for storage techniques appropriate for the wild flowers included in this volume.

Seed Dormancy and Pregermination Techniques

Sooner or later every wild flower gardener experiences the disappointment of planting seeds that do not germinate. When seemingly viable seeds fail to germinate in two to three weeks under favorable conditions, you can assume they are in a period of dormancy. You are more likely to run into dormancy problems with seed produced by native plants than with seed from cultivated plants offered in general nursery seed catalogs. Seeds offered by commercial seed companies are generally harvested from plants bred through many generations to produce extremely high percentages of viable seed that have no dormancy requirements by the time they are delivered to the individual gardener. On the other hand, freshly harvested seeds of many native plants have dormancy requirements that, as indicated in the previous section, can delay germination for up to two years.

Seed dormancy in nature is related to survival; biochemical mechanisms within the seed prevent germination until favorable conditions, usually of temperature and moisture, exist. The seeds of Jack-in-the-Pulpit, for instance, mature in the fall, but do not germinate until spring. If the seeds germinated immediately, it is unlikely that the immature seedlings would survive the winter. Gardeners can simulate the natural influences on Jack-in-the-Pulpit seed and "break" its dormancy by stratifying the seed in a moist medium and placing it in the refrigerator for the winter months before sowing in spring. Appropriate seed storage techniques are an essential first step in propagating many wild flowers.

A number of different mechanical and chemical mechanisms cause dormancy and delay seed germination in wild flowers. Seed coats of some species are hard and impermeable to water, other seed coats contain chemicals that inhibit germination, and still other seeds contain immature embryos at the time of dispersal and require a period of after-ripening before they are viable.

In the natural environment numerous processes and events break seed dormancy. Consistently low temperatures during winter months break down the chemical germination inhibitors in some seeds. Seeds that fall to the ground when mature and remain in the soil for some time are acted upon by microorganisms that can break down seed coats and hasten germination; or hard seed coats can be weakened by freezing and thawing during cold months. Some seeds with fleshy coverings are food for birds and other animals; as they pass through the digestive tracts of these animals, the inhibiting fleshy parts are removed and the hard seed coats are broken down somewhat by digestive acids.

Prolonged dormancy is a problem in propagation, and it is one reason why certain native species are wild collected rather than propagated by the nursery trade. Seeds of many wild flowers have dormancy requirements which must be met before germination can be expected. Seeds of Fire Pink and Purple Cone-flower, for example, germinate in a rapid, uniform manner after a four-week moist chill or stratification at 40°F. (For specific information on the stratification procedure, refer to the section on seed storage and the species descriptions.) If seeds of these species are not stratified, germination is uneven and less than 5 percent.

To break dormancy artificially in wild flower seeds, you must use the appropriate treatment. Carolina Bush Pea, White Wild Indigo, and other legumes, for example, produce seeds with hard coats. However, these seeds germinate in just a few days when subjected to scarification or immersion in hot water.

Scarification involves making a small cut in a hard seed coat to allow the seed to absorb water. As the newly planted seed takes in water through the cut, the embryo expands and ruptures the seed coat, making germination possible. Hard seeds can be scarified by filing a shallow groove in the coat or by cutting away a small piece of the coat with a pocketknife or a pair of small wirecutters.

Immersion in hot water can soften seed coats and may also deactivate chemical inhibitors in the seed coat. Place seeds in hot water (170–212°F) and allow them to remain there overnight as the water cools. Like seeds of many legumes, seeds of Blue Star benefit from combining the two treatments: after notching an end of the seed coat and immersing the seed in hot water for an hour or so, germination often occurs within one to two days.

Dormancy may be broken in some seeds that contain chemical inhibitors by the *stratification* method discussed earlier. Seeds kept moist and at a low temperature for four to eight weeks may lose their germination inhibitors. Seeds of Wild Bleeding Heart, for example, germinate promptly when stratified for six weeks.

Exposure to light is another pregermination technique that can break the dormancy or speed up germination in certain species such as Columbine. After stratifying Columbine seeds for four weeks, sow them on a medium and leave uncovered; germination should take place within a week.

Seeds of some wild flowers, such as Turk's Cap Lily, have a double dormancy and, in nature, require two years to germinate fully. The root is produced during the first dormancy period and the shoot during the second. A convenient way to handle seeds of Turk's Cap Lily and to satisfy their dormancy requirements is to stratify seeds at room temperature for three months, or until tiny white bulbs are evident, and then place the container in the refrigerator for an additional three months until tiny leaves have formed.

Sometimes if seeds are planted "green," before they ripen completely, they do not go dormant; the embryo merely continues its development, and the seeds germinate immediately. Such a procedure is worth a try on species that would otherwise need special treatment once the seed coats have hardened and the seeds become dormant.

For the gardener, recognizing that seeds of some species require special treatments to induce germination is half the battle. It is then a matter of timing the treatments so that germination occurs at a convenient time for your propagation schedule.

Propagation by Seed

Sowing

Plan your seed sowing according to how many plants you want and when you want them for setting out in the garden. First, however, assess the available space for new plantings in your garden and decide upon the kind of plants you want there. In your decision making, consider color scheme, blooming time, dimensions of the plant, and any special cultural requirements. Once you have decided on which species to sow, refer to the species descriptions regarding pregermination treatments and any special seed-handling techniques for the species you wish to grow.

In most of the mid-South area, which is our point of reference, the best time to sow seed outdoors is between February and August. (Greenhouse production can begin as early as January.) Outside of this period the risks involved in producing seedlings outdoors increase, due to uneven temperatures and shorter days. Seeds of certain slow-growing plants, such as Foamflower, Alumroot, and Thimbleweed, should always be sown indoors.

The months of February and March call for sowing indoors or in a well-insulated cold frame. It is important not to sow seeds too early. In general, seedlings remain in the seed flat for three to four weeks after germination and then in individual containers for five to six weeks more. To set plants out at the beginning of the frost-free period in spring you must sow eight to ten weeks before the average last date of frost in your part of the country, about May 1 here at the Garden in central North Carolina.

During the remaining months, say May to August in the Southeast and a slightly shorter period elsewhere, seeds can be safely sown outdoors in a seedbed or frame. Outdoor sowing offers one great advantage: less of your time will be needed to maintain the seedlings. For late-winter sowing select the south-facing area in or around your home that receives the greatest amount of sun. Remember that many plants can be started in a small space; seeds sown at a density of only three per square inch will produce 432 seedlings per square foot.

When seed is to be sown in pots, flats, or other containers, follow this procedure:

1. Make sure containers are at least 3 inches deep (to avoid their drying out so quickly) and fill them to their tops with seed mix.
2. Tamp the mix lightly but firmly to ½ inch below the top of the container.
3. Moisten the mix; it should be moist but not wet at the time of sowing.
4. Scatter tiny seeds on the surface and cover with a dusting of soil. When possible, sow seed thinly to avoid crowding later. Larger seeds should be sown in rows at ¼-inch spacing and covered with an amount of soil twice their diameter.
5. Label containers of newly sown seed with the species and sowing date.
6. Water small seeds from below, that is, immerse the container in a shallow tray of water until the surface of the soil is moist. Water larger seeds from above using a water breaker or rose.
7. A thin layer of milled sphagnum moss may be spread over the surface of the seed mix after sowing to further retain moisture and to inhibit fungal growth.

After the first watering, place seed containers in a shallow (2-inch), watertight tray or saucer lined with 1 inch of pea gravel. This arrangement will allow you to water thoroughly and avoid water problems indoors by providing good drainage for seedlings. Excess water in the tray will add moisture to the air as its evaporates, a condition beneficial to young seedlings.

When sowing indoors in February and March, place the seed flats in a sunny, south-facing window. Seedlings need six to eight hours of direct light per day; less light produces a spindly seedling.

Rapid, uniform germination is most likely to occur when a constant soil temperature of 70–75°F is maintained day and night. You can facilitate this with rubberized heating mats with thermostatic controls or heating cables placed immediately below the germinating medium. Alternatively, place a pane of glass or piece of clear plastic over the container to conserve heat and moisture.

After germination, remove the cover for gradually longer periods each day to allow the seedlings to acclimate to room temperatures. These temperatures should vary from 60–70°F days to 45–50°F nights—which produces a slow-growing but hardy seedling. When the time comes for transplanting, your space requirements will of course increase; allow 4 square inches for a seedling to develop to planting size, or 1 square foot per thirty-six seedlings.

To get a headstart on outdoor sowing, in the late winter sow seeds in a seed frame, cold frame, or hot bed. These structures differ in the amount of labor and expense necessary to construct them and the amount of protection they provide for the new seedlings, but all have certain minimum features, including:

· good drainage
· a south-facing exposure receiving six to eight hours of direct light per day
· ventilation to moderate inside temperatures
· protection from the wind.

The simplest of these and cheapest to construct is the seed frame, which can add a month to the growing season. This structure is simply a wooden frame (concrete blocks or other building materials will suffice) sitting on the ground and covered with a half-cylindrical wire fencing (or hardware cloth) frame supporting 4-mil clear plastic with ends closed. The frame should be deep enough to accommodate 6 inches or more of soil mix. The Botanical Garden uses 12-by-6-foot frames built with pressure-treated 2-by-12 boards. This is the basic outdoor seed frame referred to frequently in this book. You can of course design whatever size frame is appropriate for your own space and needs.

You can sow seeds directly into the soil or in flats placed in the frame. Make sure you have proper drainage below the frame and make the seedbed at least 4–6 inches deep. For best exposure orient the ends of the frame east and west. A plastic-covered seed frame should provide a 10–15°F increase in daytime temperatures, but only a 5°F temperature increase at night. You can achieve

slightly higher temperatures in the frame if you mound soil against the outside of the frame. The only heat source here is the sun. Ventilation, though, is still important, especially on bright days; prop the covering open or remove it altogether.

A properly constructed cold frame is a step above the simple seed frame in performance (and expense) and can extend the growing season by at least two months. A cold frame is an outdoor growing structure where the sun is the only source of heat. The basic site characteristics are the same as those for other outdoor seed structures, but the cold frame makes more efficient use of heat from the sun and the insulation of the earth. There are numerous designs for cold frames, and any good guide to general gardening techniques should give you instructions for making your own; all, however, should have these features:

· the glazing (glass, fiberglass, or plastic) should face only south
· the east, west, and north sides of the frame should be walls of wood, masonry, or other material that can be insulated
· inside walls should be painted white to reflect light
· the frame should be sunk in the ground at least 4–6 inches to take advantage of the earth's heat and insulation and to reduce wind chill.

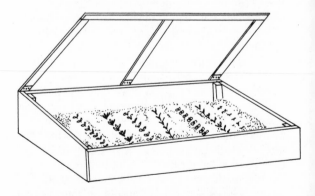

The cold frame can be used to sow seeds, root cuttings, and overwinter containerized plants.

To ensure a tight, efficient structure, all walls should be insulated in sandwich fashion—for example, a 1-inch styrofoam piece between outside and inside walls. Glazing should be double layered with an air space in between.

Cold frames require careful monitoring to avoid overheating the plants on bright winter days and to allow for ventilation and shading during summer use. Saran shade cloth and reed mats can be laid over the sashes for summer shading. Regular watering checks are a must to keep young seedlings from drying out and to maintain high humidity. The cold frame also minimizes disturbances by animals and weather.

Sow seeds directly in the soil in the cold frame, or if only a few plants are desired, sow in pots and bury them to the rim in the frame. As plants begin to establish themselves in the frame, the sash may be opened slightly during the day to provide ventilation and a slightly drier environment. The cold frame can also be used to root summer cuttings and overwinter container plants.

A hot bed is similar in design and construction to the cold frame, except that it incorporates a source of bottom heat for cloudy days and cold nights. Some hot beds use thermostatically controlled heating cables and mats positioned below the propagating medium. In some areas gardeners often bury fresh manure below the medium, but the heat output and duration are variable with this method, depending on what kind of manure is employed and how fresh it is. If you choose this method, you will want to experiment with temperature range and ventilation requirements before attempting to produce seedlings. Another option is to run a heating duct from a home heating system into the frame. To check excessive heat build-up, it is essential to open the sashes of the hot bed at the right time during the day.

If you choose to germinate seeds in an outdoor structure, you will need to harden off the seedlings prior to planting them in the garden. This means finding a midway point between the amounts of light, humidity, heat, and moisture in the frame and the amounts they will obtain in the garden. The hardening-off process, which should begin one to two weeks before permanent planting, is best done by opening the sash to the frame a bit earlier each day and closing it a bit later. Also, let seedlings dry out a little more each time between successive waterings during this period. A cool, cloudy day is the best time to move seedlings into the garden.

Outdoor sowing is practical when the soil temperature remains above 60°F, from mid-May through August in central North Carolina. You could sow seeds directly in the places where you want mature plants. But since the germination percentage is typically low for seeds sown in their permanent locations and since you have less control over water and light, it is difficult to produce a uniform stand of seedlings.

The easiest, least costly, and most effective method of sowing outdoors is to sow seeds in a small bed of prepared soil. Such a bed should include the following:

· a soil mix that drains freely and is raised 4 to 8 inches above ground level
· a nearby water source
· a rectangular shape narrow enough (3 to 4 feet across) to allow you to reach the middle without stepping in the bed and compacting the soil
· location in an area receiving some protection from the summer sun.

If you want to locate your outdoor seedbed in full sun, consider building a simple lath structure to support saran cloth shading, which can be obtained from horticultural supply companies. Saran cloth is available in grades that provide different percentages of shade and can significantly lower summer temperatures without seriously reducing the amount of light needed by most seedlings.

Structures are not needed during the summer, although a simple uncovered frame constructed with pressure-treated lumber provides a convenient unit for summer sowing. Among the advantages of outdoor sowing in carefully prepared seedbeds are rapid, uniform germination, fewer maintenance and disease problems, and fast-growing seedlings. In particular, watering is not as critical because the moisture content remains more uniform in deeper earth beds. Plants started outdoors in the summer can be moved to permanent spots in the garden in the fall, where they will flower the following year.

Outdoor sowing is also practical for nurseries offering native perennials. Seeds of Rose Mallow (*Hibiscus moscheutos*), for example, sown in an outdoor seedbed on 1 July would be ready for potting into 3-inch containers by 20 July; by 15 August the seedlings would be large enough to transfer to 4-inch pots and by mid-September could be moved to quart containers and overwintered or transplanted into the garden.

Soil Mixes

Garden soils alone are usually inadequate for seed and potting mixes as they are typically not porous enough to provide proper aeration and drainage. When these soils dry, they often shrink and harden and water tends to run down the sides of the pot and drain away. The addition of coarse sand, shredded pine bark, and perlite improves these soils.

If you need only modest amounts of seed bed or potting soil you can save time, and possibly some expense, by purchasing these mixes already prepared. Such materials are sterile (free of weeds, insects, and harmful organisms) and properly blended; they also often have dry fertilizers already mixed in. Prepared mixes can be purchased at garden centers, agricultural supply houses, and some department stores. Seed mixes that contain fertilizer should not be bottom watered because salts can leach upward and impair seedling development. Mixes that do not contain fertilizer will require weekly applications of fertilizer.

A good seed mix must drain properly but still retain enough moisture to be taken up by roots. A poorly drained, muddy soil prevents proper air circulation around roots, invites disease, and produces inferior seedlings. Both seed and potting mixes that you prepare yourself should be screened (using 1/4-inch mesh) after mixing to remove any large particles. Commercial seed mixes and the homemade mixes described below are appropriate for indoor and outdoor sowing.

Seed mixes 1 and 2 will need to be sterilized at 140°F for ninety minutes in the oven. At this temperature nematodes and most plant pathogens will be killed, but some beneficial organisms will remain that can later check an outbreak of harmful organisms. Mix 3 requires no sterilization.

Seed Mix 1
  1 part: good garden soil
  1 part: leaf mold or peat moss
  1 part: coarse sand

Seed Mix 2
  1 part: loamy soil
  1 part: peat moss
  1 part: sand

Seed Mix 3
  2 parts: peat moss
  1 part: perlite
  1 part: sand

The following potting mix is adequate for seedlings and larger container-grown plants.

Potting Mix
  3 parts: pine bark—soil mix grade (1/2-inch nuggets and smaller)
  2 parts: peat moss
  1 part: sand—coarse grade
  6 lbs. dolomitic lime per cubic yard (27 cubic feet)
  5 lbs. super phosphate per cubic yard
  6 oz. trace elements per cubic yard
  (Or, for 4.5 cubic feet [a normal wheelbarrow load], 19 oz. lime, 12 oz. super phosphate, and 1 oz. trace elements)

To prepare a soil mix, moisten the main ingredients and arrange them in layers; add the lime and other items and then mix by turning them with a shovel. The finished mix should be crumbly. For artificial mixes the dry fertilizers should be incorporated with other materials at the time of mixing. These include dolomitic lime or gypsum, super phosphate, trace elements, and others.

Transplanting Seedlings

Transplanting at the proper time is critical to the survival of a seedling. After germination, the cotyledons, or "seed leaves," are the first to emerge. The next leaves to appear are the first "true" leaves, which are often somewhat similar in shape to the leaves of the mature plant. The best time to transplant seedlings is while the first set of true leaves is enlarging. The seedlings should not be disturbed before this time, as leaf, stem, and root tissues are soft and easily damaged. If you transplant after this time—for instance, when the second set of true leaves has appeared—you run the risk of tearing the roots when lifting seedlings from the flat.

The containers that will hold the transplanted seedlings should be sterilized to reduce fungal infection (damping off) of the seedlings. Prepare a drench using ten parts water to one part all-purpose bleach. After rinsing the container with water, dip it in the drench for a few seconds, remove, and allow to dry.

Use a thin wooden plant label or flat stick to remove the seedlings from the flat, lifting out a few at a time. A thorough watering prior to transplanting will ease removal. Slide the stick under the seedlings and gently pry them loose from the soil. When transplanting a seedling, grasp a leaf, and not the stem, between thumb and forefinger. After removing a clump of seedlings from the flat, mist the seedlings with an atomizer to keep them from drying out. Be careful not to leave roots exposed any longer than is necessary, as this can quickly weaken the seedlings. Separate individual seedlings from the clump and pot them immediately. Dibble a hole deep enough for the roots, plant the seedling, and gently firm the soil next to the roots, allowing the surface of the soil to remain loose. Tap the pot several times on the bench to settle the soil and eliminate air pockets.

Your potting technique will depend on where new growth appears on the seedlings of the species you are working with. Seedlings that have an erect stem, such as White Wild Indigo and Bur-Marigold, produce new growth at the tip of the stem. When potting "stem seedlings," you can insert stems in the soil to just below the first set of

Removing seedlings from the flat.

true leaves. This technique also helps stabilize the seedling in the container. A second type of seedling does not elongate but produces new basal growth, and forms rosettes; Black-eyed Susan and Cardinal Flower are good examples of "rosette seedlings," which must be planted at precisely the same depth as they grow in the seed flat. The rosettes should "sit" on the surface of the soil.

When transplanting species that have rosettes with densely hairy leaves, such as the Maryland Golden Aster and Purple Cone-flower, you should mound the potting mix slightly at the base of the plant to facilitate surface drainage, for the fine hairs on the leaves can trap water and lead to leaf rot.

Pot seedlings in small containers. A convenient size is 3 inches wide to 2 ½ inches deep. Alternatively, space seedlings 2 inches apart in a flat; al-

Mound the potting mix slightly to accommodate seedlings with hairy leaves.

low the seedlings to grow until their roots fill up the container.

To remove well-rooted seedlings from the flat, cut the soil into squares so that each plant has a proportionate amount of soil around its roots. Do not let seedlings become pot bound. Check root growth at least once a week. When roots reach the bottom of the pot or when they begin to spiral around the sides, it's time to transplant seedlings either to a larger container or into the garden.

Maintenance

After seedlings are potted, move them to a well-lighted area with good air circulation. Inadequate lighting and poor ventilation invite disease. Check seedlings often during the three to four days after transplanting. Make sure that "stem seedlings" are upright in their pots and have not fallen over. A heavy hand with the hose or watering can can topple and kill young seedlings. Check to see that leaves of "rosette seedlings" are not in contact with the soil and remove any soil that may splash onto their leaves. Wilting is a sign that seedlings may not be moist enough. If leaves lighten in color or show signs of burning, move seedlings to a location with indirect light or shade them with cheesecloth, saran cloth, or other screening material until they recover.

Watering is the most important aspect of seedling maintenance. The condition of the soil determines when to water. The surface of the soil, however, is not a reliable indicator. The best way to determine whether a plant is dry and needs water is to tap the plant and its ball of soil from the container and note the moisture level. This can be done by placing the foliage between your fingers and inverting the container, tapping the bottom, and lifting it off. If the surface is dry but the rest of the soil moist, the plant does not need watering. If most of the soil is dry, as evidenced by a lighter color, then it's time to water.

Hefting the pot is another way to determine degree of dryness. A light pot can indicate a dry soil; peat soil will feel very light when dry; a sandy soil, heavier. Experiment for a few days using pot weight as a measure of dryness. Avoid leaving water on leaves at night, which can encourage disease; this means watering before mid-afternoon on a sunny day. Be aware that a plant with a leaf area larger than its soil area will dry out faster than a plant with a smaller leaf to soil area ratio.

Various watering devices are helpful when watering plants in their seedling stage. A fog nozzle can be attached to a standard hose connection to produce a fine, foglike spray, which is useful for watering seed flats and containers until seedlings are established. There are numerous commercially available water breakers and watering roses that attach to hoses and watering cans. They serve to break or soften, and evenly distribute, the flow of water. An aluminum extension or watering wand is a convenient device for watering more plants from a given spot. It is important to move rapidly over the seedlings when watering; otherwise puddling may result and seedlings may be knocked over. To ensure thorough penetration, move water over the plants two to three times, allowing water to drain before returning for another sweep. Seedlings will dry out faster on sunny days and will need to be checked several times during the day. Watering should be avoided on cloudy days because damp, low-light conditions can cause disease problems. Refer to the species descriptions for specific recommendations. Inspect your seedlings after you water and attend to any that have fallen over.

Crowding is a common problem in seed flats and pots. As discussed earlier, sowing seeds evenly can control crowding to some degree, but this is difficult with tiny seeds, such as those of Sundrops. To relieve a crowded condition, just thin the seedlings with tweezers to $1/4$-inch spacing. While they remain in containers, fast-growing "stem seedlings," such as Bee-balm and Mountain Mint, should be pruned back every two to three weeks to encourage bushier plants.

Most native plant seedlings respond favorably to fertilization. Weekly applications of an all-purpose fertilizer, like 20–20–20, for example, will produce faster-growing seedlings. The three sets of numbers (8–8–8, 10–10–10) printed on containers of commercially available fertilizers represent nitrogen (N), phosphorus (P), and potassium (K). Nitrogen affects vegetative growth; phosphorus aids in root development; and potassium enhances flower bud production. All-purpose liquid and granular fertilizers are available at garden centers and at some hardware and department stores. Instructions are clearly printed on the label.

Unless you are working with large numbers of seedlings, a watering can is the most efficient means of applying fertilizer. For large-scale production of seedlings, the use of a proportioner or fertilizer applicator attached to a hose lets you fertilize many plants without having to stop and replenish the fertilizer solution. Fertilize on sunny days when the soil is dry or nearly so. The build-up of soluble salts in the soil—a potentially fatal condition to seedlings—can result from heavy or too frequent fertilization. When over-fertilized, seedlings exhibit discoloration in their foliage and a general decline in appearance. Be sure to flush seedlings thoroughly with water at least once before you fertilize again.

Some commercial germination and potting mixes contain dry fertilizer. When using such a mix, no additional fertilizer is needed in the flat. If you prepare your own sowing medium or use a commercial one without dry fertilizer included, however, a starter fertilizer, such as 9–45–15, applied at weekly intervals after germination is helpful.

Native ferns and plants of certain wild flower genera, such as members of the Lily family, may exhibit adverse reactions to fertilization; leaf burn is the primary symptom; other species respond more favorably to solutions applied at a strength of one-quarter of the recommended amount. Refer to the species descriptions for specific recommendations. Use a light hand when fertilizing and watch seedlings closely during the next few days. When working with large numbers of seedlings, it is a good practice to apply the fertilizer to just a few plants initially to ascertain the results. Particularly when working with very sensitive species or species about which you have little information, such precautions can avoid the possible loss of most or all of the seedlings from improperly mixed fertilizer solutions.

Asexual Propagation

When only a few new plants of a particular kind are needed, asexual, or vegetative, increase is, for several reasons, often a logical alternative to propagation by seed. Increasing wild flowers by cuttings and division can produce new plants in a shorter period of time and with less effort to the gardener, and these plants will require less maintenance. Blue-eyed Grass and Foamflower, for example, require three to five months to develop into plants large enough for permanent planting when grown from seed but dividing mature clumps of these species will yield sizable plants, ready for immediate transplanting into the garden.

Another advantage of asexual propagation is that the new plants will be exactly like the parent plant genetically and in appearance, while it is not uncommon to find considerable variation in appearance in a batch of seedlings. When propagating by asexual means, then, it is important to select a vigorous, disease-free stock plant.

Division

Division is the easiest method of asexual propagation. In general, spring-blooming plants should be divided in the fall and fall-blooming plants in the spring to minimize interruptions in flowering. Also, you avoid disturbing the plant in hot weather.

Some wild flowers, however, such as White Wild Indigo, the Mallows, Blazing Star, and Bloodroot, should be divided during their dormant season when no foliage is present. For some other species, including Wild Bleeding Heart and Blue-eyed Grass, division is a way to rejuvenate a planting in the garden as well as to make new plants. As it matures, Wild Bleeding Heart develops a tough rootstock with numerous small crowns, or eyes, bunched together. Each crown is a potential new plant. If the crowns are not separated out, the center of the parent plant will steadily decline in vigor, spread out more, and become less attractive.

New plants created by division are often more vigorous and attractive than the stock plant from which they were taken. Blue-eyed Grass, for instance, which develops a dense, ingrown habit, must be divided at least every other year to maintain a healthy stand of plants. A single clump can be separated into smaller clumps or individual plants.

Use the following procedure when dividing herbaceous perennials:

1. Before dividing, decide how many new plants you want and prepare the planting area where the divisions are to be set out.
2. In the early spring or fall, lift a mature plant from the garden with a spade or trowel and shake the excess soil loose.
3. To further remove the soil and view the entire plant, rinse the roots in water.
4. Prune any stems back to the basal foliage.
5. Decide upon the appropriate technique for division. Shallow-rooted species with multiple crowns, such as Foamflower, the Beard Tongues, and Green-and-Gold, are easy to separate by hand by simply teasing the crowns apart. Plants that have dense, overlapping rosettes, such as Stokes' Aster, can be divided at random by hand. Clumps of Carolina Bush Pea and Rose Mallow, which have deep, woody rootstalks and large crowns, have to be divided with a shovel. Cardinal Flower, Black-eyed Susan, and other plants that produce basal offsets can be divided by simply separating the offsets by hand from the parent plant.
6. When single crowns are broken away from the stock plant and some root or rhizome tissue is exposed—as when dividing Stokes' Aster—apply a thin coating of a commercial fungicide to protect the exposed area.
7. Replant and water divisions immediately and tamp the soil to remove air pockets.

Root Cuttings

Propagation by root cuttings is also easy and reliable, and since it requires little in the way of materials, this method is an inexpensive option for producing plants of certain species; Stokes' Aster, and Butterfly Weed are examples of wild flowers readily increased by this technique. Take root cuttings to-

A clump and division of Blue-eyed Grass.

ward the end of the dormant season—late February and March in most parts of the East.

First, decide on the number of new plants you want to produce per species. If you want, say, fewer than ten, section off several pieces of the root system around the edges of a mature plant with a sharp spade or trowel. If you want more plants, lift the entire stock plant out of the ground.

Select the largest roots in the sectioned piece or clump; ideally, they should be pencil-size in diameter. Rinse the soil from the roots, and cut the larger roots into 2-to-4-inch lengths. When you later place the root pieces in the growing medium, you must position them with the same polarity—that is, their orientation up and down. To mark a root piece for correct polarity, make the cut on the end

49

toward the crown straight across and make the cut on the other end at a slant. Thin, delicate roots can be cut into 1-to-2-inch pieces and laid horizontally in rows in a flat of screened soil or sand and covered with a half inch of sand.

Root cuttings can be set in a pot, a flat, an outdoor seed frame, or a cold frame. Pots and flats containing cuttings should be sunk in the cold frame or seed frame or heeled-in in a protected spot outside. Cuttings may also be inserted directly in the soil of the cold frame or seed frame. Make sure your rooting mix is well drained; equal parts peat moss and sand will serve the purpose well.

Insert the root cutting vertically in the medium so that the "top" is at soil level. Cover the surface of the soil with a half inch of sand and firm it lightly. After watering, cover the pot, flat, or frame with a pane of glass or polyethylene plastic to maintain high humidity in the rooting environment. When shoots appear in the spring, they can be fertilized weekly with an all-purpose fertilizer; when shoots are 3 inches tall, they can be transplanted to individual containers and grown on until the plants are large enough to move into the garden.

When rooting a small number of cuttings, you might want to try the following method:

1. Cut a piece of polyethylene plastic twice the length of the root cuttings.

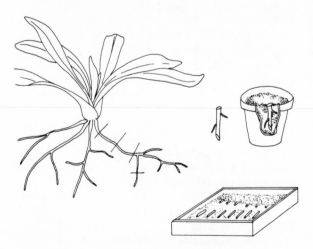

Root cuttings planted horizontally and vertically.

2. Spread a layer of damp, whole-fiber sphagnum moss across the upper half of the plastic.
3. Lay the cuttings vertically on the sphagnum. Be sure to maintain correct polarity, with the straight cut up.
4. Fold the bottom half of the plastic up over the cuttings and, beginning at one end, roll the cuttings up in the plastic.
5. Place the tube or roll of cuttings in an upright position in the cold frame or in a window receiving indirect light in the house and look for shoots in the opening at the top of the tube in several weeks.
6. Once 2-to-3 inch shoots have formed, pot up the separate cuttings as described above.

Stem Cuttings

Although more difficult to work with than root cuttings and divisions, stem cuttings are another means of propagating wild flowers at home. Sanitation is very important when you are working with stem cuttings. Tools and equipment—pruning shears, knives, flats, and pots—should be sterilized in a solution of ten parts water to one part all-purpose bleach and then rinsed in fresh water.

When handling stem cuttings, you must not let them dry out. Maintaining correct moisture conditions in the rooting environment is essential if cuttings are not to become too dry (or too wet).

Softwood cuttings are more susceptible to disease than seedlings, divisions, and root cuttings, and they require considerable attention. Regular inspection is your best way to head off diseases and produce healthy, well-rooted cuttings.

The following procedures will help you in propagating from stem cuttings:

1. Gather cuttings in the early part of the day. Wrap them in a moist material, such as dampened whole-fiber sphagnum moss, until they are placed in the rooting medium.
2. Avoid exposing the cuttings to direct sunlight and do not store them in water.

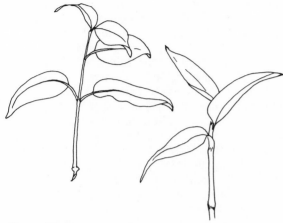

Stem cuttings.

3. Make sure your stock plants are vigorous and disease free; often roots develop faster when juvenile or seedling stock plants are used.
4. Use the terminal portion of the stem for the cutting. Make your cut just below a leaf bud and include at least two nodes.
5. Remove any flower buds or fruiting structures from the top of the cutting and the leaves from the lower half.
6. Remove the tip of the cutting to encourage side shoots.

Fresh cuttings should be put in a rooting medium as soon as possible after collection. To conserve space, cuttings can be positioned close to each other, with leaves touching. The rooting medium should be sterile, 4–5 inches deep, well drained, and premoistened. A satisfactory mix can be made of equal parts peat moss and perlite or equal parts peat moss and sand. Hormones and nutrient additions are not required when rooting most herbaceous cuttings.

The rooting environment should include the following features:
· a temperature of 65–75°F
· high humidity
· indirect light
· perfect drainage to avoid rotting.

Stem cuttings can be rooted in a variety of inexpensive structures, or rooting chambers. A wooden flat 7 inches deep, covered with a glass panel, is adequate. A larger cover for this flat can be constructed by arching hardware cloth or 2- or 4-inch wire fencing over the flat and covering it with a piece of clear polyethylene. This structure can also be used for germinating seeds. A cold frame can also be used to root cuttings, but shading must be provided.

A rectangular aquarium with a glass or polyethylene cover serves well as a rooting chamber. You must provide coarse material in the bottom layer of the rooting medium for drainage. Do not allow excess water to sit in the bottom, and keep the structure out of direct sunlight.

A rooting method using two clay pots, one inside the other, can be used for rooting a few cuttings in a small space. Sink the smaller clay pot, with the drainage hole plugged, in the center of the rooting medium in the larger pot. Stick cuttings in the circle of rooting medium exposed between the lips of the two pots. Position a clear polyethylene cover over the larger pot, supported on a frame of wire or some other material. Keep the smaller pot filled with water. This maintains a high humidity within the plastic enclosure and the clay sides allow moisture to seep slowly into the medium.

Heat must not be allowed to build up in the rooting chamber. Locate the structure out of direct sunlight and ventilate when necessary. As an indicator of humidity, some condensation should appear on the inside of the glass or polyethylene cover.

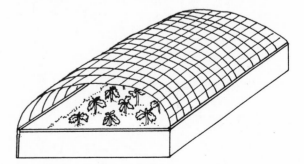

This frame for rooting cuttings can also be used to germinate seeds.

Cuttings should be "watered in" thoroughly following insertion into the medium. Check cuttings once or twice on bright days and mist leaves if they are dry. A plastic atomizer is handy for this purpose. Because cuttings initially do not have roots and are thus restricted in their uptake of water, care must be taken to ensure that they do not dry out. Cuttings can die if their leaves are allowed to become dry for even a few hours on a bright day. Though the medium should be well drained, it should be checked regularly and saturated when it becomes dry. In the commercial production of herbaceous plants in a greenhouse, an automated mist system is typically used to keep cuttings uniformly moist; the system emits a mist at timed intervals from overhead nozzles.

Cuttings are ready to be transplanted when roots are 1–2 inches long. Harden off cuttings several days before you transplant them to individual containers. The hardening-off process can be achieved by reducing the humidity within the chamber; cut back on watering and increase ventilation.

Using a spoon or wooden stick label, gently lift the cuttings, being careful not to tear roots and making sure to include a generous amount of soil around the roots. Pot them in your seedling mix, water thoroughly, and locate containers in a protected spot outdoors, out of direct sunlight.

When roots fill up the container, rooted cuttings can be transplanted into the garden. Make sure that this final transplanting is carried out at least a month prior to the first expected frost to allow plants to establish themselves before the onset of winter. The species descriptions will help you gauge the time required for the rooting of cuttings from particular species.

Part 3. Wild Flowers

Passion Flower vine in flower and fruit (photograph by NCBG Staff).

Painted Trillium in flower in May (photograph by George Pyne).

Painted Trillium berries in July (photograph by James Ward).

Painted Trillium berries split open; ants seeking the fleshy white arils often carry off the seeds (photograph by James Ward).

Jack-in-the-Pulpit in flower in April (photograph by NCBG Staff).

Jack-in-the-Pulpit berry cluster in August (photograph by Rob Gardner).

Cross Vine in flower (photograph by Ken Moore).

Beard Tongue (Penstemon smallii) (photograph by Rob Gardner).

Yellow Jessamine vine trained on a low wall (photograph by Rob Gardner).

Foamflower massed in the woodland garden (photograph by Rob Gardner).

Carolina Bush Pea in bud and flower (photograph by Rob Gardner).

Black-eyed Susan and Butterfly Weed in the sunny border (photograph by Rob Gardner).

Seashore Mallow (photograph by Ken Moore).

Green-and-Gold trailing over rocks (photograph by Ken Moore).

Joe-Pye-Weed (photograph by Ken Moore).

The flowers of Horsemint (photograph by Rob Gardner).

Seashore Mallow with Rudbeckia fulgida *in the foreground and Joe-Pye-Weed and Wild Sunflower in the background (photograph by Ken Moore).*

Cardinal Flower and ferns planted next to a deck (photograph by Rob Gardner).

Green-and-Gold and Cinnamon Fern (photograph by Ken Moore).

Ox-eye Daisy, Fire Pink, Calliopsis, and Moth Mullein interplanted on a dry, sunny roadbank (photograph by Rob Gardner).

Spiderwort and Coreopsis auriculata *(photograph by Rob Gardner).*

Boltonia and Rough-leaved Goldenrod (photograph by Rob Gardner).

The woodland garden in spring (photograph by Rob Gardner).

A goldfinch feeding on Purple Cone-flower (photograph by Rob Gardner).

Rough-leaved Goldenrod and New England Aster (photograph by Rob Gardner).

White Wild Indigo in bud and a volunteer Columbine (photograph by Rob Gardner).

Cardinal Flowers are often visited by hummingbirds (photograph by Rob Gardner).

Phacelia and Cinnamon Ferns on a wet margin (photograph by Rob Gardner).

Sunlight illuminates delicate fronds of New York Fern (photograph by Charlotte Jones-Roe).

Plastic-lined display bed for Pitcher Plants at the North Carolina Botanical Garden (photograph by Rob Gardner).

Sensitive Fern adds color to areas that are poorly drained (photograph by Charlotte Jones-Roe).

Yellow Pitcher Plant grown in a dishpan (photograph by Larry Mellichamp).

Introduction

The information provided here is intended as a guide to the propagation and cultivation of a variety of native and naturalized wild flowers found in the eastern United States. Much of the information, however, should also be helpful for growing related native species over a much greater area. Most of the plants treated are perennials—enduring for three years or longer; *Daucus*, *Phacelia*, and *Verbascum* are biennials—completing their life cycles in two years or seasons; and *Bidens*, *Gaillardia*, and *Trichostema* are annuals—completing their life cycles in a single year or season.

The specific propagation data and cultural suggestions are drawn from our experience in the on-going native plant research program at the North Carolina Botanical Garden, Chapel Hill, North Carolina (35°54′ north latitude, 79°2′ west longitude; altitude 290 feet above sea level), and represent only a small percentage of the many native plants suitable for cultivation. The blooming dates and seed maturation dates we give also reflect our experience, and they will of course be earlier for areas south of Chapel Hill and a bit later for areas to the north. The dates may also vary from year to year according to local weather trends.

Each species entry provides certain specific information for the plant treated, but many of the methods and handling techniques referred to assume a familiarity with the general information provided in the introductory sections on propagating and cultivating native plants. The horticultural and botanical terms used in the species descriptions are defined in the glossary. The species described are presented in their natural blooming sequence, referenced to the blooming chart in appendix 2.

The Garden maintains source lists of nurseries offering propagated wild flowers, concerns offering wild flower seeds, and native plant societies and their current mailing addresses. All are available without charge. To order any of these lists, send a stamped, self-addressed envelope to:

North Carolina Botanical Garden, GNP
Totten Center, 457-A
University of North Carolina at Chapel Hill
Chapel Hill, N.C. 27514

Format

Names. Common, scientific, and family names are given for each plant treated. Of course common names can change from one state or region to the next; the common name chosen was the one judged to be that most widely used by wild flower enthusiasts. If you desire more information on a particular plant, it is always best to use the scientific name to cross-reference it in a regional flora or other source to avoid possible confusion.

Illustrations. The outline drawings are provided to help the reader recognize the flower, fruit, and seed of each plant. Drawings for some plants also show rosettes, roots, and rhizomes where these are of special interest or importance. The drawings of the fruits were made at or very near the time of seed maturation. The scale line beside each seed drawing represents 1 centimeter of actual size; for example, a line 2 centimeters long indicates that the drawing has been enlarged to twice normal size.

Description. This section includes the range and general habitat of the species as it occurs in the eastern United States, that is, east of the Mississippi River; its general height and habit of growth; when the plant flowers; flower shape, color, and size (in inches and metric equivalents for ease of comparison with regional floras); leaf characteristics; and other distinguishing features of the plant.

Fruit and Seed. The size (in inches and metric equivalents), color, shape, and other distinguishing features of the fruiting structure and seeds, as well as the time between flowering and maturation of the seed, are given for each entry.

Seed Collection, Cleaning, and Storage. This section, which is critical to any efforts to propagate from seed, describes the fruits and seeds at maturity and gives suggestions to facilitate collection, such as how to recognize mature seeds and when to collect seeds to catch them before they disperse. Suggestions on how to remove seeds from the fruits and whether to store seeds "dry" or "moist" are also provided.

Propagation. Each section on propagation is broken down into as many as three subsections covering particular propagation techniques appropriate for each plant.

The subheading *Seed* includes recommendations for pregermination treatments if needed; what time of year and where to sow seeds; the approximate time required for germination and the percentage of germination to expect; how long (in weeks) is required for seedlings to develop to a size large enough for transplanting to containers; how to care for seedlings (watering, fertilizing, potting medium, and so forth); and when to set out plants in the garden.

The subheading *Cuttings* includes recommendations on cutting type (stem, root, and so forth); cutting size and when to make them; what rooting medium is best; how to care for cuttings; and how long (in weeks) it should take plants to root.

The subheading *Division* includes recommendations on the best time of year to divide a mature plant and specific handling techniques for divisions.

Cultivation. This section provides information on how to establish the plant successfully in a garden setting. Our approach treats wild flowers as culti-

vated plants that need the same care and attention you would give to traditional garden varieties. All the species discussed will require attention during the growing season, a given species' reputation for hardiness notwithstanding. Such considerations as proper exposure, preparation of the planting area, and regular maintenance activities during the growing season are treated under this heading.

Uses in the Garden and Landscape. This section gives suggestions for how best to display the plant, whether in a border planting, informal setting, or naturalized area. Also, we suggest other wild flowers with which the plant might be effectively combined and comment on the plant's adaptability to container culture and the suitability of its cut flowers for use in arrangements.

Related Species. Other species in the same genus which have ornamental potential are discussed briefly here, along with notes on their special requirements.

Production Notes. If the plant lends itself to large-scale production in a commercial nursery operation, any special recommendations or notes for propagation and handling techniques that have not already been mentioned earlier in the description are given in this last section.

Skunk Cabbage

Symplocarpus foetidus
Araceae

Duration: perennial

Blooming time: January–March

Flower color: purple, spotted with green

Height: 2 feet

Soil: boggy

Exposure: shade to sun

Description

These interesting, malodorous plants occur in wet meadows and swampy woods and thickets throughout the northeastern and north-central states, where great sweeps of skunk cabbage, covering an acre or more, can commonly be observed growing in with White Hellebore (*Veratrum viride*). The southern limit of the plant's range is North Carolina, where Skunk Cabbage is found in only a few piedmont and mountain counties. The plants are among the very earliest to flower, typically blooming in the snow in February. In an artificial bog at the North Carolina Botanical Garden, however, the plants are predictably in flower at Christmas.

Marking the end of the bloom period, tightly wrapped leaf buds push up through the ground to produce the large, basal, heart-shaped leaves (up to 2 feet long on 1-foot petioles). These are malodorous only when crushed or broken, giving off a skunklike smell.

The inflorescence, like that of Jack-in-the-Pulpit, is composed of a spathe and spadix. The fleshy ovoid spathe, 3–4 inches tall, is hooded, abruptly pointed, and purple with greenish spots or stripes. The spadix, which bears the minute male, or staminate, flowers above and the female, or pistillate, flowers below, is located within the protective cover of the spathe and is somewhat globular in outline and 1–2 inches (2.5–5 cm) broad.

Fruit and Seed

Skunk Cabbage requires the whole of the growing season to mature its seeds. The rounded seeds, ⅓ inch (8 mm) long at maturity, are embedded in the spadix, which can expand to 4 inches across by October. The fruiting spadix darkens and takes on a soft spongy texture as it develops. It resembles a blackjack and can frequently be found on

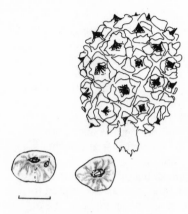

the ground after the foliage has gone.

Seed Collection, Cleaning, and Storage

Since the spongy ripe spadix is on the ground at the base of the leaves, it is easily overlooked when ripe; make a note on the calendar to collect the fruit, with its enclosed "seeds," in the early fall.

To clean, simply break apart the spadix and remove the seeds. Plant immediately. Stored dry, the seed coats dehydrate and the embryos shrivel; stratified, the seeds break down into a watery mass.

Propagation

Seed. Sow freshly collected seeds in a shaded outdoor bed in early fall and expect germination the following spring. Allow the seedlings to remain in the bed until they go dormant in the fall and then transplant them into the garden. Make sure the seedlings are watered regularly during the growing season.

Alternatively, seeds may be sown outdoors in flats or deep pots in the fall and then placed in trays in the spring and subirrigated through the season.

Division. Skunk Cabbage grows from a thick offensive-smelling rhizome that penetrates 2 feet or more into the ground. The plant can be taken up in the fall or when the plant goes dormant; just dig down around the plant and remove as much of the rhizome as possible. Cut the rhizome into pieces that include one or two nodes. Plant each piece horizontally several inches below soil level and look for new shoots the next spring.

Cultivation

The best way to establish plants is to naturalize them in conditions that closely resemble their native habitat. A low, wet area with a heavy, fertile soil that remains wet through the season is ideal. In the South a moderate to lightly shaded setting is best; more light will cause the leaves to be somewhat lighter green and to yellow prematurely. Open exposures in cooler northern areas are satisfactory. A mature plant can spread to 4 feet across, so space seedlings and divisions accordingly.

Unless new plants from division are desired, Skunk Cabbage should remain undisturbed. If proper growing conditions can be provided, seedlings should establish well and plants are long-lived and maintenance-free.

Uses in the Garden and Landscape

Establish Skunk Cabbage where conditions permit, for its interesting early flowers and arresting leaves will add interest to the garden for many months. Seepages and boggy areas bordering a stream, pond, or tumbling brook are perfect sites.

If optimum conditions are not naturally available, you might want to construct an artificial bog to accommodate Skunk Cabbage and other bog plants, such as Turtleheads, the Lobelias, Queen-of-the-Meadow, Grass-of-Parnassus, and many native ferns. To construct a bog, remove the native soil to a depth of 2 feet or so and backfill with a mixture of rotted leaves and peat moss. The soil from the excavation may be used to form a berm, or rim, to your bog, which will add a small area for special raised plantings, especially at the back of the bog.

If your soil drains well (which would be too well in this case), line the excavation with heavy-duty plastic to retain moisture before adding the leaf and peat moss planting mix. If you are working in a heavy clay soil, no lining will be necessary. Leave a low area somewhere in the bog where the water level can be observed and add water during prolonged dry periods.

Dog-tooth Violet, Trout Lily

Erythronium americanum
Liliaceae

Duration: perennial

Blooming time: March–April

Flower color: yellow

Height: to 8 inches

Soil: deep, fertile, evenly moist

Exposure: shade

Description

In very early spring, late February in piedmont North Carolina, the nodding blooms of the Dog-tooth Violet—and the conspicuous pollen-bearing catkins of the Tag Alder and Hazel-nut—signal the start of the growing season. This species of *Erythronium* occurs in bottomlands, coves, and moist deciduous woodlands throughout nearly the whole of the eastern United States, often forming vast colonies.

The flowers are borne only on the larger and presumably older plants that have a pair of leaves; single-leaved plants in a colony are apparently either too young or too crowded to flower. The small (generally, less than an inch long), triangular bulb is covered by a thin brown scale, has a short tuft of fibrous roots, and usually grows at a depth of at least 3 inches.

The attractive flowers notwithstanding, it is the unmistakable fleshy foliage that draws many gardeners to this spring ephemeral. The dark green, elliptic basal leaves are up to 7 inches long and 3 inches wide and are prominently mottled with irregular maroon-purple splotches.

The flower stalk, or scape, which may be as much as 8 inches long, bears a single nodding flower. The sepals and petals of the solitary flower, collectively referred to as tepals, overlap at the base of the flower forming a short tube. The sepals are yellow on their inner surface, purplish on the back; the petals are entirely yellow save for a band of purple along the midrib. The purple stamens are conspicuous when the longer tepals recurve.

Fruit and Seed

The light green capsules develop during the six-to-eight-week period after flowering. They are roughly oval in outline, narrowed at the base, with three distinct valves or divisions, and may lengthen during development to nearly an inch. The scape eventually arches downward with the weight of the maturing fruit, so you must look for the capsules on the ground. The leaves yellow and wither during this period and have usually disappeared when seeds are ripe. The numerous crescent-shaped seeds are about ⅛ inch (3 mm) long.

Seed Collection, Cleaning, and Storage

It is a good idea to mark the locations of flowering plants. Other plants emerging later in the season can alter the appearance of the area and further obscure the whereabouts of the small capsules. A colony of plants will include capsules of different sizes. Seeds in small capsules, however, mature at the same rate as those in larger capsules. Open a capsule when it begins to yellow and, if the seeds are dark or show signs of darkening, collect the capsules.

For best results, sow the seeds immediately. Stored seeds lose much of their viability. If you have no alternative, however, store seeds in damp, whole-fiber sphagnum moss in a sealed container in the refrigerator.

Propagation

Seed. Sow freshly harvested seeds in a shaded outdoor seedbed. If seeds are allowed to dry out, they take longer to germinate, sometimes two years or more; so be careful to maintain a constantly moist seedbed through the season. Seeds may also be sown upon collection directly in the garden where mature plants are desired.

The tiny first-year plants, which have single, narrowly elliptic leaves, should be left undisturbed in the bed until the leaves yellow. The small bulbs can then be transplanted to their permanent planting sites. Plants will likely not flower before their fourth season, although Edwin S. Steffek, in his book *The New Wild Flowers and How to Grow Them*, reports that flowering-sized plants may develop as early as the third year.

Division. Mature plants include one to several offsets attached to the mother bulb. Remove offsets when plants enter their dormant period, which coincides conveniently with seed maturation and collection. Be certain to replant the bulbs at their original depth, and with the narrow end up. Plants started from seed will likely require eight to ten years to produce offsets large enough to divide, and transplanted offsets or even bulbs may require two to three years to reach blooming size.

Cultivation

Plants are quick to establish in low areas, such as along a creek bank or seepage. They do best under hardwoods where their leaves are exposed to the filtered light of the spring months, as in their natural habitat. In a garden setting you can create the proper soil conditions for plants by spading over the native soil to the depth of a foot and working in generous amounts of organic matter to provide a deep, fertile planting medium.

To conserve moisture apply a mulch of rotted or finely shredded leaves to the planting area in the fall or early spring before the leaves come up. Large matted leaves or other coarse mulches, however, may prevent the emergence of leaves and flowers.

Clumps of plants that include many leaves and only a few flowers should be divided. Where conditions are favorable, plants will self-sow.

Uses in the Garden and Landscape

Like Bluebells, Toothworts, Spring Beauty, and other spring ephemerals, Dog-tooth Violets add color and interest to the woodland wild flower garden. The bare spot left when the plants go dormant in late May or early June should be filled by native plants with a preference for moist, shaded areas, such as Deciduous Wild Ginger, Waterleaf, and ferns.

A lightly shaded rock garden is an ideal situation for displaying Trout Lily. In time, plants may be produced in sufficient numbers to create sweeps through the garden. Small groups and individual plants may also be effectively highlighted against a prominent background, such as a tree trunk or large rock.

Related Species

Erythronium albidum has pinkish to bluish white flowers and leaves with little or no mottling. Propagation and cultivation requirements are the same as for *Erythronium americanum*.

Bloodroot

Sanguinaria canadensis
Papaveraceae

Duration: perennial

Blooming time: March–April

Flower color: white

Height: 1 foot

Soil: well-drained

Exposure: shade

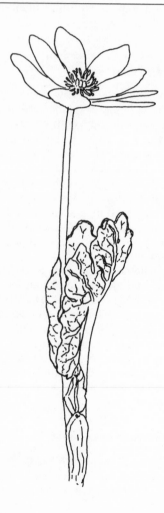

Description

Bloodroot occurs in rich soils of mixed deciduous forests and wooded slopes throughout the cooler portions of the eastern United States. Both the scientific and common names of this wild flower refer to the reddish orange sap in its thick rhizome.

Bloodroot is a spring ephemeral; the flower bud, borne on a separate stalk, or scape, is completely enclosed by the developing leaf as it first pushes up through the leaves and opens in earliest spring, when the ground is still cold. The attractive flowers are short-lived and seeds ripen and are shed by the time leaves have fully emerged on the hardwoods overhead. Each flower is 2–4 inches (5–10 cm) in diameter and has eight to twelve narrow white petals and numerous yellow stamens. The distinctive rounded leaves are up to 7 inches across, whitish on their undersides, and irregularly lobed.

A popular and striking garden variety, *S. canadensis multiplex,* has double flowers with extra petals.

Fruit and Seed

A week or two after the petals drop, a long, slender, light green capsule will be noticeable atop the scape. The leaf of Bloodroot is fully developed shortly after the fleeting blooming period and may conceal the developing capsule. Make a note on your calendar to check capsules four weeks after flowering and every few days thereafter.

At maturity the narrowly elliptic capsules, which may be up to 3 inches long and contain twenty-five or more seeds, are slightly swollen but are still green. The small ellipsoidal seeds, which turn from pale green to brown at maturity, are approximately ⅛ inch (2–3 mm) long and bear a distinctive white fleshy crest, called an aril or elaiosome, which is eaten by ants that disperse the seeds.

Seed Collection, Cleaning, and Storage

Except for a slight yellowing and puffiness in the capsules, there is no outward sign of seed maturity: one day the capsules are intact and the next they have split and shed all of their seeds. To harvest seeds, you must collect the capsules just before they split. To help judge the right time, pinch open one or two swollen capsules and, if the seeds are brown or show signs of darkening, collect the ripe capsules into a small plastic bag with a scant handful of moist soil in it to keep the aril from drying out. Keep the plastic bag in a cool place and out of the sun.

As soon as the capsules in the bag split and shed their seeds, remove the capsules and sow the seed and soil mixture at once. Storage of Bloodroot seed has not been successful as yet at the Botanical Garden. When seeds are stratified in moist sand, they tend to rot. On the other hand, if seeds are stored dry, the elaiosome dries out and either renders the seed inviable or at best delays germination for a year or longer. Seeds should be sown immediately upon collection. Obviously, much remains to be learned of the biology of Bloodroot.

Propagation

Seed. If freshly collected seeds are sown immediately, before the aril dries out, good germination can be achieved. Sow the seeds in half-inch deep furrows directly in a shaded outdoor seedbed of loose, humus-rich material, such as a mix of rotted leaves, aged manure, and topsoil. Cover the seeds with soil, tamp lightly, and keep the seedbed evenly moist through the growing season.

Sown and cared for in this manner, seeds should produce a row of seedlings the following spring, with some plants producing flowers two years from sowing. If seeds dry out, germination will be delayed a year and will be low.

Division. When leaves begin to yellow and fade, lift a large, mature plant with a trowel and break away the soil from the rhizome. Cut the rhizome into pieces that include one or more buds, dust the cut ends of the rhizome with a fungicide, and replant and water immediately. However, propagation from seed may be faster and more reliable.

Cultivation

Establish Bloodroot in a shaded setting, such as under hardwoods or some other place where protection from full sun is available.

Plants are tolerant of a wide range of soils provided they are not excessively moist, which would tend to rot the rhizomes. In nature, Bloodroot is often found on slopes and in rather dry soils, suggesting the need for good drainage.

Bloodroot benefits from a yearly application of a general fertilizer and a mulch of rotted leaves or compost. The plants are relatively slow-growing and will rarely need dividing; indeed, the more compact clumps are spectacular in bloom and do not seem to suffer from crowding. Established plants self-sow readily (with the help of ants), and seedlings will appear in the garden even at surprising distances from the parents.

Uses in the Garden and Landscape

Bloodroot is a natural for the shade or woodland garden. If some attention is given to im-

proving the soil by adding organic matter, plants can be naturalized. Combine Bloodroot with other spring ephemerals, such as Trout Lily, Dutchman's Breeches, and the Trilliums. The burgundy flowers and mottled leaves of Toad Trillium (*T. cuneatum*) and the white flowers of Bloodroot make a dramatic early-spring combination.

The bold leaves of Bloodroot will persist throughout the growing season unless a drought intervenes. They make an interesting textural contrast against the finely cut foliage of Wild Bleeding Heart, Phacelia, and New York Fern. Bloodroot is effective grown singly, in clumps, or in drifts contrasted against various stone surfaces or tree trunks in a shady rock garden.

Whether on a shady rocky slope or in a flat woodland, Bloodroot combines dramatically with such evergreen plants as Christmas Fern and the southern Wild Gingers to create beautiful summer shade gardens where the emphasis is on leaf shapes, textures, and variations of green rather than the bright flower colors of sun-loving plants.

Twinleaf

Jeffersonia diphylla
Berberidaceae

Duration: perennial

Blooming time: late March–April

Flower color: white

Height: ½–1 foot

Soil: rich, moist

Exposure: shade

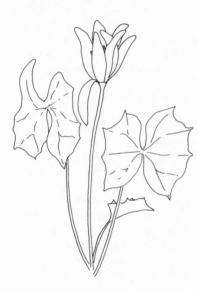

Description

Twinleaf occurs infrequently throughout the eastern United States in rich moist woods, often in soils strongly influenced by limestone. The plant, named in honor of Thomas Jefferson, third president of the United States, is one of only two species belonging to the genus, the other being Asiatic.

The attractive paired leaflets, which give the plant its common name, are borne on petioles 6–12 inches (15–30 cm) long. The leaves remain through much of the season.

The flowers, however, are among the most fleeting of spring wild flowers. Borne on leafless stems, or scapes, a few inches below the partially opened leaves, they have eight clean white petals and eight stamens. The flowers are 1–1½ inches (2.5–4 cm) in diameter and appear in April, but a sudden gust of wind or even a light shower may cause the fragile petals to drop within a day or two after they open.

A dense network of yellowish roots, penetrating 4–6 inches below soil level, is produced from a short, stocky rhizome.

Fruit and Seed

The follicle develops rapidly during the three-to-four-week period after flowering. It is green, roughly pear shaped, and about an inch (2.5 cm) long; toward its apex it has a groove extending about halfway around the follicle. Numerous small seeds, each with a fleshy aril (which appears to aid their dispersal by ants), are arranged in rows within the follicle. When the seeds are mature, the follicle splits along the groove to form a lid, which opens to allow the seeds to disperse.

Seed Collection, Cleaning, and Storage

The leaves of *Jeffersonia* are fully opened after flowering and may conceal the follicle. Make a note to check on the plant in early May, as the seeds are often ripe before the follicle splits. Three to four weeks after the bloom period, open a follicle and note the color of the seeds. If they are dark or beginning to darken, collect them; if they are whitish, check again in a few days. Like the petals, the seeds are quick to drop and should be checked daily if possible as they reach maturity.

Propagation

Seed. Seeds must be sown fresh, immediately after they are collected, or you run the risk of no germination whatsoever. As with the seeds of Trillium and Bloodroot, the fleshy arils must not be allowed to dry out.

Sow seeds in a shaded outdoor seedbed, high in organic matter and well drained. The bed must be kept evenly moist throughout the growing season. The rate of germination is typically low; some is possible the first spring after sowing, with more likely the second spring.

Seedlings are slow-growing and may take four to five years to develop into flowering-sized plants. Allow them to remain undisturbed in the seedbed for two years; then move plants into the garden when they go dormant during their second season.

Division. At the end of the growing season or when leaves begin to yellow, lift mature plants from the garden and completely remove the soil from the mass of roots. Select the largest plants for division, as the stubby rhizome is crowded with buds and the larger plants are much easier to divide. With a razor blade or sharp knife, cut the rhizome into pieces that include two or more buds and as many roots as possible. If the rhizome divisions are too small, they may have too few roots to establish themselves. Replant the divisions, positioning rhizomes a half-inch below the surface of the soil, and water thoroughly.

Cultivation

Establish these plants in areas of light to moderate shade. If your soil is acidic, dust the area at the base of the plants with agricultural lime once a year. These plants require a rich soil, one with plenty of compost, rotted leaves, or aged sawdust, and regular watering during dry periods. Otherwise the leaves will yellow and drop, and the plants will go dormant too soon to develop vigorously and will eventually die.

Apply a mulch of shredded leaves or compost at both ends of the growing season to help conserve moisture. Where there is ample moisture in the soil, the plants will self-sow, with the seedlings popping up in the immediate area of the parent plants. Young plants do not compete well and should be kept free from weeds and other aggressive, spreading plants.

Uses in the Garden and Landscape

Twinleaf makes a fine addition to the shade or woodland wild flower garden, where the plants can be effectively highlighted against darker backgrounds, such as evergreen foliage and tree trunks. Foamflower, Deciduous Wild Ginger, and New York Fern work well with Twinleaf, but all must be curbed seasonally so that they do not encroach.

Twinleaf has long been admired by rock gardeners in the cooler Northeast; southeastern gardeners must take care to establish plants in the shaded rock garden. Over time, and with careful attention to proper cultural practices and a regular propagation schedule, plants may be produced in sufficient numbers to create sweeps through the garden.

Related Species

Jeffersonia dubia, native to Eastern Asia, has scalloped heart-shaped leaves and blue flowers and is highly regarded by American gardeners. Propagation techniques and cultivation requirements are the same.

Toothwort, Pepperroot

Dentaria diphylla
Brassicaceae

Duration: perennial

Blooming time: April

Flower color: white

Height: ½–1 foot

Soil: rich, moist

Exposure: shade

Description

Toothwort is a spring ephemeral which is often found in association with Jack-in-the-Pulpit, Wake Robin, Deciduous Wild Ginger, and Trout Lily on wooded slopes and in ravines throughout much of the eastern United States.

The attractive three-lobed, conspicuously serrated basal leaves are usually present during the winter months, and two stem leaves with narrower lobes occur just beneath the inflorescence. The flowering stems, which are 6–12 inches tall, bear a small cluster of white, four-petaled, salverform, or bell-shaped, flowers ¾ inch (1.85 cm) long in a loose raceme.

The common names of this species refer to characteristics of the shallow rhizomes. The angular ribs or teeth (actually, they are leaf scars) that occur irregularly along the length of the rhizome give the plant its common name Toothwort, and the strong, peppery flavor of the rhizome is the basis for the less commonly used Pepperroot.

Where there is shade, ample moisture, and rich soil, Toothwort is quick to naturalize, spreading readily and requiring minimal care.

Fruit and Seed

The long, slender, and somewhat flattened fruit, called a silique, develops four to five weeks after flowering. It remains green during the course of seed development. Most pods are riddled with holes from insects, a warning that only a few, if any, seeds will mature within.

The brown seeds, which are arranged in a single row running the length of the silique, are shed when the valves of the mature silique split and recoil sharply from base to apex at dehiscence. The valves dry and fall to the ground within a day or two.

Seed Collection, Cleaning, and Storage

Beginning three to four weeks after flowering, closely monitor the development of the fruits. Siliques grow to their full length of 1½ inches (3.75 cm) in two to three weeks and remain essentially unchanged in appearance until they split. Open a mature silique every few days and, if the seeds are dark, collect the ripe pods immediately—few seeds adhere to the valves for more than a few hours after the fruit splits. Allow the fruits to dry and pop open in a paper bag, then separate out the small, round seeds.

It is advisable to sow seeds fresh. If seeds must be stored, place them in damp sphagnum in a sealed, labeled container and refrigerate.

Propagation

Seed. For best results sow seeds in a shaded outdoor bed immediately upon collection. Allowing seeds to dry for any length of time will reduce the germination percentage appreciably. Make sure the seedbed remains moist

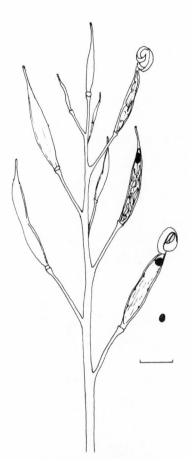

and transplant them to 3- or 4-inch pots. At this stage the whitish, bulblike rhizome, only a few millimeters long, is easily moved. Allow plants to grow on in pots if their moisture and shade requirements can be met or move them into the garden after the second season.

Division. The white rhizomes do not penetrate the soil but run along the surface, just below the layer of leaf litter. However, a network of slender white roots reaches 4 to 6 inches into the soil. When the plants are dormant, remove the litter to expose the rhizomes and cut away sections of the plant with a trowel. Keep the soil intact around the roots and relocate divisions to a site where soil and moisture conditions are appropriate. Be careful, as the rhizomes are easily broken.

through the growing season, which means regular watering during dry periods.

Look for tiny seedlings early the following spring; they are typically dormant by early summer and should remain undisturbed in the bed through their first season. Transplant second-year plants to the garden as they go dormant and expect flowering-sized plants the third or fourth season.

These plants are also readily grown in containers; sow fresh seeds in a pot or flat outdoors, thin seedlings the next spring,

Cultivation

Grow Toothwort in shaded areas. Plants are tolerant of all degrees of shade except the very deep shade cast by evergreens. Direct sunlight may cause the foliage to lighten, detracting from the plant's appearance, and send the plant into an early dormancy if ample moisture is not available.

Establish plants in your very best soil, incorporating generous amounts of rotted leaves and compost, and rework the soil whenever plants are divided. Plants begin to shed their leaves before the seeds are mature, and as summer draws near, the leaves and stems disappear completely. Plants may also enter an early dormancy if the soil becomes dry for extended periods. The basal leaves reappear in the late-summer and fall months, making a groundcover during the winter in southern areas.

Weed the area around plants regularly and promptly remove aggressive neighbors, which can quickly encroach upon, and choke out, the Toothwort. Apply a mulch of rotted leaves at the base of plants in early spring and again when plants go dormant.

Uses in the Garden and Landscape

The Toothworts are useful in the shaded rock garden and naturalized in rock outcroppings. In these settings they combine well with Stonecrop, Jack-in-the-Pulpit, the Phacelias, Wild Geranium, and the Trilliums. Plants are also at home in the woodland wild flower garden, where the creamy white flowers are effectively highlighted by darker backgrounds of evergreen perennials and ferns and tree trunks.

Once a few clumps are established in the garden, new plants are likely to appear even at some distance from their parents. If possible, allow them to grow and spread, for these volunteers often prove to be faster growers and showier plants.

Related Species

The leaves of *Dentaria laciniata*, which also has white to pinkish flowers, usually have five segments and are more coarsely serrate; *D. douglassii* is a smaller plant with more rounded leaves and beautiful lavender flowers in early spring. Propagation and cul-tivation of these species are the same as for *D. diphylla*.

Production Notes

Grow plants in shaded nursery beds, irrigating regularly during the growing season. Divide clumps every second year, pot in quart containers, and market the following spring.

Dentaria douglassii

Yellow Jessamine

Gelsemium sempervirens
Loganiaceae

Duration: perennial

Blooming time: April

Flower color: yellow

Height: climbing vine

Soil: fertile, well-drained

Exposure: full sun

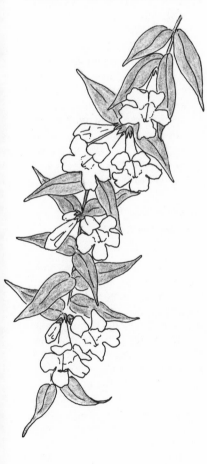

Description

This high-climbing evergreen vine, which produces a profusion of fragrant yellow flowers in March and April, occurs along woodland margins, fencerows, and roadsides of the southeastern coastal plain. The plant is easy to grow and can be used in a variety of ways around the home landscape, but in regions where the minimum winter temperature is below 0°F, the plant's hardiness as a cultivated plant is questionable.

Yellow Jessamine is one of the few spring-blooming native plants that have yellow flowers. On mature plants grown in full sun, the bright, tubular flowers, about 1½ inches (3.75 cm) long with five expanded terminal lobes, cover nearly the entire vine. The opposite, narrow, dark green leaves remain on the vine over the winter in warmer climates.

Fruit and Seed

Seeds develop slowly over the season and mature in the fall, October and November. The flattened and oblong capsules, about ¾ inch (1.85 cm) long and ½ inch (1.25 cm) wide, can be easily missed, as they are usually hidden by the foliage. Numerous dull brown seeds, each about ¼ inch (6 mm) long with thin, flat wings at the end, are produced within the capsule.

Seed Collection, Cleaning, and Storage

Younger vines or those trained to a low fence or trellis pose no problem when it comes time to collect seeds. Simply part the leaves to locate the ripe, brownish capsules and, if the seeds within are brown, the capsules may be collected. Capsules split within a few days after they begin to darken.

Vines of Yellow Jessamine that are allowed to climb very high typically lose their lower leaves and produce most of their flowers and capsules higher up, out of reach. If you are intent on collecting seeds for propagation, you will likely need a ladder and the steadying influence of a friend to harvest the capsules.

Allow the collected capsules to air-dry for a few days, then break them open, if necessary, and remove the seeds. Store the seeds dry in a sealed container and refrigerate until they are to be planted.

Propagation

Seed. Sow stored seeds indoors or in a cold frame in late winter or in a seedbed in late spring. Germination is uneven; expect some germination within two weeks and sporadic germination over the next few months.

When seedlings produce a second true leaf, amend your potting mix with half again as much sand and step them up to 2- or 3-inch containers; apply an all-purpose fertilizer at weekly intervals. When roots fill the containers, in three to four weeks, the young plants can be moved to their permanent planting site in the garden.

Cuttings. Take stem cuttings from the current season's growth in June or July. The stems should be firm, but not brittle, and dark red. Each cutting should be 2–4 inches long and include at least two pairs of leaves. Remove the bottom pair of leaves so that the leaf node is exposed; moisten the area of the stem below the node and cover it thinly with a rooting hormone in powder form, such as Hormodin no. 2.

With a dibble or wooden stick label, make a hole in the rooting medium and insert the cutting; firm the medium around it. A rooting medium of equal parts peat moss and sand is recommended. Place the flat of cuttings in a covered rooting chamber, where high humidity can be maintained. Water in the cuttings thoroughly after they are stuck and mist them when the leaves are dry. The rooting chamber should be situated out of direct sunlight and the cover opened to provide ventilation when temperatures inside exceed 85°F.

In five to six weeks the cuttings should be well rooted and ready for potting in 3-inch containers in a sandy mix. Transfer plants to the garden when roots fill up the pots, usually after another three to four weeks. Permanent planting should be carried out at least a month prior to the expected first frost.

Division. An entire clump need not be taken up to make divisions. Instead, use a spade or shovel with a sharp blade and remove small sections from the outer edges of the clump. Make sure each section has a few green shoots and some roots. Divisions may be made in this manner anytime it is convenient as long as the new sections are pruned appropriately and well watered until they become established.

Contact with the roots when handling divisions may cause slight irritation to the skin; wear gloves or wash your hands in warm, soapy water after divisions are transplanted. And do not be tempted to chew the leaves, as they contain a toxic compound.

Cultivation

These attractive vines are dense and fast-growing when planted in full sun. A lightly shaded setting is acceptable, but the vines will be thinner and leggier.

Plant Yellow Jessamine in fertile, well-drained soils. Add plenty of organic matter and a shovelful of sand to the planting site. Top-dress plants in early spring with 2–3 inches of compost, leaf mold, or aged manure.

Vines trained on a trellis or post tend to become top-heavy in three to four years, a condition you may find tolerable for the mass of flowers they produce in spring. If you desire a tidier plant, however, you will need to prune more frequently to maintain a dense habit from bottom to top.

Uses in the Garden and Landscape

Yellow Jessamine is versatile around the home garden as well as commercial landscapes. Because the Loblolly and Short Leaf pines typically lose their lower limbs and thus allow more direct sunlight to reach the trunk, they make ideal natural supports for the vines. Select free-standing pines or those at the edge of a wooded area. Also, the vines are easily trainable on trellises and posts. For best effects, make sure the support is at least 8–10 feet tall and prune the vine freely to maintain the desired height and form.

They may also be trained up or along a fence and are especially effective along a split-rail fence. Mail carriers are fast becoming familiar with Yellow Jessamine, as many homeowners are using the plant to beautify mail boxes. Judging from observations of its vigorous, dense, sprawling growth in the full sunlight of recently cutover forests, the vine has potential as an evergreen groundcover in the southern states. It has been observed sprawling densely in sunny road banks and flowering well in coastal areas. We have not been successful in getting it to flower as a groundcover in our North Carolina piedmont setting, however.

The plant can successfully be grown in a large container for several years with or without staking. Used as a cut flower, the blooms will last three to four days in arrangements.

Production Notes

Stick individual cuttings in 3-inch pots under mist; 90–100 percent rooting can be expected. When cuttings are well rooted, transplant them to quart pots and insert a short trellis or stake along the side of the pot. Overwinter plants in a greenhouse or cold frame and market the following spring.

Green-and-Gold, Golden Star

Chrysogonum virginianum var. *virginianum*
Asteraceae

Duration: perennial

Blooming time: April–October

Flower color: yellow

Height: groundcover

Soil: fertile, well-drained

Exposure: full to filtered sunlight

Description

Green-and-Gold, an outstanding, long-blooming semievergreen groundcover, is one of the best small wild flowers for garden use. It is among the earliest-blooming species in the Aster family. In the Middle Atlantic states March is not too soon to expect a few flowers nesting in the basal foliage.

Warmer days bring a regular procession of bloom, peaking in early-to-mid May, when dozens of flowers, borne on short, densely hairy stems, bloom neatly atop the tight clump of foliage. The flower heads are star shaped, about 1 inch (2.5 cm) across, and consist of a small central green disk of sterile flowers and five evenly spaced golden yellow fertile ray flowers with blunt tips. After the spring rush of flowers, the plant blooms sparsely but regularly for the remainder of the growing season.

The oval leaves are fuzzy, or heavily pubescent, on both surfaces. After spring flowering the rosette steadily expands and develops a loose sprawling habit with long stems useful for cuttings. New basal rosettes develop as the winter months approach and flowers may occasionally be observed, tightly held within the basal foliage, as late as mid-December and as early as February.

Fruit and Seed

Each of the five fertile ray flowers may produce a single small, flattened, dark brown nutlet shortly after blooming. The plant changes little in appearance from time of flowering through seed development and maturation of the individual heads.

Seed Collection, Cleaning, and Storage

The nutlets have a short maturation period—two to three weeks after the ray flowers fade and drop. Because only the five ray flowers of each head produce seed and flowering occurs over a long period, it is impossible to make a large seed harvest at any one time. However, a few ripe seeds can be collected just about any time during the growing season, the greatest number of course being available in late spring just after the time of peak bloom.

Often the nutlets will fall to the ground rapidly after they ripen, so collect any that exhibit any brown coloration. Completely darkened heads should be gathered at once, lest they fall and become lost in the soil below. To clean, simply remove seeds from the heads. They should be stored dry in a sealed, labeled container in the refrigerator.

Propagation

Seed. Although germination is often uneven, some seedling production can be counted on with almost every sowing. Sow seeds indoors, or outside when the soil has warmed to 70°F. Transplant to containers and then into the garden as soon as roots begin to work their way down into the pot because Green-and-Gold will not survive a pot-bound condition for very long.

An easier method of obtaining new plants is simply to observe the area around a parent plant in mid-spring for small seedlings. Green-and-Gold self-sows prolifically, especially where a pea-gravel mulch is used. When seedlings are of sufficient size, transfer them directly into the garden.

Cuttings. Mallet cuttings, which include a piece of the rootstock with the stem, will root in a sand and perlite medium. Older stems root more successfully. To gather mallet cuttings, use a knife, razor blade, or pair of sharp pruning shears to cut small sections of the brittle rhizome. Place the cuttings under intermittent mist or in a rooting chamber, where high humidity can be maintained. In four to six weeks you should have well-rooted plants of a suitable size to pot. Young plants need a loose, well-drained potting mix, so add extra sand or fine pine bark to your standard potting mix.

Division. Division of the clumps offers the backyard gardener the most dependable method of vegetative increase, and fall or late-winter months (October–November, February–March) are optimum times to divide your plants. Lift large, mature plants from the garden and wash the soil from the roots. Look for individual rosettes of leaves, or crowns, and carefully separate them. The brittle rhizomes are easily broken by hand, but a knife or pruning shears make for a cleaner cut. As you work, plunge the divisions into a container of water to prevent them from drying out. Reduce the leaves by half, replant divisions in the garden, and water immediately.

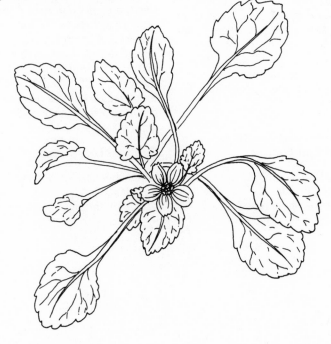

Cultivation

Green-and-Gold prospers in areas receiving at least a half day's full sunlight; shaded exposures give looser, less flowery specimens.

A well-prepared garden soil, fortified with organic material—compost, leaf mold, or humus—is preferable, but the plant fares reasonably well on a dry, sunny road bank in clay soil. The overall performance of the plant in the wild, however, is less vigorous than in garden cultivation. Heavy organic mulches are not necessary and may in fact hinder the development of new seedlings. A thin pea-gravel mulch, on the other hand, will aid the germination of new-fallen seeds and the subsequent growth of young plants. Good drainage is essential to maintaining vigorous plants.

Like Blue-eyed Grass (*Sisyrinchium angustifolium*), Green-and-Gold appears to benefit from periodic disturbance. At least every other year lift plants, shake the soil free, and divide or transplant to another spot in the garden.

Uses in the Garden and Landscape

This long-blooming, semievergreen groundcover has wide application in the home garden. Although striking when displayed singly, Green-and-Gold has enormous potential in the planned landscape planted in masses. It is effective as a continuous edging plant along a path, staggered in small groupings at the front of the perennial bed, and at the base of evergreen foundation plantings close to the house. The plant also fits well in a rock garden that utilizes low, spreading specimens.

Green-and-Gold should be considered for areas that need a uniform, continuous groundcover, such as a flat, open area or a bank with a moderate slope. It is particularly effective interplanted with Fire Pink or Columbine. Finally, consider interplanting this species on a dry road bank with other roadside wild flowers that need little care.

Related Species

Chrysogonum virginianum var. *australe* has above-ground stolons and shorter stems. Although not as showy as *C. virginianum* var. *virginianum*, it has many possibilities for the garden. Its spreading habit is perhaps best used on banks or rocky ledges.

Production Notes

When choosing stock plants, select plants that retain their compact habit throughout the growing season.

For propagation by seed, establish rows of stock plants in nursery beds in half day to full sun. Provide a loose mulch of small pea gravel, grit, or other porous material along both sides of each row of plants, which will catch the seeds as they drop from the plants throughout the growing season.

"Letting nature do it" will result in hundreds of seedlings all along the line of stock plants the following year in mid-to-late spring. The seedlings can then be potted up from the gravel mulch beds just as you would seedlings started in seed flats. Keep the area around the stock plants free of other competing plants in order to provide optimum conditions for the Green-and-Gold seedlings. Don't forget to look under the spreading foliage of stock plants for additional seedlings.

If propagating by division, field-grow Green-and-Gold in an open, sunny plot. As many as a dozen sizable divisions can be obtained from each stock plant if they are raised in humus-rich, well-drained soil. The shallow root system develops rapidly in such a mixture, whereas root penetration is slower in a heavy clay soil. Occasional watering during dry periods is beneficial. Plants to be marketed should be divided and potted in 4-inch or quart containers in the late winter for early-spring sales.

Bluebells

Mertensia virginica
Boraginaceae

Duration: perennial

Blooming time: April

Flower color: blue

Height: 1–2 feet

Soil: rich, moist

Exposure: light shade

Description

Like Trout Lily and the Spring Beauty, Bluebells push up their leaves at the very onset of the growing season, flower, fruit, and then go dormant in little more than two months' time. They are classic spring ephemerals—important perennial elements in the woodland wild flower garden—

and not as difficult to propagate as you may have been led to believe.

The bell-shaped flowers are loosely arranged in pendulous cymes at the top of a 1-to-2-foot stalk. A single flower is nearly an inch long (18–25 mm) and has a slender, funnel-shaped tube which broadens into a cup-shaped opening with shallowly lobed margins. In the bud stage and again after pollination the corollas are pink and make a pleasing contrast with the vivid blue of the opened flowers. The yellow green, oval, alternate stem leaves may be up to 8 inches long and may be sessile or have short petioles; the basal leaves have long petioles.

In her book *Wild Flowers for Your Garden* Helen Hull ranks Bluebells third on a recommended list of dependable wild flowers with which to begin a native plant garden. Bluebells flower in April or early May and occur infrequently in rich woods, clearings, and bottomlands throughout almost all the cooler portions of the eastern United States.

Fruit and Seed

The leaves begin to yellow and the stems begin to sag shortly after the bloom period. During the next two to three weeks the ovary at the base of the spent flower develops into a four-seeded fruit (called a schizocarp because it splits into 4 nutlets) which fades to yellow as the conspicuously wrinkled, or rugose, nutlets, ⅛ inch (3 mm) long, ap-

proach maturity and turn from yellowish green to brown.

Seed Collection, Cleaning, and Storage

There is a good chance that when the nutlets are brown and ready for collection the stems will have collapsed. However, prostrate stems are still no guarantee that the nutlets are fully developed and you may need to make several return trips, ideally on a daily basis, to catch the nutlets when they are ready.

To clean, shake or pluck the nutlets from the fruiting stems. If you are not planning on planting immediately, dry nutlets and store them in a sealed, well-labeled container in the refrigerator.

Propagation

Seed. For best results, sow the nutlets immediately upon collection in a shaded outdoor seedbed. This allows them to undergo a natural, moist cold period over the winter, a condition necessary to break their dormancy. Keep the seedbed evenly moist after sowing and look for tiny seedlings with a single leaf the following spring. Allow young plants to remain undisturbed in the bed until just before they yellow and go dormant, whereupon they may be transplanted into the garden and expected to flower during their third season.

Alternatively, stored nutlets may be sown six weeks prior to the average last frost date in your area in a flat of moistened standard sowing mix and covered lightly with soil. Secure a piece of plastic over the flat (or place it in a large, closed plastic bag) and place it in the refrigerator; six weeks later remove the flat from the refrigerator and place it in a protected place outside. Transplant seedlings into the garden as they go dormant in the summer.

Division. Plants may be divided just as they go dormant, an event which coincides conveniently with the maturation (and collection) of the nutlets. Using a shovel, lift the clump from the garden and begin separating the russet rhizomes from the soil. The rhizomes are brittle and easily broken; therefore, separate them with care and keep them in larger rather than smaller clusters, say, 2 to 3 inches across per division. Replant the new divisions at least 2 inches deep and water thoroughly.

Cultivation

Bluebells thrive in moist soils with a lot of humus, where they will spread into robust, full-flowering clumps. Plants also adapt readily to drier clay soils, but will typically have fewer stems.

Moderate to light shade, or areas receiving a few hours of direct sunlight, are suitable exposures; an ideal setting is under a canopy of tall hardwoods whose lower limbs have been removed, thus creating a high, open shade.

To help conserve moisture, spread a two-to-three-inch mulch of rotted leaves at the base of plants when the leaves emerge in early spring. To establish plants in a drier area, work plenty of organic matter into the soil and water regularly, if needed, in the spring.

Clumps may be left undisturbed indefinitely or divided when new plants are desired.

Uses in the Garden and Landscape

Work toward establishing Bluebells in drifts through the shaded areas of your garden by regular increase by seed and division. As plants are dormant by late spring or early summer, fill the bare spots with longer-growing moisture-loving shade dwellers, such as the native ferns, Wild Bleeding Heart, and Wild Ginger. For an effective spring color scheme, combine plants of Bluebells with Wild Geranium, Jack-in-the-Pulpit, Foamflower, Columbine, and the Trilliums. Bluebells are also appropriate for the herbaceous border where some protection from too much direct light is available.

Bird-foot Violet

Viola pedata
Violaceae

Duration: perennial

Blooming time: April

Flower color: violet, lavender

Height: 2–6 inches

Soil: sandy, well-drained

Exposure: full to filtered sunlight

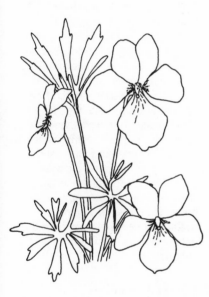

Description

This most attractive of our native violets is a favorite among gardeners. Its rather demanding requirements for successful cultivation, however, have severely restricted its use. Bird-foot Violet is found in rocky or sandy upland woods and in dry, sunny clearings in much of the eastern United States. Often the soil is barren, containing little, if any, organic matter, which suggests that this is a species for the problem area of a garden that has lean, dry soil.

The plant's common name refers to its palmately dissected leaves, which arise from a short, erect, cormlike rhizome. Flowers measure 1–1¾ inches (3–4 cm) across and are borne on arching peduncles 2–6 inches (5–15 cm) long. A single flower bears five petals, the upper two violet or lavender, the lower three lavender, and a cluster of bright orange stamens in the center. Plants bloom in April and May and often produce a second crop of flowers three to four months later.

Bird-foot Violet exhibits considerable variation in leaf shape and flower color, which further enhances its ornamental potential in the garden.

Fruit and Seed

Capsules develop rapidly after the blooming period. They are green, smooth, less than ½ inch (1.25 cm) long, and divided into three locules, or seed compartments. Seeds are expelled from the capsule during dehiscence, at which time the three valves of the capsule explode open and then fold down against the peduncle. T.? seeds are oval, ⅟₁₆ inch (1–2 ɯ.ɯ) long, and typically golden brown.

Seed Collection, Cleaning, and Storage

Watch the plant closely after it flowers. Seed collection can be easily overlooked amid the excitement of other spring gardening activities. A week or two after the last flowers fade, pinch open a few capsules and note the color of the developing seeds. Let them begin to darken before you harvest. If capsules show signs of opening, collect them immediately.

Pinch open the capsules to release the seeds over a clean surface indoors. Or place the capsules in a paper bag or other closed container and allow the capsules to dehisce. Store the seeds dry in a sealed container and refrigerate until spring sowing or sow immediately upon collection.

Propagation

Seed. Sow fresh seeds in a pot or small flat and overwinter in a nursery area where the container can be heeled or mulched in. Before sowing, add a generous amount of sand to your sowing medium to insure good drainage. Keep the medium evenly moist after sowing and look for tiny seedlings early the next spring.

When second leaves appear on the seedlings, transplant them to individual containers. The garden medium in which seedlings are to mature is critical. Anything less than a fast-draining soil will cause young plants to rot. Add sand and fine-particle pine bark to your potting mix and allow plants to grow on in pots until the fall, when they should be moved to their permanent planting site.

A more direct method is to sow the seeds directly in the garden where violets are desired, being careful to keep the site free of other plants and to watch closely for germination the following spring.

Cuttings. We have had success with mallet cuttings, as described by Will C. Curtis, founder of Garden in the Woods in Framingham, Massachusetts. After the bloom period, lift a plant and remove a leaf with a piece of the rhizome. Insert heel cuttings into sand in a rooting chamber and expect rooting in several weeks. Rooted cuttings should be grown in pots for the rest of the growing season

and moved into the garden in the fall.

Division. In late winter take up a mature plant from the garden, pot it, and bring it indoors or into the cold frame to force. In two weeks the plant will have leafed out and will be ready for division. Using a razor blade or sharp knife, slice off sections, each with a leaf, a piece of the rhizome, and several roots. Dust exposed areas on the rhizomes with a fungicide and pot divisions in individual containers. Grow them on until they are well rooted and producing new leaves, at which time you can transplant them to the garden.

These procedures may also be successfully carried out later during the growing season; new divisions will flower the following year.

Cultivation

Grow Bird-foot Violet in full sun or where the plants receive at least a half day's direct light. A lean, fast-draining soil is essential. Before setting each plant, remove several shovelfuls of soil and replace with a sandy or gritty mix. To lessen the chances of the plants developing crown rot, to which they are particularly susceptible, cover the area around them with coarse sand or pea gravel. Or establish Bird-foot Violet on a slope or bank, where drainage is naturally excellent.

Several gardeners from southern New England report that, when grown in acid, well-drained soils, plants reliably flower a sec-

ond time in late summer and continue blooming until the onset of frost.

Uses in the Garden and Landscape

Because Bird-foot Violet is low growing and has attractive leaves and flowers, it is a natural choice for a sunny rock garden or naturalized on a dry, sunny bank where drainage is rapid. The most unlikely spots in your garden, dry gravel or sandy areas almost devoid of vegetation, often provide the optimum natural conditions for Bird-foot Violet. They are displayed to advantage in small groups or masses, and a single clump is a show in itself.

If your plants are naturalized, make a point to weed the area several times during the season, since they do not tolerate competition. This species also takes well to pot culture; overwinter the pots heeled in outside or in a cold frame.

Related Species

There are several forms of *Viola pedata* which differ in leaf shape and flower color, including pale blue, rose pink, and white; *Viola papilionacea* has heart-shaped leaves and purple flowers or, frequently, white flowers with purple variegations. Sometimes called the Confederate Violet, it is a vigorous summer groundcover in both sun and shade and many gardeners consider it too aggressive. In areas where its aggressive nature will not prove objectionable, however, the Purple Violet is easily naturalized and provides a colorful and fragrant spring show.

In spite of the problems with the classification of our violets, there are many other natives, including yellow- and white-flowered species (as any regional flora will describe), which would be very appealing in a garden. Through seed exchange and sharing, enthusiasts of native violets have the opportunity to propagate and grow a wide variety of species.

Great White Trillium

Trillium grandiflorum
Liliaceae

Duration: perennial

Blooming time: April

Flower color: white

Height: 1–1½ feet

Soil: moist, rich but well-drained

Exposure: shade

Description

It is difficult to describe the special beauty and form of the Great White Trillium, one of our most dazzling spring wild flowers. Frequently the first wild flower that gardeners and amateur botanists learn, this spectacular Trillium occurs in rich wooded coves and slopes throughout the eastern United States.

Vigorous plants may approach two feet in height with three ovate dark green leaves 2–6 inches (5–15 cm) long at the top of the solitary, unbranched stem. Flowers, which appear in late April and early May, are borne singly on a pedicel above the leaves and have three sepals and three pure white petals up to 3 inches (7.5 cm) long; the petals usually turn a pink or rose after pollination or with age.

Deservedly, the Great White Trillium has long been a standard in woodland wild flower gardens but, like some of the Trilliums that are considered difficult to grow, such as the Painted Trillium (*T. undulatum*), it can be quite short-lived out of the rich, moist conditions of its native habitat. While Trilliums have been the target of plant collectors, both individuals and commercial nurseries, for many years, they frequently do not survive transplanting from the wild. The solution to this problem, which has severely depleted the species in our natural areas, is to propagate Trilliums ourselves and encourage nursery operators to do so on a large scale.

Fruit and Seed

The fruit of this Trillium is a white, oval berry ½–¾ inch (1.2–1.5 cm) long, with 3 prominent angles or ridges which develop over a period of six to eight weeks after flowering. In the Botanical Garden the pulpy berries are usually fully developed during the latter part of June, and begin to split along the three seams. As

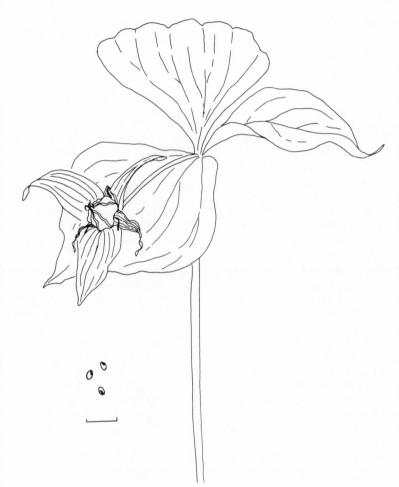

they develop, the seeds turn from white to russet and each seed bears a prominent white appendage, or elaiosome. The condition of the elaiosome is critical in determining when, or if, the seed will germinate, as indicated below.

Seed Collection, Cleaning, and Storage

Seeds are often mature before the berry begins to split, making reg-

ular inspection essential. Five to six weeks after the plant flowers, pinch open a berry and note the color of the seeds. If they are dark or beginning to darken, collect the berries.

If you are after seeds from plants occurring in a natural population and find that seeds are still white but fully developed, collect a few berries, but do not take the leaf, as this would weaken the plant. The seeds should continue to ripen in the

berry, and if you cannot return to the site regularly, this method should provide you with enough seeds to begin propagation.

To remove the ripe seeds, just break open the berry and rake them out. Fresh seeds should be sown immediately upon collection. If seeds must be stored for short periods, for example, to share with others, pack the whole berries, with the seeds, in damp whole-fiber sphagnum moss in a sealed container and refrigerate.

Propagation

Seed. Sow seeds in a shaded outdoor seedbed with plenty of humus immediately upon collection; keep the bed evenly moist during the growing season. If the elaiosomes are allowed to dry out, germination will be severely reduced and uneven. One gardener reported germination of Trillium seed eight years after sowing dry seeds she had received in the mail.

Trillium seeds should overwinter in the ground to break their dormancy. Leave seedlings, which bear a single ovate leaf, undisturbed during the first year. As they go dormant, separate plants and move directly to nursery beds or move into containers heeled in for winter protection; for nursery production space plants 2 inches apart. Flowering may begin as early as the third year, but is unlikely until the fourth or fifth season.

Gardeners have also reported success with the following method: sow seeds immediately in pots in a medium consisting of

81

equal parts peat, sand, and soil taken from the site of a natural population. Pots should be dug into the ground in the fall and germination should follow the next spring.

Division. Increase by wounding the rhizomes, as reported by Winder, in *How to Propagate*, vol. 1, has been used successfully at the Garden. After the flowering period, lift a large clump from the garden and wash the soil from the thick woody rhizome. With a sharp knife, cut a shallow groove around the rhizome just below the new season's growth, dust the wound with a fungicide, and replant. Small bulblets should form along the damaged area. After the parent plant blooms the next year, take up the clump again and remove the new bulblets and their roots. Replant these and water thoroughly, and you should have blooming-size plants in one to two years.

Another method, and one which leaves the roots undisturbed, is to remove the soil, exposing only the top of the rhizome, then cut a V-shaped groove along the upper length of the rhizome. Dust the wounded area with a fungicide and cover with the removed soil. Uncovering the rhizome a full year later should expose bulblets along the old wound. These bulblets can be separated from the parent rhizome without ever disturbing the main roots.

Cultivation

Trilliums thrive in a moist, well-drained soil where the pH is neutral or slightly acid. Plants grow noticeably larger in soils fortified with generous amounts of organic matter, such as compost, aged manure, or rotted sawdust or leaves. Growing plants in a medium of rotted leaves has proved satisfactory for many years. A mulch of shredded or rotted leaves applied at the beginning and end of the growing season is also beneficial.

Trilliums are shade dwellers and will tolerate all such exposures, save that of the dark shade cast by evergreens. The Painted Trillium will prosper even there, as it grows naturally in the very acid soils beneath Rhododendron and Hemlock and in fact seems to require such conditions in cultivation.

Take care to water plants during periods of dry weather. Space new plants 10–12 inches apart and set rhizomes at a depth of 4 inches.

Uses in the Garden and Landscape

The Great White Trillium is effectively displayed in mass plantings. If you give some attention to improving the soil, plants are not difficult to naturalize. The great sweeps of this species observed in nature are difficult to duplicate, although with regular irrigation and an ongoing propagation schedule sizable patches may be established in the woodland or shade garden.

Interplant the Trilliums with Hepaticas, Bloodroot, Wild Gingers, Wild Geranium, Phacelias, and native ferns. The various Trillium species are interesting when interplanted, where their differences and similarities can be observed. The plant is also desirable in clumps in a shaded rock garden.

Related Species

All the Eastern American Trilliums, without exception, are worthy of cultivation, although some, such as *T. pusillum*, are so rare that they are protected by state and federal regulations and should *not* be removed from their native habitat.

Trilliums may be grouped generally according to whether the flower is peduncled (with a stalk) or sessile (without a stalk). Species with peduncles include *T. catesbaei* (pink or white petals), *T. cernuum* (white), *T. grandiflorum*, and *T. undulatum* (white and red). Species with sessile flowers include *T. cuneatum* (maroon), *T. cuneatum* var. *luteum* (yellow), *T. discolor* (cream to pale yellow), *T. erectum* (maroon to cream), *T. lanceolatum* (maroon), *T. pusillum* (white), and *T. viride* (dark purple to yellow and green).

All prefer basically the same moist soil, rich in humus, and shaded conditions, but careful attention must be given to their differing soil pH requirements. The maroon-flowered *T. cuneatum*, with mottled leaves, naturalizes readily under beech trees and makes a striking show when in-

Trillium cuneatum *in fruit*

terplanted with Bloodroot either in natural beech woods or in an artificial setting such as a shady rock garden.

Trilliums, as we noted, are often collected from the wild to be sold in nurseries, but plants collected in this way often do not make the adjustment to private gardens. In addition to nurseries that offer propagated native plants, the best source of plants is gardening friends and members of wild flower societies who have succeeded in cultivating Trillium and will likely be happy to share the natural seedlings occurring in their gardens.

Columbine

Aquilegia canadensis
Ranunculaceae

Duration: perennial

Blooming time: April–May

Flower color: red and yellow

Height: 1–3 feet

Soil: light, well-drained

Exposure: light shade

Description

Columbine, one of the most familiar wild flowers of the eastern United States, is among the first plants to break ground in early spring. Typically it occurs in well-drained sites on cliffs and ledges, in dry rocky woods, and scattered across cool, open-sloped meadows.

The compound light green leaves, numerous at the base of the plant but reduced in size and number along the stem, are divided into segments of three-lobed leaflets. The pendant flowers are borne above the foliage on loosely branched stalks, 1–3 feet tall. Each flower is about 1½ inches (3.7 cm) long and consists of an outer whorl of five red sepals and an inner whorl of five yellow petals with a column of bright yellow stamens extending out from the center.

Projecting backward from the petals are the conspicuous nectar-bearing spurs. The many garden varieties of Columbine often have spurs of different lengths and colors. Hummingbirds seeking the nectar produced at the base, or pointed portion, of the spurs, are regular visitors to the flowers.

Fruit and Seed

Immediately after the flowers wither and drop, the five light green papery follicles are evident; each follicle, similar in appearance to a slender capsule, contains many seeds. The follicles are quick to expand and turn brown, and the seeds quick to

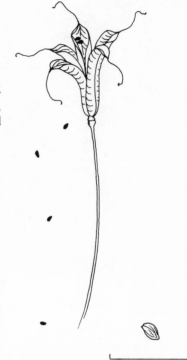

mature. The follicles split at their apexes and the small, shiny black seeds are shed as the breeze shakes the slender stalk.

Seed Collection, Cleaning, and Storage

At the Botanical Garden Columbine finishes blooming in early May, and the seeds are mature and ready for collection in late May to early June. It is only a matter of two or three days from the time the seeds turn black to when the follicles dehisce. Since the seeds may ripen and be shed before the follicle turns brown, it is wise to begin checking seeds before the follicles open. Split a follicle or two; if the seeds are black, they are ready to collect.

Cut the fruiting stalks below the top of the clump of basal leaves and drop them into a collection bag. Allow the follicles to dry in the bag for a few days. Dark green, almost ripe, seeds in the pods will usually ripen and turn black during this time. Close the bag and shake it vigorously; all the seeds will be in the bottom of the bag. Plant at once or store seeds dry in a sealed, well-labeled container and refrigerate.

Propagation

Seed. Columbine seeds need a moist cold period to break dormancy. Sow seeds immediately upon collection in a seedbed outside and look for seedlings the following spring. As Columbine self-sows freely in the garden, look for small plants at the base of parent plants.

Or, when you want to start plants later, mix the stored seeds with a small amount of damp vermiculite, place in a sealed container, and return to the refrigerator for three to four weeks. Sow the seed and vermiculite mixture thinly and evenly over your sowing medium in a flat and tamp the soil lightly to help hold the seeds in place. Make sure you can see the seeds on the surface, as they need light to germinate. Make certain that the sowing mix does not dry out. You should observe rapid and uniform germination during the next week.

Though young seedlings are small and slow-growing, do not fertilize them, for you might burn the foliage. Allow the plants to make strong root systems in the flat—probably six to seven weeks from sowing—before transplanting to individual containers and finally into the garden.

Division. Mature plants can be divided in the fall. The tough, woody rootstock bears several crowns that can be divided with a sharp knife. As Columbine transplants with some difficulty, take care during the procedure not to break too many roots. Replant and water immediately.

Cultivation

Columbine does best in a well-drained soil amended with modest amounts of organic material. Avoid poorly drained clay soils and very rich garden soils. A rich soil encourages lush vegetative growth and weak stems. Interestingly, Columbine does well in a thin, gravelly soil, where it maintains a tight, compact habit. Although tolerant of either direct

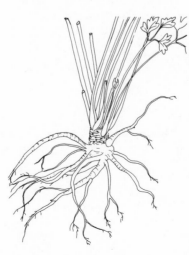

sun or deeply shaded exposures, Columbine develops best in light shade or in a setting that receives only a few hours of direct light during the day.

Older plants seem to become less attractive; consider dividing, or replacing, the plants every three to four years after they are established in the garden. During dry summer weather a weekly watering or two makes for better-looking plants. Faded blooms can be removed, but let a few remain for seed production. Columbine can also be raised successfully in a deep container. When Columbine becomes well established in a garden, it freely self-sows with many seedlings resulting in garden walks and in any bare patches where seeds may fall.

Uses in the Garden and Landscape

Columbine is best used in small groups or singly in the front of the flower border, in rock gardens, and in the shaded woodland garden. If space allows, it produces a magnificent spring show when grown in masses in the open or in a shady woodland area. It should be included in any naturalized garden where several species are mixed together in a meadowlike situation. It makes a fine cut flower.

Production Notes

Sow heavily and thin seedlings in the flat to ½-inch spacing. Allow ten weeks production time from seed to a salable plant.

Foamflower

Tiarella cordifolia var. *collina*
Saxifragaceae

Duration: perennial

Blooming time: April–May

Flower color: White

Height: 6–12 inches

Soil: rich, moist

Exposure: shade

Description

Foamflower has been a favorite groundcover among gardeners for many years. The small white, star-shaped flowers, in compact showy racemes 6 inches or more tall, begin blooming in mid-April at the Garden and continue for nearly a month. Close inspection of the flowers reveals bright yellow stamens extending out from the base of the petals. The long-petioled, downy, maplelike leaves, which form attractive mounds of foliage, are 2–3 inches wide and 3 inches long.

The Foamflower that we recognize as *Tiarella cordifolia* var. *collina* (called *Tiarella wherryi* by some authorities) may have burgundy red variegation along the veins and may turn completely light to dark burgundy during winter months. Foamflower occurs in rich wooded areas in the mountain and piedmont provinces from northern Georgia to Canada.

Fruit and Seed

The unusual capsules consist of a small upper convex flap seated in a larger spoonlike base approximately ¼ inch (6 mm) long. As they mature, they change rapidly in color from light green to dark brown. The small, shiny black seeds are generally ready for collection about one month after the first flowers open.

Seed Collection, Cleaning, and Storage

Seed development occurs immediately following the flowering period. Because flowering occurs first at the bottom of the inflorescence and then proceeds upward, there will be a progressive maturation of seed from the bottom to the top of the stalk. Approximately five to seven days after the uppermost flowers have faded is a good time to begin looking for ripe seed.

When the seeds are mature and shiny black, simply cut the stalk below the bottom capsules and deposit in a paper bag. Care

Propagation

Seed. Although the seedlings grow slowly, Foamflower can be reliably grown from seed. As seeds are very small, direct sowing in the garden is not recommended. In early spring sow seeds thinly in a seed flat or pot and place either indoors in a warm, sunny spot or in a protected location outside, such as a cold frame. Germination is usually high.

Since crowded seedlings suffer in the seed flat, thin them to a 1-inch spacing soon after the appearance of the first true leaves. Pricked-out seedlings may be transferred to additional seed flats if quantities are important. Seedlings are ready for transplanting to 2- or 3-inch containers some six to eight weeks from the sowing date.

Division. Mature clumps of Foamflower can be divided in the fall or in early spring before flowering. Look for the crowns, or growing points, at the base of the plant. To make divisions, simply lift the plant from the soil and separate the crowns. A mature plant will yield from four to eight divisions, and plants should be divided at least every third year.

Cultivation

Three things are necessary for the successful cultivation of Foamflower: first, the shallow, spreading root system requires a well-drained soil high in organic matter—a compost of well-rotted oak leaves is satisfactory; sec-

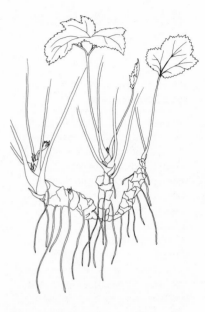

should be exercised while collecting capsule stalks because the ripe seeds frequently roll right off the lower spoon-shaped base when handled. Place a collecting bag next to you, cut the stalks with as little movement as possible, and hold the stalks over the bag before tilting them into the bag.

Spread the seed stalks on newspaper and allow them to air-dry for a day or two; the capsules will split open and the seeds can be shaken free. Be sure to check the bottom of your collection bag for loose seeds. If necessary, use a sieve to separate litter from the seeds. Cleaned seeds should be stored in a sealed, labeled container and refrigerated until time of sowing.

ond, regular watering during dry periods is essential for healthy plants; and, finally, a shaded site, protected from direct sunlight, is recommended.

In southern regions, plants grown in a half day or more of direct sunlight flower and seem fine in the spring, but the foliage takes on a burned look for the remainder of the season. Sunny exposures are better tolerated in cooler northern regions.

A mulch of shredded oak leaves or fine bark nuggets applied around the base of the plants during the growing season will help reduce the necessity for watering and weeding.

Foamflower is easily cultivated in containers as long as they are watered frequently during the growing season and the root zone is protected from freezing during the winter. Pots taken indoors in late winter will produce flowering specimens before the normal flowering period for plants grown outside.

Uses in the Garden and Landscape

Foamflower is an ideal ground-cover for the shade garden, and the massed effect is spectacular when it is in flower. It may be used as an edging plant along a path or border or massed at the base of trees and shrubs. It is also effective singly or in small groups, particularly in the rock garden.

Because the plant has a shallow root system, deeper-rooted wild flowers can be planted among a stand of Foamflower. These could include Cardinal Flower, True and False Solomon's Seal, Blue Cohosh, and Bluebells, among many other wild flower and fern species. Also, the combination of the evergreen Christmas Fern (*Polystichum acrostichoides*) and Foamflower in a shaded window box or a shaded entrance is very attractive.

Related Species

Tiarella cordifolia var. *cordifolia*, native to the mountains of North Carolina and common in northern areas, differs from *T. cordifolia* var. *collina* in that the leaves are smaller, lighter green, and closer to the ground and it actively spreads by stolons. *T. cordifolia* var. *collina* remains as a clump and is effective in southern regions as an evergreen until weathered down in late winter by snow and ice. Cultivation and propagation techniques are the same for both.

Production Notes

Divide Foamflower in the fall and plant divisions one foot on center in prepared nursery beds, or pot directly into 4-inch pots, making certain to provide the pots with good winter protection.

Bleeding Heart

Dicentra eximia
Fumariaceae

Duration: perennial

Blooming time: April–September

Flower color: pink

Height: 1½–2 feet

Soil: rich, moist

Exposure: light shade

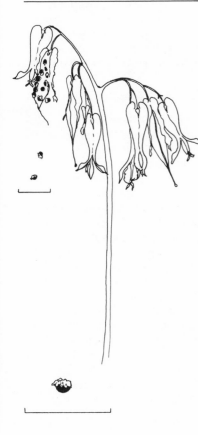

Description

Bleeding Heart inhabits rich wooded slopes and rocky places in the eastern United States. From March to November it is a steady attraction in the woodland garden.

Leaf buds break ground in early spring, followed shortly by the flowering stems. The light green, much dissected, fernlike leaves arch outward. The plant is quick to send up new leaves and in no time forms a finely textured mound 1½ to 2 feet tall, spreading to nearly 3 feet across at maturity.

Bleeding Heart softens a planting area and should occupy a prominent place in the garden. The raceme of somewhat flattened pink flowers, each about 1 inch (2.5 cm) long, is borne just above the leaves. The plant flowers without interruption from the beginning to the end of the growing season. Many horticultural varieties have been derived from this species.

Fruit and Seed

The seeds mature throughout the growing season, and in most cases faded flowers remain attached to the developing capsules. The light green capsules, obvious on the stalk immediately after the flowers fade, expand steadily and lengthen to ½ inch (1.25 cm). As the numerous tiny seeds develop and swell against the walls of the fruit, the outer surface of the capsule takes on a bumpy appearance. As seeds ripen, they change from a moist white to green and at maturity are shiny black. Attached to each seed is a moist, white crest, or aril.

Seed Collection, Cleaning, and Storage

New leaves, which are produced continually, can hide developing capsules. When you check for ripe seed, part the leaves from above and you will likely find some capsules just below the level of the taller leaves. Periodically, split a capsule along a seam and examine the seeds, as they are often black and mature before the capsule splits.

With Bleeding Heart you can afford to take a casual approach to seed collection, as seed production is continuous over the season. Do not let seeds dry out after they are collected, however; delayed germination may result if seeds are not cleaned and stored at once. Split unopened capsules and tap or scrape out the seeds onto a clean piece of paper. If you are not planting immediately, store seeds in damp whole-fiber sphagnum moss in a sealed container and refrigerate until sowing.

Propagation

Seed. First, look for seedlings around parent plants. They may be all you need for additional plantings in the garden.

Sow seeds outside as you collect them in a prepared bed of fine soil and look for seedlings the next spring. Bleeding Heart seeds will not germinate without a moist cold period of four weeks or more.

When sowing seeds that have been stored, spread the seed and sphagnum mixture over your sowing medium, cover lightly, and keep moist. Frequently the seeds will clump together in layers within the sphagnum and can easily be separated out for sowing. If the seeds remain generally scattered throughout, the sphagnum and seeds can be shredded and sown together in a thin even layer on the sowing medium. Some gardeners may find milled sphagnum easier to use both for storage and sowing.

Seedlings are small and slow-growing, but eight to ten weeks from germination they should be large enough to move to small containers. An additional four weeks should yield plants of sufficient size to transfer into the garden.

Alternatively, sow a few seeds in a 4- or 6-inch pot upon collection and hold seedlings in the pot until large enough for permanent planting.

Division. A mature plant of Bleeding Heart develops a tough rootstock with several crowns which can be divided in the fall or the early spring. With a knife or sharp pruning shears, separate the smaller crowns, paint the exposed rootstock with a fungicide, replant the divisions, and water thoroughly.

Cultivation

Plant Bleeding Heart in a lightly shaded setting. It luxuriates in a rich, well-worked garden soil under a canopy of tall hardwoods where light is filtered. Deep shade is better than full sun, particularly in the South, since in direct light the leaves yellow, become spindly, and are most unattractive. When grouping plants, be sure to allow enough room for a 3-foot spread per plant.

Uses in the Garden and Landscape

Bleeding Heart is a natural for the woodland garden. Its beautiful form is constant through the season, so use it liberally for interest during the summer and fall months. When massed, it creates a lush, airy presence. Try it at the base of a tree, a large rock, or a broad-leaved shrub such as Rhododendron for a pleasing textural contrast.

In spring, it blends well with Trillium, Bloodroot, Jack-in-the-Pulpit, and Foamflower. Plant both True and False Solomon's Seal and Blue and Black Cohosh in the immediate background for accent. Cardinal Flower and the White Wood Aster (*Aster divaricatus*) are enhanced in late summer and fall with *D. eximia* planted nearby. For an exciting effect where dappled light is available, interplant Bleeding Heart and Green-and-Gold. The plant also does well in a large container with regular watering and, as noted above, not too much light.

Related Species

Dutchman's Breeches (*D. cucullaria*), with white flowers in early spring and many fewer leaves, has long been a favorite in shade gardens; it takes its name from the shape of the fused petals. Squirrel Corn (*D. canadensis*), which derives its name from the small yellow tubers on the rootstock, is similar in appearance to Dutchman's Breeches, but has longer and more narrow flowers. Fleeting spring ephemerals, these two are dormant by June and can be propagated by seed or separation of the bulblets on the rootstock.

Crested Dwarf Iris

Iris cristata
Iridaceae

Duration: perennial

Blooming time: April

Flower color: blue, violet

Height: groundcover

Soil: rich, well-drained

Exposure: sun to light shade

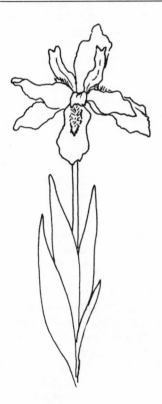

Description

Colorful and fetching in flower, Crested Dwarf Iris is attractive throughout the growing season and useful as a seasonal ground-cover and edging plant. Clusters of narrow, pointed leaves from a network of surficial rhizomes, or runners, vary in height from 4 to 16 inches. The flowering stems, 1½–2½ inches tall, are shorter than the leaves, and the showy blue flowers frequently appear nestled within the clumps of foliage.

The flower itself is, botanically, a symmetrical arrangement, in three series, of three sepals, three petals, and three elaborately petaloid styles. The sepals, 1¼–2¼ inches (3–6 cm) long, are bluish to violet and distinctly marked with a central white or yellow purple-lined band having two crested ridges frequently called beards. The shorter petals are uniformly bluish to violet; the showy petaloid styles extend closely out over the basal portion of the bearded sepals, concealing the stamens beneath.

Crested Dwarf Iris flowers for a short period, one to two weeks, in early-to-mid spring. White flowering forms are sometimes seen and are enthusiastically shared among gardeners.

In nature, Crested Dwarf Iris is found throughout the southeastern and south central United States on rich wooded slopes, bluffs, and ravines, suggesting that they need good drainage. In some areas large colonies of the plant are common along sunny road banks where the soil has been recently disturbed.

Fruit and Seed

More often than not, only a small percentage of the flowers in a given population develop capsules, and it is not unusual for no capsules to form in some years. Propagation by seed cannot always be counted on as a method of increase.

The leathery elliptic capsules, about ½ inch (1 cm) long and with three sharp angles, develop over a six-to-eight-week period after flowering; they remain light green as they expand, but turn brown at dehiscence.

Each of the three locules of the capsule usually contains two rows of flat, ovoid, tan, smooth seeds approximately ⅛ inch (3–3.5 mm) across, with an aril along one side.

Seed Collection, Cleaning, and Storage

Capsules cease expanding several weeks before they split, and seeds appear to be mature and fully developed at this time also. Collect the capsules when they have turned brown.

To clean, split open the capsules and rake out the seeds. If seeds are sown fresh—and the fleshy aril not allowed to wither and dry—germination seems better, and more uniform. Or store seeds dry in a sealed, labeled container and refrigerate until sowing. Germination of stored seeds cannot be guaranteed.

Propagation

Seed. For best results, sow seeds immediately upon collection in an outdoor seedbed and look for seedlings the following spring. A seed lot that is allowed to dry before sowing will germinate sporadically over a two-year period.

Let seedlings remain in the seedbed until they have produced a full fan of leaves (one to two months after germination), and then transplant them into 2- or 3-inch pots. When plants are well rooted, move them into the garden. Light applications of an all-purpose fertilizer every two weeks enhances seedling growth and should be continued through their first season. Amend your standard potting mix with half again as much sand or fine pine bark to assure proper drainage.

Division. The short, inch-long, stubby rhizomes are connected by slender runners. Plants should be divided in the early fall when leaves begin to yellow, signaling the onset of the dormant period. To divide, remove the runners from a fan and lift the rhizome from the soil, making certain to keep the stringy roots attached. Divisions may include one or several fans.

If plants are to be divided earlier in the season, cut the leaves in half before lifting clumps from the garden. Replant divisions at the same level and water thoroughly.

Cultivation

Establishing the Dwarf Iris in the garden is problematical for many gardeners, but need not be. These plants do not take well to pampering; they typically lose their attractive, compact habit when lavished with rich soils and regular irrigation. "Just ignore them," remarked a local gardener, "and they'll do fine."

Plants are most likely to do best in very ordinary, dryish soils where water drains away rapidly. Plants set in soils high in organic matter are likely to make excessive vegetative growth at the expense of flower production. Clay soil loosened with modest amounts of sand or gravel and leaf mold is a more desirable medium. Plants typically succeed when established on an incline, as opposed to flat or poorly drained sites.

An exposure where sunlight is direct most of the day makes for tight, attractive colonies, though

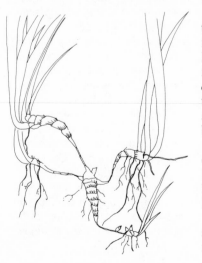

foliage is apt to yellow and tip-burn by mid-summer if moisture is inadequate. A setting in light or dappled shade with perhaps a few hours of direct light is ideal, as the foliage can be expected to remain a pleasing medium green through the season and flower production is plentiful.

Space new plants, seedlings and divisions, 6 inches apart. A light mulch can be applied in the fall, and a light feeding with an all-purpose fertilizer in the early spring is beneficial. Bone meal worked into the soil in the fall is also recommended.

Once established, these plants are essentially self-sustaining and may remain undisturbed for years.

Uses in the Garden and Landscape

Crested Dwarf Iris is useful in the rock garden, in the foreground of a herbaceous border, in the woodland garden, and naturalized.

The plant is a good choice for the southern rock garden, where it combines handsomely with Fire Pink, Green-and-Gold, Robin's Plantain, and *Coreopsis auriculata*. Plants should be allowed to spread freely, as the foliage is so effectively highlighted by rock backdrops.

In the border, plants make fine edge or corner plantings; their foliage softens the lines of a formal bed, and the blooms inject a lively blue accent.

Establish plants in a lightly shaded woodland setting with the native ferns, Wild Bleeding Heart, and Columbine; or naturalize plants on a road bank or in a rock outcropping; plan to make soil improvements initially and remove any aggressive competitors that might encroach upon the planting.

Related Species

Iris verna, Dwarf Iris, is slightly taller and native to sandy and peaty soils; it has a yellow or orange band on the sepals and no crest. *I. virginica*, Blue Flag (2 feet tall, blue sepals marked with yellow), and *I. pseudacorus*, Yellow Flag (3 feet tall, large yellow flowers), are native to wet sites and ideal for naturalizing in wet, sunny areas. Propagation is by division and seed.

Production Notes

Grow plants in raised nursery beds in a lightly shaded or open setting. Divide plants every second year into one or two fans, pot these divisions in quart containers, and market the following season.

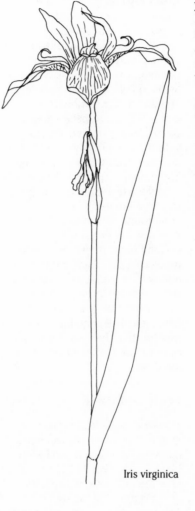

Iris virginica

Phacelia, Scorpion Weed

Phacelia bipinnatifida
Hydrophyllaceae

Duration: biennial

Blooming time: April–May

Flower color: lavender blue

Height: 1–2 feet

Soil: rich, moist

Exposure: shade

Description

A member of the Waterleaf Family, Phacelia is an attractive yet little-known spring-blooming biennial, native to moist wooded areas in the southern mountains and the cooler Northeast. The plant, 1–2 feet in height, has an open, loosely branched habit with light green leaves divided into five deeply lobed segments. The numerous, round, lavender blue flowers are about 1 inch (2.5 cm) in diameter.

Although an individual specimen does not readily hold the eye, the plant is striking when massed in the shade garden. Its ability to reseed itself makes for drifts of color throughout the garden within two years after it is established. The peak blooming period for this Phacelia is from late April to late May, depending on the area.

Fruit and Seed

The seed capsules are light green, changing to brown when mature, and contain two to four black seeds. One to two weeks after the last flowers have faded the lowermost of the round capsules should be starting to ripen. After flowering, the plant begins a steady decline in appearance and by mid-June has disappeared entirely. Phacelia is thus typical of many ephemeral spring wild flowers in that it produces seed soon after the blooming period and quickly goes dormant.

Seed Collection, Cleaning, and Storage

Since Phacelia begins flowering at the bottom of the stalk and progresses upward, seeds will mature first in the basal fruits. A good time to collect the seed is when the lower capsules have split. At this time seeds in the upper capsules are still white, but a majority of these seeds will continue to mature in the capsules following collection.

To collect seeds, simply cut off the plant or pull it, roots and all, and deposit in a large bag. Because Phacelia is a biennial and has a scant root system, the plant is easily taken up and removing some plants does not harm the population.

Plants should be allowed to air-dry at room temperature, and most capsules will open within a week's time. Shake the capsules in a bag to release all of the ripe seeds. Seeds can be separated

from chaff by running through a series of sieves. Cleaned seeds should be stored dry in a sealed, labeled container and refrigerated until time to sow.

Propagation

Seed. Phacelia propagates readily from seed. Direct sowing in the garden, a prepared seedbed, or a cold frame at the time of collection or later indoors in a seed flat is reliable. In most cases Phacelia self-sows freely in the garden, allowing you to bypass seed collection and sowing; simply transplant seedlings about to get the distribution you want. Phacelia is fast-growing in containers, so transplant to a permanent location as soon as possible.

Cultivation

Phacelia requires a shaded environment with little direct sunlight, a loose soil rich in organic material, and plenty of moisture. If you can, determine the drainage patterns in the protected areas of your garden and plant Phacelia in the low areas. Some

watering may be necessary during dry periods, and mulching will of course help conserve moisture.

Uses in the Garden and Landscape

Phacelia is most effectively displayed in groups or masses. When the plant is established in the garden, seedlings can easily

be transplanted to achieve the massed effect. As Phacelia is low and spreading in habit and has a very shallow root system, it is appropriate interplanted with tall, deeper-rooted wild flowers. Consider planting a groundcover of Phacelia at the base of shrubs and trees. If you give some attention to improving the soil, Phacelia can also be naturalized in a wooded area.

Related Species

Both *Phacelia purshii*, which has pale blue flowers with white centers, and the white-flowered *Phacelia fimbriata*, a somewhat smaller annual species native to the mountains and cooler areas of the Northeast, are worthy of garden cultivation. Both require growing conditions similar to *P. bipinnatifida* and self-sow freely.

Production Notes

Seeds should be sown in flats and stepped up to 4-inch containers in four to five weeks. Plants reach salable size in six to eight weeks from time of sowing.

Blue Star

Amsonia tabernaemontana
Apocynaceae

Duration: perennial
Blooming time: April–May
Flower color: blue
Height: 2–3 feet
Soil: rich
Exposure: light shade to sun

Description

Among many native plant gardeners, Blue Star enjoys a reputation as a handsome, long-lived, low-maintenance perennial that remains attractive throughout the growing season. The plant occurs on rich, wooded slopes and in bottomlands in the southeastern and south central United States. In cultivation plants develop into thick clumps with many stems spreading to at least 2 feet across and reaching a height of 3 feet.

The smooth stems are crowded with narrow, ovate to lanceolate, alternate leaves, 3–6 inches long, which turn an attractive golden yellow in the fall. Small, star-shaped, steel blue flowers, ½ inch (1.25 cm) across, are borne in panicles at the tips of the stems. A vigorous specimen will be covered with flowers for a short two-week period in the spring.

Fruit and Seed

Pairs of smooth, slender, light green follicles are evident a few weeks after flowering, but are essentially hidden among the leaves for the remainder of the growing season. The slender follicles are ⅛ inch (2–3 mm) in diameter and 2–4 inches (5–10 cm) long; they turn darker green and finally tan when they are mature, four to five months after flowering.

The corky, cylindrical, cinnamon brown seeds, which are sharply angled at both ends and round in cross section and re-

semble broken pieces of twig, are arranged tightly in a single row in the follicle.

Seed Collection, Cleaning, and Storage

Remember that the follicles are often concealed by the foliage and that the seeds require several months to mature. Since you can easily overlook, or forget them, make a note to check your plants for seeds in late August or when the follicles change from green to brown or when they begin to split along one side. Mature follicles have been collected in our North Carolina piedmont area as early as August and as late as October.

When the seeds are brown, collect the follicles immediately, spread them over clean newspaper, and let them air-dry for a week or until they are papery to the touch and begin to crack and curl. To clean, simply peel apart the follicle and remove the seeds.

Store seeds dry in a sealed, labeled container in the refrigerator until sowing. Seeds have a storage life of at least four years when refrigerated.

Propagation

Seed. Sowing can be carried out upon collection in an outdoor seedbed, and good germination can be expected the following spring.

For indoor or cold frame sowing in late winter, rapid and uniform germination will be obtained if you cut away a small piece from one end of each seed with scissors and then soak the seeds in water for two or three days. Cutting off the end of the seed allows more water to be absorbed quickly and germination to occur, usually in two or three days. (Seeds that are merely soaked in water for a few days will also germinate, but germination will be sporadic and will extend over a much longer period.)

Seedlings should be transplanted to 2- or 3-inch containers when the second set of true leaves appears, about four weeks from germination. Apply an all-purpose fertilizer at half strength to potted plants on a weekly basis.

The root system of Blue Star develops rapidly, so move the seedlings to the garden as soon as the roots reach the bottom of the container. Some flowering can be expected from second-year plants, but plants do not ap-

proach their mature habit until the third season.

Cuttings. A high percentage of tip cuttings taken from lateral branches in May will root rapidly. Cuttings taken later in the season are not as successful and require more time to root. Remove the lower leaves from the cutting and insert at least two nodes in pure sand or in a medium of equal parts sand and peat moss. Maintain cuttings in a rooting chamber out of direct light. Mist the cuttings and saturate the rooting medium when it becomes dry.

Your cuttings should be well rooted and ready to be potted in six weeks. Overwinter rooted cuttings in containers in a protected spot outdoors and transplant them to the garden the following spring.

Division. Plants three or four years old will have developed deep, thick, woody root systems just a few inches below the surface of the soil; the root system or crown will have several "eyes," or buds, where stems emerge. When plants go dormant in the fall, use a shovel to lift them from the garden (in this operation you will probably break some longer roots, but this is not a problem because divisions are quick to recover). With pruning shears or a sharp knife, cut through the crown so that each new piece or division includes an "eye" and a mass of roots. Replant the divisions immediately and water thoroughly.

Cultivation

Blue Star, much like Green-and-Gold, Spiderwort, and Fire Pink, thrives in cultivation when it is planted in a setting with more light than is available to it in its native woodland habitat. Indeed, for best results, put these plants in full sun or in high, open shade, such as under hardwoods whose lower limbs have been removed.

Plant Blue Star in a rich, well-prepared soil high in organic matter. Water during dry periods and mulch plants in the spring to conserve moisture. Unless the plants encroach upon neighbors or need to be divided to provide new plants, they can remain undisturbed in the garden for many years to develop into dense, shrublike specimens.

Uses in the Garden and Landscape

Use plants in the front or middle ranks of the herbaceous border where they should be planted in small groups of threes and fives at intervals along the border. Their dense, leafy habit contrasts well with many other plants through the growing season.

Plants are also very appropriate for woodland wild flower gardens, naturalized at the edge of a wooded area, or planted for color and accent in the sunnier spots of a fern garden.

In a sunny exposure integrate Blue Star with Butterfly Weed, Sundrops, Black-eyed Susan, or White Wild Indigo. In shadier locations work in Blue Star with Bleeding Heart, Columbine, and Wild Geranium. Although they last only a day or two as cut flowers, Blue Star is attractive in arrangements.

Related Species

Amsonia ciliata, native to the southeastern United States, occurring in the sandhills and in sandy, open woodlands, has a finer texture and is more delicate in appearance than *A. tabernaemontana*; the stems can reach to 3 feet and bear their blue flowers in April. These plants demand an open setting and a well-drained soil. Propagation is by division and seed.

Robin's Plantain

Erigeron pulchellus
Asteraceae

Duration: perennial

Blooming time: April–May

Flower color: lavender

Height: 1–2 feet

Soil: light, well-drained

Exposure: sun to light shade

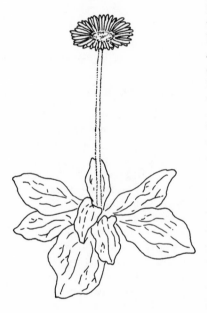

Description

Robin's Plantain, which occurs throughout the eastern United States on rich, wooded slopes and in open woods and meadows, is a good choice for the southern rock garden and requires only minimal maintenance once established. The attractive lavender ray flowers of Robin's Plantain somewhat resemble those of some species of fall-blooming asters, such as *Aster novae-angliae*, *A. grandiflorus*, and *A. puniceus,* but the rays are much slenderer and more numerous. Plants spread via slender stolons and in cultivation, where the soil is well prepared, make dense, mat-forming colonies— and an attractive groundcover during the growing season.

The oblong, spoon-shaped, dentate (or "toothed") leaves which form the basal rosettes are rough textured and densely hairy on both surfaces; the stem leaves are smaller, narrower, and clasping at their bases. Flowers are borne in heads that are either single or in branched clusters (corymbs) on 1-to-2-foot stems. The individual flower heads are 1–1½ inches (2.5–3.75 cm) across and have numerous lavender to white ray flowers around a cluster of yellow disk flowers.

In the mountains of western North Carolina and northward, Robin's Plantain occurs in broad sweeps and makes a beautiful floral display in spring as it begins to flower in late April and May.

Fruit and Seed

In the two to three weeks following the bloom period the nutlets develop rapidly. The tiny, hairlike, tan pappus bristles, 4–5 millimeters long, form a fluffy mound typical of the fruiting heads of many species in the Aster family. The small, shiny, greenish tan nutlets are triangular and ribbed along the margins.

Seed Collection, Cleaning, and Storage

Usually only a small percentage of the nutlets in each head develop. By late spring the fruiting heads and stems have withered and all but disappeared, so begin checking the nutlets when the pappus bristles turn tan. To do this simply grasp the pappus and pinch out a few nutlets; if they have any brown coloration, collect the seed heads immediately into a paper bag.

Allow the heads to air-dry for a few days and then separate the nutlets by rolling the heads between your fingers. There is no need to remove the pappus. If you are not planting immediately, store the dry, cleaned nutlets in a sealed container and refrigerate until time of sowing.

Propagation

Seed. Since only a small percentage of nutlets generally develop, they should be sown very thickly. Sow nutlets directly in an outdoor seedbed as soon as they are collected in late spring or early summer. Cover the nutlets lightly, keep the bed evenly moist through the summer, and look for tiny seedlings the next spring. Let the seedlings remain in the bed until they have formed strong rosettes that measure about an inch across.

Transplant them to 3-inch pots containing a well-drained potting mix; when roots fill the containers, move the plants to the garden, watering as needed until they establish. The time from germination until the plants are ready for permanent planting is usually eight to ten weeks. Of course, by judicious thinning the seedlings may be left in the seedbed until large enough to plant directly into their permanent location.

Alternatively, sow stored nutlets in the cold frame or an outdoor seedbed in the spring, but expect a lower percentage of germination than would result from direct sowing at the time of collection.

Division. This is the most practical method of increase. After the plants have flowered in the spring, select the largest clumps for division, those with at least six rosettes. Lift a clump with a shovel and begin separating rosettes from the edge of the clump—they pull apart easily. Put the separated rosettes in a container of water to keep them from drying out while making other divisions, then replant and water immediately.

Cultivation

Robin's Plantain grows naturally in full sun, at the edge of a

wooded area, or in light shade. Ideally, plants should be located in an open setting with taller herbaceous plants nearby to give some protection—something you can easily achieve by siting them carefully in the sunny border. Provide a soil that is loose, organic, and well-drained; amend average garden soil with a shovelful each of compost or rotted leaves and sand per plant.

Where plants can spread unobstructed, growth is rapid, and a colony may enlarge to 3 feet across in two to three years. Divide mature plants when they become crowded—when the rosettes overlap.

If you do not need seeds, remove the flowering stems after the bloom period. Regular watering during dry periods will of course make for healthier plants. Remove the fallen leaves that accumulate from nearby trees in the fall, as they can smother the rosettes and cause them to rot.

Uses in the Garden and Landscape

Robin's Plantain is a natural choice for the front rank of the perennial border and should be included in your spring color scheme. Combine them in the border with Sundrops, Ox-eye Daisy, Blue-eyed Grass, and Blue Star. In the sunny rock garden, plant them near Bird-foot Violet, Green-and-Gold, and Wine-leaved Cinquefoil. Plants may be naturalized in moist, fertile soils and along the margins of wooded areas. Plants may also be used in "openings" in the shade garden.

Container culture is appropriate where watering is regular.

Related Species

Although most of the related and somewhat similar native Fleabane Daisies, such as *Erigeron annuus*, *E. strigosus*, and *E. canadensis*, are generally considered to be weeds (and may be in your garden unintentionally), the Philadelphia Fleabane (*E. philadelphicus*) and especially the western Oregon Fleabane (*E. speciosus*) are excellent garden plants, with propagation and cultivation essentially the same as for Robin's Plantain.

Production Notes

Field-grow plants in an open, sunny plot in loose, well-drained soil. Space plants a foot apart in the row, divide and pot transplants in pint containers in the fall or early spring, and market when the plants are in flower.

Deciduous Wild Ginger

Asarum canadense
Aristolochiaceae

Duration: perennial

Blooming time: April–May

Flower color: maroon

Height: groundcover

Soil: rich, moist

Exposure: shade

Description

Deciduous Wild Ginger is a common inhabitant of rich, moist woods in many eastern states. With its attractive, heart-shaped foliage, it is an excellent plant in the shade garden as a fast-spreading groundcover.

When the leaves or rhizomes are broken, they give off a pleasant, pungent gingerlike aroma, which accounts for part of the plant's common name; "deciduous" refers to the fact that, unlike those of the Wild Gingers in the genus *Hexastylis*, the leaves are not evergreen. These other native American wild gingers are not related to the true ginger (*Zingiber*) of the tropics, which produces the pungent rhizome used as seasoning.

Deciduous Wild Ginger is first seen in early spring as the tightly wrapped, light green, wrinkled leaves appear at ground level and slowly unfold over the next few weeks. The wide, reniform (or kidney-shaped) leaves, which are 4–6 inches (10–15 cm) across, are borne on petioles up to a foot in length. Thick spreading rhizomes just below the surface produce a network of finely branched roots that penetrate deeper into the soil.

The curious flowers are borne at ground level beneath the leaves, each on a short pedicel between the paired petioles. The leaves are fully expanded at the time of flowering (April–May) and completely conceal the blooms. The flower, which has no petals, consists of a maroon, bell-shaped calyx, ½ inch (1.25 cm) long, terminating in three spreading, pointed lobes.

Fruit and Seed

Since the fleshy calyx persists as the capsule develops, the appearance of the fruiting structure is essentially unchanged from that of the flower. The oval, grayish seeds, about 4 millimeters long, are formed in the lower, or basal, portion of the fleshy capsule.

Seed Collection, Cleaning, and Storage

Seeds ripen four to six weeks after the first flowers appear. Because the capsules, now enclosed by the withered calyx, are so effectively hidden by the leaves, they are easily forgotten. As a reminder to check on the seeds, make a note on your calendar.

To collect, simply pinch off the pulpy capsules and peel apart over a clean, dry surface to remove the seeds. A markedly higher rate of germination can be expected when the seeds are sown fresh, but, if necessary, they may be stored in moist (not wet) whole-fiber sphagnum in a sealed container in the refrigerator.

Propagation

Seed. Sow seeds in a shaded outdoor seedbed immediately upon collection. Keep the bed well watered throughout the summer for uniform germination early the following spring. If the seeds are allowed to dry prior to sowing, germination will be uneven and may not occur for several years, if at all.

As with some other shade-loving native perennials, such as the Trilliums, Bloodroot, and Wild Bleeding Heart, a moist cold period is a prerequisite for germination, a condition best satisfied by outdoor sowing. Seeds may also be sown in a pot which is then plunged into the soil or a cold frame to just below its rim and kept evenly moist.

The first true leaf on a seedling appears several weeks after germination, whereupon the seedlings should be transplanted to a nursery row or a suitable container for the remainder of their first season, then moved to a permanent planting site in the spring of their second year.

Cuttings. Mallet cuttings, taken in late spring and summer, are a reliable method of increase. With a pocket knife remove a small piece of the rhizome with a pair of leaves attached. Insert the cutting in a rooting chamber in a medium consisting of equal parts peat moss and sand and place in the shade where high humidity can be maintained. A high percentage of cuttings treated in this manner should root.

In four to five weeks, when cuttings have developed masses of fine roots, transplant them into a nursery bed or 4-inch containers for the remainder of the season. Plants should be moved to a permanent site the following spring.

Division. Divide mature plants (the mats should be at least 1½–

2 feet across) in the fall when they begin to go dormant. Lift the mat and with a trowel or sharp spade cut through the rhizome at intervals of 6–8 inches. Alternatively, leave the mother plant in place and section off pieces from the edges of the clump. Replant the new divisions immediately and water thoroughly.

Cultivation

As with Foamflower, another spring-blooming groundcover, shade and moisture are necessary for success with Deciduous Wild Ginger; light, moderate, and deep shade are all acceptable.

Plants establish rapidly in loose, rich, organic soils. Make sure the planting site is primed to a depth of 8–10 inches, with generous amounts of compost, rotted leaves, or aged manure. A mulch of leaves applied in early spring and again in the fall will help conserve moisture and improve the soil.

Deciduous Wild Ginger is a good indicator plant during the summer months, as its leaves are among the first to wilt at the onset of a dry period and signal the need for regular watering until the weather changes.

Space new plants 10–12 inches apart in the garden and plan to divide large clumps when they become crowded or when new plants are needed.

Uses in the Garden and Landscape

This species is a natural for the shade or woodland garden. It is

effective when used as an edging plant along a path or trail, in a mass, or when interplanted with other shade-loving natives. Try it as a spreading groundcover at the base of clump-forming (*not* spreading) ferns, such as Cinnamon, Maidenhair, Marginal Shield, Southern Lady, and Fancy Fern or Silvery Spleenwort. An attractive woodland scene can be created by combining the spreading mats of Deciduous Wild Ginger with taller species, such as Solomon's Seal, Cohosh, Cardinal Flower, Bane Berry, and the Bellworts.

Related Species

Hexastylis is a closely related genus of attractive evergreen wild gingers with fleshy brown flowers borne at ground level beneath the leaf litter. Of the eight species found in our region, *H. arifolia* (Wild Ginger) and *H. virginica* (Heart Leaf) have the widest dis-

tribution. Both form tight clumps, are among the first plants to flower in early spring, and produce attractive mottled foliage. The leaves of *H. arifolia* are arrowhead shaped and the fleshy calyx is urn shaped; *H. virginica* has shiny, rounded heart-shaped leaves (with considerable variation in their mottling) and a more open, bell-shaped calyx. Cultivation is essentially the same as for *Asarum* except that the evergreen species are more tolerant of dry conditions. Propagation is by seed, division, and mallet cuttings.

The various evergreen *Hexastylis* species scattered throughout the South are among the most ornamental of our native plants because of their year-round attractiveness and usefulness as accent plants. Though they frequently occur as only single- or double-leaved specimens in dry piedmont woods, it is not uncommon to find spectacular clumps in humus-rich locations bearing a dozen to two dozen or more leaves. Sometimes such clumps are the result of seeds germinating and growing at the base of the parent plant.

There is such wonderful variation in these species in leaf size, shape, and mottling that a rock garden or wooded slope with nothing but evergreen gingers would be garden enough in itself. Single large clumps at the edge of a patio or next to entrance steps make enduring attractions.

Production Notes

In nurseries, where sufficient stock plants are available, mallet cuttings are the most efficient propagation technique for large-scale production of *Asarum* and *Hexastylis*.

Jack-in-the-Pulpit, Indian Turnip

Arisaema triphyllum
Araceae

Duration: perennial

Blooming time: April–May

Flower color: green, green and maroon

Height: 1–3 feet

Soil: rich, moist or wet

Exposure: shade

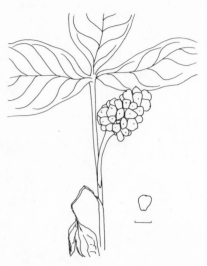

Description

Jack-in-the-Pulpit occurs on stream banks, in boggy areas, and in rich woods throughout the eastern United States.

In early spring a narrow, pointed bud bearing both leaves and the solitary "flower" emerges from the ground; one to two weeks later the bud scales unfold and reveal the most unusual "flower." It consists of a leaflike hood, or spathe (the pulpit), around a central column, the spadix, which bears small clusters of pollen-bearing male flowers near the top and often a cluster of minute female flowers near the base. Typically light green, the hood can vary in color from plant to plant, sometimes taking on a striking pattern of alternating maroon and greenish white stripes.

One or two leaves, each divided into three (rarely, five) leaflets, also expand from the bud and are usually from 1 to 3 feet in height. With proper attention to moisture, Jack-in-the-Pulpit can be a stalwart in the garden, enduring for many years. Unless the plants are well nourished, however, female flowers may not be produced every year, and fruit production may be sporadic.

Fruit and Seed

Shortly after the spathe withers, a small, dense cluster of green berries appears. As the growing season continues, the cluster slowly expands; green gives way to orange, and by September the berries are bright red, making the plant once again very prominent in the garden. Five or six months elapse between flowers and mature fruit. Often the leaves deteriorate before the fruit matures so that at the time for seed collection the gardener finds just a single green stalk supporting the cluster of brilliant red fleshy berries.

Seed Collection, Cleaning, and Storage

The clusters of berries can be safely gathered as soon as they have turned brilliant red. Each fleshy berry contains from one to five white seeds.

Seed cleaning should be started within a few days from collection while the pulp around the seeds is still soft and easy to remove. To clean the seeds separate the berries from the cluster and place them in a sieve. Moving to a sink, run a steady stream of water over the berries until the red pulp loosens and seeds can be removed.

Alternatively, soak the berries in a container of water for a few hours and free the seeds by hand or by placing the berries between several folds of newspaper on the floor and walking on them (with soft-soled shoes). Excessive handling of the pulp may cause a slight irritation to the hands, which can be quickly remedied by washing with soap in warm water.

Wash the seeds thoroughly to float off all the pulp and skin. Seeds should be stratified right away in damp, whole-fiber sphagnum moss in a sealed container and refrigerated. If seeds are allowed to dry out, germination may be delayed for a year.

Propagation

Seed. Seeds can be sown indoors or outside with the same good results.

Indoor sowing can begin after seeds are moist-cold treated in the refrigerator for at least sixty days. Sow seeds evenly in a flat of standard sowing medium, cover with a quarter-inch of soil, and keep constantly moist. Germination can be expected within two weeks. First-year seedlings are small, 2–3 inches tall, have only one undivided leaf, and are completely dormant within three months' time. At this stage pot the small corms individually and place them in a shaded spot outside. Move corms into the garden at the end of the second season. Plants should flower the third season.

Outdoor sowing is easier. After collection and cleaning in the

fall, sow seeds 3–4 inches apart in a prepared seedbed. Plants can remain in this bed through the second season, at which time they can be moved into the garden.

Do not fertilize Jack-in-the-Pulpit during the growing season, as this may cause premature dormancy, but fertilize lightly in winter for larger plants and more fruit.

Cultivation

To produce superior specimens, Jack-in-the-Pulpit requires a constantly moist or wet garden soil and moderate shade. Direct sunlight makes for lighter foliage and less attractive plants. For naturalizing, native woodland soil with a pH of around 5.5 is adequate; heavy clay soils, however, should be amended with rich garden soil or compost.

Uses in the Garden and Landscape

Jack-in-the-Pulpit belongs in the woodland shade garden. An ar-

rangement of single plants spotted in and among fern plantings is effective, especially in late summer and fall when the red fruit is conspicuous against the green fern fronds.

Interesting combinations can be created when these plants are interplanted with shade-loving groundcovers, such as Foamflower, Phacelia, Stonecrop, and Wild Ginger. A low, wet area is an ideal place in which to naturalize these plants; once established, they require little, if any, care. Jack-in-the-Pulpit also makes a fine container plant if kept out of direct sun and watered regularly. To force blooms for mid-winter moisten the soil in the pot after the plant has gone dormant in the fall, place the pot in a closed plastic bag in the refrigerator for two to three months, and then put it in the greenhouse or a sunny window and water.

Related Species

Green Dragon, *A. dracontium*, is taller than Jack-in-the-Pulpit, bears a single horizontally oriented leaf with seven to fifteen leaflets, and has a light green spathe terminating in a long, thin, ascending projection. Its cultural requirements are the same as for *A. triphyllum*, but Green Dragon can tolerate a sunnier exposure.

Production Notes

Pot corms as plants go dormant at the end of the second growing season for sale the following spring.

Wild Geranium

Geranium maculatum
Geraniaceae

Duration: perennial

Blooming time: April–May

Flower color: pink

Height: 1–2 feet

Soil: rich, moist

Exposure: light shade

Description

Wild Geranium has long been a standard in the wild garden—and for good reason: the plants have attractive flowers and foliage, require little, if any, maintenance once they are established, and are easy to propagate from seed and division. The plant is found throughout the eastern United States in alluvial woods, coves, and wet meadows.

The large, rounded leaves, which are borne on long, smooth petioles 1–2 feet long, are deeply cut into five to seven segments. Each segment is pointed and coarsely toothed with prominent venation. The leaves resemble in a general way those of some of the Wild Anemones, especially *Anemone canadensis*. The notched ends of the leaf segments give the plant another, although rarely used, common name—Crowfoot. In addition to the distinctive basal leaves, the plant produces smaller leaves, in pairs, on the stems at the bases of flowers.

Wild Geranium blooms for two to three weeks in May, and each inflorescence consists of one or two individual flowers borne on long (to 5 inches) peduncles from the leaf axils. A single flower, with five purplish-pink, whitish, or rarely white petals, can measure to 1½ inches (4 cm) across. The flowering stems arise from stout, dull orange, sharply angled rhizomes which have knobby leaf scars from the previous season's growth and a few long, slender roots.

Fruit and Seed

The fruiting structure and its dispersal mechanism are intriguing. During the three to four weeks after the flowering period the fruit, a schizocarp, develops into a beaklike structure that gives the plant yet another name—Cranesbill. The beak, situated in the center of a persis-

tent, five-pointed calyx, is really the styles of the pistil. At maturity the schizocarp splits into five separate threads; each recoils sharply backwards, remaining attached at the apex of the beak and taking with it one of the five seeds from the base of the pistil.

The mature seeds are smooth, oval to kidney shaped, dark brown, and 1/16 inch (2–3 mm) long. Sometimes the seeds are catapulted away from the plant as the style threads recoil. Or they may remain attached for a short while at the ends of the recoiled threads.

Seed Collection, Cleaning, and Storage

Seeds are essentially lost when the fruit splits; a few may hang on for a short time after the meri-carps recoil, but you should not count on this. The fruit turns darker shades of green as seeds develop, and in many cases seeds may be brown and mature before they are released. Collect the intact mericarps as soon as they begin to darken and place them in a paper bag, where they will split open and spill their seeds. If you are not planting the seeds immediately, store them dry in a sealed container and refrigerate until time to sow.

Propagation

Seed. Sow seeds in a shaded outdoor seedbed upon collection and look for seedlings the next spring. Allow the plants to remain undisturbed in the bed during their first season and transplant them into the garden when they go dormant.

With some sowings, it may take a second year, or second period of extended cold, for seeds to germinate. If germination is poor the first year, leave the flat or row in the seedbed undisturbed until the next growing season.

Alternatively, sow stored seeds indoors or in the cold frame in late winter; the seeds should germinate, though perhaps only a low percentage, in a week or less and may be potted in two weeks' time. Seedlings develop a tiny rhizome and are easily handled. Allow six weeks for the seedlings to become large enough for permanent planting.

Division. The rhizomes of Wild Geranium may be up to 6 inches long and support several clusters

of stems. In the fall lift a clump from the garden and with pruning shears cut the rhizome into pieces, each with two to three buds and several roots. Often a rhizome will form right angles and thus further simplify division. Replant divisions an inch below the soil and water.

Cultivation

As its native haunts suggest, Wild Geranium does best in moist, rich soils and shaded settings. The plant's requirements are similar to those of Deciduous Wild Ginger, Waterleaf, and the Trilliums.

Its performance through the season will depend largely on how regularly the plants are irrigated during summer dry periods. If plants remain dry for two weeks or more, the stems are apt to die down for the remainder of the season.

A good time to rework the soil is when you divide your plants, adding plenty of organic matter. Apply a mulch of shredded leaves or compost at both ends of the growing season. If left unchecked, Wild Geranium may encroach upon other plantings and should be curbed as necessary.

High, open shade, such as under hardwoods that have been limbed up to let in more light, and even as much as a half day's full sun are acceptable exposures and seem to produce plants with more flowers.

Uses in the Garden and Landscape

Use Wild Geranium in the shade garden, where it can spread freely and mix with other shade-loving species. New York and Maidenhair Ferns are especially appropriate companions, as are Cardinal Flower and Wild Bleeding Heart. It is a marvelous plant for the front or middle ranks of the shaded perennial border.

The plant adapts readily to brighter settings in cultivation, rewarding the gardener with dense clumps of foliage throughout the season. Where conditions are favorable, naturalize these plants in sweeps and at the bases of large trees.

Production Notes

Grow plants in shaded production beds with rich soil and water regularly. Divide plants every second year, pot into 4-to-6-inch containers, and market the following spring.

Atamasco Lily

Zephyranthes atamasco
Amaryllidaceae

Duration: perennial

Blooming time: May

Flower color: white

Height: 8–10 inches

Soil: rich, moist or wet

Exposure: filtered to full sunlight

Description

Atamasco Lily is a charming, low-maintenance perennial wild flower ideally suited for eastern gardens, since it occurs in rich woods, damp clearings, and open meadows throughout the southeastern United States. It has sometimes been compared with such other attractive spring-blooming plants as the Trilliums, Bloodroot, and the Wild Gingers as notoriously difficult to propagate. Like those plants, however, Atamasco Lily can be started by a number of straightforward propagation techniques and, furthermore, establishes readily in the garden or naturalized setting.

Shiny, narrow, grasslike leaves are grooved, 8 to 10 inches long, and form loose clumps. The white or, rarely, pink, funnel-form flowers, up to 4 inches (10 cm) long, are borne singly on leafless stalks, or scapes, 8 to 10 inches tall. Because flowers appear in April and have the look of the classic funnel-shaped lilies, plants are sometimes referred to as Easter Lilies. With age, or after pollination, the white flowers turn pink.

Fruit and Seed

The flowers are followed in five to six weeks by a green, three-lobed, spherical capsule. Since the plant is not conspicuous after it flowers, make a note on the calendar to remind you when to begin looking for seeds and attach a bit of bright-colored flagging to the scapes so you will be able to find them when you return.

The capsules expand steadily as they mature and each of the three lobes, or locules, holds numerous flattened, shiny black, wrinkled seeds, which measure approximately ¼ inch (5 mm) across and vary considerably in shape. Some are nearly rounded, while others are distinctly crescent shaped and sharply angled.

Seed Collection, Cleaning, and Storage

Allow the seeds to turn black within the capsule before collecting. At the Botanical Garden in central North Carolina the capsules are typically collected during the first week in June.

After collection, break open the capsules and let the seeds spill out. The small amount of litter that will mix with the seeds can be easily removed by hand, by gentle vibration, or by blowing it away. Store the seeds dry in a sealed, labeled container and refrigerate until time of sowing.

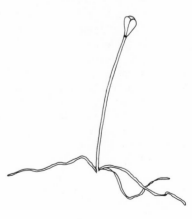

Propagation

Seed. Sow stored seeds in a flat indoors or in the cold frame in late winter. Space seeds ¼ inch apart in the flat and cover them with ¼ inch of soil. Germination, which occurs over a three-to-four-week period after sowing, is typically 50 percent or greater. Seeds may also be sown in an outdoor seed bed upon collection.

During their first season the seedlings look like small tufts of grass, so be sure to place a label at the beginning of the row in your seed bed as a safeguard against weeding out the young seedlings. Eight to ten weeks after germination, when roots approach an inch in length, move the seedlings into 3-inch pots and apply an all-purpose fertilizer weekly. A month or so before the expected first frost date, move the plants to the garden; or overwinter them in the cold frame or heeled-in outside and plant the next spring.

Division. Mature plants can be increased by separating the basal offsets or by division of the cluster of bulbs. Toward the latter part of the growing season, when the plant begins to go dormant, lift it and shake loose the soil. Basal offsets, which are smaller in size and connected to the mother bulb, can be separated by simply pulling them away at the base. Replant offsets or bulbs at a depth of 2 inches and water thoroughly.

Cultivation

Establish Atamasco Lilies in areas that receive at least a few hours of direct light during the day. An opening in or at the edge of a wooded area is ideal. Shadier settings make for fewer flowers.

The soil should be humus rich, so incorporate plenty of organic matter like rotted leaves and compost in the planting area. Since these native lilies are frequently found in wet areas, drainage is not a consideration, and the plants are appropriate for naturalizing in wet areas. The soil should not be allowed to dry out during the growing season, and provision should be made to water plants during dry periods. A leaf mulch should be applied during the spring and again in late summer.

Space new plants, first-year plants, and divisions 6 to 8 inches apart. Unless new plants are desired, the clumps can remain undisturbed indefinitely or until they become so crowded that flowering is reduced.

Burrowing rodents may be a danger for the bulbs. To deter them, plant the bulbs in large pots and then plant the pot and mulch over the top. Alternatively, mix in two shovelfuls of coarse, ¾-inch, sharp-edged gravel with the soil around each plant. The latter method is also appropriate for other plants in the perennial border if you have a problem with rodents. To work gravel into a large bed spread a 2-inch layer of gravel over the surface of the bed and mix it in using a rototiller.

Uses in the Garden and Landscape

Atamasco Lilies are most effectively displayed in groups, either in a border planting or naturalized. Establish plants in the first rank of the border with other low-growing natives, such as Green-and-Gold, Blue-eyed Grass, Wild Bleeding Heart, and Buttercup (*Ranunculus bulbosus*).

Where a naturally moist area or bog exists, combine plants with the native ferns, the Gentians, Turtleheads, and Cardinal Flower. In the colder northern states, the bulbs should be brought in at the end of the season and stored in a cool location or treated as a container plant.

Related Species

Zephyranthes candida, native to South America, has become naturalized in a few coastal areas of the Southeast. The beautiful white or occasionally pink star-shaped flowers, 1½ inches (3.75 cm) long, bloom in the fall. It forms a tighter clump than *Z. atamasco* but is only marginally hardy in the North and is perhaps best treated as a container plant.

Stonecrop

Sedum ternatum
Crassulaceae

Duration: perennial

Blooming time: May

Flower color: white

Height: groundcover

Soil: rich, moist

Exposure: light shade

Description

Stonecrop occurs in rich, often rocky woods and along stream banks throughout nearly the whole of the eastern United States. The plant has value in the shade garden as a nearly prostrate spreading groundcover since, once established, it will require little, if any, maintenance. It is attractive at the bases of rocks and large trees and as a mat-forming carpet around taller, shade-loving plants.

On nonflowering stems the succulent, slightly rounded leaves, which vary in size and may be up to ¾ inch (1.85 cm) long and ½ inch (1.25 cm) wide, are in whorls of three, terminating in a rosette of usually six leaves. On flowering stems, which arise from a basal rosette, the few leaves are alternate.

The small white flowers, about ¾ inch (1.85 cm) in diameter, first appear in May (in our area) and continue for several weeks. A flower has five green sepals, five spreading white petals, and ten stamens with prominent dark anthers.

Fruit and Seed

Four-pointed, star-shaped clusters of follicles, not quite ½ inch (1.25 cm) across, develop soon after flowering. Each follicle bears a thin, hairlike appendage at its apex. As the seeds develop, the follicles change from white to tan and split along the single suture.

Seed Collection, Cleaning, and Storage

Seeds are mature and ready for collection two to three weeks after the plants flower. They are dark brown, elliptic, and very small—less than a millimeter long. The follicles remain slightly opened on the stalk for several weeks after the seeds mature, allowing some flexibility in when they may be collected.

To harvest the seeds, snip the stalks with pruning shears and drop them into a collection bag. Spread the stalks on a clean, dry, white surface indoors and let them air-dry for a few days. Replace the stalks in a bag and shake vigorously. Remove the stalks from the bag and run the loosened seed and debris through a sieve. Ripe but unopened follicles may be crushed with a rolling pin or by hand. Without sophisticated seed-cleaning equipment, it is difficult to obtain a perfectly clean seed lot, but a bit of chaff in with the seeds will do no harm. Store seeds dry in a sealed, labeled container and refrigerate until time of sowing.

Propagation

Seed. Because the seeds are tiny, they should be mixed with some sand and the mixture sown in a flat and placed in a protected location outdoors, such as a cold frame, or indoors, where they should germinate in one to two weeks. Water carefully, as the small seeds are easily washed away. Watering by setting seed flats in a tray of water is a safe method to avoid splashing seeds off the medium.

Allow the seedlings to produce three to four leaves before transplanting them into individual containers. Amend your standard potting mix with half again as much sand, as seedlings grow faster in a loose, fast-draining mix. When roots fill the containers, transfer plants into the garden.

Cuttings. Take cuttings from sterile, nonflowering shoots at any time during the growing season. Make cuttings approximately 3 inches long, remove the lower leaves, and insert the cuttings in a medium of fine sand. Allow cuttings a few days to callus before the initial watering. A rooting chamber is not required. Place cuttings out of direct sunlight and keep the sand evenly moist. In two weeks root development should have proceeded far enough that the cuttings may be potted; a month later they can be moved into the garden.

Division. Plants form a shallow-rooted mat and are easily divided at any time during the year with a trowel. Simply cut out divisions of the size and number desired, replant, and water thoroughly.

Cultivation

Stonecrop does best in a lightly shaded setting. Plants tolerate direct light, but the leaves tend to lighten in color and lose their distinctive luster. In nature populations typically occur on slopes, suggesting adaptation for a well-drained soil. Thus Stonecrop may be established on an incline or in a raised bed or prepared soil. A loose, organic soil is recommended. Keep the soil evenly moist through the growing season.

Uses in the Garden and Landscape

Stonecrop is an ideal ground-cover for the woodland wild flower or rock garden. Deeper-rooted plants, such as Trillium, Solomon's Seal, Cohosh, Bellwort, Trout Lily, and Jack-in-the-Pulpit, may be interplanted with Stonecrop without fear of competition. Naturalize plants on a creek bank or in a shaded, moist (but not wet) area and in rocky outcrops.

Related Species

Sedum smallii is a low winter annual which occurs in the shallow soil of vernal pools on flat granite outcrops; its attractive red leaves and white flowers make it a choice rock garden plant. *S. telephioides* has pale pink to whitish petals and grows to 16 inches tall.

Production Notes

Take cuttings at several times during the growing season and insert them directly into 2- or 3-inch containers; market the plants in the fall or following spring.

Coreopsis

Coreopsis auriculata
Asteraceae

Duration: perennial

Blooming time: May

Flower color: yellow

Height: ½–2 feet

Soil: well-drained garden soil

Exposure: sun to light shade

Description

This hardy, low-growing Coreopsis occurs in rich woodlands and thickets throughout the southeastern United States. In the garden the plants perform equally well in either full sun or light shade and require little, if any, maintenance, save for an occasional watering during summer dry periods.

Plants spread and form colonies via stolons, or runners, which terminate in leafy rosettes. Some of these leaves are auriculate, or basally lobed; both the rosette leaves and the stem leaves are densely hairy.

The bright flowering heads are 1–1½ inches (2.5–3.8 cm) in diameter with yellow disk flowers and yellow ray flowers that are toothed along their outer margins. Plants begin blooming in late April and continue through most of May.

This Coreopsis is unique in its size (it is essentially a dwarf, only 6–24 inches tall), its slowly spreading habit, and its attractive foliage, which persists through most of the winter.

Fruit and Seed

The ray flowers, subtended by two whorls of overlapping bracts that make up the bell-shaped involucre, turn dark brown after the bloom period and remain attached to the head during nutlet development. The ovoid nutlets are small, ¹⁄₁₆–⅛ inch (2–3 mm) long, smooth, dark brown or black, and are slightly concave. A slender, light brown wing encir-

cles the darker body of the nutlet and under magnification the upper edge, or rim, on the front of the nutlet is often deep red or maroon.

Seed Collection, Cleaning, and Storage

Nutlets are mature and ready for harvest approximately four weeks after the flowers wither. Watch the inner series of bracts; when they begin to darken, it is time to collect. At this stage the bracts begin to spread, the seed head "opens" a bit, and the nutlets are dispersed in the next few days.

You will almost certainly collect considerable chaff, consisting of the dried pieces of ray and disk flowers and bracts, with the nutlets as you remove them from the head. Clean the seeds with a sieve, or blow away the chaff with a fan. Store the nutlets dry in a sealed, labeled container and refrigerate until sowing. Stored correctly, the nutlets have a "shelf life" of at least three years.

Propagation

Seed. Sow seeds in an outdoor seedbed at any time during the growing season or in the cold frame or indoors in late winter. Unlike many other species in the Aster family, most of the nutlets produced are fully developed and viable; you can expect a high percentage of germination within a week.

The seedlings grow rapidly and in about three weeks will have two or three true leaves; at that time they can be moved to individual containers. Allow roots to fill the pots, then transfer plants into a permanent planting site in the garden.

If you plan a summer sowing, make sure you allow enough time for seedlings to develop so that they may be transplanted into the garden at least a month prior to the expected first frost date. This will enable the plants to become established before the onset of cold weather, which is especially important for gardeners in the middle Atlantic and northeastern states.

Seedlings in containers benefit from weekly applications of an all-purpose fertilizer. When potting, mound the soil slightly to prevent the leaves from remaining in contact with wet soil— which can be fatal for young plants.

Division. Although colonies of Coreopsis may be dense, especially when grown in a rich soil, individual basal rosettes are readily discernible. In the fall lift a clump from the outer edge of the planting and separate the rosettes by hand or cut away with a trowel. Remove a few of the leaves from each new division to reduce moisture loss, replant, and water thoroughly. Divide the plants every third year or when the planting becomes crowded.

Cultivation

Flower production will be nearly as prolific in a lightly shaded setting as it will in direct sunlight. Plants are not unduly specific as to soil requirements although

they seem to spread faster in a rich, well-drained medium primed with plenty of compost and rotted leaves. A planting may be selectively thinned to improve its appearance by removing clumps from the interior of the planting. Apply a mulch of rotted leaves at both ends of the growing season to conserve moisture and control weeds. Remove faded flowers after the bloom period but save a few for seed, of course.

Uses in the Garden and Landscape

Plant this dwarf Coreopsis in groups of fives and sevens in the front of the sunny border. They also make excellent filler material in and among other low-growing plants and at the bases of larger plants in the border. Use Coreopsis as an edging plant along a sunny walk or shaded path.

Plants also work well in the woodland wild flower garden where the golden yellow flowers are conspicuous in the darker, shaded setting. So versatile is this Coreopsis that it may be interplanted with dry roadside species such as Butterfly Weed, Blue-eyed Grass, and Sundrops, or with shade-loving plants such as Bloodroot, Columbine, and Deciduous Wild Ginger. Coreopsis may also be grown in large pots or window boxes provided watering is regular.

Related Species

Coreopsis auriculata "Nana," Dwarf-Eared Coreopsis, 4 to 6

inches tall, is a cultivated strain of our native species that is available from many nurseries.

Many other wild species of Coreopsis are suitable for cultivating in the border or naturalizing in the garden. Among them are *C. angustifolia* (to 3 feet), *C. falcata*, and *C. gladiata* (both to 6 feet), which occur in wet places along the coastal plain; *C. lanceolata*, *C. major*, and *C. pubescens*, which grow in drier soils and reach 3–4 feet; *C. verticillata*, the most popular among the taller Coreopsis, has fine-textured, dissected leaves, a more rounded bushy habit, grows to 3 feet tall, and has numerous small (1 inch across) flowers that continue

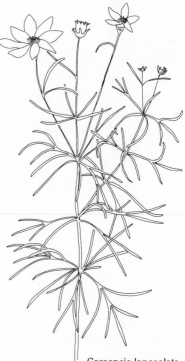

Coreopsis lanceolata

through much of the summer. All the above species do best in sandy, well-drained soils and full sun. Propagation is by seed and division.

Coreopsis tinctoria is a beautiful winter annual with an attractive fernlike rosette; the numerous flower heads have bright yellow rays with a red band in the center, or they may be entirely red or yellow; this species does well in a well-drained soil and full sun or light shade, and propagates from seed.

Production Notes

Work Coreopsis into a production program for bedding plants in the greenhouse. Basal leaves overlap the edges of the pot nine to ten weeks from time of sowing. Market plants in the spring in 3- or 4-inch containers.

White Wild Indigo

Baptisia pendula
Fabaceae

Duration: perennial

Blooming time: May

Flower color: white

Height: 2–3 feet

Soil: average garden soil

Exposure: sun to light shade

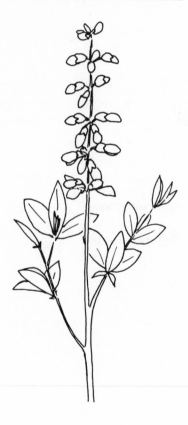

Description

Attractive in bud, in flower, and in leaf, White Wild Indigo is a choice native perennial. The young leaf and flower buds appear in spring on long, charcoal grey, asparaguslike stems. The older flower buds, which are also charcoal grey, are especially striking against emerging creamy white flowers. As the stalks push upward, attractive gray green leaves gradually unfold. Each leaf is divided into three segments, or leaflets, and, like the rest of the plant, has a thin white or gray powderlike surface.

The white bilateral, or zygomorphic, flowers, typical of the Pea family (with the characteristic wing-and-keel petals), are about ¾ inch (18 mm) across and are borne on long racemes. Viewed from a distance during flowering, even a single mature plant is spectacular—a mass of snow white. After the bloom period the plant is still attractive as a low mound of textured foliage.

Fruit and Seed

The characteristic pods, or legumes, are conspicuous on the stalk a few weeks after the bloom period, and they steadily inflate over the next few weeks as they turn from a dull light green to purplish black before they open. The texture of the 1½-inch-long (3.5–4.5 cm) pod is at first soft and pliant, then harder and brittle. The numerous small seeds, ⅛ inch (3 mm) long, are arranged in a row along the bottom of the pod. An unusually dry sum-

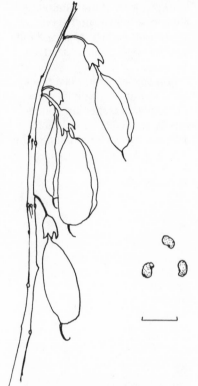

mer can cause the pods to shrivel before the seeds are mature. Supplemental watering during this period aids seed production.

Seed Collection, Cleaning, and Storage

Since the seed stalks are several inches taller than the foliar mound, they are easily seen. About six weeks past flowering (late June to early July), the seeds should be at or near maturity. Shell a few pods and examine the seeds, which are pliant and green as they develop and harden and turn light, medium, or dark brown when mature. Harvest the pods when they are black or show signs of opening along the top suture.

Comb the seeds from the pod, discarding the smaller shriveled ones. It is not uncommon to find a few insects, which feed on the developing seeds, inside the pods. If insects remain after cleaning, place an inch-long piece of No-Pest Strip in with the seeds and store in a sealed container at room temperature for two weeks. At the end of that period, remove the strip and refrigerate the seeds until time of sowing.

Propagation

Seed. Germination is typically slow and uneven with the Baptisias. Soak seeds overnight in hot water before sowing. A warm soil temperature (70°F) will hasten germination. Sow seeds outdoors in a prepared seedbed in April. Alternatively, sow indoors or in a cold frame in February. You can expect some germination in two to three weeks and sporadic germination during the next month.

Avoid overwatering. The thin young stems are very susceptible to damping off. Allow the surface of the soil to become dry between waterings. Regular fertilization can cause seedlings to burn, but a weekly application of an all-purpose fertilizer applied at half-strength enhances seedling development.

Seedlings raised indoors should be transferred to containers after the second set of true leaves appears—three to four weeks after germination—and planted in the garden in late spring. Started in a seedbed or cold frame, seedlings can be moved directly to the garden seven to eight weeks from germination when vigorous, well-rooted plants have developed.

Division. The tough rootstock can be divided in the fall, every two to three years. As the roots are deep, dig deeply when removing the clump to avoid breaking them. Make the divisions with a sharp knife or pruning shears; paint exposed parts of the crown with a fungicide; replant the divisions and water immediately.

Cultivation

White Wild Indigo is a hardy, deep-rooted perennial that needs no tending in the garden except for an occasional watering during dry periods. The plant thrives in an open, sunny setting, but tolerates light shade. While ordinary garden soil is sufficient, young plants seem to benefit from a rich, well-prepared medium.

Established plants need little care. They do, however, produce many branching stems that will ultimately give the plant a crowded, ingrown appearance. Regular division, as described previously, will relieve this condition. Space plants at least 2 feet apart at planting time.

A young plant sends up only a few stems the first season, but develops an impressive root system. Second-year plants flower modestly and plants flower prolifically the third season and thereafter.

Uses in the Garden and Landscape

This Baptisia is a must for the sunny perennial border. It is among the taller early-spring-blooming species and should be planted toward the rear of the bed. Plants are effective singly, in small groups, or in masses. After flowering, the plant's dense, shrubby habit makes an effective background for lower summer-blooming plants.

A few plants of the yellow-blooming Carolina Bush Pea (*Thermopsis*) planted nearby and a plant or two of the Blue Wild Indigo (*B. australis*) in front of the taller *B. pendula* make for a very colorful contrast with White Wild Indigo. With some attention to improving the native soil, White Wild Indigo can be naturalized in open, sunny areas.

Related Species

Baptisia australis (blue flowers), *B. cinerea* (yellow flowers), and *B. alba* (white flowers) should all be considered for use in the garden. *B. australis* tolerates a moist, sweet (pH 7+) soil and ranges from 3 to 6 feet in height. *B. cinerea* prefers dry, sandy conditions, has a looser form with spreading stems, and reaches 2 feet. *B. alba* grows to 5 feet and seems to grow well in dryer soil. Cultivation and propagation requirements for these species are essentially the same as for *B. pendula*.

Umbrella-Leaf

Diphylleia cymosa
Berberidaceae

Duration: perennial

Blooming time: May

Flower color: white

Height: 1–3 feet

Soil: rich, moist or wet

Exposure: shade

Description

Umbrella-Leaf is native to cool mixed deciduous forests and moist wooded coves and seepage slopes in the southern Appalachians. The large, coarse leaves are an effective contrast for other wild flowers with similar light and moisture requirements, such as Cardinal Flower, Turtlehead, and Bee-balm. The striking leaves notwithstanding, the plant is perhaps most interesting in fruit, when the deep blue berries stand out in sharp relief against the bright red stalks.

The loose, prominently toothed basal leaves measure 12 to 20 inches across and are divided into two major lobes and numerous small lobes. The two stem leaves are smaller, to 16 inches across, and more deeply lobed. Both basal and stem leaves are peltate, that is, they are attached to the long petioles from near the center of their lower surfaces.

The terminal cluster of white flowers, which appear in May and June, extends above the leaves; each separate flower measures ½–¾ inch (12–18 mm) across.

Fruit and Seed

Plants require approximately eight to ten weeks after flowering to produce mature seed. The rich dark blue, rounded berries, which reach ½ inch (1.25 cm) in diameter when fully expanded, are borne on long pedicels. Each fruit is covered with a whitish bloom and usually contains six or fewer seeds. The kidney-shaped seeds are about ¼ inch (6 mm) long and are an attractive reddish pink.

Seed Collection, Cleaning, and Storage

Because Umbrella-Leaf is not commonly cultivated, you may find that natural populations are your only source of seed. Learn the plant's habitat and then go after the seed at the height of summer—late July and August. Open a few berries and, if the moist, shiny seeds within show any pink coloration, they are ready to collect.

If you must wait a day or two before cleaning them, pack the berries in damp whole-fiber sphagnum in a sealed plastic bag to prevent the seeds from drying out. To clean, simply squeeze or mash the seeds out of the soft berry. If you are cleaning seeds from more than a few berries, you will likely pick up a purplish stain on your hands that will remain for a few days.

If seeds cannot be sown fresh, they may be stored in damp sphagnum in a sealed container and refrigerated. Stored seed take longer to germinate, often as long as two years, and germination is usually poor. For best results sow seeds immediately.

Propagation

Seed. Sow seed as soon as collected in a shaded outdoor seedbed and keep the soil moist during the growing season. (Allowing the soil to dry after sowing may delay or prevent germination; allowing it to dry after germination will send seedlings into an early dormancy or kill them.) Look for seedlings the next spring and leave them undisturbed in the seedbed for most of their first season. Then move plants into their permanent planting area when the leaves yellow in late summer.

The rate of growth of young plants appears to be dependent on soil moisture—more moisture produces larger plants. Flowering-sized plants are not likely before the fourth or fifth year.

Division. Plants have a thick rhizome with a mass of tough white roots and must be of flowering size before they can be divided. To divide, lift a plant from the garden in the fall, shake the soil from the roots, and section off a piece of the rhizome that includes at least one white bud and several roots. If you are dividing more than a few plants, plunge each new division into a bucket of water to keep it from drying until the procedure is completed; replant the divisions and water thoroughly.

Cultivation

Umbrella-Leaf is a shade garden plant that enhances both formal and naturalized settings. Plants should be established under a canopy of hardwoods where most of the lower limbs have been removed, creating a high, open shade and simulating the plant's natural environment. Prepare the soil in the planting area to a depth of at least a foot and work in generous amounts of rotted leaves, aged manure, and compost. If planting in a prepared bed, improve the moisture-holding capacity of the soil by adding plenty of rotted leaves or peat moss.

To produce fast-growing plants, locate them in a wet spot or near a water source so that irrigation can be regular during dry periods. To conserve moisture apply a leaf mulch at both ends of the growing season. Mature plants have a spread of nearly 4 feet, so space nearby plants accordingly.

Uses in the Garden and Landscape

Incorporate Umbrella-Leaf with any of the shade- and moisture-loving native ferns, where the textural contrast between the coarse leaves and the finely dissected fronds is most effective. Plants also combine well with many summer and fall-blooming wild flowers that have a preference for moist or wet soils, for example, Spiderwort, Bugbane (*Cimicifuga americana*), and Bee-balm. Plant groundcovers, such as Deciduous Wild Ginger, Waterleaf, and Stonecrop, at the base of plants. The spectacular leaves of Umbrella-Leaf make a strong focal point in your garden; where conditions permit, naturalize them in large groups.

Production Notes

Sow seeds 6 inches apart in rows in a deep, fertile bed. When plants go dormant at the end of their third season, pot them in quart containers and market the following spring.

Wine-Leaf Cinquefoil, Three-Toothed Cinquefoil

Potentilla tridentata
Rosaceae

Duration: perennial

Blooming time: May

Flower color: white

Height: groundcover

Soil: thin, well-drained

Exposure: full to filtered sunlight

Description

This attractive evergreen ground-cover, well suited to rock garden settings, occurs in rock crevices and balds in gravelly, sandy, and peaty soils usually at high elevations throughout the northeastern United States and as far south as Georgia. Both names, Wine-Leaf and Three-Toothed, refer to the attractive foliage—the former to its deep reddish color during the fall and winter months where plants are exposed to direct light, the latter to the three prominent dentations, or teeth, at the apex of each leaflet.

Although flowering enhances the plant's appearance, it is the lustrous, dark green foliage and tight, mat-forming habit that make it so desirable in the garden. The leaves, which are borne on short petioles, are composed of three leaflets, each tapering from apex to base and up to 1 ½ inches long. Botanically, the plant is classified as a "suffrutescent perennial," from its very low, shrubby habit and woody stems and runners.

The open cymes of flowers are on slender stems which may be a foot tall: each flower has five white petals and is approximately ⅓ inch (8 mm) wide. Flowering begins in early June with a burst of blooms lasting one to two weeks, followed by a two-to-three-week period of sporadic flowering.

Fruit and Seed

The achenes, or seeds, are held together in an "epicalyx" consisting of a series of sepals and bracts. The smooth, dark brown seeds, each ¹⁄₁₆ inch (1.5 mm) long, develop on the receptacle within the epicalyx, which turns from green to grayish brown during the three-to-four-week period after flowering. It may remain closed for several weeks after the seeds are mature—typically early July at the Garden. The dark seed stalks are conspicuous a few inches above the leaves if for no other reason than that they often seem to detract from the handsome foliage below.

Seed Collection, Cleaning, and Storage

To collect the ripe seed, snip the fruiting stalk below the lowermost cyme and lay the sprays of seed heads on a clean, dry surface indoors for several days to air-dry before cleaning. Remove the epicalyxes, place them in a small jar or bag, and shake vigorously to free the seeds.

If you do not wish to sow seeds immediately upon collection, store them dry in a sealed, labeled container in the refrigerator.

Propagation

Seed. For best germination, the seeds require a period of moist chilling; this can be most easily accomplished by sowing fresh seeds as soon as they are collected in an outdoor seedbed. Fresh seeds sown in the summer can be expected to germinate early in the next spring.

Alternatively, sow stored seeds indoors in early spring in a pot or seed pan of premoistened sowing medium; cover the pot or pan with plastic and return to the refrigerator for a six-week stratification period. At the end of that time remove the container from the refrigerator and place it in a protected area outside. Look for seedlings in one to two weeks.

Let the young plants produce three to four leaves before transplanting them into 2- or 3-inch pots filled with one part potting mix to one part sand or fine gravel. Slender white roots develop rapidly and are easily torn when plants are moved. To minimize damage during transplanting, slide a wooden stick label or spoon underneath the seedlings and gently pry them up. Put the plants in a lightly shaded area during the summer months and transfer them into the garden in the fall. Young plants benefit from weekly applications of an all-purpose fertilizer.

Cuttings. Take stem cuttings at any time during the growing season, being careful to include a piece of old (last year's) wood at the base of each cutting. Apply a rooting hormone, such as Hormodin number 8, to the bases of cuttings and insert them in pure sand or a mix of three parts sand to one part peat moss.

Rooting occurs at a significantly higher rate when a mist system is used; however, a 50 percent "take" can be expected if you use a rooting chamber where high humidity can be maintained. Mist cuttings when they become dry and keep the rooting medium evenly moist. When cuttings have formed a mass of roots an inch or so long, transplant them into 3-inch pots, overwinter in the cold frame or in a protected spot outside, and move into the garden the following spring.

Division. Plants are best divided in the fall. New divisions establish with some difficulty because roots are usually broken during handling. To reduce the danger of root damage, select three to four large stems in close proximity to each other and with a shovel or long trowel lift the clump, making sure to include a large amount of soil around the roots. Because plants form a dense foliar mat, hiding the stems, you might need to simplify the procedure by tying stems together and isolating the division you wish to dig. Replant and water the divisions immediately.

Cultivation

Once established, plants require very little attention. Well-drained, stony soils that include a minimal amount of organic matter are ideal. Where possible, locate plants on a slope to further enhance drainage.

Although plants are often found in sterile soils in nature, they may be acclimated to prepared garden soils by mixing in a shovelful of sand or gravel per square foot of planting area. Apply a gravel mulch annually, a half inch deep, at the bases of the plants to keep roots cool and facilitate drainage during periods of wet weather.

If seeds are not needed, prune away flowering stems after the blooms fade. Divide plants every three to four years or when they appear crowded—this will also be a good time to rework the planting area with drainage material. The more direct sunlight the plants receive, the more bronze or reddish the foliage will be during the dormant season.

Uses in the Garden and Landscape

With Nodding Onion, Bird-foot Violet, Dwarf Crested Iris, Yellow Star-Grass (*Hypoxis hirsuta*), and Fire Pink, Wine-Leaf Cinquefoil makes a fine addition to the southern rock garden; with attention to proper soil preparation, it makes an effective edging plant for lining a path or forming the front of a herbaceous border. Or try locating plants in pockets of a rock wall, in crevices of a patio, or along the edge of a stone or brick walkway.

Cross Vine

Anisostichus capreolata
Bignoniaceae

Duration: *perennial*

Blooming time: *May*

Flower color: *red or orange*

Height: *climbing vine*

Soil: *average soil*

Exposure: *full sun*

Description

The attractive high-climbing, evergreen Cross Vine occurs throughout the central and southern states in alluvial forest, bottomlands, and mixed or deciduous woodlands.

The dark green, opposite, compound leaves have only two leaflets and a strong, twining terminal tendril. The individual leaflets are leathery, up to 6 inches long and 1–3 inches wide. They typically overlap each other as vines climb, forming dense layers of foliage which may hide some of the flowers.

Blooming begins in early May and lasts several weeks. The large, colorful tubular flowers, each about 2 inches (5 cm) long, occur in groups of two to five in the axils of the leaves and bear some resemblance to those of the Trumpet Vine. The tubular corolla, dull red or orange outside and yellow or red in the throat, flares into five lobed segments.

Flowers appear on the previous season's growth and are more numerous higher up on the vines. In nature one seldom sees the flowers because the leafy, flowering portion of the vine is usually high in the treetops and essentially lost within the foliage of tall canopy trees.

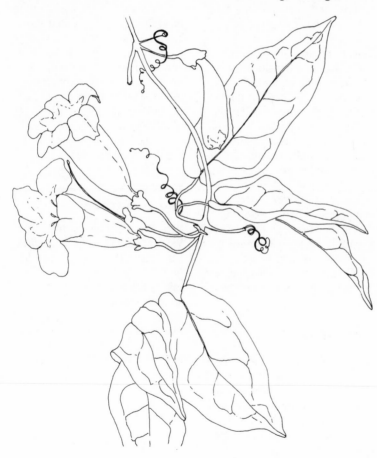

Fruit and Seed

The flattened, sword-shaped capsules, 5–6 inches long, develop over a three-to-four-month period after flowering and are typically covered by the foliage during most of the season. The numerous, flattened, papery winged seeds are an inch (2.5 cm) in length.

Seed Collection, Cleaning, and Storage

Seeds are mature and ready for collection in August, but they remain on the vine for one to two months beyond this time. Because you could forget the capsules in the dense leaf cover, it is not a bad idea to make a note to check on the seeds.

Collect the capsules when they begin to split and when the seeds are brown. Split the capsule lengthwise and rake out the seeds; there should be little or no debris. Store the seeds dry in a sealed container and refrigerate until time of sowing.

Propagation

Seed. Seeds can be sown in an outdoor seedbed upon collection or stored and sown in the spring after danger of frost is past. Both late-winter and early-spring sowing of stored seeds are appropriate in a cold frame or indoors. Space seeds an inch apart and cover them with ¼ inch of soil or sowing mix. Germination is typically slow and uneven, and seedlings are slow-growing.

After the second pair of leaflets appears and the roots are at least an inch long, transplant the seedlings into 2- or 3-inch containers and then into the garden when roots fill up the pots. Application of an all-purpose fertilizer at weekly intervals is beneficial to young plants.

Cuttings. Take stem cuttings, about four inches long, from new wood in June or July. (As you make the cuttings, look closely at one of the larger cut ends and you can see the four distinct strands of woody cells in the stem that form a cross and give the plant its common name.) Remove the bottom pair of leaflets, dip the bottom of the cutting in a rooting hormone, and insert into sand or a rooting mix of equal parts peat moss and sand. The lower node on the cutting should be about an inch below the surface of the rooting medium. Cuttings should be placed under mist or in a rooting chamber, where humid conditions can be maintained. Move cuttings into containers when they are well rooted and into the garden a month or so before the expected first frost in the fall.

Division. A portion of the vine will likely spread over the ground, and the rooted trailing stems will provide numerous divisions. So as not to disturb the main roots, select sprouts furthest from the center for division. Using a sharp spade, remove small rooted shoots containing five or six leaf nodes; prune shoots down to two or three leafy nodes and replant and water the divisions immediately.

Cultivation

Cross Vine is an aggressive, fast-growing plant that can climb to 50 feet or more as its strong tendrils grip surrounding plants and structures. Therefore, establish the vines in areas where you can control their spread. When trained on a post, trellis, or fence, vines tend to become top-heavy and will need thinning, which is best done in the spring just after flowering. To thin or shape Cross Vine drastically, just cut away until you arrive at the desired shape. This kind of pruning is best performed in late winter before new growth begins; however, you will lose the flowers for that season.

Cross Vine grows well in a variety of soils provided adequate moisture is available; the vines flower profusely in sunny areas, less so in the shade.

Uses in the Garden and Landscape

Cross Vine is especially useful as an evergreen cover for fences and rock walls and as a screening material. Once established, vines will rapidly sweep up the side of a house, garage, or carport or effectively cover nearly any fencing material. Vines are easy to establish on posts and trellises and make attractive specimen plantings, especially if you place a wire cage or fence around the post to provide the vines more growing area.

Production Notes

Pot rooted cuttings into quart containers and insert a stake or small trellis next to the plant. Overwinter pots in a protected area outside and market plants the following spring.

Blue-eyed Grass

Sisyrinchium angustifolium
Iridaceae

Duration: short-lived perennial

Blooming time: May

Flower color: blue

Height: 1–1½ feet

Soil: average garden soil

Exposure: full to filtered sun

Description

One or more species of Blue-eyed Grass grow along open sunny roadsides and in moist meadows and old fields throughout the eastern half of the United States. *Sisyrinchium angustifolium* thrives in cultivation, producing lush growth and prolific blooms; garden specimens far outshine the smaller, sparser flowering plants of native habitats. A moist soil, sunshine, and freedom from competition are all that are required.

A member of the Iris family, the plant has numerous, narrow, light green leaves that form dense, tufted clumps, which steadily grow with new foliage during the fall and persist during mild winter months, adding interest to the garden in the dormant season. The flattened, leaflike flowering stems, or scapes, may be up to 18 inches long. In May small, light blue, star-shaped flowers open on the scapes a few inches above the leaves.

Fruit and Seed

Shortly after the bloom period, round green capsules appear on the scapes. Because the plant blooms over a four-to-five-week span, capsules produced by the first flowers may appear at the same time that later flowers are just opening. Capsules slowly expand and darken to brown over the next month. They contain numerous tiny (1 mm) round seeds, which are black when mature.

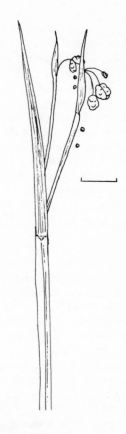

Seed Collection, Cleaning, and Storage

The capsules wrinkle slightly before they fall from the scape—a signal that seeds are ready for collection. The capsule has three inner compartments, each holding many seeds. Over a clean, light-colored surface, break open the drying capsules and shake loose the seeds. Run the seeds and debris through a sieve and allow seeds to air-dry for a day or two before storing in a sealed, labeled container in the refrigerator.

Propagation

Seed. Late summer or fall is the best time to set out plants of Blue-eyed Grass. Sow seeds in mid-summer in the cold frame or in a flat placed in a protected spot outside. Be sure to cover the cold frame with shade cloth at this time of year to protect young plants from the drying and burning effects of direct sunlight. Also, make sure cold-frame sashes remain open to allow for proper ventilation to prevent excessive heat buildup. Seedlings sown in the frame should be moved directly into the garden in early fall. Seedlings in the flat can be potted up when they have three or four leaves; keep them well watered and then transplant into the garden in early fall. Since the plant also self-sows in the garden, it may pay to check for seedlings at the base of parent plants in the fall and early spring.

Division. Early spring is the best time to divide clumps of Blue-eyed Grass. With a trowel lift plants from the garden and wash off the soil. You will notice numerous small crowns and a mass of white, fibrous roots. Make divisions by tugging apart small pieces of the clump, with three to four crowns per piece. From a mature specimen, you can expect to get several dozen divisions. Replant the divisions at once and keep them well watered until established.

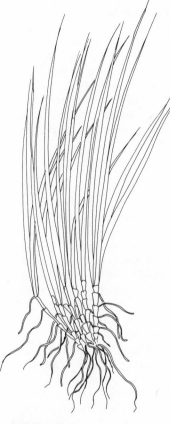

Cultivation

Blue-eyed Grass thrives in open, sunny sites and ordinary garden soil that is kept moist; plants will decline if they dry out. Avoid heavy mulches because, like Iris, these plants may develop crown rot. The plant declines in crowded conditions and thus benefits from periodic division; lift and divide plants at least every other year. Average garden soil is preferable to a rich, organic one; average soil keeps the plant low and compact, whereas a rich medium encourages rank vegetative growth that detracts from the appearance of the plant.

Uses in the Garden and Landscape

Blue-eyed Grass is very versatile. It is a fine specimen plant for tucking in rock gardens for winter interest and spring blooms. In the front of the perennial border it creates a miniature hedging effect, quite unexpected of this plant. As the plant is actively growing during the fall and much of the winter, it is striking as an unbroken edging plant along a path or walk when many plants are dormant. At the base of a rock wall its form and flowers are effectively highlighted. Its low, compact character makes it useful in spaces between other low to medium plants, such as Green-and-Gold, Ox-eye Daisy, Fire Pink, and Sundrops. In addition, Blue-eyed Grass is also suitable for container culture.

Production Notes

Field-grow plants in an open, sunny plot and irrigate regularly. Make divisions in late winter and pot several crowns together in 3- or 4-inch pots for spring sales. Single crowns potted up in spring and watered and fertilized through the growing season will produce vigorous plants for sale in the fall.

Spiderwort

Tradescantia virginiana
Commelinaceae

Duration: perennial

Blooming time: May–June

Flower color: blue

Height: 1–2 feet

Soil: average garden soil

Exposure: sun to light shade

Description

This native Spiderwort is one of the most versatile and reliable of the many native species suitable for use in the garden. Indeed, it is so adaptable and vigorous a grower that some inveterate gardeners question the wisdom of passing along information on "how to raise the thing." However, by dividing plants every second year and by regular removal of slumping stalks (which root at the nodes when in contact with the soil), the plants can easily be confined to their allotted space in the garden.

Tradescantia virginiana produces a thick clump of slender, fleshy, rounded stalks, 1–2 feet tall. The linear leaves are 6–18 inches long and have a prominent, grooved midrib. The bright blue flowers, 1–1.5 inches (2.5–4 cm) across, have three prominent petals and are in crowded terminal clusters. Rarely, the flowers may have purple, rose, or white petals, but all have a central tuft of purple and yellow stamens. An individual flower opens for only a day, but because there are so many buds in a cluster, the blooming period lasts three to four weeks, through most of May and into early June. In nature, Spiderworts are found in open woods and meadows and along roadsides in many eastern states.

Fruit and Seed

After flowering, the pedicels curve sharply downward. The small, light green, oval capsule, ⅜ inch (1 cm) long, is surrounded by three green bracts; it is mature two to three weeks after flowering. A few days prior to dehiscence, the bracts and capsule dry to a papery texture and darken to medium brown. The three compartments, or locules, of the capsule, each holding one or two seeds, split along the sutures. The dried, opened capsules look like dried flowers in their symmetry. The gray, oval seeds are about ⅛ inch (2 to 3 mm) long and conspicuously pitted.

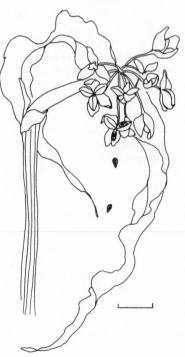

Seed Collection, Cleaning, and Storage

Several years' experience collecting seed from Spiderwort indicates that most capsules never produce viable seeds and those that do, open at different times and spill their seeds rapidly. So that the seeds are not lost as they are shed, enclose the cluster of capsules with a piece of nylon hose, cheesecloth, or a small bag. Another approach is to cut the stem when some capsules in the fruiting cluster have opened and place it in a container of water on a bench or table; the capsules will continue to develop and seeds may be harvested more conveniently.

Sow seeds immediately or store them dry in a sealed container and refrigerate until sowing later in the year or the following spring.

Propagation

Seed. Seeds sown fresh in an outdoor seedbed will normally germinate within two weeks. Thin the seedlings in the bed and allow plants to grow on for several months before moving them into the garden. Alternatively, seeds stored in the refrigerator over the winter can be planted in late winter in the cold frame or in a flat indoors. Seedlings need little attention, save regular watering and containers large enough to accommodate the spreading root system. When the danger of frost has passed, move plants into the garden and expect flowering-sized specimens the following year.

Cuttings. Stem cuttings may be taken at any time during the growing season. Remove the flower cluster, cut the stem in sections, each section with at least two nodes, and insert the sections (and their nodes) into a sandy rooting mix in a rooting chamber; saturate the mix when the surface becomes dry. Excellent rooting usually occurs within three weeks (sooner when cuttings are placed under mist). Pot the newly rooted plants and transplant them into the garden when roots fill the containers.

Division. The separation of large clumps during the early fall or very early spring offers a faster and much easier method of increase. Spiderworts form colonies via stolons or underground runners. A planting established for several years typically includes tight clumps—the original stock plants—and numerous smaller clumps and single shoots. To divide a large clump, lift it from the garden and with a shovel or trowel cut it into pieces that include four to six shoots each. Smaller clumps and individual shoots with a few roots may be taken up and treated as new plants without taking up the whole parent plant. Replant and water the divisions at once.

Cultivation

Spiderworts spread rapidly in an open, sunny setting and average garden soil, but they also grow well in light to moderate shade, which makes for darker, more attractive foliage. Rich soils encourage rampant spreading and should be avoided when interplanting Spiderwort with less aggressive plants. A dry, sunny road bank may be one of the very few settings generally unsatisfactory for cultivating Spiderwort.

Rejuvenate older clumps by division every three to four years. Immediately after plants flower in the spring, cut off the flowering stems and the plants will produce a second crop of flowers in the late summer and fall. Plants benefit from regular watering during summer dry periods.

Uses in the Garden and Landscape

Use Spiderwort in the front or middle layers of the perennial border and in the woodland wild flower garden. Plants work well in open settings with the Sundrops, Beard Tongues, the Purple Coneflowers, and Fire Pink. Native ferns, Wild Bleeding Heart, and the Phacelias are apt companions in shaded areas. Spiderwort is recommended for bog plantings and other naturally wet sites.

Related Species

Tradescantia rosea, native to dry sandy coastal areas in the Southeast, is a truly outstanding, low (to 1 foot) plant especially suited to the southern rock garden. The leaves are narrow, less than ⅛ inch (3 mm) wide. The deep rose flowers are smaller than those of *T. virginiana*, but propagation of the two species is the same.

Production Notes

Stick rooted cuttings directly into 3- or 4-inch pots, overwinter, and market plants the following spring.

If propagating by division, field-grow Spiderwort in a fertile, well-drained soil. Lift clumps from soil in the fall and divide into single shoots by grasping a shoot from the edge of a clump and pulling it down and away from the clump, making sure a few roots are attached. Line out the shoots or pot them directly into quart containers.

Alumroot

Heuchera americana
Saxifragaceae

Duration: perennial

Blooming time: May

Flower color: pink or purple

Height: groundcover

Soil: average garden soil

Exposure: full to filtered sun

Description

Alumroot occurs throughout the eastern United States in dry woods and on rock outcrops, and its tolerance for a wide range of growing conditions makes it a versatile garden plant. The primary value of Alumroot in the garden is as an evergreen foliage plant; the basal leaves are solid

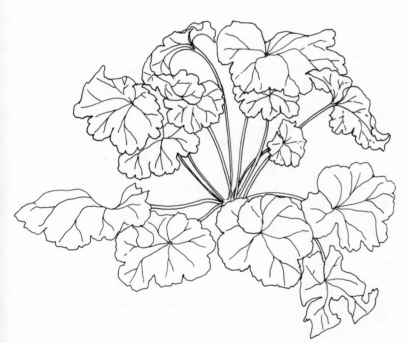

green when they first appear in early spring, but later they become attractively mottled with patches of gray. When the plants are grown in a sunny spot, the leaves take on a bronze or burgundy cast several months into the growing season.

A mature clump produces numerous, shallowly lobed, rounded leaves, 2–5 inches (5–12 cm) in length, borne on long petioles. In their seedling stages Alumroot and Foamflower, both members of the Saxifrage family, are easily confused. The leaves and petioles of Alumroot, however, are often smooth or only sparsely hairy, whereas the petiole and leaf surfaces of Foamflower are densely hairy. In midspring slender flowering stalks, 2–3 feet or more tall, bear dozens of very small, green, pink or purple, bell-shaped flowers less than ¼ inch (6 mm) broad.

When plants are grouped, the flowering stalks create an airy presence which can be especially effective at the front of the flower border. One would not, however, compare the flowers of our native species with some of the horticultural varieties in the nursery trade.

Fruit and Seed

A few weeks after flowering, clusters of light green, oval capsules appear, which expand gradually to a length of about ⅛ inch (3 mm). At maturity the capsules are dark brown and protrude slightly from the papery calyx. Seeds are numerous within the capsule, and change from white to green and then rapidly to black. Under magnification, the seeds are covered with tiny dark red barbs. As seeds are less than a millimeter long, this coloration cannot be picked up by the naked eye.

Seed stalks of Alumroot are not conspicuous in the garden and are easily overlooked; thus a reminder to check for ripe seeds is in order. Attach a strip of bright-

129

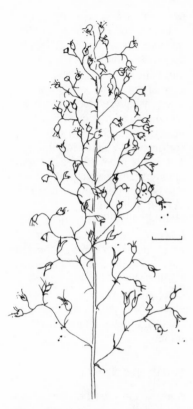

colored flagging to one of the stalks, or make a note on your calendar to check on the seeds three to four weeks after plants flower.

Seed Collection, Cleaning, and Storage

Seeds are usually ripe and ready for collection during the first two weeks in June in our area and a bit later northward. Pinch open a few of the plump, dark capsules and shake the seeds into your hand. Remember that they are tiny, smaller than grains of black pepper, and will appear as flecks. If they appear black, then it is time to collect. Cut the fruiting

stalks at their bases and put them heads down in a paper collection bag, where they can air-dry indoors for three to four days.

To make the seeds more visible, open the capsules over a white background, such as poster board or typing paper. If you need only a small amount of seed, make a hole in the top of the capsule and tap the seeds out. If you want more seeds, crush the capsules with a rolling pin or the bottom of a jar.

You can process more seeds in less time with this second method, but the crushed capsules will mix with the seeds and create more litter. The larger litter can be removed with a sieve, but the smaller litter may fall through with the seeds; no harm will result from storing and even sowing the fine litter with the seeds. Store seeds dry in a sealed, labeled container and refrigerate until time of sowing.

Propagation

Seed. Because the seeds of Alumroot are tiny and can be easily washed away or buried, direct sowing in the garden is not recommended. Seeds should be sown in early spring directly in a cold frame or indoors in a seed flat. When sowing seeds that include some litter left from the cleaning procedure, mix the seeds (and litter) with a small amount of sand and spread the mixture evenly in the flat, and then cover them with a dusting of fine soil. The sand allows for a more even distribution of seeds and is a safeguard against crowd-

ing later on. Water carefully, preferably with a mist, to avoid washing away the tiny seeds. Germination can be expected within ten days.

During the first month after germination seedling growth is slow; a weekly application of a starter solution during this period will accelerate seedling growth. Remove larger seedlings (those with two and three leaves) from the flat and put them in small containers. Seedlings grow faster from this point, producing strong roots and a healthy rosette over the next three to four weeks. Apply an all-purpose fertilizer at weekly intervals to container plants.

Move plants into the garden when the danger of frost is past. Use a light hand when watering and be sure to check that the young leaves do not remain in contact with the soil.

Division. Your plants will likely need dividing every third year. Divide mature clumps in early spring or fall. Lift the plant with a fork or spade, shake loose the soil, and divide by working individual crowns free from the clump. Each crown should include several well-formed roots. Replant new divisions immediately and water well.

Cultivation

Although Alumroot often occurs in shaded sites in nature, a shaded exposure does not produce as tight a clump and thus makes for a less attractive specimen. In the garden it is best

130

planted in full or filtered sunlight. The plant thrives in rich, well-drained soils high in organic matter. When plants are divided, rework the planting area, adding plenty of compost or leaf mold. Keep plants well watered during summer dry periods. If seeds are not needed, remove the flower stalks after the bloom period.

In time plants will develop a woody center, become more open in habit, and generally decline in appearance; thus, as noted above, division of Alumroot every third year should become part of your maintenance schedule. If planted in low areas or in poorly drained soils, the plants are susceptible to rot.

Uses in the Garden and Landscape

With its mound of silvery, evergreen leaves, Alumroot makes an

attractive rosette in the winter garden. Use it in the first layer of the perennial border, where its full, rounded habit can be shown off in front of taller plants, or in a sunny rock garden, at the base of a rock wall, or as a groundcover in and among foundation plantings. It is also effective as an edg-

ing plant in the flower border or lining a path. For best effects, plant in groups of three or five.

Alumroot can also be displayed in a one- or two-gallon pot, provided care is taken to water plants on a regular basis.

Related Species

Heuchera villosa and *H. parviflora*, which inhabit shaded rocky areas and ledges in the Appalachian mountains, make fine additions to the rock garden. Plant them where some protection from the sun is available. Both species are smaller than *H. americana* and do not form as dense a clump. The leaves of *H. villosa* are pointed and sharp lobed; they have hairy petioles and bear a close resemblance to the foliage of Foamflower. The leaves of *H. parviflora* are rounded, and the lobes not as deeply cut.

Beard Tongue

Penstemon smallii
Scrophulariaceae

Duration: short-lived perennial
Blooming time: May–June
Flower color: purple or pink
Height: 1½–2½ feet
Soil: light, well-drained
Exposure: full to filtered sun

Description

Perhaps the most beautiful eastern Beard Tongue is *Penstemon smallii*, which typically occurs along woodland margins and on exposed cliffs and banks in a few areas of the Southern Appalachians, where it is endemic. The numerous tube-shaped flowers, borne on upright branched stalks up to 2½ feet tall, are purple or pink with white throats that have purple nectar guidelines on the lower inner surface. This Beard Tongue differs from other eastern Penstemons in that the flowering branches extend down into the axils of the leafy stems, giving a bushy appearance.

The shiny, opposite leaves are lanceolate with prominent dark veins. The basal rosette of leaves, which develops after flowering, frequently turns pink or burgundy in the fall and adds color to the garden in winter. Like so many native perennials, this species thrives in cultivation and is a fine companion to exotics as well as other native plants. Our attractive and versatile native Penstemons should be more utilized by native plant gardeners.

Fruit and Seed

The ovate seed capsules, which darken from green to a brown or maroon luster at maturity, are ¼–⅜ inch (6–9 mm) long and are conspicuous after flowers fade and drop. The withered style frequently persists as a thin twisted thread attached to the apex of the fully developed capsule. Numerous seeds, approximately ¹⁄₁₆ inch (1.1–1.5 mm) long, develop within the capsule. At first white and moist, they turn green and, finally, dark brown or black at maturity.

Seed Collection, Cleaning, and Storage

Seeds are ready for collection in late July to early August, about six to eight weeks after flowering. At maturity the capsules begin to dehisce, or split open, slightly at the apex. If the capsules have not begun to dehisce but are darkened and contain dark seeds, then the fruiting stem may be collected. The removal of the fruiting stalks accents the attractive basal foliage.

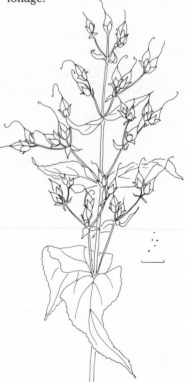

Cut the seed stalks at the base, near ground level, and, so as not to lose any seed, insert the stalks, seed heads first, into a collection bag. Alternatively, cut the stalks and carry them upright to a location indoors where they can be spread on newspaper for drying. Allow the fruits and seeds to air-dry for several days before processing. Seeds can be rapidly removed by placing the capsules, which should have split open during drying, in a bag and shaking vigorously. If the capsules have not split open, crush them with a rolling pin and put the seeds through a sieve to displace unwanted stem pieces and litter. Store seeds dry in a sealed, well-labeled container and refrigerate.

Propagation

Seed. Mature seeds may be sown immediately in seedbeds or flats set in a protected site outdoors where at least a half day of sunlight is available. The site should be regularly monitored to prevent excessive drying and to note first germination. Seeds that germinate before the arrival of the dormant winter months develop rapidly, and seedlings can be transplanted to a permanent garden location in the early fall.

However, most of the seeds will probably germinate the following spring, after a period of natural chilling. Approximately four weeks after germination in the spring the seedlings can be thinned, transplanted to permanent garden sites, rowed out in nursery beds, or put into 2½-to-4-inch pots. For indoor sowing see the production notes below.

Penstemon smallii should be regarded as a short-lived perennial, and it is a good idea to start some seedlings each year for incorporation into the garden or, perhaps easier, to allow the plants to self-sow and transplant seedlings from the area of the parent plant.

Cuttings. Stem cuttings may be taken in early summer, after flowering, and stuck in a rooting medium of half sand and half perlite. When preparing cuttings, be sure to remove seed capsules and insert at least one node into the medium. A mist system is best for maintaining constant humidity, but a cold frame or rooting chamber where cuttings can be misted several times a day will yield satisfactory results. Cuttings should be well rooted in five to six weeks and ready for potting.

Division. Division offers the easiest method of increasing your stand of Beard Tongue, and it is practically foolproof. In fall or early spring simply lift a mature clump and separate the crowns. The crowns are individual rosettes of leaves with roots that can be pulled or cut free from one another. Washing the soil from the clump prior to division renders the procedure simpler. For each new division, prune back the foliage to reduce water loss, replant, and water immediately.

Cultivation

Penstemon smallii demands a light, well-drained soil; planted in a poorly draining soil high in organic matter, it is likely to rot. Piedmont gardeners would do well to amend their best soil with sand or gravel, or both, to ensure that the root zone does not retain an excessive amount of moisture.

To establish this particular Beard Tongue in a perennial border, add a shovelful of coarse sand or gravel to the soil per plant and do not extend leafy mulch to the base of the plant. A mulch of ½-to-1-inch gravel is ideal. At the Garden this plant has been successfully cultivated in a gravel-filled drainage ditch. It requires exposures with at least a half day's sun; full sun is preferable. A shaded site produces a leggy, less flowery specimen.

Uses in the Garden and Landscape

If sun and proper soil conditions are available, Beard Tongue has numerous applications in the garden. In the perennial border the pink and purple flowers harmonize beautifully with other plants that bloom in the late spring. *Penstemon smallii* blooms up to four weeks or more, longer than other eastern Penstemon species. For best effects, plant in the front or middle of the border in groupings of threes and fives. Use it as an edging plant along a busy path, where the attractive rosettes add color during the winter months. Along a gravel path the gravel itself can serve as a mulch.

Specimens potted in gallon containers are attractive in flower on a deck or patio. Beard Tongue also makes a fine cut flower suitable for use in arrangements. Though it does not develop as fully as it would with frequent waterings, Beard Tongue is effective interplanted with such drought-tolerant natives as Black-eyed Susan, Butterfly Weed, Ox-eye Daisy, Stokes' Aster, and Sundrops on a dry sunny road bank.

Related Species

Penstemon canescens, P. digitalis, and *P. laevigatus,* all nearly identical in appearance, bear white, pink, or purple flowers. All are late-spring bloomers, prefer open, sunny exposures, and range in height from 3 to 4 feet taller than *P. smallii.* Propagation is the same as for *P. smallii;* in cultivation they all tolerate poorly drained soils much better than *P. smallii.*

Penstemon
canescens

Production Notes

Sow seeds in the greenhouse in late winter and move seedlings to individual containers four weeks after sowing. Four to six weeks later the seedlings will have become robust plants of salable size. A regular fertilization program will hasten seedling growth. A good way to proceed is to use a starter solution in the seed flat after germination, followed by an all-purpose liquid feed, administered at half strength, to transplanted seedlings. Plants thus produced indoors and planted outside by early May may bloom the latter part of the first growing season. The plants will subsequently bloom normally during the late spring to early summer.

In the nursery, field-grow Beard Tongue in an open, sunny plot in well-drained soil. Space plants 18 inches on center. Under these conditions, spring-planted seedlings grow remarkably, spreading rapidly and yielding eight to ten large divisions per plant in early fall.

134

Ox-eye Daisy

Chrysanthemum leucanthemum
Asteraceae

Duration: short-lived perennial

Blooming time: late spring–summer

Flower color: white

Height: 1–2 feet

Soil: ordinary garden soil

Exposure: full sun

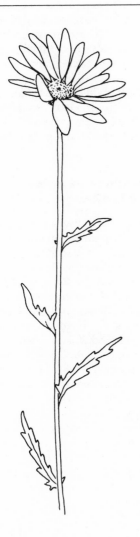

Description

Introduced into America by early settlers, Ox-eye Daisy is a favorite "naturalized" roadside wild flower. It is colorful, long blooming, and easy to raise and survives quite well in a sunny area. Flower heads are made up of white ray flowers up to 1 inch (2.5 cm) long encircling a central compact cluster, up to ¾ inch (2 cm) broad, of small yellow disk flowers. These daisies begin blooming in late May and continue through June. Stems range in height from slightly less than 1 to more than 2 feet, depending on growing conditions. Whether naturalized or in conventional garden settings, daisies are a bright feature each year and, like so many other hardy species of roadsides and fields, require little maintenance.

Fruit and Seed

After the ray flowers fade, the yellow head, or disk, darkens and slightly expands as the nutlets are produced; each tiny yellow disk flower, if pollinated, produces a single nutlet. Like some other members of the Aster family, such as Purple Cone-flowers, Stokes' Asters, and Black-eyed Susans, nutlets do not have a conspicuous pappus. Splitting open a seed head will expose the tight arrangement of the numerous developing nutlets. Shortly after flowering, they are white, but over the next several weeks they darken to green and finally to a grayish black at maturity.

Since the developing seed heads are rather unsightly in the garden, any not needed for seed production should be cut back (deadheaded). Cutting back also increases the possibility that this short-lived perennial will flower a second time in the current season, or persist into another season.

Seed Collection, Cleaning, and Storage

Seed is mature and ready for collection about a month after flowering. Check seed heads regularly during this period. If possible, allow the heads to begin falling apart before collection. This is a

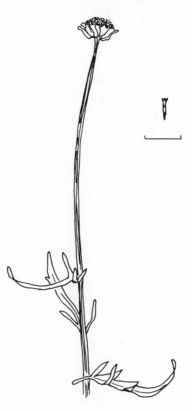

135

matter of timing on your part, for at this stage a high wind or rain-storm can take seeds to the ground and they will be lost.

Collect the heads and let them air-dry for a few days indoors. Break apart the heads by hand and, using seed screens, sieve the material down to pure seed. Most of the chaff collected with the seed is composed of dried disk flowers, larger in size than the seed and easily held back in the sieve. Store seed dry in a well-labeled, sealed container in cold storage until needed for planting.

Propagation

Seed. Before you sow a single seed, examine the ground at the base of mature plants in the garden for small seedlings. You may find your propagation already done and in a quantity sufficient to make further sowing unnecessary.

If you are starting plants for the first time, sow seed indoors in late winter. Spread seed evenly in a flat and lightly cover with your sowing medium. As is true with many species in the Aster family, many nutlets in a seed head may not mature, and thus only a small percentage of the seeds will germinate. Therefore, sow seeds generously to ensure adequate seedling production. With a warm soil temperature (70°F) to hasten germination, you can expect some seedlings within two weeks, and seedlings large enough to be potted eight to ten weeks from your sowing date. Seedlings grow faster in a well-

drained medium, so add an extra measure of sand to both sowing and potting mixes. Seedlings can also be raised in a cold frame.

If you are planning a naturalized planting, sow seeds out-doors in late summer to early fall directly on the sites where plants are desired. Some seeds will germinate immediately and slowly develop through the winter as basal rosettes to produce flowers the following spring and summer. However, it is wise to start some plants indoors to be certain you have plants, if needed, to "plug" into the site.

Cuttings. Stem cuttings root in four to six weeks in a sand and perlite medium. From vigorous plants take tip cuttings 2 inches long and remove all flower buds. Place cuttings in an enclosed chamber and mist several times a day. When well rooted, cuttings should be grown in containers for a month and then set out in the garden.

Division. The Ox-eye Daisy produces short rhizomes, and a single plant will have several overlapping basal rosettes. To make divisions, lift the plant in early

fall or early spring and shake the soil free. Separate the rosettes by gently tugging them away from the clump, replant the divisions, and water immediately.

Cultivation

Plant Ox-eye Daisy in full sun and ordinary garden soil. Planted in a rich soil, high in organic material, the plant produces tall, spindly stems, easily toppled by wind, rain, and their own weight. Native soil, improved only slightly, produces a more compact, tighter plant with sturdy stems. Plant away from taller plants that could crowd and shade it. Avoid heavy mulches and water established plants weekly during dry periods.

Uses in the Garden and Landscape

The Ox-eye Daisy is appropriate in the perennial border as well as on a dry, sunny road bank. In a border, place the plants in the foreground and mix with other low spring-flowering species, such as Green-and-Gold, Fire Pink, Beard Tongue (*Penstemon smallii*) and Stokes' Aster.

On the dry road bank, inter-plant with the Purple Cone-flowers, Black-eyed Susan (*Rudbeckia hirta*), Butterfly Weed, and Sun-drops. Plants can also be "plugged" into dry, gravelly areas where soil conditions are poor. It should be included in any meadow or open naturalized areas. The plant also fares well in a large container and makes a fine cut flower.

Production Notes

Sow seeds in summer in a prepared seedbed and move seedlings to 4-inch containers in the fall. Overwinter containers and offer for sale in the spring. When propagating from stem cuttings, bring plants into the greenhouse in January and take cuttings from the new growth. Cuttings root faster under mist.

Moneywort

Lysimachia nummularia
Primulaceae

Duration: perennial

Blooming time: May–June

Flower color: yellow

Height: groundcover

Soil: fertile soil

Exposure: full to filtered sun

Description

Moneywort is a trailing ground-cover in moist, sunny areas. Where it is not shaded by surrounding vegetation, plants will reward the grower with numerous bright yellow flowers in May or June. Moneywort was introduced from Europe and is now naturalized over much of the eastern United States in wet meadows, alluvial woods, and damp roadsides. The fast-creeping stems have given the plant a reputation as a bit of a pest; however, with proper placement and regular pruning during the season, these plants make attractive and interesting additions in the garden.

The shiny, opposite, round leaves, ½–1¼ inches (1.5–3 cm) in diameter, are borne about an inch apart on slender, angled stems. Flowers are borne singly in the axils of leaves; the colorful yellow, open-rounded corolla, ¾–1½ inches (2–3 cm) broad, has five oval lobes and is finely dotted with black.

Fruit and Seed

The tiny capsule, only 1–2 millimeters broad, is mature some three months after flowering and is usually hidden by several layers of foliage. It is almost entirely enclosed by the pointed, keeled lobes of the light green or yellow calyx, which is borne on an inch-long (2.5 cm) stem. The brownish, triangular seeds, less than a millimeter long, are few per capsule.

Seed Collection, Cleaning, and Storage

The seeds are ripe in late summer, August and September. To find the capsules, which are usually located in small groups along the stems, part the stems and look for the distinctive, sharply angled calyx and a slender black style protruding upward from the capsule. At dehiscence, the capsules are plump and split along sutures to their bases.

To collect, break off the fruits and bring them indoors to air-dry for a few days before cleaning. Break open the capsules by rolling them between your fingers, separate the seeds, and store them dry in a sealed, well-labeled container and refrigerate until time of sowing.

Propagation

Seed. If you sow the seeds in an outdoor bed upon collection, keep the bed moist through the season; after germination, let the young plants grow on until they

have several stems and begin to trail, then transplant them to a permanent planting site. Stored seeds can be sown in an outdoor seedbed in the spring when the danger of frost is past. Follow the same procedure recommended for fall sowing above.

A light application of an all-purpose fertilizer will "green up" the plants and make them grow faster. For best results, keep the soil evenly moist.

Cuttings. This is the easiest method of increase. Take stem cuttings at any time during the growing season and simply lay the cuttings down in the area where you wish to establish plants and secure stems to the ground by lightly covering both ends with soil. Provided the site is fairly moist, you can expect thin white roots to form at nodes along the stem in one to two weeks. Cuttings may also be rooted in a rooting chamber using a standard potting mix; when the cuttings are well rooted, in about three weeks, they may be transplanted directly to the garden.

Division. After plants flower, divide established clumps into pieces with a trowel; the pieces may be of any size and should include a mass of roots. Alternatively, take up a clump and pull it apart with your hands into as many pieces as you need. Replant the new divisions and water thoroughly.

Cultivation

Plants are not difficult to establish. They adapt readily to a wide variety of soil types and exposures; for best results, however, provide a fertile, humus-rich medium and locate the plants in full or filtered sunlight. Sunnier sites will make for more flowers.

Under good conditions clumps spread rapidly, forming thick, overlapping layers of foliage; on drier sites the plants are slower-growing. Where growth is rapid, curb plants several times during the growing season lest they spread into areas where they are not desired.

Application of an all-purpose liquid fertilizer will improve the appearance of the plants, and regular irrigation during summer dry periods will of course be of benefit. Divide the clumps when they become crowded—and this is a good time to rework the planting area with organic matter.

Uses in the Garden and Landscape

Moneywort may be used to good advantage along the front of the herbaceous border, but for best effects it should be maintained as a clump and not allowed to spread. The plants are also well displayed at the bases of tree trunks and among rocks or naturalized in moist, sunny areas, in a bog, or at the edges of ponds or creeks where they can be allowed to spread freely and form a continuous and attractive ground-cover. In these areas, interplant deeper-rooted plants, such as the Lobelias and Grass-of-Parnassus, for effective contrast. Moneywort can also be grown in wide containers or trough gardens if they are divided annually to avoid stunting.

Related Species

Lysimachia terrestris, Swamp Candles, has terminal clusters of yellow flowers, grows to 3 feet, and does best in open, boggy areas. *Lysimachia fraseri* has beautiful yellow flowers in a leafy raceme, grows to 4 feet, and requires a moist, sunny location. *Lysimachia ciliata*, *L. lanceolata*, *L. quadrifolia*, and *L. tonsa* all grow to 2–3 feet tall, have attractive yellow flowers, are excellent filler plants in the border, and are ideal for naturalizing. Propagation of these erect species is by seed and cuttings, or by vegetative axillary buds in the case of *L. terrestris*.

Carolina Bush Pea

Thermopsis villosa
Fabaceae

Duration: perennial

Blooming time: May

Flower color: yellow

Height: 4–5 feet

Soil: rich, well-drained

Exposure: sun

Description

Carolina Bush Pea is a rather infrequent but attractive plant of forest openings and clearings in the mountains of North Carolina and other southeastern states. In the garden the plant can reach 4–5 feet in height. The dense terminal racemes are generally a foot long and bear many deep yellow flowers; the trifoliate leaves are alternate. The bright flowers begin in mid-May in our area and continue for several weeks.

Fruit and Seed

A week or two after the flowers fade, the characteristic legumes become evident. They are set tightly against the stalk, point upward, are covered with a dense mat of hairs, and, as they lengthen, turn from light green to dark gray to near black. Unlike the inflated legumes of White Wild Indigo, the pods of *Thermopsis* are flattened. The small brown beans, or seeds, are arranged in a single row in the legume.

Seed Collection, Cleaning, and Storage

Five to six weeks after the flowers fade—early July in central North Carolina—is a good time to check the condition of the seeds. Legumes usually begin to split along their sutures when the seeds are mature. Remove a legume or two and look at the seeds: if they are brownish, they may be collected; if they are still green and moist, check again in a week.

To collect seeds, snip the stalks below the lower legume and deposit them in your collection bag; then spread the legumes out and let them air-dry for a few days, whereupon most will open slightly. You can remove some of the seeds by placing the legumes in a large paper bag and shaking; however, most will need to be extracted by hand—just split open the legume and rake out the seeds.

You may notice some insects, adult weevils or small larvae, in with the seeds. If so, insert a 2-inch piece of No-Pest Strip, or some equivalent fumigant, in a bag with the seeds, close the bag tightly, and store in an out-of-the-way place for two weeks. Following fumigation, store seeds in a sealed container and refrigerate until time of sowing.

Propagation

Seed. Seeds may be sown outdoors in a seed frame or seedbed upon collection for germination the following spring. Grow seedlings on in containers and transplant to the garden when plants are well rooted.

For sowing seeds indoors or in a cold frame after a period of cold dry storage, germination is more uniform if the seeds are presoaked. Pour boiling water over the seeds and allow them to soak and cool for at least twelve hours. Seedlings will begin to appear within ten days after planting and continue to germinate new divisions recover slowly. The problem is that the deep roots are easily broken when the plant is moved. Nevertheless, you may safely divide plants if you are careful. When plants go dormant in the fall, dig down around a plant to a depth of 16–24 inches and ease the clump out of the ground. Remove the soil from around the roots and with pruning shears section off pieces of the clump. Each piece should include several well-formed roots. Dig a deep hole, prime it with compost and good garden soil, replant the divisions—taking care not to break the roots—and water thoroughly. Healthy, flowering-sized specimens can be expected the second year following division.

Cultivation

Plants do best in full sun, or only light shade, in rich, well-drained garden soil fortified with plenty of organic matter. Dig into the subsoil a foot or so to accommodate the root system, space young plants or divisions 3 feet apart, and be patient. Much of the first two seasons is given over to root development; thereafter, you can enjoy long-lived plants requiring little care. To keep foliage dark green and attractive during the season, water deeply during summer dry periods. If seeds are not desired, remove flower stalks immediately after the bloom period.

Uses in the Garden and Landscape

Carolina Bush Pea is a natural for the middle or rear of the sunny border. The yellow flowers mix well with the Baptisias and Penstemons, especially the white flowering *P. digitalis*. *Thermopsis* may be naturalized in sunny areas where the soil is fertile and well-drained. The flowering stalks

over the next two weeks. Transfer seedlings to individual containers after the first set of true leaves appears. Weekly applications of an all-purpose fertilizer are helpful. When roots fill up the pots (in four to five weeks) and when the danger of frost is past, move the plants into the garden. Some flowering will occur during the second year, but full flowering should not be expected until the third season, and then it becomes more prolific each year.

Division. Mature plants may be lifted in the fall and divided, but

141

are excellent in cut arrangements. Dense foliage during the remainder of the growing season makes an effective backdrop for plants of low and medium heights. Once established, plants require little, if any, attention and will persist in the garden for many years, frequently attaining bushlike size with many stems.

Related Species

A member of the pea family, *Thermopsis* is very similar to White Wild Indigo in flower structure and both species share the same propagation and cultivation requirements as well.

Production Notes

If plants are to be held in containers during their first season, move them into quart pots in early summer to allow space for their long taproots and provide them with protection over the winter.

Sundrops

Oenothera tetragona
Onagraceae

Duration: perennial

Blooming time: May

Flower color: yellow

Height: 2 feet

Soil: average garden soil

Exposure: full sun

Description

Unlike the flowers of some members in the Evening Primrose family, which open in late afternoon and close in early morning, the light yellow flowers of Sundrops open during daylight hours. This species, and the related *O. fruticosa*, which is quite similar in appearance, occurs throughout most of the eastern United States in dry woods and meadows and along roadsides.

Flowering begins in mid-May and extends over several weeks, occurring sporadically thereafter. Plants are about 2 feet tall and heavily branched, with numerous four-petaled flowers, 1½–2 inches (4–5 cm) across, borne singly in axils of the smaller leaves at the top of the plant. The simple, alternate, elongate leaves are about 5 inches (12 cm) long and 1½ inches (4 cm) wide and are often mottled with red. These plants are easily propagated by a number of methods and need little attention either in the garden or naturalized.

Fruit and Seed

The numerous tiny seeds, held in oblong capsules less than half an inch long, mature slowly after flowering. The capsules expand steadily and lengthen, darkening to light brown as they approach maturity. The interior of the capsule is four valved, that is, it is divided into four seed compartments running the length of the capsule, which split open at the distal (top) end to release the seeds.

Seed Collection, Cleaning, and Storage

Late June or early July is a good time to begin checking the condition of seed. The capsules, which become rather hard as they develop, are best opened with the aid of pruning shears. Cut a capsule in half and examine the seeds; if they are not easily removed or are still pale or whitish, check again in a week or two. When mature, some seeds should fall from the split ends of the capsule when you shake it.

To collect seeds, cut individual capsules and drop them into a bag or cut off the entire fruiting stalk and put upside down in a large paper bag. Leave the bag open and allow the capsules to air-dry for a few days. Then vigorous shaking of the closed bag will get most of the seeds out of the capsules. Empty the contents of the bag onto a white surface and remove the larger debris by hand. Some litter, mostly larger pieces, will mix with the seeds, but this can be quickly separated out with a sieve.

As with other species that produce very small seeds, such as Yarrow, Goat's Beard, and Monkey Flower, the cleaning process is much easier when you know precisely what you are looking for. Examining a few seeds under a hand magnifier will help familiarize you with their shape and general appearance. Store seeds dry in a sealed, well labeled container and refrigerate until time of sowing.

Propagation

Seed. Sow seed indoors or in the cold frame in late winter. As germination is usually very good, sow the seeds thinly by combining them with a small amount of sand and then spreading the mixture evenly over the sowing medium. Expect germination in a week to ten days.

During the next three to four weeks, the seedlings will form tiny rosettes with fine roots; when the roots approach an inch in length, transplant the seedlings to individual containers. Take care to avoid contact between the leaves and the soil; mound the leafy rosettes in the center of the pot so that, when watered, the leaves are not forced onto the soil. Mounding also allows water to drain away from the rosette.

From this point, seedling growth is rapid, with leaves overlapping the edges of the pot within the month. Allow the soil to become almost completely dry between waterings. Seedlings respond to a weekly application of an all-purpose fertilizer.

Cuttings. Stem cuttings, taken after flowering, are a fast, reliable method of increase. Because rooting occurs rapidly at the nodes along the stem, the easiest approach involves simply bending the very flexible stems to the ground and covering the nodes with a bit of soil. In a few weeks look for small rosettes at the nodes and, when they are well rooted, detach them from the parent stems and transplant to the garden. Alternatively, take stem cuttings 6 inches long and lay them down in a flat of soil. Cover the stems lightly with soil and proceed as before. The latter method is best carried out in a rooting chamber, where high humidity can be maintained.

Division. In the fall, when several basal rosettes have developed, lift a clump from the garden and shake loose the soil. Small rosettes, or basal offsets, are produced close to the larger central rosette and these can be quickly separated. Replant the new divisions and water thoroughly.

Cultivation

Plant Sundrops in full sun or in a setting that receives at least a few hours of direct sun during the day. Although the plant will survive a shaded location, specimens are typically leggy and sparse-flowering.

Sundrops are tolerant of a wide range of soil types, except those that retain excessive moisture and become soggy. Planted in a rich soil, high in organic matter, Sundrops tends to produce stems that are taller but somewhat less sturdy; they may benefit from staking a week or so before flowering. If seeds are not needed, remove the stalks after flowering; divide the clumps every second year.

Uses in the Garden and Landscape

Sundrops are an excellent low-growing filler plant for the sunny border. Spot plants in the front of the border, where the yellow flowers can be "held" by taller, leafy plants in the back. Interplant Sundrops with Blue-eyed Grass, Stokes' Aster, and Spiderwort for an effective blue and yellow combination. The plant also does well with *Penstemon smallii* and Butterfly Weed. Use this plant to edge a path, where you can enjoy the winter rosettes and the many seedlings in the spring. Plants are quick to naturalize on dry, sunny road banks, as they possess that trait so endearing to gardeners—drought tolerance.

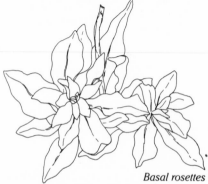

Basal rosettes

Related Species

Oenothera fruticosa, with slightly smaller but still quite attractive flowers and leaves spotted with purple, has a looser habit with flowering stems not as upright. Cultivation and propagation are the same as for *O. tetragona*. *O. biennis*, a 4-foot or taller biennial species native throughout the region in old fields and along roadsides, has few ornamental possibilities for the well-kempt garden but adds color and interest to the naturalized wild yard or meadow garden. The bright yellow flowers are showy in the mornings, but generally are closed by early afternoon on bright sunny days. The tall fruiting stalks are useful in dried arrangements.

The foliage of *O. biennis* is a preferred food of Japanese Beetles. Local experience has demonstrated that more desirable ornamental plants are generally spared as long as those insect pests have this weedy, biennial primrose growing nearby. It is easily propagated by seed in much the same manner as the other described species. Self-sown seedlings are usually common in the garden during the winter and early spring. They are easily recognized as flat basal rosettes of lanceolate leaves with a prominent white mid-vein.

Production Notes

Sundrops can be incorporated in a winter bedding plant production schedule in the greenhouse. Allow ten weeks from seed to salable plants.

Fire Pink

Silene virginica
Caryophyllaceae

Duration: short-lived perennial

Blooming time: May, June

Flower color: crimson

Height: 1–2 feet

Soil: average, well-drained

Exposure: full to filtered sunlight

Description

Vivid crimson flowers, opening in late May and June, make Fire Pink an immediate focal point in the garden. The flower is a whorl of five petals prominently notched at the tips and forming a tube-shaped base enclosed in a sticky, glandular pubescent calyx. The tubular base of the flower is up to l inch (2.5 cm) long from which each of the separate petals flares open for another inch (2.5 cm); each petal has a pair of small appendages at the top of the corolla tube. The flowers measure ½–2 inches (1.25–5 cm) across and are borne on loosely branched stems that range from 1 to 2 feet in height. Flowers are occasionally pink and, rarely, white.

Basal rosettes of narrow, elliptic-to-lanceolate leaves are prominent in the fall and spring and may persist where winters are mild. Since Fire Pink is frequently a short-lived perennial, it is a good idea to start a few new plants each year to ensure its permanence in the garden. The plant normally occurs in dry, rocky woods and on road banks and exposed slopes throughout our area, but it is more common in the mountains and piedmont.

Fruit and Seed

Shortly after the flowering period, conspicuous green capsules appear which are sticky to the touch because the glandular pubescent calyx persists around the developing capsule. During the next week or two, the capsules rapidly mature, becoming ½–¾ inch (1.25–1.85 cm) long and approximately ³⁄₁₆ inch (5 mm) wide as the numerous small brown seeds develop within the swollen capsule. The plant itself declines steadily after the bloom period; the stem leaves yellow and fruiting stems often fall to the ground. Pieces of brightly colored flagging attached to stalks while the plants are still prominent will make it easier to locate them when the time comes for seed collection.

Seed Collection, Cleaning, and Storage

Capsules split and curl back at the apex when the seeds are mature. However, the capsules hang down when they dehisce and the seeds immediately fall, so it is a good idea to check seed development before this time. Since seeds mature within one to two weeks, vigorous plants may have flowers and dehisced capsules at the same time; there is really no single time at which a large harvest of seeds can be made. To be sure of obtaining some seeds collect the capsules as they approach full maturity: they should be swollen and pale green to tan, and should split open readily when pinched in the middle, containing well-formed seeds about ¹⁄₁₆ inch (1.5 mm) broad that separate easily. The capsules should be stored in a dry location where, within a day or two, they will dehisce.

In this manner one can enjoy the plant as it continues to flower and collect a few capsules every other day or so. This method is a

146

bit tedious, but foolproof. Do not be surprised if many of the capsules do not develop. Our experience has been that less than 50 percent of the flowers on a given plant set fruit, probably because of an absence of natural pollinators.

To remove seeds from dried capsules simply shake them free from the capsules onto a clean, dry surface. Little, if any, litter should accumulate during the cleaning procedure. Refrigerate dry seeds in a sealed, properly labeled container.

Propagation

Seed. Seeds can be sown immediately upon collection outdoors in a prepared bed, and germination should occur the following spring. For indoor sowing in winter, sow stored seeds in a flat, spacing them ¼ inch apart and covering lightly with soil. The open spacing of seeds will allow maximum uncrowded development of seedlings. To insure rapid, uniform germination, moisten the soil and stratify the seeds by covering the flat with plastic and placing it in the refrigerator for three to four weeks. Alternatively, store seeds in moist vermiculite or peat moss after cleaning.

Following the chilling period, a warm soil temperature should produce germination within a week. Seedlings are best transplanted after they have developed four to six leaves and vigorous root systems in the seed flat; they should be large enough to pot four to five weeks from the germi-

nation date. Allow seedlings to dry out between waterings as a constantly moist soil can promote fungal attacks on Fire Pink seedlings. Allow roots to fill containers before moving into the garden.

Cuttings. Take cuttings from the upper third of the stem after flowering. Remove seed capsules and insert a node into a sand or perlite rooting medium. Cuttings should be placed under mist or in a rooting chamber and misted several times a day. Expect some rooted cuttings in four to five weeks; these plants can be grown on in containers until large enough to transfer into the garden.

Division. In the late fall or early spring, take up a mature plant from the garden and shake loose the soil. The clump will consist of several basal rosettes. Make divisions by gently separating rosettes from the clump. Replant and water the divisions immediately.

Cultivation

Fire Pink thrives in average, well-drained garden soils; a soil high in organic matter is likely to produce rangy stems that are easily toppled at flowering time. A fine gravel mulch is ideal at the base of the plant. Although in nature the plant is frequently found on wooded slopes, Fire Pink produces many more flowering stems and more basal leaves in a sunnier exposure. Good locations for Fire Pink are at the

wood's edge or in a garden spot receiving a half day's direct sunlight.

Amazing results have been noted when Fire Pink was cultivated in full sun, mulched with pine bark, fertilized, and regularly watered. One such plant attained a height of 1½ feet and a breadth of 2 feet and produced hundreds of flowers.

Because the plant is short-lived, make a point to divide some clumps at least every year.

Uses in the Garden and Landscape

Fire Pink is effectively displayed in the perennial border in pockets and gaps between other low-growing plants. Combine it with Ox-eye Daisy and Green-and-Gold in the front of the border or on a dry road bank. Although it will do better in sunnier sites, Fire Pink is still well suited to the woodland garden and it is an excellent plant for accent in rock gardens. Spot plants at the base of large rocks, tree trunks, and broad-leaved plants to highlight its crimson flowers. Fire Pink also grows well in containers and can provide several weeks of color on a deck or patio.

Related Species

Starry Campion, *S. stellata*, which has white flowers with fringed petals, is slightly taller than Fire Pink and flowers more prolifically on loosely branching stems with fewer basal leaves. Propagation and cultivation are the same as for *S. virginica*.

Moth Mullein

Verbascum blattaria
Scrophulariaceae

Duration: biennial

Blooming time: May–June

Flower color: white or yellow

Height: 2–4 feet

Soil: ordinary, well-drained

Exposure: full to filtered sunlight

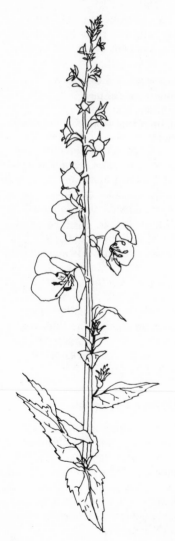

Description

A European plant by origin, Moth Mullein has naturalized in fields and along roadsides throughout the United States. This easy-to-grow biennial, with its flat, shiny green basal rosettes of scalloped leaves, is one of the many roadside plants suitable for cultivation in the home garden. During the winter the leaves take on a purplish cast and add to the prominence of the attractive rosette.

The flowers, each with five white or occasionally yellow petals, are 1 inch (2.5 cm) across and are borne in a single 2-to-4-foot raceme. The center of the flower is distinguished by five conspicuous stamens, which are very pubescent. Mullein flowers, which open in the evening and stay open through the following midday, are pollinated by moths. At the Botanical Garden the plant blooms for several weeks in late May and early June.

Fruit and Seed

Small, green globular capsules, approximately ¼-inch (6 mm) broad, are visible shortly after the blooming period and mature to a deep brown three to four weeks later. The capsules are divided into compartments, or locules, and split along those divisions when the seeds are mature. Since, as in most plants, the flowers open first at the bottom of the stalk and progress upward, the seeds mature first in lower capsules. Numerous dark brown or black seeds, less than ¹⁄₁₆ inch (1.5 mm) long, are enclosed within the capsules. After flowering, the plant declines rapidly as seeds develop and the basal leaves deteriorate completely.

Seed Collection, Cleaning, and Storage

As each capsule contains many seeds, you will need to gather only a stalk or two for your seed supply. About four to six weeks after the flowers fade, the lower capsules should be opening. Cut the fruiting stalk and put it upside down in your collection bag or pick individual capsules from the stalk and drop them into a small bag and let them air dry, and continue to ripen, for a few days. Seeds of Moth Mullein are readily removed by shaking the capsules in a paper bag or crushing capsules with a rolling pin and separating seeds from debris with screen sieves. Store seeds dry in a sealed container in the refrigerator.

Propagation

Seed. Sow seeds indoors or in a cold frame in March or outdoors in April to May or late summer to early fall. Provided the soil temperature is above 60°F, good germination should occur within a week. Sow seeds thinly and evenly over the medium to avoid crowded and stunted seedlings later on. It is safe to transfer seedlings to small containers when individual rosettes measure ½ inch across—four to five weeks from your sowing date. In another three to four weeks plants will be well rooted in the

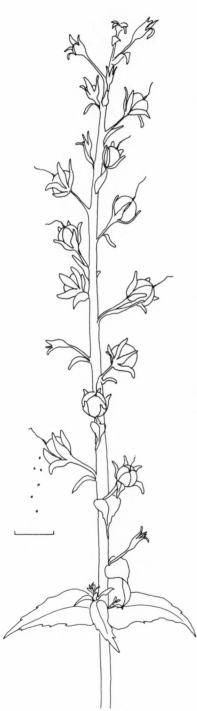

containers and need to be transplanted into the garden.

Seedlings respond aggressively to small amounts of fertilizer, and they should be allowed to dry out thoroughly between waterings. A continuously wet soil may result in seedling loss. Too much moisture can also be detrimental to Moth Mullein in the garden.

Some self-sowing can be expected in the garden, but to assure having plants every year, set out seedlings early each spring.

Cultivation

Ordinary soil is sufficient for Moth Mullein but it must be well drained. A rich organic soil with high moisture retention hinders the plant's development, and a rainy period or two may be enough to cause the plant to rot. If you wish to interplant Moth Mullein with more moisture-tolerant plants, add a shovelful of coarse sand or gravel per Mullein plant for drainage. Allow enough room at planting time for a 1-foot spread at maturity. An open, sunny exposure is best, but a site with a few hours of direct sunlight will do. Avoid excessive watering and do not mulch. The rosettes grow actively through mild winters.

Uses in the Garden and Landscape

Moth Mullein is perhaps most interesting during its shiny green flat rosette stage, from late fall up to the time it blooms in May or June. During this stage it resembles a large green doily, quite unlike most other winter rosettes. It is very noticeable when planted in groups of three or five close to walkways and patios, at edges of borders, and even in the cracks of brick and stone walks and terraces.

Planted close to frequently used paths and doorsteps, the attractive rosettes, which never fail to attract comments from visitors unfamiliar with them, can be enjoyed during the long late winter. The flowering stems, though as tall as 3 feet, are not disruptive when situated in front of other plants because the open racemes are not heavy and do not hide plants behind them. Such close siting is also appropriate because it brings the delicate white flow-

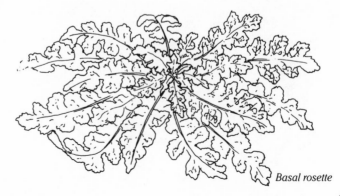

Basal rosette

149

ers, which open in the evening and fade by noon on the following day, up for close viewing.

Related Species

The familiar Woolly Mulleins, *V. thapsus* and *V. phlomoides*, also found on sunny roadsides, can be used in a similar manner. Since these species form cabbagelike rosettes of densely woolly leaves up to 3 feet across, they are also effective when planted in the middle or rear of garden beds. The large rosettes are very attractive into the early summer, at which time the tall (4–8 feet), yellow-flowered spikes reach above the foliage of other garden plants. *V. thapsus* has a single dense spike, and *V. phlomoides* can develop a very showy branched candelabralike inflorescence of spikes. On hot sunny days the fragrant flowers fade by early afternoon. Propagation and cultivation are the same as for Moth Mullein.

Production Notes

Sow seeds no more than eight weeks prior to the sale period; step up seedlings to 4-inch pots when plants are ½ inch across, approximately four weeks after sowing.

Waterleaf

Hydrophyllum canadense
Hydrophyllaceae

Duration: perennial

Blooming time: May

Flower color: white to lavender

Height: 1–2 feet

Soil: moist, rich

Exposure: shade

Description

Waterleaf works well in the shade or woodland wild flower garden as an attractive groundcover and foliage plant. In nature the plants occur on rich wooded slopes, along stream banks, and in alluvial woods in many of the eastern states.

The first leaves to appear in early spring are conspicuously marked with splotches of gray, somewhat resembling large droplets of water, which perhaps account for the plant's common name. These leaves lose the grayish coloration and assume a uniform dark green color at about the time plants flower in early May. Several weeks later, a second series of leaves, larger and darker green, overtops the early leaves and persists through the growing season. These larger leaves are 4–6 inches across and resemble a maple leaf in shape.

The cymose flower clusters, which are borne in the leaf axils, are slightly below the leaves. The small, white to lavender, bell-shaped flowers are about ¼ inch (5–7 mm) long.

Fruit and Seed

Tiny capsules with the dried styles still attached appear soon after flowering. Over the next eight to ten weeks, the capsules enlarge to nearly ½ inch (10–12 mm) long and change from light to dark green and finally dark brown or black at maturity. Each capsule contains one to three rounded seeds that are light brown and ⅛ inch (3 mm) wide at maturity.

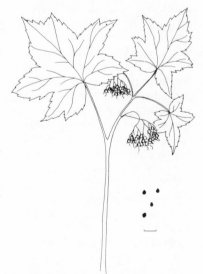

151

Seed Collection, Cleaning, and Storage

Because seeds require two to three months to mature and because the capsule cluster is hidden beneath the leaves, make a note to check on the seeds in mid-summer. At the Botanical Garden the seeds are ripe in late July and early August. When capsules turn brown, split open a few; if the seeds within are light brown, it is time to collect. Snip off the cluster of capsules, break out the seeds, and, for best results, sow immediately. If you wish to store seeds, stratify them in damp sphagnum moss in a sealed container and refrigerate.

Propagation

Seed. Best results will be obtained by sowing freshly collected seed in a shaded outdoor seedbed. Keep the bed well watered during the remainder of the season and look for germination the next spring. Allow the seedlings to spend their first season undisturbed in the seedbed; thin them if necessary. Transplant seedlings in the fall of their first year to a permanent planting site in the garden. Stored seeds may also be sown in the spring in an outdoor bed, but germination may not occur until the following year.

Division. Division of the rhizome in the fall, or when plants go dormant, is the most practical method of increase for Waterleaf. The long brittle rhizomes, ribbed with a series of leaf scars along their length, lie an inch below the

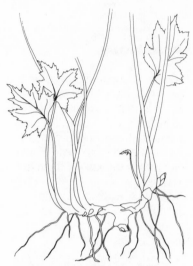

soil and produce a network of tough, stringy roots which penetrate another 3–4 inches into the soil. With a trowel or shovel, cut out 8-to-12-inch sections from the colony. Shake off the soil and with pruning shears cut the rhizome into pieces that include a few leaves (or leaf buds) and some roots. Replant the divisions a foot apart at the original depth and water thoroughly.

Cultivation

Waterleaf thrives in shaded, naturally moist sites. Your major maintenance concern will thus be keeping the soil evenly moist during dry periods. Like Deciduous Wild Ginger, another shady groundcover, leaves of Hydrophyllum are among the first to wilt when the soil begins to dry out and repeated drying may push the plants into early dormancy.

Grow Waterleaf in your very best soil; a display area where the soil has been raised and includes plenty of rotted leaves and compost is ideal. Apply a mulch

of shredded or rotted leaves, 2–3 inches deep, at both ends of the growing season. Plantings can become crowded in time and benefit from selective thinning and division. Because of their spreading rhizomes, plants in favorable habitats can become invasive if left unchecked.

Uses in the Garden and Landscape

Waterleaf makes an effective, albeit a tall (1–2 feet), spreading groundcover for the shade garden. Interplant Waterleaf with taller, deeper-rooted plants such as Jack-in-the-Pulpit, the Turtleheads, and the native lilies and ferns. Where conditions permit, plants should be naturalized and encouraged to spread freely, as they are very effective in drifts. Or try Waterleaf as a groundcover at the base of flowering shrubs and foundation plantings where shade and moisture are assured.

Related Species

The leaves of *H. macrophyllum* and *H. virginianum* are more dissected and the cymes borne on longer peduncles which rise above the leaves. Propagation and cultivation of all three species, however, are the same.

Production Notes

Grow plants in shaded nursery beds of fertile soil and irrigate regularly through the season. Divide plants every second year, pot them in quart containers, and market the following spring.

Prickly Pear, Indian Fig

Opuntia compressa
Cactaceae

Duration: perennial

Blooming time: June

Flower color: yellow

Height: groundcover

Soil: average, well-drained

Exposure: full sun

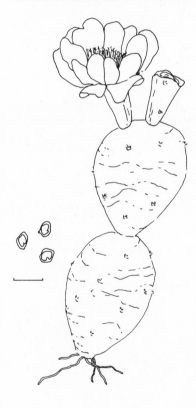

Description

Perhaps because the genus *Opuntia* is strongly associated with the arid Southwest, Prickly Pears are seldom considered for use in eastern gardens. *Opuntia compressa*, however, occurs throughout the eastern United States in dry, sandy, and rocky areas. Acclimatizing readily, *Opuntia* can be propagated easily in a garden setting where the soil drains rapidly.

Photosynthetic action in the green, oval segmented stems, or "pads," characteristic of the genus, essentially replaces that of the minute ephemeral leaves. Areoles, the small, regularly spaced areas on the stems, bear mounded clusters of tawny, hair-like spines, or glochids, which are invisible to the naked eye but quick to lodge in the skin upon contact, where they can cause mild irritation.

The large, colorful flowers are produced singly or in small groups along the upper edges of the pads in May and June and sporadically thereafter. These waxy, yellow flowers are nearly 3 inches (5–7 cm) across and have masses of showy stamens. The plant's common names are derived from the edible fruit, which may also bear clusters of glochids.

Fruit and Seed

The intriguing fleshy fruit, botanically a berry, develops three to four months after flowering. It is obovoid or club shaped, tapering to the base, and approximately 1–2 inches (2–5 cm) long and about half as broad. As seeds approach maturity, the fruits turn from green to purple or reddish brown. Two to three dozen rounded, compressed seeds are encased in the sticky, whitish pulp of each berry.

Seed Collection, Cleaning, and Storage

At the Botanical Garden seeds are mature and ready for harvest in early August; however, the fruits typically remain attached to the stems after the seeds are mature, often persisting for several weeks past the first frost. Break open or cut a fruit and, if seeds are dark, collect them immediately. Remember that the fruits are also armed with glochids, so wear gloves while collecting.

Removing the pulp from the seeds does not appear to affect germination. If you want to store the seeds, simply rake them from the berry and allow them to air-dry for a few hours. Then store seeds dry in a sealed labeled container and refrigerate.

Propagation

Seed. For best results, sow freshly collected seeds in an outdoor seedbed. To assure good drainage work generous amounts of sand into the top 2–3 inches of your seedbed. Look for tiny seedlings the next spring and allow young plants to remain in the bed until early fall, when they may be transplanted to a permanent planting site.

Cuttings. Take cuttings anytime during the growing season by breaking off one or more pads at their joints. If the soil has been properly prepared, as discussed in the cultivation section, the cuttings can be put directly in their permanent locations. Roots should be established within three to four weeks.

Alternatively, put cuttings in a rooting medium of three parts sand to one part soil and place them in a protected area outside. A rooting chamber and regular misting of the foliage is not necessary; however, the rooting medium should be moistened when dry. Rooted cuttings may be transplanted directly into the garden or potted and overwintered for planting the next spring.

Division. In the fall or early spring large clumps may be divided by pulling one or two pads and their roots up from the periphery of the clump. (Individual pads may break off during this procedure; if they do, simply plant them and root them as cut-

tings.) Or lift an entire clump with a shovel and break it apart to get larger divisions with more pads. Replant and water the divisions. Again, be sure to wear gloves and a long-sleeved shirt while handling these plants to avoid contact with the small spines.

Cultivation

Grow Prickly Pear in dry, sandy, fast-draining soils. Mix two or three shovelfuls of sand or fine gravel into each planting hole. In cultivation Prickly Pear withstands soils wetter than those in which it naturally occurs, but during periods of extremely wet weather drainage becomes vital.

Locate plants in open, sunny settings or in areas receiving at least a half day's full sun, such as at the edge of a wooded area. Where soil and light conditions are favorable, the plants can spread to 3 feet across in three to four years. Once established, plants are virtually maintenance-free; if they encroach upon other

plantings, they are easily cut back, or they may be taken up and divided.

Uses in the Garden and Landscape

Prickly Pear is an excellent choice for the rock garden, where it can be combined effectively with Bird-foot Violet, Fire Pink, Green-and-Gold, and Tennessee Cone-flower (*Echinacea tennesseensis*). Or naturalize the plants on dry, sunny banks with other stout, sun-loving species, such as the Mulleins, Sundrops, and Butterfly Weed. Use Prickly Pear as an accent plant in a planter, at the edge of a patio, or against a tree trunk, where the beautiful yellow flowers can be highlighted.

Production Notes

Take cuttings in spring and put them directly in pint or quart containers for market the following spring.

Black-eyed Susan

Rudbeckia hirta
Asteraceae

Duration: short-lived perennial

Blooming time: June–July

Flower color: yellow

Height: 1–2 feet

Soil: average, well-drained

Exposure: full sun

Description

Black-eyed Susan, one of our most common and attractive "roadside weeds," occurs in meadows, old fields, and along roadsides throughout the eastern United States, and is a versatile plant for the garden. It fits well in the herbaceous border or naturalized area and is a good source of cut flowers for use in summer arrangements.

This species exists as an annual, a biennial, or a short-lived perennial, depending upon local growing conditions. To keep the plant in the garden from year to year, allow plants to self-sow and retain the larger seedlings.

Plants produce basal rosettes of hairy leaves that are among the first to emerge when the weather breaks in early spring and which may persist through the winter months in milder climates. The grooved, bristly stems, 1–2 feet tall, are solitary or sparsely branched. The flower head, subtended by an attractive whorl of green involucral bracts, is a beautifully symmetrical circle of bright yellow ray flowers (or "petals"), often with darker yellow or orange at the base, 1½–2 inches (3.5–5 cm) long. The central cone (or "eye"), ½–¾ inch (1.25–1.85 cm) across, is composed of numerous minute disk flowers that are typically dark purple. Black-eyed Susan flowers through most of June, into early July, and sporadically thereafter.

Fruit and Seed

After the flowers fade, the dark central cone expands steadily during the next several weeks as the nutlets develop. Unlike many other species in the Aster family, Black-eyed Susans typically produce a high percentage of fully developed, viable nutlets, tightly arranged on the receptacles. The tapered nutlets, charcoal gray at maturity, are approximately ⅛ inch (2–3 mm) long, have four longitudinal ridges, and lack a pappus.

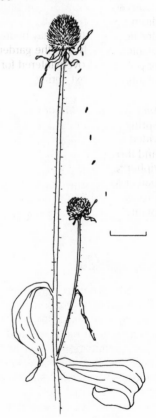

Seed Collection, Cleaning, and Storage

The color of the nutlets is a good indicator of when to collect. Three to four weeks after flowering, break open a few cones, or fruiting heads, and if nutlets are dark, they may be collected. A better time to collect, however, is when the cones lose their tight, compact structure and turn grayish. At this stage removal of the nutlets is easier, as they can be simply shaken or tapped out of the heads. If a large quantity of seed is desired, care should be taken while collecting at the mature stage, since the nutlets can fall from the heads with the slightest movement of the stems. If you harvest the cones before they age to gray, you may get more seed but will need to pry the heads apart by hand and comb out the nutlets; also, considerable chaff will accumulate with the nutlets and should be separated out with a sieve. Store cleaned nutlets dry in a sealed, well-labeled container, and refrigerate.

Propagation

Seed. Sow seeds in late winter in a flat indoors or in a cold frame, or at any time during the growing season in an outdoor seedbed. Expect germination in a week or two and let seedlings grow three to four leaves before transplanting them into small containers. Allow the surface of the soil in the pot to dry between waterings. A constantly wet soil can cause

A cone in cross-section

seedlings to rot. Weekly applications of an all-purpose fertilizer are beneficial to young plants.

Division. Large plants with numerous overlapping basal leaves, all from a single woody crown, may be divided in late winter or early spring. Lift the clump and shake loose the soil and with a sharp knife or clippers cut through the crown and make several divisions, making sure each new division has some vigorous roots. Exposed sections of crown are best treated with a fungicide. Cut back some of the foliage to reduce water loss and replant and water the divisions at once.

Cultivation

Plant Black-eyed Susans 2 feet apart in full sun. A setting that is shaded for more than a few hours during the day makes for leggy plants. Rich soils, or soils high in organic matter, usually produce lush growth, resulting in long, weak stems, easily toppled in

rain and windstorms or by the weight of multiple flowers. Plants grown in poor to average, but well-drained, soils develop a tighter, more compact habit. If you wish to establish plants in a sunny border in your "best" soil, stake the plants as they approach flowering.

Rudbeckias are well suited for a sunny border mixed with other roadside plants tolerant of poor soils and dry conditions, such as the Mulleins, Yarrow, Butterfly Weed, the Penstemons, Ox-eye Daisy, and the Goldenrods, to name only a few. Black-eyed Susans self-sow freely in the garden and even in the lawn, so there should always be extra plants to move around or share with friends. The number of volunteer seedlings can be limited by removing the seed heads after flowers fade.

Uses in the Garden and Landscape

Work plants into the summer border with the Purple Cone-flowers, Stokes' Aster, and Butterfly Weed for lively contrast. Black-eyed Susan is ideally suited for meadow gardens, for it is easily naturalized in open, sunny areas. Immediately after the soil has been broken, sow seeds or transplant potted seedlings to the site. Try them on a dry road bank with Queen Anne's Lace, Chicory, Fire Pink, Coreopsis, Sundrops, and other species of *Rudbeckia*. This species is also easily grown in containers to provide weeks of color on a deck or patio.

Related Species

Other *Rudbeckia* species are easy to cultivate and very appropriate for gardens and naturalized areas. The tallest, 3–8 feet, is *R. laciniata*, Cone-flower, which may be grown in a moist soil in shade or in the woodland garden as well as a sunny border. In mid-summer it bears numerous flower heads of bright yellow rays, 1½ inches (3–4 cm) long, slightly re-flexed from a green cone of disk flowers. Before flowering, this pe-rennial is a handsome plant with pinnately dissected leaves which emerge early in the spring. *Rud-beckia triloba*, 3–4 feet tall, bears numerous small yellow flowers from mid-summer to fall. It is tol-erant of drought and several hours of shade. The very variable *R. fulgida* spreads via rhizomes, stands 2½–4 feet, and flowers from mid-summer into the fall. The yellow ray flowers vary in size from ½ to 1½ inches (1–4 cm) long. The southeastern forms of this species are smaller flowered, though equally as handsome, than the midwestern forms, from

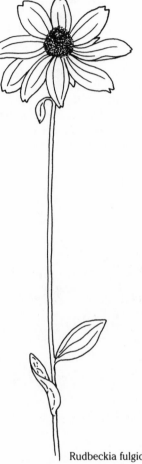

Rudbeckia fulgida

which was derived the popular floppy-petaled cultivar "Gold-strum."

Growing all four of these Rud-beckias will extend the Black-eyed Susan season from late spring into fall. Remember that while *R. fulgida* and *R. laciniata* are vigorous perennials spread-ing by rhizomes, *R. hirta* and *R. triloba* are short-lived perennials and best treated as biennials, re-quiring growing of seedlings each year for continued maintenance in the garden.

Production Notes

Nurserymen can incorporate Black-eyed Susan in a green-house bedding-plant production schedule. The fast-growing seed-lings reach salable size eight to ten weeks after sowing. Direct late-summer sowing in a garden bed, nursery field row, or natural-ized area will result in some ger-mination and growth in the fall and, in turn, more established and earlier-blooming plants in the spring.

157

Butterfly Weed, Pleurisy Root

Asclepias tuberosa
Asclepiadaceae

Duration: perennial

Blooming time: June–July

Flower color: red to yellow

Height: 1–3 feet

Soil: average, well-drained

Exposure: full sun to light shade

Description

Butterfly Weed, one of the few members of the Milkweed family that does not produce a milky sap, is among the most common and popular of our cultivated native milkweeds. The conspicuous orange flower clusters, which beautify woodland margins and open roadsides in the summer months, have long made this native perennial a favorite of home gardeners. Butterfly Weed can vary in height from 1 to 3 feet and has narrow alternate leaves 3–4 inches (7–10 cm) in length.

Flowers are borne in compact clusters, or umbels, generally appearing at the top of the stem above the leaves. Flower color ranges from red to yellow; however, orange flowers are most common. Butterflies are frequent visitors to the flowers, as there is copious nectar and the flattish surfaces of the umbels make convenient landing areas.

Although Butterfly Weed has been the object of plant collectors over the years, it has a long taproot and does not move easily. If the brittle taproot is broken, the plant is usually lost. A number of reliable propagation techniques, however, can provide gardeners with plants for their gardens.

Fruit and Seed

The long pods, or follicles, of Butterfly Weed are produced either singly or in pairs and develop gradually after flowering. Pods slowly expand and lengthen to about 4 or 5 inches at maturity, when they split along one side and shed the wind-dispersed seeds; they are ready for collection six to eight weeks from the time of flowering. The flat, dark brown, mature seeds, each attached to a tuft of silky down which aids in dispersal, are beautifully and efficiently "packaged" in the mature follicle.

Seed Collection, Cleaning, and Storage

The best time to collect the pods is when they first begin to split and before the down emerges, but if you find that the seeds have already turned brown, you can collect the pods before they split. If you are able to check the development of the seeds only infrequently, you might want to tie a piece of string around the center of the pod to prevent it from splitting and losing the seeds.

Soon after collection the seeds should be cleaned; keeping the seed intact in the pod until cleaning will make the process easier. Carefully split the green pod and remove the cylindrical mass of seeds and down. Grasp the seeds with one hand and the down with the other and, with a firm tug, pull the seeds free from the down. This technique eliminates the laborious task of separating individual seeds from the down. If not sown immediately, the seed should be stored dry in the refrigerator in a sealed, labeled container.

Propagation

Seed. Fresh seed of Butterfly Weed does not require a cold period to germinate and thus can be sown immediately upon collection. A high percentage of the seeds usually germinate whether sown indoors or out. If seeds are sown in a flat, seedlings should be removed promptly when the second set of true leaves appears.

Because the taproot is fast-growing, seedlings should be stepped up to at least a 4-inch container. Hold them here only until the plants are established and growing and then transplant to a permanent spot in the garden; if they become pot-bound, seedlings deteriorate rapidly. If you sow in an outdoor seedbed or frame, simply transplant seedlings directly into the garden when they are large enough, but, again, be careful of the taproot.

Cuttings. Terminal stem cuttings, 3–4 inches in length, can be taken before flowering. Remove half the leaves and stick the cuttings in pure sand or a mix of equal parts peat and sand. Make a tent with clear plastic over the cuttings and mist them enough to maintain constant high humidity. Cuttings should be rooted and ready for potting within six weeks.

An easier method of propagation is from root cuttings; in the fall carefully take up a mature plant from the garden and cut the taproot into 2-inch sections. Position each section vertically in a sandy rooting mix outdoors and keep the area slightly moistened.

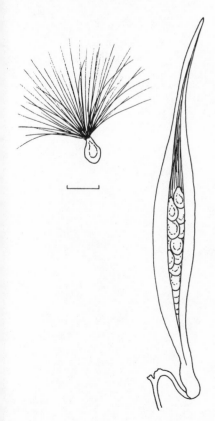

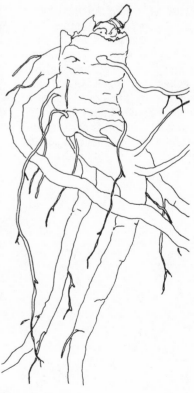

159

Cultivation

Butterfly Weed thrives in ordinary soils and open exposures, but will tolerate light shade. The only soil requirement is that it be well drained. Roots are subject to rot if planted in a rich soil that retains moisture. Mulching is not advised. Once you have established Butterfly Weed, benign neglect, with only occasional extra water or fertilizer, may prove the best caretaker.

Uses in the Garden and Landscape

Butterfly Weed is striking when planted singly or in groups. It also harmonizes well with other sun-loving natives. Interplanted with Ox-eye Daisy, Fire Pink, and Stokes' Aster, the effect is spectacular. Try it in a dry roadside planting with Chicory, Queen Anne's Lace, and Sundrops. There is nothing quite as striking as a few clumps of Butterfly Weed spotted in an expanse of green lawn, and it is also a good choice for the hot, dry problem spot where nothing else seems to grow. The cut flowers are superb in arrangements, lasting a week or more.

The plant may also have potential for mass plantings along the roadsides and in the median strips of some of our major thoroughfares, for it quickly recovers and flowers after mowing; plants mowed in May would be blooming by July.

Related Species

Swamp Milkweed (*Asclepias incarnata*), with clusters of pale to dark pink flowers in mid-summer, is a good choice for the sunny perennial bed. Despite its name, the plant does not require particular attention to moisture, and it propagates readily from seed. Also, if an appropriate place is available toward the back of the perennial border for a few plants of the Common Milkweed, *A. syriaca*, the tall plants (3–6 feet) with their large leaves and large globose clusters of fragrant flowers are easy to grow—and easy to control if the rhizomes spread too far.

Asclepias incarnata

Queen Anne's Lace, Wild Carrot

Daucus carota
Apiaceae

Duration: biennial	
Blooming time: June–July	
Flower color: white	
Height: 4–5 feet	
Soil: average garden soil	
Exposure: full sun	

Description

Queen Anne's Lace, native to Afghanistan and the parent species of our cultivated garden variety carrot, is an early introduction from Europe which has become thoroughly naturalized throughout the eastern United States in waste places, along roadsides, and in abandoned fields. It is an attractive roadside species that lends itself to a variety of uses around the home landscape.

Its bold basal rosette is prominent during late winter and early spring and, during winter warm spells in the southeastern states, the plant creates interest as the rosette develops into a lush clump of fernlike leaves.

The flowering stems are usually branched and may be 4–5 feet tall. Each stem bears one terminal and several lateral flattish flowering heads, or umbels, measuring to 4 inches (10 cm) across. Each compound umbel consists of many small white flowers and often one central maroon flower. In cultivation plants begin flowering in late May and continue through most of June, and, as in nature, sporadically throughout the summer months.

Fruit and Seed

During the weeks after flowering, the umbel folds sharply inward, creating a nestlike structure, as the small, oval, bristly fruits, or "seeds," about ⅛ inch (3–5 mm) long, develop and turn grayish brown.

Seed Collection, Cleaning, and Storage

Collect umbels when the fruits are brown, three to four weeks (or more) after flowering. Spread open the umbel and rub or shake loose the paired seeds. Store seeds dry in a sealed, labeled container and refrigerate. Under these conditions seeds have a storage life of at least six years.

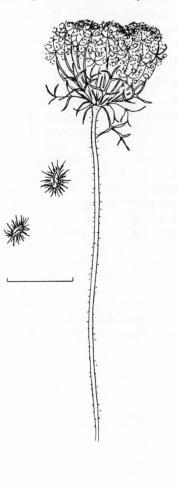

Propagation

Seed. Sow stored seeds in June in an outdoor seedbed and expect a high percentage of germination within a few days; in two to three weeks the seedlings are large enough (have two to three leaves) to transplant to individual 4-inch pots. When roots fill the containers, move the seedlings to their permanent planting site.

From this point growth is rapid; the rosettes enlarge quickly and the taproot, which looks and smells like a carrot, works its way rapidly down into the soil. The plants will overwinter as a rosette of leaves and flower the following year in late spring or early summer.

If you want a great many plants for naturalizing, sow seeds directly into the display area, such as an old field or meadow. Germination and seedling survival will probably be greater if seeds are sown at the beginning or end of the growing season. Dig or rototill the area first, broadcast the seeds, and then make a second pass with a garden rake to cover and protect the seeds. At least one annual mowing in the fall to redistribute seeds will help maintain Queen Anne's Lace, as well as other plants, on the site.

Cultivation

Plants grow well in nearly any soil, even rather dry, barren soils; however, improving the soil will enhance their appearance. Since stems can range to 6 feet or more when plants are grown in prepared garden soil, they are likely to need some support. Establish plants in an open, sunny area or one that receives at least a half day's full sun.

Since *Daucus* is a biennial, it loses all decorative value shortly after blooming, so just pull up the plants promptly after it flowers; otherwise you are likely to find the area around last season's parent plants crowded with seedlings a few months hence.

Plants naturalize most readily in areas recently disturbed and will not establish well in areas already thickly covered with perennial flowers and grasses.

Uses in the Garden and Landscape

Queen Anne's Lace is an effective filler spotted at the rear of the sunny border. They require little space, and the lacy foliage adds a nice textural touch.

In the border or naturalized, Queen Anne's Lace mixes well with Black-eyed Susan, Butterfly Weed, Purple Cone-flower, and the summer-flowering Blazing Star. It also softens the bright yellows, reds, and oranges of cultivated Daylilies. As a cut flower it is long lasting and combines well with Butterfly Weed and other natives to make a striking arrangement.

Related Species

The perennial March Parsley (*Cicuta maculata*) and the annual or biennial Poison Hemlock (*Conium maculatum*) are also in the carrot family and also have small white flowers in compound umbels. Although *Cicuta* can be used at the back of the bog garden, both *Cicuta* and *Conium* can be fatal if eaten and are best not planted where children might use the hollow stems as toys.

Stokes' Aster

Stokesia laevis

Asteraceae

Duration: perennial
Blooming time: June
Flower color: lavender blue
Height: 1–2 feet
Soil: average, well-drained
Exposure: full sun to light shade

Description

Stokes' Aster occurs infrequently in moist pine woods in the coastal plain of the southeastern states. The numerous solitary flower heads are 3–4 inches (7–10 cm) across, flat or shallowly cup shaped, and borne on stems 1–2 feet tall. The flowers, which are lavender blue to purplish or, occasionally, white, bloom throughout the month of June and sometimes thereafter. The ray flowers are larger than the central disk flowers and have five distinct teeth, or lobes. Stems arise from a dense basal rosette of narrow, overlapping leaves. These hardy, attractive plants need little more than well-drained soil to thrive.

Fruit and Seed

After the flower heads fade and shrivel, the numerous papery brown bracts that surround the developing cluster of nutlets become conspicuous. Mature nutlets are about ¼ inch (6 mm) long and sharply angled and darken to medium brown.

Seed Collection, Cleaning, and Storage

At the Botanical Garden seed is mature and ready to be collected in mid-to-late August—almost two months after flowering. Begin checking the nutlets when the head expands and the bracts curl back from the head. For easier cleaning, allow the tight seed head to dry a bit and loosen before collecting them. Nutlets will

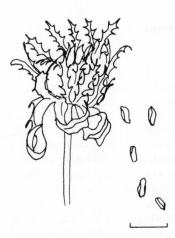

remain intact in the head for several weeks after they mature, reducing the risk of seed loss.

Cut the fruiting stalks and place them head down in a large paper bag to air dry for a few days; then shake the nutlets free or remove them by hand. You will notice right away that at least half of the nutlets are smaller and shriveled—an indication, so frequent in members of the Aster family, that many seeds did not mature. Separate and discard undeveloped nutlets either by hand or by the flotation method, that is, empty all nutlets into a container of water, scoop out the immature nutlets floating on the surface, and retain the heavier, viable ones on the bottom. Let the viable nutlets dry for a few days and store them in a sealed container in the refrigerator until time of sowing.

Propagation

Seed. Indoors, sow seeds in a well-drained sowing medium in late winter. Germination of a high percentage of the seed is rapid,

163

one to two weeks, and the seedlings quickly develop strong roots and can be transferred to individual containers two to three weeks after germination. Four weeks in containers should yield well-rooted plants of suitable size to move into the garden. Fertilization is beneficial to young plants; apply a starter solution to seedlings in the flat and an all-purpose liquid feed at full strength to plants in containers. During the first season plants develop an aggressive root system but few leaves.

Outdoors, sow seeds in the cold frame in February and transplant directly into the garden after the last spring frost. Alternatively, sow in a prepared seedbed during the summer and move plants to the garden in the fall.

Cuttings. Try raising Stokes' Aster from root cuttings. In the fall lift a mature plant from the garden and shake loose the soil. Snip off some of the longer, thicker roots. Cut the roots into 3–4-inch sections and lay them in a flat of well-drained potting soil. Cover the cuttings with an inch of sand, water thoroughly, and place the flat in the cold frame or in a protected spot outside. Subsequent watering should be necessary only during prolonged dry periods. The following spring, new shoots will emerge, which should be potted and then moved into the garden when strong plants have developed.

Division. In the spring or fall take up a large plant from the garden.

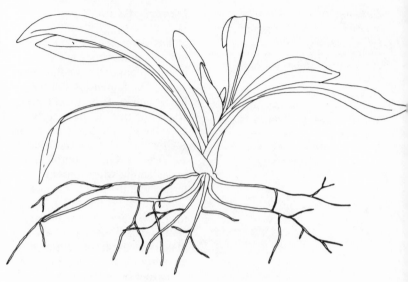

With a sharp knife, cut through the crown and make three or four large divisions. These clumps can be further divided, but make sure that each division includes several roots. Paint exposed portions of the rootstocks with a fungicide, cut the leaves in half to reduce moisture loss, replant the divisions, and water thoroughly. This is also a convenient time to take root cuttings.

Cultivation

Stokes' Aster grows best in full sun, but tolerates a lightly shaded setting. An ordinary garden soil amended with a shovelful of coarse sand or gravel per plant for drainage is recommended; the plant will not endure a poorly drained, heavy clay soil. When setting out plants in the garden, allow 1½–2 feet between plants. Remember that a small first-year plant will spread to a foot across by the second or third season.

Uses in the Garden and Landscape

Plant Stokes' Aster toward the front of the sunny perennial border and interplant it with other low, sun-loving species that flower in June, such as Fire Pink, Beard Tongue (*Penstemon smallii*), and Green-and-Gold. On a dry sunny road bank you might naturalize Stokes' Aster with Ox-eye Daisy, the Purple Cone-flowers, Butterfly Weed, and Sundrops. The blues of the Stokes' Asters are particularly effective in softening the bright yellows and oranges of Sundrops, Butterfly Weed, and Black-eyed Susans.

The basal rosettes are especially attractive during the winter months and can be worked in with other species with attractive winter foliage, such as the Mulleins, Yarrow, Beard Tongue (*P. digitalis*), Blue-eyed Grass, and Alumroot. Stokes' Aster can be successfully grown in a large container for patio and deck gardening, and the flowers provide nice blues for flower arrangements.

Production Notes

For commercial production sow seeds outdoors in July and move plants to 4-inch pots in September for fall sales or overwinter them and offer them for sale the following spring. Smaller plants in pots can be offered in spring from late-winter sowing as described above.

Yarrow, Milfoil

Achillea millefolium
Asteraceae

Duration: perennial

Blooming time: June–July

Flower color: white

Height: 1–4 feet

Soil: average garden soil

Exposure: full sun

Description

The value of Yarrow as a ground-cover, an evergreen, and a durable, long-blooming perennial in mild climates is considerable. Perhaps because it is frequently labeled a "roadside weed" and persists in poor growing conditions throughout the eastern United States, gardeners have been slow to use this plant but, like other common roadside species, Yarrow excels in cultivation.

Thick basal mats of finely dissected, woolly, fernlike leaves produce flowering stems 1 to 4 feet high. In good garden soil, the rhizomes spread rapidly, and by fall a spring seedling may grow into a dense clump 2 feet across. Flat-topped flowering heads are made up of numerous small flowers with white (or rarely pink) ray and disk flowers. Yarrow will readily adapt to a wide range of growing conditions and in a sunny location will bloom prolifically in early summer and sporadically thereafter.

Fruit and Seed

The flower heads turn dark brown after the bloom period, and the tightly woven whorls of bracts, which are just below the receptacle holding the nutlets, are most conspicuous. The small, nearly flat nutlets are gray with a white border; an imposing quantity of chaff—dried floral parts—surrounds the developing nutlets.

Seed Collection, Cleaning, and Storage

A month or more after flowering, collect the seed heads and bring them indoors to air-dry for at least a week before cleaning. Crush the heads with a rolling pin to remove the nutlets, which are tiny and difficult to identify at first. When you spot one, though, you will quickly notice many more. Put the nutlets and chaff in a sieve and screen the material down, as near as possible, to just seeds. Obtaining pure seed is difficult, if not impossible, without sophisticated cleaning equipment, and a bit of fine debris with the seeds does no harm. Store seeds dry in a sealed, labeled container in the refrigerator. (Cleaning Yarrow seeds is a good way to learn the virtues of patience; division is an easier and quicker propagation technique.)

Propagation

Seed. Sow stored seeds indoors in late winter or outdoors in a seed flat when the weather breaks in late April. Spread the seeds as evenly as possible over your sowing medium to avoid crowding later on. Germination should occur in a week or less. Seedlings can be transferred to containers in six weeks then moved to a permanent spot in the garden a month later.

Division. A mature Yarrow plant is composed of a cluster of numerous basal rosettes of leaves. Thus division is a simple, straightforward technique for propagation. Preferably in the early spring, lift a healthy plant from the garden and shake loose the soil; then separate individual or small groups of rosettes from the clump. For each new division, cut the leaves back to reduce moisture loss, replant, and water thoroughly. Divisions respond quickly with a flush of new growth. Mature plants should be divided at least every other year.

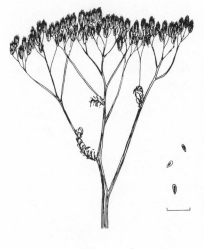

Cultivation

Yarrow can endure dry, impoverished soil and survive with little, if any, maintenance. With even modest attention from the gardener, however, the plant's appearance improves dramatically, resulting in plants that bear little resemblance to the stunted roadside plants. Bear in mind that the richer the soil, the larger and more aggressive will be the plant, perhaps requiring staking of flowering stems and controlling of its tendency to crowd out less aggressive species. Plant Yarrow in a sunny location with a 2-to-3-inch mulch to reduce weeds and keep the soil from drying out.

Uses in the Garden and Landscape

Yarrow works well in the front of the sunny perennial border. Consider integrating the wild plants with some of the many horticultural varieties of Yarrow, or try it as an edging plant bordering a path where it can be free to spread. To encourage vegetative production and more attractive clumps of basal foliage, prune away most of the stems after flowering—leaving just a few for seed collection later.

The tight, fernlike clumps of foliage provide effective contrast for other plants in the border. Use Yarrow as an evergreen groundcover or as accent clumps in an open sunny area where winters are mild. The plant's lush, verdant presence during the dormant season is perhaps its most endearing trait. The white-flowering Yarrow is one of the easiest perennials to maintain throughout the garden to soften the bright red, yellow, and orange flowers so predominant in the summer. Yarrow is one of the species which should certainly be included, by direct seeding or setting out transplants, in any meadow planting.

Production Notes

For production purposes, field-grow plants in a light, organic soil in an open, sunny plot; divide the plants in the spring and again in late summer and pot in quart containers.

Gaillardia, Indian Blanket

Gaillardia pulchella
Asteraceae

Duration: annual

Blooming time: June–October

Flower color: red and yellow

Height: 1–2 feet

Soil: sandy, well-drained

Exposure: full sun

Description

Gaillardia occurs in sandy soils throughout the southern United States. The plant is drought resistant, blooms from July to the first frost, and is easy to propagate. It has a loose, sprawling habit, and attains a height of 1–2 feet. The ray flowers are typically red, tipped with a narrow yellow border at the apex. Occasionally, these flowers are solid orange or yellow. Rarely, the ray flowers are tube shaped, a trait frequently seen in some of the horticultural varieties.

Fruit and Seed

The rounded seed heads, prominent after the ray flowers fade, are grayish and measure ½–1 inch across. The mature seeds, or nutlets, are gray, 1/16–1/8 inch (2–3 mm) long, four angled, and wider at the apex than at the base; they are densely hairy and have long awns at the apex. One seed head will produce three to four dozen nutlets.

Seed Collection, Cleaning, and Storage

The best time to collect the seed heads of Gaillardia is in October, after the first few frosts. Although seed heads are produced during the growing season, the seeds collected after flower production has ceased are much more likely to be viable. Be selective when collecting seed heads: heads with considerable dried flower parts still attached are probably not ready. Look for uniformly gray heads with no dried petals persisting. Examine the nutlets by grasping the white appendages, the awns, that protrude from the seed head and pulling out a few nutlets. If they are gray and swollen, rather than green and flat, they are probably mature and ready for harvest. To clean, simply break up the seed head and separate the individual nutlets. Store the seeds dry and refrigerate. If stored correctly, Gaillardia seeds remain viable for at least four years.

Propagation

Seed. Gaillardia is best started indoors in pots or flats of good soil in late winter. Allow eight weeks for the development of well-rooted seedlings before transplanting into the garden at the start of the frost-free period.

In a bed where Gaillardia has grown one season, a few seedlings will likely appear the next spring, and occasionally a plant will overwinter. But you cannot count on Gaillardia to self-sow, and should plan on producing

new plants each year. Gaillardia is generally treated as a short-lived perennial, which it in fact is in the warmer coastal areas. Gardeners in the mountain regions and northern areas, however, should treat this species as an annual.

Cuttings. Under mist, cuttings root well and in a high percentage. A mixture of equal parts sand and perlite is satisfactory as a rooting medium. Take cuttings in June, make them 3–4 inches long and remove the lower leaves before inserting them in the rooting medium. Cuttings root rapidly in two to three weeks, whereupon they can be moved directly into the garden.

Cultivation

Gaillardia grows best in an open, sunny location and a well-drained garden soil. Amend heavy clay soils with generous amounts of coarse sand for improved drainage and to promote a better-developed root system. Remove spent flowers for more blooms, but as the end of the growing season approaches, leave some flowering heads intact to make seed.

Uses in the Garden and Landscape

For best effects, Gaillardia should be planted in groups. Staggered plantings of, say, five to seven plants per group create drifts of color in the garden when viewed from a distance. Gaillardia can also be used in much the same manner as a bedding plant: at the edge of a perennial border, along an entrance walk, or simply massed by itself. As the plant does not begin to branch and spread until mid-season, it can be effectively interplanted with other low-growing plants that bloom earlier, in the spring and summer months.

Production Notes

Overwinter healthy plants in the greenhouse and prepare cuttings in late winter.

Bee-balm

Monarda didyma
Lamiaceae

Duration: perennial

Blooming time: June–July

Flower color: red

Height: 3–6 feet

Soil: moist or wet

Exposure: full to filtered sun

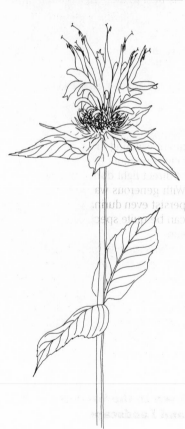

Description

Bee-balm occurs along stream banks and in wet meadows throughout the northeastern United States and as far south as the southern Appalachians. It has several uses in the garden, not the least of which is as a naturalized planting in a wet area. Owing to its vigorous stolons, or runners, the plant develops a dense mat of basal foliage during the fall and early spring.

Healthy plants with square stems, typical of the mints, can reach 6 feet or more. The large, lanceolate, opposite leaves give off a pleasant mint odor when crushed. The showy, terminal flower clusters, which appear in mid-summer, are surrounded by a whorl of several purplish or reddish leafy bracts. Each single flowering head, or compact cyme, contains many narrow tubular flowers, each with a five-toothed calyx and a red or scarlet two-lipped corolla; the upper lip is smooth or entire, while the lower lip is three lobed. Stamens are conspicuous, protruding out from just under the longer upper lip.

Our wild Bee-balm is a parent of some hybrid Monardas popular in contemporary gardens. Bee-balm blooms in June and early July.

Fruit and Seed

After the corollas shrivel and drop, the round head gradually expands and darkens. The fruiting head consists of numerous ⅜-inch-long (1 cm), tightly ar- ranged, tubelike, persistent calyxes, each of which contains 1–4 separate seeds, ⅟₁₆ inch (2 mm) across, which turn dark brown as they near maturity, and which you can see with a hand lens. Often one or more of the nutlets does not mature.

Seed Collection, Cleaning, and Storage

Seeds mature in late July and early August, one to three weeks after flowering. To check the condition of the seeds, bend the stem over and tap the bottom of the fruiting head. If the seeds are brown and fall out readily, they are mature and should be collected. If the seeds are still green or if, upon tapping, no seeds fall out, wait another week and then check again. If frequent monitoring of the plants is not possible, cut the stalks with seed heads containing well-developed but green nutlets, put them in water, and let the seeds mature.

When seeds are mature, snip off the seed heads and spread them over a clean, dry surface indoors to air-dry for a few days. Then place fifteen or so heads at a time in a bag and shake vigorously. Most of the seeds will fall out. To be sure all seeds have been removed, air-dry heads again for a few days and repeat the shaking procedure. To clean further, run seeds and accumulated litter through a sieve. Store seeds dry in a sealed, labeled container in the refrigerator.

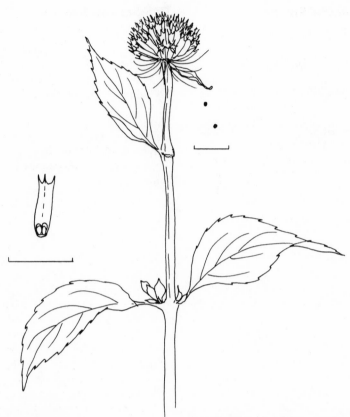

Propagation

Seed. Seeds sown indoors in January should germinate in a week or two. Since the seedlings are tiny and slow growing, they should remain in the flat 6–7 weeks after germination before being transplanted to 3-inch containers. Allow roots to fill the container before planting in the garden. During the container stage, pinch out the tops of the plants several times to encourage branching and bushier specimens. Seedlings respond favorably to fertilizer; a starter solution for seedlings in the flat and a weekly application of an all-pur-pose fertilizer for the transplants are recommended.

Cuttings. Take stem tip cuttings, 3–4 inches long, any time from May to August. Remove the lower leaves and all flower or seed heads and insert at least one node into a sand and perlite rooting medium. Place cuttings in an enclosed chamber and mist them several times a day. Cuttings can also be taken from vigorous seedlings when you are pinching out the tops. In four to five weeks cuttings are well rooted; grow them on in containers and transfer plants to the garden in the early fall.

Division. Divide mature clumps of Bee-balm in March before they send up stems. Dig up the plant and using a pair of pruning shears or a sharp shovel cut the clump into sections. Replant and water the divisions immediately.

Cultivation

It is best to plant Bee-balm in an area that remains moist during the growing season, as the plant's appearance is largely dependent on the availability of moisture. Plants in a border planting benefit from at least weekly watering and require more regular irrigation during extended dry periods. Bee-balm will require less frequent watering in a site that receives no more than a few hours of direct light during the day. With generous watering it can persist even during a drought and can be quite spectacular in full sun.

Plants benefit from division every two or three years. The shallow root system spreads best in a light soil, so work generous amounts of leaf mold and compost into your soil. However, under ideal growing conditions the plant can become very aggressive.

Uses in the Garden and Landscape

Naturalize Bee-balm in moist areas along stream banks, pond edges, seepages, and in low areas in the garden. In the perennial border, plant Bee-balm in groups to create masses of color. Space plants 1½–2 feet apart.

(Remember to lift and divide plants when they become crowded.)

Established along the outside edge of a deck or patio, Bee-balm is beautiful to look through or over and, like Cardinal Flower, attracts hummingbirds, making close observation of their fascinating habits possible. Bee-balm is also a versatile flower for arrangements.

Related Species

Monarda fistulosa has shorter stems (to 3 feet), a looser habit, and pink, lavender, purple, or, rarely, white flowers; it tolerates a slightly drier and sunnier condition in the garden. Propagation and cultivation are the same as for *M. didyma*.

Production Notes

Take cuttings from seedlings in the greenhouse in late winter and root them under mist. Continue to pinch the tops until two weeks before plants are offered for sale. To increase by division, break clumps into small, 1-inch sections and pot in 3- or 4-inch containers. A large clump or mat of runners may yield as many as two hundred divisions.

Purple Cone-flower

Echinacea purpurea
Asteraceae

Duration: perennial

Blooming time: June–July

Flower color: pink

Height: 1–3 feet

Soil: fertile, well-drained

Exposure: full to filtered sun

Description

For many gardeners Purple Cone-flowers are old standbys in the summer border. These plants are long-lived, and the bright pink blooms make excellent cut flowers. *Echinacea purpurea* is abundant in midwestern prairies and has a sporadic distribution in woodlands and along road banks in the mountain and northern areas of the eastern states.

The coarsely textured and coarsely toothed basal leaves, 3–6 inches (7.5–15 cm) long, arise in a central clump from the rootstock. Flowering stems are sturdy, usually unbranched, and 1–3 feet tall. The striking flower heads are about 4 inches (10 cm) across and consist of an outer whorl of pink ray flowers and a central disk, or cone, of very small dark purple disk flowers. The plants maintain a moderately tight habit through the season and require little care once established.

Fruit and Seed

After the ray flowers fade, the "cones," or heads, of disk flowers, now in fruit, become prominent as they expand steadily and the seeds mature over the next four to five weeks. The seeds, or nutlets, are seated tightly against the receptacle, or central tissue of the head, in a symmetrical spiral. Like other members of the Aster family, Purple Cone-flowers typically produce only a single seed, or nutlet, per small flower and only a small percentage of these are viable. The quadrangular nutlets range in color from

light to medium brown, and are barely ⅛ inch (3.0 mm) long.

Seed Collection, Cleaning, and Storage

Don't be too hasty to collect seed. For easier seed harvest allow the bristles on the cone to loosen their hold on the nutlets; three to four weeks after flowering is a good time to begin checking cones. Bend the seed stalk over and tap or shake the cone; if nutlets fall out, it is time to collect. If nutlets do not fall out, check again in a few days. You have one to two weeks and a running battle with the goldfinches between the time the cones loosen and the nutlets fall to the ground to collect the seed.

Just snip the stalks at the base and drop them headfirst into a large paper bag. Hold the bag closed around the stems and shake the bag vigorously to free the loose nutlets. No doubt some

Cone in cross-section

nutlets will remain attached to the cone, and these will require hand cleaning if you really need every seed. For maximum recovery of seeds sever the cones from the stalks and break them apart. Considerable chaff will accumulate with the nutlets, but it can be quickly separated with a sieve. A large percentage of nutlets will be small and shriveled, and are either empty or contain undeveloped embryos. Separate the good nutlets from the bad by hand and place them in a sealed, labeled container and refrigerate until sowing.

Propagation

Seed. The nutlets can be sown immediately after harvest in an outdoor seedbed, and seedlings should appear the following spring.

Alternatively, sow stored seed indoors or in a cold frame in late winter or early spring. For uniform, high-percentage germination stratify the seeds for four weeks or more. To do this, sow nutlets in a flat of standard soil mix, cover them with ⅛ inch or so of the mix, and water thoroughly. Then seal the flat in a plastic bag (or tightly cover the top of the flat with a piece of plastic) and refrigerate (34–44°F) for four weeks. At the end of the stratification period, move the flat to a sunny window or the cold frame and expect germination in a few days.

The seedlings grow rapidly when in a commercial soil mix that includes dry fertilizers or when weekly feedings of a starter solution (9–45–15 or equivalent) are applied to other seed mixes. Transplant seedlings into 3-inch containers when their second true leaves appear. In three to four weeks these plants should be well rooted and can be moved into the garden when danger of frost is past.

Cuttings. When only a few new plants are desired, propagation by root cuttings is a practical method. In late winter use a sharp spade or trowel to remove a few sections of roots from the edges of a mature clump. Select the thickest roots from each section and plant them vertically in a deep pot so that the tops of the roots are at soil level. Maintain the correct polarity when planting the cuttings: that is, the portion of the root that was closest to the crown should be at soil level. When the weather warms, look for new shoots. Allow time for the cutting to make a root system and then transfer to 3- or 4-inch containers. Move plants into the garden when roots fill the container.

Division. When plants go dormant in the fall, lift a mature clump from the garden and shake the soil loose. Clumps consist of multiple crowns which separate readily when teased away from the parent clump. Make sure each new division includes several well-developed roots. Replant the divisions an inch below the soil and water thoroughly.

Cultivation

Purple Cone-flowers thrive in a fertile, well-drained soil in direct sunlight but tolerate light shade, where they tend to develop a looser, more open habit. Good drainage is essential; the plants are likely to rot in soils that retain excessive moisture. If you have doubts about how well your soil drains, work a shovelful of sand into the soil where each plant is to be set.

Unlike the acid soil tolerance or preference of many eastern American wild flowers, Purple Cone-flower grows better in circum-neutral soils having a pH of 6–7. Therefore, limestone amendments are recommended for acidic soils. Space plants 1–2 feet apart and divide every three to four years. Rework the soil, adding organic matter and sand, when plants are taken up for division. If seeds are not needed, cutting the flowering stems at their bases after blooming encourages vigorous vegetative growth.

Uses in the Garden and Landscape

Purple Cone-flowers are a natural choice for the front or middle layers of the sunny perennial border. Plant them in groups of threes and fives at intervals in the border. The pink flowers mix well with such other colorful, sun-loving native species as Gaillardia, Black-eyed Susan, and Butterfly Weed. Cone-flowers stand out when set in front of taller species with dense foliage, such as White Wild Indigo, Carolina Bush Pea, the Goldenrods, and Boltonia. Because established plants can tolerate extended periods of dry weather, they can be naturalized on dry road banks. Plants can also be grown quite successfully in large containers.

Related Species

Echinacea laevigata and *E. pallida* occur infrequently on road-

Echinaceae laevigata

sides and in open woodlands in a few states. Both species deserve a place in American gardens; *E. laevigata* is spectacular, with drooping ray flowers three inches long and heads on stems that can reach to 3 feet or more. Both plants flower earlier than *E. purpurea* and are similarly demanding of good drainage. Propagation of all three species is the same.

Production Notes

Allow ten to twelve weeks from seed to salable plant. When field grown, young plants develop rapidly through their first season and can be potted in quart containers.

Trumpet Vine, Cow-Itch Vine

Campsis radicans
Bignoniaceae

Duration: perennial

Blooming time: June–July

Flower color: orange

Height: climbing vine to 30 feet

Soil: rich soil

Exposure: full sun

Description

Trumpet Vine occurs commonly throughout the eastern United States in woodlands and along fencerows and roadsides, where the vines climb to 30 feet or more, attaching to tree trunks or other supports by means of aerial, rootlike holdfasts.

The opposite pinnately compound leaves, which have nine to eleven coarsely toothed leaflets, are well spaced along the stem and do not form the dense habit of some native vines, such as Yellow Jessamine and Cross Vine, which have overlapping layers of foliage. The large terminal clusters of spectacular orange to crimson trumpet-shaped flowers, 3 inches (7.5 cm) long and flaring into five lobes, appear in June and July and sporadically thereafter.

These woody vines are hardy as far north as southern New England, but do not climb or spread as rapidly as in the middle Atlantic and southeastern states. Through considered a weed in the Southeast, it is beautiful in cultivation and a number of cultivars are being marketed.

Fruit and Seed

The long, green, crescent-shaped capsules develop slowly during the two to three months after flowering and are 4–7 inches (10–17 cm) long at maturity. They are attractive and remain on the vine through the growing season and often through the winter. The numerous winged, papery seeds are 1 inch (2.5 cm) long and bear a close resemblance to those of the Cross Vine. The transparent light brown wings completely surround the dark brown seed.

Seed Collection, Cleaning, and Storage

The seeds, which mature in September and October, should be harvested just before the cap-

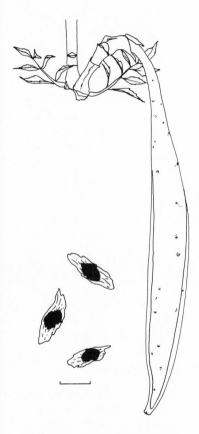

sules split open. When the vines are grown in full sun, collection is easy as the branches often arch downward, bringing the ripe capsules within easy reach. A single capsule should contain all the seeds you will ever need for propagation of the vines.

Remove a capsule and crack it open with pruning shears; or, if the capsules have turned dark brown and brittle and have split along their central seams, you can collect the seeds by simply shaking them out. Note, however, that it has recently been discovered that the green capsules have nectar glands (called extra-floral

nectaries) on their surface and that the large ants, which are attracted to the nectar, may afford some degree of protection for the smooth fruits from other insects or predators. So be careful! The seeds should be stored dry in a sealed container and refrigerated.

Propagation

Seed. The easiest method of seedling production is to sow the seeds in an outdoor seedbed upon collection and look for seedlings in the spring.

Plants can also be started in flats indoors or in the cold frame at any time after a 6-week moist chill (stratification) period, which breaks dormancy and yields more rapid and uniform germination. Seeds that have been stored should be mixed with a small amount of damp vermiculite in a plastic bag and refrigerated for the six weeks prior to sowing.

Pot seedlings in 4-inch containers and move them to their permanent location when plants are well rooted.

Cuttings. Take stem cuttings before flowering and include a piece of last season's wood. Insert cuttings, old wood down, in a deep pot of equal parts peat moss and sand. After thoroughly moistening the rooting mix, place the pot in a rooting chamber or in a sealed plastic bag to maintain high humidity. Some cuttings should root during the next three to four weeks, whereupon they can be moved to 4-inch pots and overwintered in the cold frame or heeled-in outside.

Division. Older vines typically produce runners terminating in new shoots. Dig around the new shoot, making sure to keep roots and soil intact, and transplant the clump to its new location.

Cultivation

Trumpet Vines tolerate a wide range of soil conditions. Young plants, however, grow faster during their first few seasons when established in rich, organic soils and watered during dry periods. An early-spring application of an all-purpose fertilizer and a mulch of rotted leaves is beneficial for new plants.

The vines should be grown in full sun, where flower production is profuse. The young vines may need to be attached to the structures on which they climb until aerial rootlets develop, and older vines sometimes tend to pull away from their supports and may need tying.

If you wish to confine vines to an area or shape them, prune branches in the fall or late winter. Pinching new growth will stimulate vines to branch more, but remember that flower buds are formed on new growth in the spring. Also, be aware that contact with the plant may cause a skin rash on some people (and, presumably, cows, as indicated by one of the common names).

Uses in the Garden and Landscape

In the southeastern states Trumpet Vines are common on pines whose lower limbs have fallen away, letting in more light. Thus it is appropriate to establish young plants at the base of pines or other trees where direct light is available.

These vines can also be used as a loose, spreading ground-cover to conceal a stump or lap over a rock wall, and they can be spectacular when allowed to sweep up the side of a stone building. Regular shaping usually enhances the vine's appearance in this setting.

Trumpet Vines are often seen growing up fence posts along the expressways. Just a single such fence post with a cascading trumpet vine will provide a point of interest in the home garden; Trumpet Vines, by the way, are a favorite of hummingbirds.

Queen-of-the-Prairie

Filipendula rubra
Rosaceae

Duration: perennial

Blooming time: late June

Flower color: pink

Height: 3–6 feet

Soil: rich soil, moist or wet

Exposure: light shade

Description

There are few sights in the garden more pleasing and spectacular than a massed planting of Queen-of-the-Prairie. Clusters of fragrant pale pink blooms and large, deeply cut leaves make an engaging textural contrast. Where moisture is constant through the season and sunlight plentiful, the plants are quick to establish and spread, requiring minimal maintenance from one year to the next.

Many gardeners use these perennials in the herbaceous border; their lush foliage remains attractive throughout the growing season. In nature, these plants occur in bottomland prairies, wet meadows, and bogs in the upper South and northward throughout the eastern United States.

They flower over a two-week period in mid and late June. The numerous small flowers are borne on ascending branched stalks, forming a loose, nearly flat-topped panicle. The tiny pink petals of the individual flowers are up to ¼ inch long (4–6 mm).

The alternate, pinnately dissected leaves are borne on tall, 3- to-6-foot stems, topped by larger, palmately dissected terminal leaflets. All leaf segments are toothed along their margins and sharply pointed at the apex.

Fruit and Seed

Several weeks after the short-lived flowers fade, the panicle begins darkening from green to varying shades of brown. The one-seeded fruits are smooth, narrow, slightly twisted, and about ¼ inch (6 mm) long. Since the fruits do not dehisce to expel their seeds, the achene itself may be treated as a seed for cleaning, storing, and sowing.

Seed Collection, Cleaning, and Storage

Clusters of seed heads can be collected when they turn grayish brown, about four to six weeks after the blooming period. Cut the heads from the stems, then spread them on clean, dry newspaper to air-dry for a few days prior to cleaning. Brush or shake the follicles free from the heads and store them in a sealed, airtight, labeled container in the refrigerator until sowing. Further cleaning—that is, removing the tiny seeds from the follicles—is troublesome and unnecessary for propagation.

Propagation

Seed. For best results sow seeds (follicle and all) fresh, upon collection, in an outdoor seedbed and look for seedlings the following spring. Since from our experience only a small percentage of the seeds are viable, sow heavily to assure some germination. Keep the seedbed evenly moist for the remainder of the growing season and through the following spring, even after germination.

When the seedlings have two or three leaves and roots about an inch long, transplant them into 2- or 3-inch pots. Keep the potted plants out of direct sunlight and give them a weekly treatment with an all-purpose fertilizer.

Move them to a permanent planting site when roots fill the containers. Plants grown from seed can be expected to flower the second year.

Division. Division offers the fastest and most reliable method of increase. Plants of *Filipendula* spread by short rhizomes running just below the surface of the soil. The rhizomes terminate in rosettes which bear several stems. A rosette includes a dense network of roots that run only a few inches into the soil and is easily taken up.

In the spring just as leaves emerge or in the fall before the plants go dormant, work from the edges of the clump and remove individual or small groups of rosettes with a trowel. Transplant new divisions to their new place in the garden and water thoroughly.

Cultivation

Plants remain lush and attractive through the summer and early-fall months, provided moisture is constant and the plants are not allowed to dry out. Make certain that you plant your *Filipendula* close to an irrigation source or in a naturally wet area.

Prepare a soil high in organic matter; use plenty of rotted leaves and compost and then mulch the area where the plants grow each spring. Flowers last longer when plants are grown in a slightly protected setting where sunlight is not direct for the entire day.

Once established, plants can be left undisturbed for many years, although in time they may become less floriferous due to crowding and then should be thinned. Plants are not terribly aggressive, but do spread steadily; to curb clumps if they begin crowding other plants, simply remove stems and roots from the edges of the clump. If seeds are not wanted, prune away the heads when flowers fade.

Uses in the Garden and Landscape

Use Queen-of-the-Prairie in the middle or back of the perennial border. It is also a useful foliage plant, providing a backdrop for shorter plants or a foreground for such taller, fall-blooming plants as the Goldenrods, the Asters, Blazing Star, and Boltonia.

Naturalize plants in wet areas; combine Queen-of-the-Prairie with Bee-balm, Joe-Pye-Weed, the Turtleheads, the Lobelias, Bur-Marigold, and the native Mallows. Plants are especially attractive at the edge of a pond or stream. Cut flowers are outstanding in arrangements.

Production Notes

Field-grow plants in a rich, organic soil and irrigate regularly through the growing season. Divide clumps in the fall and pot divisions in quart containers, which should be overwintered in a protected area outdoors. Market plants the following spring.

Ruellia

Ruellia caroliniensis
Acanthaceae

Duration: perennial

Blooming time: June–August

Flower color: lavender or blue

Height: 1–1½ feet

Soil: dryish garden soil

Exposure: light shade

Description

The lavender, blue, or, rarely, pink flowers of Ruellia are borne in clusters of two to four along the stem in the middle and upper leaf axils. Each flower has a short, hairy calyx tube with threadlike lobes, up to ¾ inch (22 mm) long, which persist as the capsule develops. The funnel-shaped corolla, up to 1¾ inch (2.5–4.5 cm) long, has a slender tube, an open throat, and five equal spreading lobes. The un-branched stems range from 1 to 2½ feet tall and bear opposite, densely hairy, oval to lance-shaped leaves. The short-lived flowers, which appear sparsely from June to August, often re-main open for less than a day.

Its much smaller size notwith-standing, Ruellia, which occurs throughout the southeastern United States in dry woods, sandy fields, and rock crevices, invites comparison with the cultivated petunia in its shape and erect habit.

Fruit and Seed

The capsules, which slowly ma-ture and change from yellow green to brown over a two-month period after flowering, may num-ber as many as one dozen in a cluster. Because flowers are pro-duced over a long period, indi-vidual capsules within a cluster may be of different sizes and stages of maturity at any point during the growing season. At maturity the smooth capsule is about ½ inch long (12–16 mm) and approximately ¼ inch

(6 mm) wide and has four com-partments containing eight flat, round, dark brown seeds, each seed measuring nearly ⅛ inch (3 mm) across. At dehiscence the capsule explodes open to expel the seeds.

Seed Collection, Cleaning, and Storage

Capsules may be collected indi-vidually as they ripen (when they are a light or medium brown) over the late-summer and fall months. A stand of plants should include several mature capsules at any one time. Care must be taken to collect capsules before they show signs of splitting since shortly after a capsule splits the seeds are lost in the leaf litter.

Seeds can also explode from the capsule after collection, so harvest the capsules and store in a closed bag or envelope to catch seeds as they eject. To remove the seed from unopened cap-sules, split them open by hand

and rake out the seeds. Store them dry in an air-tight, labeled container and refrigerate until time of sowing.

Propagation

Seed. Freshly collected seeds may be sown immediately in an outdoor seedbed and should germinate the following spring. Stored seed may be sown indoors or in the cold frame in late winter; add an extra measure of coarse sand or horticultural-grade pine bark to your standard potting mix to insure good drainage.

The fast-growing seedlings are large enough to transplant into individual containers in three to four weeks from germination. Locate the potted seedlings away from direct sunlight. When plants are well rooted, in another three to four weeks, transplant them to the garden. Weekly applications of an all-purpose fertilizer will enhance seedling growth.

If new plants are in the ground early in the growing season, some flowering can be expected during the first year. Plants will attain their full maturity during their second season.

Cuttings. In our experience stem cuttings taken in July root well. Take cuttings that include two nodes, remove the lower pair of leaves and any flower buds and developing capsules, and insert the cuttings in a medium of equal parts sand and perlite in a root-ing chamber or in a flat covered with plastic. Mist the cuttings and saturate the medium when dry.

Cuttings are typically well rooted and ready to be potted in four to five weeks. Plan to overwinter the rooted cuttings in pots and transplant them to the garden the next spring.

Cultivation

Ruellia tolerates a wide range of garden soils, but not excessive moisture. A well-prepared garden soil supplemented with organic matter, however, will promote larger, more robust plants. If you intend to naturalize plants, amend the native soil with one shovelful of prepared garden soil per plant.

A lightly shaded setting or one where some protection from direct sun is provided is recommended. For example, the edge of a wooded area or in borders where neighboring plants cast some shade during the day are ideal locations for Ruellia. After new plants are established, little, if any, maintenance will be required, although regular irrigation during summer dry periods will make for more floriferous specimens.

Uses in the Garden and Landscape

Use Ruellia in the front rank of the border, where the plants prove especially valuable in fill-ing the sizable gaps in the blooming season that occur during the summer months.

Few plants are less conspicuous than the Ruellias when they are not in flower, so you can feel comfortable planting them liberally, encouraging their spread, and enjoying the blooms throughout the summer season.

Integrate plants with *Coreopsis auriculata*, Blue-eyed Grass, Green-and-Gold, and other low-growing wild flowers. Ruellias can be naturalized in sparsely vegetated, somewhat dry shaded areas, such as along entrance driveways and paths. During mid-to-late summer the blue flowers, though sparse, are quite attractive in a naturalized planting, where they appear just above the loose mat of foliage.

If you have only a few plants, a most effective use is to locate one to three plants at the base of frequently used steps, at the edge of a shady patio, or just outside a breakfast room window. In such situations the elusive beauty of the single flowers can be enjoyed frequently during routine activities.

On dryish, well-drained sites, naturalize plants with Butterfly Weed, Fire Pink, and Black-eyed Susan. Try plants as a colorful deciduous groundcover at the base of evergreen foundation plantings. Ruellias are also fitting in the shade garden where individual flowers are striking against darker backgrounds.

Button Snakeroot

Eryngium yuccifolium

Apiaceae

Duration: perennial

Blooming time: July

Flower color: white or greenish

Height: 1–4 feet

Soil: sandy, well-drained

Exposure: full sun

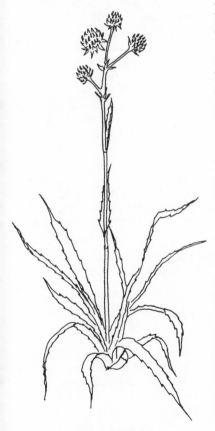

Description

Button Snakeroot, unknown to many gardeners, is noteworthy for its compact and intriguing flower clusters and seed heads and for its durability in cultivation. Its garden interest is more in its form and texture than in any floral beauty. In nature, these plants occur on sandy roadsides and in open woods, prairies, and thickets nearly throughout the eastern United States.

The distinctive narrow, linear, leathery, yuccalike basal leaves, which may be as long as 2 feet, account for the descriptive specific epithet *yuccifolium*, which means "yucca-leaf." The plants usually produce a single upright stem, 1–4 feet tall, that branches toward the top and bears the terminal globose flowering heads. The leaves along the stem are greatly reduced.

An individual inflorescence, or flower head, is about ¼–¾ inch (7–20 mm) across, subtended by a collar of pointed involucral bracts. A head consists of many small, tightly arranged flowers, each with five white or greenish petals. Each flower is also subtended by a hard, pointed bract, giving the head a very hard spiny feel. The plants flower throughout the month of July; toward the end of the blooming period, the heads take on a bluish cast.

Fruit and Seed

After the petals fade, the heads harden and darken to a dull brown, remaining attached to the stalk for the remainder of the growing season. Each head holds numerous seeds (or mericarps), as each flower produces a pair of semicylindrical fruits, each containing a single seed. The short calyx lobes persist as sharp-pointed scales at the apex of the "seeds."

Each seed is ¼ inch (6 mm) long, concave on the inner face and convex with a prominent ridge on the outer face; the margins have rows of short translucent scales.

Seed Collection, Cleaning, and Storage

Collect heads when they turn brown, in September or October. Heads do not usually fall apart

183

until the first October frost, a time when many gardeners perform a fall cleanup of their gardens—and a convenient time to collect seeds of Button Snakeroot and other sun-loving plants that mature their seeds late in the season.

Bring seed heads indoors and over a clean, dry surface tap or crumble the seeds out of the heads. It may be impractical to separate the seeds from the similar-sized involucral bracts or scales (chaff), but it will do no harm if they are stored and sown together. Let the seeds air-dry for a few days prior to storing them in a sealed, labeled container in the refrigerator.

Propagation

Seed. For best results sow seeds upon collection in an outdoor seedbed and look for seedlings in the spring. Young plants make a basal rosette of three or four leaves one to two months after germination, at which time they can be transplanted to containers.

Potted plants grow steadily in a fast-draining potting medium; add extra coarse sand or horticultural-grade pine bark to your soil mix. Container plants respond favorably to weekly applications of an all-purpose fertilizer.

When roots fill the container, move plants directly to a permanent location in the garden where they will receive direct sunlight for at least part of the day. Allow the soil to become dry between waterings.

Stored seeds germinate in a higher percentage if you stratify them for four weeks. This is best done in late winter or early spring. Sow seeds in a seed flat or pot, cover with ¼ inch of soil, and water thoroughly. Cover the flat or pot with plastic and place in the refrigerator for four weeks. After danger of frost has passed, move the flat to the cold frame or a sunny spot outdoors. Uniform germination may be expected in one to two weeks. Handle seedlings in the manner described above.

Division. Where growing conditions are favorable, mature, well-established plants may form clumps containing several rosettes. In the fall use a shovel to carefully lift a clump from the ground. Separate the clump into individual rosettes, taking care not to break any roots, and replant the divisions immediately. To be safe, leave at least a few plants undisturbed, as *Eryngium* does not always move readily.

Cultivation

Plants thrive in open, sunny sites and well-drained soils. In places where water does not drain away rapidly, add several shovelfuls of coarse sand or other coarse soil amendments to the planting area. Plants will respond to an early-spring application of an all-purpose fertilizer.

Button Snakeroot is a long-lived, drought-resistant perennial requiring little maintenance from one year to the next; leave established plants undisturbed.

Uses in the Garden and Landscape

Use plants in the middle rank of the sunny border, where the clusters of round flower heads make an effective contrast to the foliage and flowers of neighboring plants. They will not make a dominant display in a mixed planting, but they are effective fillers and accent plants spotted throughout the border.

Naturalize plants in large groupings in dry, sunny areas where they will create interest from July to October. They combine effectively with Butterfly Weed, Black-eyed Susans (*Rudbeckia fulgida* and *Rudbeckia hirta*), and Purple Cone-flower. Both flowers and fruit are attractive in arrangements; they can be dried and used in winter arrangements by gathering heads before they expand fully and hanging them upside down in a well-ventilated area out of direct light.

Related Species

Eryngium aquaticum is found in marshes, ponds, and bogs on the coastal plain in the eastern United States. The long-petioled, oblanceolate leaves are attractive in aquatic and bog gardens and flowering and fruiting stems are very similar to *E. yuccifolium*. The leaves of *E. integrifolium* are rather insignificant, but the light blue flower heads are welcome in late summer and fall. Both species require constantly moist or wet soils, full sun, and propagate readily from seed.

Mountain Mint

Pycnanthemum incanum
Lamiaceae

Duration: perennial

Blooming time: July

Flower color: white, lavender

Height: 3–6 feet

Soil: average garden soil

Exposure: light shade

Description

The very aromatic Mountain Mint, which occurs in woodlands, thickets, fields, and along roadsides throughout the southeast, is rather similar to some of the native Monardas, but has small flowering heads.

The opposite, dark green, lanceolate leaves have serrate margins and are 1–4 inches (2.5–10 cm) long. When brushed or bruised, the leaves give off a strong minty odor that quickly permeates the garden. The square stems range in height from 3 to 6 feet, branch freely, and produce many terminal flower clusters approximately 1 inch (2.5 cm) across. The flowers bloom in late June and July, and the leaves just below the flowers are whitish. The small, two-lipped corollas, ¼ to ⅜ inch (7–9 mm) long, vary from white to lavender and are spotted with purple. Mountain Mint is a hardy perennial that, with minimal care, endures for many years.

Fruit and Seed

The plant's overall appearance changes little after flowering; the lower leaves remain green and the whitish upper leaves remain attractive. After the flowers fade, the flat seed head expands slightly and darkens. The individual calyx tubes, tightly arranged in the seed head, contain one to four individual nutlets less than 1/16 inch (1–1.7 mm) long. Looking down on the head (a hand lens may be necessary), you may be able to see the black, ripe nutlets in the base of the calyx tubes.

Seed Collection, Cleaning, and Storage

Collect seed in October or November after the first few frosts. Unlike the seed heads of Beebalm, which split apart after the seeds mature, the seed heads of Mountain Mint retain their structure well into the fall. To check for ripe seed, bend the stem over and shake it; if any black seeds fall out, collect the heads right away. If not, check again in a week.

When the seeds are ripe cut the seed heads and place them in a paper collection bag. Leave the bag open indoors, or spread the

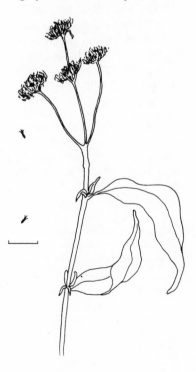

contents of the bag on a clean, dry surface, and let the heads air-dry for a few days. To dislodge the remaining seeds, shake the heads in the bag. Use sieves to remove most of the litter from the seed lot. Store seeds in a sealed, labeled container in the refrigerator.

Propagation

Seed. Sow seeds indoors or in the cold frame in early February. You can expect a high germination rate in one to two weeks; therefore, sow the seeds thinly and evenly in the flat. Seedlings are tiny and slow-growing and, after germination, they will require six to seven weeks in the seed flat before they are large enough to transplant to 3-inch pots. Let the roots fill up the pot—about another seven weeks—before moving the plants into the garden.

Pinch the tops several times during the growing season to create bushier specimens. Seedlings respond to a starter solution in the flat and to one or two weekly applications of an all-purpose liquid fertilizer in the pots. Sowing outdoors is difficult because the seeds are tiny and easily washed away or buried.

Cuttings. Tip cuttings are easy and reliable, taken in June. Remove the leaves from the lower half of 3-to-4-inch cuttings and insert at least one node in a sand and perlite rooting medium. Cuttings should be placed in an enclosed rooting chamber and misted several times a day. About 80 percent of the cuttings should

be rooted in three weeks, and 100 percent in seven weeks. Pot the rooted cuttings in 3- or 4-inch containers and transfer established plants into the garden in the fall.

Division. Mountain Mint spreads quickly, via short rhizomes, to form a dense mat. To make divisions, in late fall or early spring, just lift a mature clump from the garden and, using pruning shears or your hands, divide the clump into sections, 3 or 4 inches wide. The shallow root system makes this operation easy. Replant and water new divisions immediately.

Cultivation

Plant Mountain Mint in a partially shaded setting—such as the edge of a wooded area or under an open canopy of tall trees; in shadier sites the plant loses its compactness and in full direct sun the foliage may become scorched. Add a generous amount of organic matter to your garden soil and mulch the plants in the spring. The shallow root system develops quickly in a light soil, and will require watering during dry periods. To encourage more basal foliage, cut back the stems severely after collecting seeds; to avoid crowding, divide clumps every second season. Even in a very dry site Mountain Mint survives amazingly well, although it will not be as robust as you might want. However, in good growing conditions it can be quite invasive.

Uses in the Garden and Landscape

The mats of basal foliage are actively growing and very attractive during winter months. For best effects, plant in masses. Mountain Mint is quick to naturalize in a favorable setting, so use it as an entrance planting at the front of a wooded area or in openings along a woodland path. It is an excellent filler plant in the perennial border (as long as you remain alert to its aggressive nature in improved soil) and an effective backdrop for other native perennials, such as Butterfly Weed, Cardinal Flower, and *Penstemon smallii*. It is very useful and attractive as a "filler" in flower arrangements.

Related Species

The more coastal species, *Pycnanthemum flexuosum*, grows to 3 feet, branches above the middle, and has narrow leaves and flat, white flowering heads. *P. tenuifolium*, with very narrow, linear leaves, is well adapted to low moist areas. Propagation and cultivation are essentially the same for these species as for *P. incanum*.

Production Notes

Take cuttings in mid-summer and root them under mist. Transplant rooted cuttings into 4-inch containers. Overwinter containers and offer for sale in the spring. Regular pinching in containers will produce more compact plants.

If propagating by division, field-grow the plants in an open sunny plot and mulch heavily. With little or no irrigation, first-year plants spread to nearly 2 feet across. Make small divisions—an inch across—in the fall, pot in 4-inch containers, and offer for sale the next spring.

Turk's-Cap Lily

Lilium superbum
Liliaceae

Duration: perennial

Blooming time: July

Flower color: orange or reddish

Height: to 9 feet

Soil: deep, fertile

Exposure: open shade

Description

Lilies are among the oldest cultivated plants in the world. Hybrid and native lilies have long been revered by American gardeners for their flamboyant yet graceful blooms and their stately habits of growth. Although the native species have a reputation for being "difficult" to propagate, many gardeners report success with them, especially with *Lilium superbum*.

Turk's-Cap Lily occurs in wet meadows, swampy woods, and mountain coves throughout nearly the whole eastern United States. Sturdy, upright, purple-tinted stems, as tall as 9 feet, arise from whitish bulbs with overlapping scales. The lanceolate to elliptic leaves, 3–7 inches long, appear in whorls of five to twenty along the stem. On mature plants up to fifty nodding, or pendulous, flowers may be borne in a loosely branched inflorescence. An individual flower is magnificent: the three sepals and three petals are strongly reflexed, 2–3 inches (5–7.5 cm) long and ½–¾ inch (1.25–1.85 cm) wide. Each is green at the base, then yellowish, spotted with brown, and orange or reddish toward the apex. Six slender filaments capped by brownish anthers and a long style with a three-lobed stigma protrude from the center of the flower.

Fruit and Seed

Capsules turn from greenish to brown as they develop over a six-to-eight-week period after flowering. At maturity the elliptic cap-sules are 1½ inches (3.75–5 cm) long and ¾ inch (1.85 cm) across and have six prominent seams, or sutures. A single capsule holds hundreds of seeds neatly stacked in six narrow compartments, or locules. The lustrous, golden brown seeds are thin, nearly triangular, and about ¼ inch (6 mm) long.

Seed Collection, Cleaning, and Storage

Despite the nodding blooms, the capsules are upright. When the seeds are mature, the capsules are tan, dry, and papery in texture and they split along three sutures. To remove the seeds, simply open the capsule and let the seeds spill out. Before cleaning,

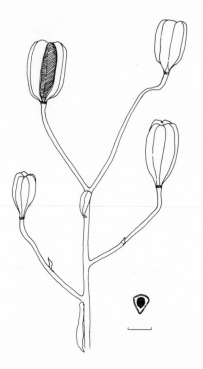

examine capsules for insect damage. Look for holes in the capsule and for insects or larvae among the seeds. If insects are present, remove seeds and fumigate immediately with No-Pest Strips. (Refer to the section on seed cleaning for the fumigation procedure.) If you do not plan to sow the seeds immediately upon collection, store them in a labeled airtight container in the refrigerator.

Propagation

Seed. Proper pregermination treatments, which are essential to successful seedling production with this species, can save gardeners an entire growing season. If you sowed fresh seed outdoors, most seedlings would not appear until their second season, eighteen months from sowing. The seeds of Turk's-Cap Lily have a complex dormancy; they need a warm, moist period, during which they develop into small white bulbs, followed by a cold period, and finally another warm period, when the plant finally puts out shoots. To meet these requirements, and produce a crop of seedlings the first season, layer the seeds in dampened, whole-fiber sphagnum moss or peat moss in a sealed jar or freezer container and store at room temperature for six to eight weeks, by which time small bulbs should have developed. Then store the jar in the refrigerator for an additional six weeks or more. Finally, plant the bulbs outdoors in fertile, well-drained nursery beds. Time these treatments so that

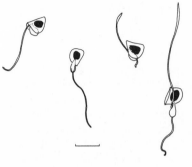

planting of the bulbs can be carried out in the spring when the danger of frost is past.

First-year plants send up a single leaf which persists for only a portion of the growing season. Lily seedlings are very sensitive to transplanting while they are in active growth; to a build-up of soluble salts in the soil or medium, usually caused by fertilizer in the soil or water; or even to merely moving the seedling tray or pot from one location to another if this causes a change in the plant's environment. Any of these may force the plants into early dormancy. (Seedlings may appear to have died, but do not discard without checking thoroughly for healthy dormant bulbs beneath the surface of the growing medium.) Plants often take five years or longer to reach flowering size. Transplant bulbs into their permanent location when they go dormant after their second growing season.

Division. Mature, well-established plants may produce smaller "daughter bulbs" on short rhizomes which may be divided in the fall by severing the bulbs from the rhizome. Replant the

bulbs immediately and water thoroughly.

The most common method of vegetative increase for this species is scale division. In late summer or fall, after the plants flower, dig a bulb from the garden and remove the outer two rows of scales; replant the mother bulb. Reject any scales showing signs of injury or deterioration and dust the remaining healthy scales with a fungicide, then row out the scales in a nursery bed. Planted at a depth of 1–2 inches, the scales will develop bulblets at their bases. Allow bulblets to grow on in the bed for two years; then transplant them into a permanent spot in the garden.

Scales can also be handled in a manner identical to that described for propagation by seed. After removing them from the bulb, layer scales in a moist medium, place them in a sealed container, subject them to alternating eight-week periods of warm (70°F) and cold (35–40°F), and then transplant the resulting bulblets into nursery beds.

Cultivation

To cultivate Turk's-Cap Lily successfully, you must provide three things. First, plants need a deep, fertile soil kept evenly moist and cool; prepare the planting area to a depth of 1 foot, working in generous amounts of organic matter. Second, plants must receive at least several hours of direct sunlight during the day. Third, they need some protection from gusts and damaging winds; plant bulbs in or near a buffer of shrubs, such as azalea or rhododendron, where the plants will also benefit from an acid soil condition.

Water plants deeply during summer dry periods; to conserve moisture apply a 2-to-3-inch mulch of rotted leaves at the base of the plants in spring. Plants also benefit from a spring dressing of bonemeal or superphosphate. Bulbs should be planted at a depth of 2 inches. When planting in groups, space the plants 1–2 feet apart; plants should be divided when the stems appear crowded and thin. If stems lean and require staking, insert a sturdy pole a few inches from the plant (to avoid disturbing bulbs) and loosely secure the stem to the stake with light cord. Coarse, sharp-edged, 1½-to-2-inch gravel liberally incorporated into the soil around the bulbs gives good protection against tunneling rodents.

Once established, bulbs endure in the garden for many years and can be left undisturbed indefinitely, or until new plants are needed.

Uses in the Garden and Landscape

Single plants spotted in the rear of the perennial border make an eye-catching mid-summer flowering display. Plants are also effective against evergreen backgrounds, where the brilliant orange flowers appear to be suspended in front of the darker foliage. Naturalize plants in areas where the soil remains moist during the growing season; woodland "openings," moist meadows, and along the edges of wooded areas are ideal locations. Turk's-Cap Lily may be grown in deep containers, provided watering is regular through the growing season.

Plants are also attractive in fruit and useful in dried arrangements, where the numerous upright capsules invite comparison with ornate candelabra.

Related Species

The other native lilies are all enormously attractive and, whenever possible, should be incorporated into your garden. They may be divided into two groups: species with upright flowers and those with pendulous flowers. Species with upright flowers include *Lilium philadelphicum* (Wood Lily), which grows to four feet, produces from one to five orange flowers, spotted with purple, borne terminally on the stem, and occurs in open woods, balds, and meadows, and *Lilium catesbaei* (Pine Lily), which grows to from 1 to 3 feet, bears one or two red flowers, and occurs in moist pine woods, savannas, and bogs. Species with pendulous flowers include *Lilium grayi* (Gray's Lily), which grows to 6 feet, has up to nine or more beautiful reddish, bell-shaped flowers, and occurs only locally in a few southeastern states in moist mountain meadows, woods, balds, and openings; *Lilium canadense* (Canada Lily), which grows to from 2 to 7 feet, bears as many as twenty reddish orange flowers, the petals flaring outward, and is found in wet meadows, bogs, and balds; *Lilium michauxii* (Carolina Lily), which reaches 1 to 4 feet, bears up to six reddish yellow flowers similar in shape to those of *Lilium superbum*, and occurs in drier upland woods and thickets. Propagation of all of these lilies is by scale division and seed.

Passion-flower, Maypops

Passiflora incarnata
Passifloraceae

Duration: perennial

Blooming time: June–July

Flower color: pale blue, white

Height: to 20 feet

Soil: fertile, well-drained

Exposure: sun

Description

With its spectacular, complex flowers and sweet-smelling fruits, Passion-flower has long attracted the interest of gardeners. Although from a plant family with a primarily tropical distribution, this native species is hardy where the average minimum winter temperature is 0–10°F and marginally hardy even in somewhat colder areas. Passion-flower is found throughout the southeastern and south central United States in fields and sandy thickets, along fence rows, and on roadsides.

Supported by solitary tendrils borne in the leaf axils, the vines can climb to 20 feet, but more commonly they trail over the ground or clamber over shrubbery. The alternate, usually three-lobed leaves are from 2 ½ to 6 inches (6–15 cm) long and wide and have finely serrated margins. At the top of the petiole (at the base of the leaf blade) are two prominent nectar-bearing glands.

The flowers, which are borne in the leaf axils, have five sepals, 1–1½ inches (2.5–3.5 cm) long, green below and whitish above, each with a single hornlike appendage near its apex, quite noticeable when the flowers are in bud. The five petals are pale blue to white and 1¼–1½ inches (3–4 cm) long. The corona, the most striking feature of the flower, is formed by several series of numerous threadlike filaments which are up to 1¼ inches (3 cm) long, white or lavender and banded with purple. The five prominent stamens are united at their bases, forming a tube; the pistil, in the center of the stamen tube, has three styles with three capitate, or headlike, stigmas. Maypops flower from late May to July, and occasionally thereafter.

Fruit and Seed

The leathery berries develop during a two-to-three-month period after flowering. They are broadly elliptic in outline, 1½–2¾ inches (4–7 cm) long (egg shape and size), and turn from green to yellowish as the seeds mature. The numerous ovoid seeds, about ¼ inch (4–6 mm) long, darken from medium to dark brown and are finely netted. Each seed is entirely enclosed by a clear gelatinous aril.

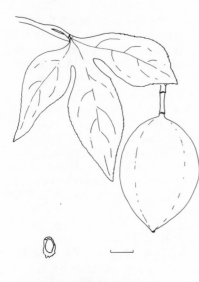

Seed Collection, Cleaning, and Storage

Depending on when the plants flower, seeds may be mature and the berries harvested as early as July or as late as October. If the berry is soft and yellowish and beginning to pucker and shrivel, break it open. If the seeds are brown, they are ready to collect; if the seeds are still whitish, check again in a week.

The berries should be cleaned within a few days of collection, if not immediately, as they are likely to rot and attract fruit flies and other insects. The seeds are easier to handle and sow if the sticky aril is removed prior to storage. This does not appear to affect germination.

To clean, scrape the seeds out of the berry and into a sieve. Run a stream of hot water over the seeds and stir them to remove the aril, continuing until the seeds are clean. Store seeds moist, layered in whole-fiber sphagnum moss in a sealed, labeled container and refrigerated until time of sowing.

Propagation

Seed. Whether seeds are sown in an outdoor seedbed upon collection or in the greenhouse after storage, germination, which may take two years, is poor and sporadic. Direct sowing in a fertile, well-drained outdoor seedbed is recommended and it should produce enough seedlings of Passion-flower for your garden. Once established, the vines can provide cuttings and divisions for further increase.

Allow the seedlings to grow three or four leaves before transplanting them into the garden. Where conditions are favorable, young plants grow rapidly, with a few flowers likely toward the end of their first season.

Cuttings. Take 6-to-8-inch stem cuttings early in the season, in May or June. Remove the leaves from the lower half and insert a node in a well-drained medium consisting of equal parts sand and perlite under mist or in a rooting chamber, where high humidity can be maintained.

If you are using a rooting chamber, mist the foliage when dry and keep the medium evenly moist. Keep the cuttings out of direct sunlight and ventilate the chamber to avoid excessive heat buildup.

When the cuttings have developed a mass of roots, transplant them to 4-inch pots and fertilize weekly with an all-purpose liquid fertilizer for the remainder of the growing season. In the fall transplant the rooted cuttings into the garden or overwinter them in a protected spot in the nursery for transplanting to the garden the next spring.

Division. Once Passion-flower is established, numerous suckers appear in the general area of parent plants. Remove the suckers and attached roots with a shovel, replant, and water.

Cultivation

Establish plants in full sun or in areas receiving at least a half-day's direct sunlight, such as at the edge of a wooded area. Although clay soils are acceptable, the plants thrive, suckering freely, in a fertile, well-drained soil amended with generous amounts of rotted leaves, compost, aged manure, and sand. Plants also benefit from applications of an all-purpose fertilizer several times during the season and by a reworking of the top 2–3 inches of soil in the spring.

Where Passion-flower is to be grown in close proximity to other garden plants, confine the vines to a trellis or other support and remove suckers regularly when they threaten to climb on nearby plants. Other suitable supports for vines are fences, tree trunks, and a post with a wire cage around it. To encourage branching, pinch the plants back during their first growing season. In the spring, thin crowded vines by removing older stems, which can be used for cuttings.

Uses in the Garden and Landscape

Passion-flower is best displayed—and easiest to maintain—in areas where it can climb or sprawl unimpeded, such as at a wood's edge. The herbaceous vines make an attractive seasonal screen along a fence, and in the Deep South leaves may persist through the winter months. Where they can be tended regularly, the plants can be trained on a trellis or post in the rear of the herbaceous border. Vines may be grown in large planters and trained, or allowed, to flow over the sides, but such container plants will require annual thinning and division.

Related Species

Passiflora lutea is a climbing or trailing vine which grows to about 15 feet long. The attractive greenish yellow flowers, an inch across, which bloom during the summer months, give way to a purple or black berry and attractive yellow foliage in the fall. These vines are more tolerant of shade than *P. incarnata*; otherwise, propagation and cultivation requirements are the same.

Meadow-Beauty

Rhexia mariana
Melastomataceae

Duration: perennial

Blooming time: July–September

Flower color: white, rose

Height: to 2½ feet

Soil: moist or wet garden soil

Exposure: full sun

Description

Rhexias are not common in American gardens, which is unfortunate, for their abundant rose, pink, or white flowers provide many ornamental possibilities in summer flower beds or in naturalized areas and they propagate readily from seed. This species of Meadow-Beauty occurs in marshes, meadows, savannas, bogs, and roadside ditches throughout the southeast and as far north as Massachusetts.

The slender, lightly hairy, angled stems can reach 2½ feet and bear attractive pairs of densely hairy, elliptic or lance-shaped leaves which may be as long as 2½ inches (6.5 cm) and have three distinctive nerves, or veins. The flowers of *R. mariana*, which are 2 inches (5 cm) across and significantly larger than the flowers of some of the other Rhexias, are loosely arranged in the leaf axils at the top of the stem. The four sepals and the four white or bright rose to purple petals are attached to the summit of a cylindrical floral tube, or hypanthium, as is the cluster of eight yellow orange stamens that stand out boldly against the petals.

These plants typically form colonies via a network of long, slender, horizontal roots, or rhizomes, running just below the surface of the soil.

Fruit and Seed

The showy petals of an individual flower last only a day or so, and immediately after they wither and drop off, the hypanthium and fruit enlarge and become strongly urceolate, or urn-shaped, and turn from green to reddish and then to a copper tone when the seeds are mature. The numerous crescent-shaped seeds are light brown, and very small, less than a millimeter long. The attractive fruiting structures are outstanding in dried arrangements.

Seed Collection, Cleaning, and Storage

Seeds are mature and ready for collection near the end of the growing season, early-to-mid October, when the capsules dry out and become brittle. At close range the distinctive capsules stand out in the garden, but it is not a bad idea to tie a piece of flagging around a stem or two

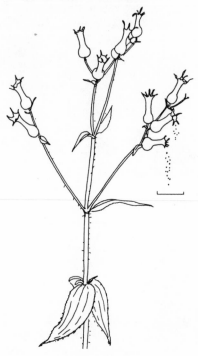

194

when plants are in flower to assure that they are not overlooked when the capsules mature and the seeds begin to drop.

Break open a few capsules and, if seeds are yellowish, tan, or brown, collect them right away. To clean, crush the capsules and allow the seeds to air-dry for a few days; then place the capsules and seeds in a bag and shake; pour the contents of the bag into a sieve to separate the seeds from the pieces of broken capsules. Store the seeds dry in an airtight, labeled container and refrigerate until time of sowing.

Propagation

Seed. Because the seeds are tiny and easily washed or smothered in an outdoor seedbed, sow seeds in flats or pots indoors or in the cold frame in late winter. To prevent damping off, cover seeds with a thin layer of sand, or milled sphagnum or charcoal dust after they are sown. A high percentage of seeds should germinate over a one-to-two-week period. The seedlings are very small and slow-growing, however, and require regular attention.

The slender stems and roots are easily damaged during transplanting; gently pry small groups of seedlings up from the seed flat, taking care to disturb root systems as little as possible, and transplant each group of seedlings into a 3-inch pot and allow the plants to grow until roots fill the container, about six to eight weeks. Then separate the individual plants out of the group and move them into the garden.

Do not allow young plants to become dry in containers and feed them weekly with an all-purpose liquid fertilizer. If planted in the garden in May, the plants are likely to bloom in late summer.

Cuttings. We have experienced much success with cuttings rooted under mist. Cuttings may also be successfully rooted in a chamber where high humidity can be maintained. Take stem cuttings 3–4 inches long at any time during the growing season and remove any flowers or flower buds. Remove the lower leaves from the cuttings and insert at least one node in a mix of equal parts sand and perlite. When cuttings develop a cluster of roots, in about three or four weeks, transplant them to 3-inch pots and overwinter in a protected spot outside. Move them into the garden the following spring.

Division. Where plants have established themselves in the garden and spread to become a colony with many stems, division is a very practical and easy method of increase. With a trowel, just remove a clump that includes several stems, replant, and water thoroughly. Dividing the plants in the fall, after flowering, will allow the new plants the fall and winter months to reestablish before they resume active growth the next spring.

Cultivation

Grow Meadow-Beauty in sunny, open sites. Plants thrive in moist or wet soils that contain plenty of sand and peat moss or other organic matter, although a clay soil amended with a shovelful of sand per plant also provides a suitable growing medium. Regular watering during summer dry periods produces more attractive plants. Division or thinning of plants is necessary only as a means of increase, as you will want to encourage plants to spread freely and form masses in the garden.

Uses in the Garden and Landscape

Plants are most effectively displayed where they can be naturalized. Combine Meadow-Beauty with other wild flowers that have a preference for wet, sunny areas, such as the Sabatias, Marshallias, Gaillardias, and Ludwigias. Bogs, roadside ditches, or low, sunny areas are ideal sites in which to establish plants.

Provided the soil remains moist through the growing season, Meadow-Beauties can be worked into late-summer and fall color schemes in the sunny border. Use them as filler plants in the first rank of the border, where they are less conspicuous prior to flowering. The stalks of flowers (although short-lived) and the developing capsules are outstanding in cut arrangements.

Related Species

Rhexia lutea has yellow flowers, blooms in spring and early summer, and grows to 2 feet. *Rhexia virginica* has pinkish petals, blooms throughout the summer, and grows to 3 feet. *Rhexia alifa-*

nus has purple petals, also blooms throughout the summer, and grows to 3 feet. *Rhexia aristosa*, with distinctive bristles along the rim of the hypanthium, has purple petals, and grows to 2½ feet. *Rhexia mariana* has several varieties that are similar in nearly all respects and have petals ranging from purple to white.

Production Notes

Sow seeds in the greenhouse in January and step up young plants first to 3- and then to 4-inch containers and market the plants later that season when in flower. In May move the containers to a lightly shaded setting outdoors, watering as needed.

Nodding Onion

Allium cernuum
Liliaceae

Duration: perennial

Blooming time: July

Flower color: pink

Height: 1–2 feet

Soil: well-drained

Exposure: open

Description

The Nodding Onion, found throughout much of the eastern United States mostly in open, rocky woods and meadows, is related to the Wild Onion and Field Garlic, but when the leaves or bulbs of this species are crushed or bruised, they give off only a mild and inoffensive odor. The name should not deter us from taking advantage of its outstanding ornamental possibilities.

The plant bears the familiar trademarks of the Alliums: a prominent bulb, leafless flower stalks terminating in umbels, narrow flattened or rounded leaves, and a plump, rounded capsule containing small black seeds. The bulb is covered with a thin coat, darkening with age to reddish purple. The slender, grass-like leaves may grow to nearly 2 feet, and the smooth scapes, or flower stalks, taller than the leaves, terminate in an umbellate cluster of flowers. There is a sharp downward arch at the top of the scape causing the inflorescence to nod, prompting the specific epithet *cernuum*, from the Latin *cernuus*—"with the head facing toward the earth." The pink, purple, or pinkish white flowers remain for about two weeks in July.

Fruit and Seed

In fruit the scape may straighten. The small, lobed, three-valved capsules, less than ¼ inch (6 mm) long, develop during a four-to-six-week period after flowering. They remain green as they develop, turning tan or straw colored shortly before they dehisce. There are one to three small black seeds, about 2 millimeters long, per locule.

Seed Collection, Cleaning, and Storage

As these plants are not conspicuous after their blooming period, mark potential seed stalks for collecting with colored yarn or other flagging while they are still in flower. In mid-August, press open a few capsules and, if the seeds are black or have some black coloration, collect the capsules immediately.

If seed is to be stored, air-dry the capsules indoors for a few days or until they become papery. Seeds may be effectively dislodged by putting the capsules in a large paper bag and shaking vigorously. An appreciable amount of litter—broken pieces of capsule—will accumulate with the seed, but this can be removed by sieving. Store cleaned seed dry, in a sealed, labeled container, and refrigerate until time of sowing. Under these conditions the seeds remain viable at least three years.

Propagation

Seed. The key factor here is not so much when you sow but where. The germination percentage is essentially the same whether seeds are sown outdoors or inside, but the seedlings grow faster when seed is sown in a fertile, well-drained outdoor seedbed. Because roots naturally tend to develop to 6 inches or deeper, stunted, inferior plants will result if seedlings are confined to a seed flat or small container. If you do plan an indoor sowing, transplant seedlings into the garden or a lightly shaded nursery bed when three or four leaves appear.

Seedling growth is slow during much of the first season, with only several wiry leaves showing for the first few months. Container plants are likely to remain in this condition through their first year, whereas field-grown specimens from fall planting put on considerable growth and are ready for removal into the garden in the early fall. Where the long, white, fibrous roots are not restricted by containers, second-year plants can be expected to flower. Add an extra measure of

sand to your growing medium to assure proper drainage and help avoid crown rot, which is a possibility in wet soils.

Division. Mature plants produce clusters of bulbs an inch or so below the soil. Individual bulbs have their own roots and tufts of leaves and are easily separated from the group. Divide plants in late summer after seed has been collected or in the spring when the leaves first appear. Replant the bulbs at their original depth and water at once.

Cultivation

Plants are excellent garden subjects when grown in well-drained soils of only average richness; a rich soil, high in organic matter that retains moisture, produces weak specimens whose leaves and scapes are likely to fall over. If you wish to establish plants in a prepared planting bed, add generous amounts of sand and gravel to the soil to ensure good drainage. A local gardener in central North Carolina has produced robust, full-flowering second-year plants in a gravelly clay soil amended with a small amount of humus.

Plants thrive in open settings, such as a woodland clearing. As these plants mature, the bulbs become crowded and flower production is reduced; divide your plants every third year or when eight to ten bulbs appear in the

clump. Nodding Onion is tolerant of moderately dry soils and requires watering only during periods of extended dry weather.

Uses in the Garden and Landscape

Nodding Onion is a good choice for the rock garden, where it combines well with Stonecrop and *Coreopsis auriculata*. It is also well displayed in the front rank of the herbaceous border in groups that include no fewer than five to seven plants. Also the bulbs may be interplanted in the border with shallow-rooted groundcovers, such as Green-and-Gold, Blue-eyed Grass, and Crested Dwarf Iris; the latter two plants are aggressive and may need to be periodically curbed when they begin to encroach upon the less aggressive Nodding Onion. The plants may be naturalized in areas where the soil is well drained. Flowers are effective in cut arrangements, but are short-lived.

Related Species

Allium tricoccum, Ramps, which grows in rich woods, is renowned for the pungent, often overpowering garliclike aroma of its flat leaves and bulb. The foliage is short-lived, however; typically, it is gone by the time the cream-colored flowers appear in June.

Rose Mallow, Wild Cotton

Hibiscus moscheutos
Malvaceae

Duration: perennial

Blooming time: July

Flower color: white

Height: to 6 feet

Soil: garden soil

Exposure: sun

Description

Rose Mallow is native to the margins of swamp forests, wet meadows, and brackish marshes in the southeastern United States. Its large shrubby habit (to 6 feet tall) and showy flowers are welcome

in the garden in the mid-summer "green interlude" between the profusion of blooms of early summer and early fall.

Rose Mallow produces numerous sturdy stems, arising from a single crown, with large, alternate, 3-pointed leaves, up to 6 inches long that are grayish green above and usually whitish and densely hairy below. The five-petaled, creamy white or, rarely, pink flowers are borne in the upper leaf axils and measure 4–8 inches across. Each petal has a conspicuous red or burgundy band at its base, creating a darker flower center from which a tubular column of yellow stamens extends. The opening flower buds are interesting to observe: a dozen or so very narrow bracts surround the green sepals and as the bud opens, the sepals and bracts fold completely back.

Fruit and Seed

Shortly after flowering, smooth, rounded light green capsules appear on the plant. The capsule tapers abruptly at the apex to form a beak. The persistent calyx and the involucral bracts enclose the capsule in a leafy green base. Over the next four to five weeks, the capsules enlarge and turn dark brown. At maturity the capsules, which have grown to 1½ inches (3.5–4 cm) long, hold numerous dark brown seeds in five compartments, or locules. A single mature plant produces dozens of capsules, and as they open, the plant again becomes rather attractive, or at least interesting.

Seed Collection, Cleaning, and Storage

The seeds are dark brown and ready for collection in late August or early September. To make cleaning easier, let the capsules open on the plant before collecting them; the capsules open slowly for about two weeks, and there is little danger of seed drop during this time. Snip the capsules from the stems, drop them into a bag, and allow them to air-dry for a few days prior to cleaning. Place twenty or so capsules in a bag and shake vigorously; most of the seeds will separate from their locules but any that still remain can be removed by hand.

You are likely to notice little boll weevils in with the seeds. To fumigate the seed lot place small pieces of No-Pest Strip and the seeds in a tightly closed plastic bag and store in a dark, out-of-the-way place for two weeks. (If you happen to touch the strips, wash your hands right away in warm, soapy water.) Separate out the good seeds, dry, and store in a sealed, labeled container in the refrigerator.

Propagation

Seed. Rose Mallow is easily raised from seeds, whether started indoors or outside. In late winter sow the stored seeds in a flat using ¼-inch spacing (the large seeds are easily spaced by hand) and expect good germination within a week. The seedlings can be moved to individual containers when they are an inch or so in height and have three or four true leaves—about four weeks from your sowing date. Apply a starter solution to the seedlings in the flat and later an all-purpose fertilizer to container plants on a weekly basis. In another four to six weeks the young plants should be large enough to transfer into the garden.

For outdoor sowing, sow stored seeds thinly in a prepared bed after danger from frost is passed. Seedling growth is rapid at this time of year; pot the seedlings when they are large enough and move the plants into the garden in September.

Cuttings. Tip cuttings root readily in a sand and perlite medium. Take them in early July and not before. Remove flower buds from the tips and the leaves from the lower half of the cuttings. A small rooting chamber or a cold frame equipped with shade cloth provides an adequate rooting environment. Mist cuttings several times during the day. The cuttings should be well rooted and large enough for containers in three to four weeks.

Cultivation

Even though it occurs in wet areas in nature, Rose Mallow does not require excessive moisture in cultivation. A constantly wet, or even moist, soil is not necessary, but of course such a site makes a natural location for this plant. Make sure, though, that young plants do not dry out during their first season.

Mature plants seem able to do without additional watering during periods of normal rainfall, but bloom less vigorously if left unwatered during droughts. A site receiving at least a half day's full sun is best. Shadier exposures produce a leggy, less attractive plant. Average garden soil is sufficient for Rose Mallow. Since plants can spread to nearly 5 feet across, allow plenty of room in your planting area. Older plants with many stems may require some staking.

Uses in the Garden and Landscape

In the sunny border Rose Mallow is effective treated as a mid-summer shrub. Plant it singly or as a background grouping. Because it is late to break dormancy in the spring, low-growing spring-blooming plants may be planted nearby. The plant is a natural at a pond's edge or in other sunny wet areas, or use it close to the house, in front of taller evergreen plants, or in front of any darker background. Take care to avoid putting other plants too close lest they be dwarfed and lost in a mixed planting. The seed stalks are interesting in dried arrangements.

Unfortunately, this is one native plant which is a preferred food of Japanese beetles. Uncontrolled, the beetles can make the plant unsightly. It is worth the trouble to try to control the beetles, however.

Related Species

Halberd-leaved Marsh Mallow (*H. militaris*) is similar in appearance, with smaller pink flowers 4 inches across. It grows to 6 feet or more and has fewer branches. It is also effective in the garden border or in a naturally wet area. Propagation and cultivation are the same as for *H. moscheutos*.

Production Notes

Sow seeds in mid-summer and move seedlings directly into 4-inch pots. Overwinter pots and offer for sale the following spring.

Joe-Pye-Weed, Queen-of-the-Meadow

Eupatorium fistulosum
Asteraceae

Duration: perennial

Blooming time: summer

Flower color: pink to lavender

Height: 10 feet

Soil: moist or wet

Exposure: full to filtered sun

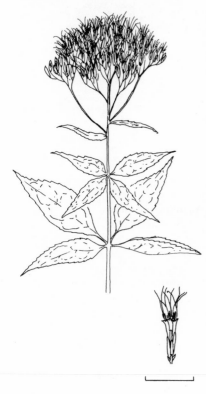

Description

The wild species of *Eupatorium*, or Thoroughworts, with their many different habits, unusual textures, distinctive foliage, and striking inflorescences, are a gift to gardeners. We should be taken to task for not using them more. They are useful in formal border plantings or in naturalized areas, require minimal, if any, maintenance, and are easy to propagate.

Joe-Pye-Weed can grow to 10 feet and taller where the soil is kept moist through the season. The narrow lanceolate leaves are arranged in whorls along the stem, which is hollow, usually waxy (glaucous), and conspicuously spotted with purple. The tiered effect of the foliage on stout stems gives the plant a certain grace and lightness, which softens an otherwise imposing appearance. The simple, narrow leaves are up to 10 inches long, 4 inches wide, toothed along their margins, prominently veined beneath, and of a soft leathery texture.

The large domed or broadly rounded terminal inflorescence, up to 20 inches across and many branched, is conspicuous even at a distance, and may persist well into October. Actually, the branches bearing the tiny florets are also arranged in whorls. The flower heads of *Eupatorium* consist of a cluster of very small disk flowers, 2 to 3 millimeters broad, which in this species are pink to lavender. Plants flower in late July or August and occur throughout the eastern United States in alluvial woods, meadows, bogs, and marshes.

Fruit and Seed

The shape of the inflorescence remains essentially unchanged after the bloom period except that as the nutlets develop over the next three to five weeks it becomes fluffier and the pink and lavender coloration gives way to dull brown. The nutlets are small (about 3 mm long), shiny black, five angled, and tapered sharply from apex to base, with tawny pappus bristles attached.

Seed Collection, Cleaning, and Storage

The nutlets are mature in mid-to-late September and remain attached to the receptacle of the seed head until about mid-October. Typically, only a small percentage of the tiny nutlets develop; the viable nutlets are usually plump and swollen, while those without embryos will be thin and shriveled. If you break some of them open, you will likely find that most are hollow.

To collect, snip off the entire top of the plant, or individual heads, and place them upside down in a large paper bag. Shake or pick loose the nutlets in an area free of drafts or seed will blow everywhere. It is helpful to shake large dried seed heads in a large plastic trash bag to loosen the seeds and then transfer the lot into smaller containers. Cleaning can be simplified if you allow the nutlets to expand fully

crown that has a massive system of fibrous roots. Insert a sharp shovel or spade between two stems and section off a piece of the plant that includes a single stem and a cluster of roots. Stems on the periphery of the clump are easier to remove than those in the center. Replant new divisions immediately and water thoroughly.

Cultivation

As their native habitat suggests, these plants are adapted to full or filtered sunlight and moist or wet soils. Seedlings of Joe-Pye-Weed should not be allowed to dry out during their first season; thereafter plants do not demand regular watering except during periods of extreme dry weather. Joe-Pye-Weed is not particular as to the soil it grows in, although a planting area that has been well worked and improved by the addition of organic matter produces faster-growing plants. In time, plants can become crowded, a condition that can cause stems to bend and detract from the plant's appearance. To avoid crowding, divide the plants every two to three years.

Uses in the Garden and Landscape

Joe-Pye-Weed can form the background of the sunny perennial border in late summer and fall. Establish the plants at the very rear of the border, allowing three feet between plants. Essentially everything in front of the Joe-Pyes

and loosen naturally within the involucre. It is difficult, and not necessary, to obtain a perfectly clean seed lot—many of the bracts that make up the involucre will mix harmlessly with the achenes. If not planted when collected, store seeds in a sealed container and refrigerate until time of sowing.

Propagation

Seed. Seeds may be sown directly outdoors upon collection in the fall for germination the following spring. Alternatively sow seeds thickly in a flat indoors or in the cold frame in late winter; germination will likely be spotty. Seedlings are large enough to transplant into 3-inch containers four to five weeks from sowing. They do not demand much attention, but do seem to grow faster when the soil is kept evenly moist. Plants should be moved into the garden after the last frost; they should reach their mature height, or nearly so, and flower during their second season.

Division. Divide plants in the fall as they go dormant or in the spring as soon as shoots first appear. Stems grow from a large will be highlighted, especially plants that develop rounded habits—Boltonia, Rough-leaved Goldenrod, the native Asters, and *Rudbeckia triloba*, for example. Where naturally moist, sunny conditions are available (such as a roadside ditch), naturalize Joe-Pye-Weed with Bur-Marigold, Ironweed, and Seashore Mallow. Its size notwithstanding, Joe-Pye-Weed may not dominate a mixed planting—it will simply be the tallest plant in your garden and should be regarded as the architectural high point in your design. Whether in flower or fruit, the plants are outstanding in arrangements.

Related Species

Eupatorium maculatum is very similar and may be grown and used in the same manner; *E. dubium* and *E. purpureum* are also similar but are shorter plants—to 4 feet; *E. perfoliatum*, Boneset, has opposite leaves that completely surround the stem; *E. rugosum*, white snakeroot, common in old fields, pastures, and open woodlands, is excellent as a filler plant for the border and in arrangements; and *E. coelestinum*, or Ageratum, with many horticultural varieties, has violet flowers and is suitable for the front of the border or naturalized area. Two species, *E. capillifolium*, Dog Fennel, and *E. hysso-pifolium*, both considered common roadside and pasture weeds, are quite beautiful in naturalized areas and in the large perennial border. Dog Fennel is quite tall, head high or more, and has attractive threadlike foliage. When the top foot or so of its many stems is covered with countless minute heads of white disk flowers, the plant has a gossamer appearance. *E. hyssopifolium*, 2–3 feet tall, consists of several stiffly erect stems with linear leaves and wide rounded or flat-topped branches of minute heads of white disk flowers. The plant is spectacular in fruit, as the white pappus bristles of the developing achenes produce billowy, cloudlike effects.

Cardinal Flower

Lobelia cardinalis
Campanulaceae

Duration: short-lived perennial

Blooming time: August–September

Flower color: red

Height: 2–5 feet

Soil: average, moist

Exposure: sun to shade

Description

Cardinal Flower occurs in marshes, wet meadows, and low woods and along stream banks throughout the eastern United States. Its bright red flowers, considered among the most vivid in nature, bloom for a month or longer in late summer.

The leafy, unbranched flowering stems, which may grow to 4 or 5 feet, arise from compact basal rosettes which are prominent throughout the winter months but are often absent during the bloom period.

The numerous two-lipped flowers, each an inch (2.5 cm) long, occur in a dense, terminal raceme, which is a sure attractor of hummingbirds, the main pollinators of this plant. The anthers are at the end of a slender red filament tube extending out over the lower lip of the corolla, where it is perfectly placed to transfer pollen to the head of a hummingbird hovering to collect nectar from the corolla tube.

More versatile in the garden than its natural habitat would suggest, Cardinal Flower need not be confined to shaded or wet environments, but can be used freely in open areas with only average soil moisture.

Fruit and Seed

The round developing seed capsules are evident on the lower portion of the stalk while the flowers on the upper portion of the still-growing, or indeterminate, inflorescence are still in bloom or even bud. The spherical capsules expand to approximately ⅜ inch (1 cm) in diameter and turn brown as the seeds mature. The seeds are small, less than 1/16 inch (1 mm) long, and numerous.

Seed Collection, Cleaning, and Storage

Seeds are usually brown by mid-October, but some early blooming plants may yield mature seeds before this time; on the other hand, a dry September may delay ripening. As seeds approach maturity, the capsule opens slightly at its apex, an indication that seed dispersal is beginning. Make sure to check capsules at both upper and lower portions of the stalk.

When the seeds are ripe, snip the stalk below the bottom-most capsule and deposit upside down in a paper collection bag. Bring the stalks inside, open the bag, and allow them to air-dry for a few days. Close the bag and shake it vigorously, then check the bottom of the bag for loose seeds—you may find enough there to satisfy your needs. If not, remove the capsules from the stalk and crush them with a rolling pin. Use a sieve to separate the seeds from litter.

Store the dry cleaned seed in a sealed, labeled container and refrigerate. Cardinal Flower seeds have a "shelf life" of at least three years when kept in this manner.

Propagation

Seed. Some germination can be expected from seeds sown immediately upon collection. A two-month cold period, however, promotes a much higher germination rate and seeds sown indoors in late winter may produce blooming plants by early fall.

Take the time to sow Cardinal Flower seeds very thinly and evenly; a spacing of ¼ inch is ideal, if very tedious with such small seeds, but it reduces the possibility of overcrowding in the seed flat later on. The rate of germination is usually quite high, and overcrowding can choke many seedlings and reduce the growth rates of survivors.

Cover the fine seeds with a dusting of soil. Since overhead watering could uncover some seeds and bury others too deeply, you should bottom water the seed flats; that is, place the flat in a shallow tray of water until the surface of the soil becomes moist. A warm soil (70°F) produces germination in a week's time.

Seedlings are small and slow-growing. They can be transplanted to individual 2- or 3-inch containers when their white roots approach an inch in length, eight to ten weeks. Four to six weeks later plants should be of suitable size to transfer into the garden, where they will spend most, if not all, of their first season developing large basal rosettes of leaves. If a dozen or more seedlings are planted, a few will most likely flower the first year.

Cuttings. Take stem cuttings 6–8 inches long in mid-summer. Lay them horizontally in a sand and perlite medium, cover lightly, and keep moist. Small rosettes of leaves with roots should develop at the nodes, and grow into well-rooted plants in four to six weeks. Simply sever new rosettes from the stalk, and pot.

Division. A healthy plant produces a dense clump of basal foliage that consists of several rosettes or crowns. Divide plants in fall or spring by separating these individual rosettes or basal offshoots from the mother plant; replant the divisions and water immediately.

Cultivation

Although a naturally damp portion of the garden is the ideal location, Cardinal Flower can adjust to a wide range of soil and moisture conditions, so long as the soil around the plant is never allowed to dry out completely.

When grown in a light, well-watered, organic soil, Cardinal Flower outdoes its performance in nature. It does best in a lightly shaded setting or an exposure with less than a half day's full sun. In full sun the plant naturally requires more frequent watering; in times of drought the foliage may be lighter or sometimes appear burned. The brilliant scarlet of the flowers can appear washed out in the glare of harsh, direct sunlight.

After seed development in the fall, one to several small leafy offshoots usually form at the base of the drying stem. Care must be taken, at least in the southern regions, to see that these offshoots are not covered by falling leaves as they remain active in food production during the winter, taking advantage of the winter sun shining through the bare limbs and branches of deciduous trees. If they are smothered by leaves or mulch during this period, the plants die. This simple fact accounts for the difficulty most gardeners have in keeping Cardinal Flower for successive growing seasons. In nature Cardinal Flower seems restricted to open meadows or to wet ditches, pond edges, and stream sides, where high moving water during the fall and winter keeps the rosettes clear of smothering fallen leaf litter.

Uses in the Garden and Landscape

Plant Cardinal Flower in small groups of threes and fives in a perennial border that receives some protection from the midday or afternoon sun. Plants placed in front of a clump or two of Goldenrod—such as *Solidago rugosa* or *S. juncea*—form an interesting color contrast, and a few clumps in front of a large planting of Black-eyed Susan, particularly *Rudbeckia fulgida*, or of a border of white-flowered *Boltonia asteroides* are startling. Against most backgrounds, Cardinal Flower is brilliant and attracts attention, planted either singly or massed.

Planted at the far side of a lawn, at a woods edge, or at the base of a tree, the flowers will attract the eye over a great distance. The plant is, of course, appropriate for naturalizing in low, wet areas and interplanted among ferns in the shade garden. It can also be cultivated successfully in large containers placed in deep saucers of water. A container-grown Cardinal Flower placed on a sunny deck or patio will bring hummingbirds up to within a few yards of observers for periods of several minutes of intimate bird viewing.

Related Species

Lobelia siphilitica, the Great Blue Lobelia, has blue flowers on frequently branched erect stems, and it tolerates a sunnier exposure. The two species can be easily grown together and create

Lobelia siphilitica

a beautiful red and blue combination. When cultivating both species in the garden, label the plants of one species while they are in flower to avoid confusion during seed collection. Or remember that the persistent calyx segments on capsules of the Blue Lobelia have "ear-lobed," or auriculate, bases, while those of Cardinal Flower do not.

If you are very fortunate, you may have a white form of the Blue Lobelia develop from one of your seedlings; they are not uncommon. Take care to keep it and multiply it by cuttings and division. Rarer still are the white and pink forms of Cardinal Flower.

Production Notes

Sow seeds in flats and place over bottom heat in the greenhouse in late winter. Begin fertilizing in the flat with a starter solution and continue with an all-purpose liquid feed after seedlings have been stepped up into containers. Robust plants of salable size are ready twelve to sixteen weeks from sowing date.

Alternatively, field-grow seedlings in a moist, organic soil and move to 4-inch or quart containers at the end of the summer growing season for sale in the fall or the following spring.

Garden Phlox

Phlox paniculata
Polemoniaceae

Duration: perennial

Blooming time: August–September

Flower color: pink to lavender or white

Height: 3–6 feet

Soil: good garden soil

Exposure: full-filtered sun

Description

Some of the many species of Phlox native to the eastern United States are parents of some of the many attractive horticultural varieties of Phlox sold by nurseries and garden centers, and are worthy of a prominent place in your garden. Indeed, Creeping Phlox has long been a standard in the woodland wild flower garden, and the varieties of the taller, sun-loving Garden Phlox are valuable in a garden setting for their long blooming period and ease of handling.

Garden Phlox occurs in rich, open woods and along roadsides and stream banks in practically the whole of the eastern United States, except for the Upper Midwest and New England. In many mountain counties in western North Carolina, for example, sweeps of Garden Phlox occur on road banks, much to the delight of passing motorists in mid and late summer, when the plants are in flower.

Garden Phlox is a clump-forming plant with many stems that can range from 3 to 6 feet tall and bear numerous, narrow, lanceolate leaves, 3–6 inches long. The showy bright pink to lavender flowers are borne in dense, branched inflorescences, or panicles, 4 inches across. The slender tubular corolla opens into five spreading lobes which measure between ½ and 1 inch (14–24 mm) across. Although the individual blooms are not long lasting, the plants remain colorful for six weeks or more in August and September.

Fruit and Seed

Seed production is scant; typically, only a few tan, oval capsules, about ¼ inch (6 mm) long, develop in a given panicle. The capsules are quite firm when developing, but later dry and become papery in texture when seeds are mature. Usually only a single oval seed, ⅛ inch (3 mm) long, which darkens to grayish

black when mature, is produced per capsule.

Seed Collection, Cleaning, and Storage

Capsules should be collected in the fall before they begin to split. At the Botanical Garden, seeds are collected in October. Hold a capsule between thumb and forefinger and squeeze lightly; if the capsule cracks and breaks into small pieces and if the seed within is dark, it is time to collect.

Cut the entire panicle from the stalk and bring it indoors to air dry for at least several days before removing the seeds by lightly crushing the capsules. Continue crushing until the capsule pieces are smaller in size than the seeds and can be easily separated by sieving. Store seed dry in a labeled, airtight container in the refrigerator.

Propagation

Seed. Garden Phlox requires a moist cold period before it will germinate. Sow seeds in late fall or early winter in areas where you want to establish the plants, or in seedbeds or an unheated cold frame and look for germination in the spring. Alternatively, stored seeds may be stratified for four weeks in a moist medium in the refrigerator and then sown in flats in the early spring. Place the flats in the cold frame or in a protected spot outside.

When seedlings have two pairs of leaves, transplant them into 3-inch containers. Move plants into the garden when roots fill the pot and water them as needed for the remainder of their first season. Young plants in containers respond favorably to weekly applications of an all-purpose fertilizer. Plants can be expected to flower during their second season.

Cuttings. Take tip cuttings, 4–6 inches long, in May or June. Remove the lower leaves and insert several nodes in a rooting medium of either straight sand or equal parts peat moss and sand. Put the cuttings in a rooting chamber out of direct sunlight; mist the cuttings and saturate the rooting medium when dry. Pot cuttings when they are well rooted in 4-inch pots and monitor their watering closely during the summer months. Move plants to the garden in the fall or when their roots fill containers.

In his fine book *Plant Propagation in Pictures*, Montague Free

described how to increase Garden Phlox by root cuttings. In the fall lift a plant from the garden, select the thickest roots, and cut them into 2-inch lengths. Fill a flat with equal parts garden soil, peat moss, and sand and lay the roots out in rows, 2 inches apart. Then cover them with ½–1 inch of sand and water thoroughly. Overwinter the flat in the cold frame or a protected spot outside.

When cuttings have produced several leaves and new roots the following growing season, move them into 4-inch containers and handle as potted stem cuttings. It is likely that new plants will not flower until their second season.

Division. Divide mature plants in the fall, after flowering. Prune away stems to within an inch or so from the ground and pry apart the clump so that each new division has the remains of three or four stems and a mass of roots. Replant the divisions immediately and water thoroughly.

Cultivation

Grow Garden Phlox in areas receiving at least a half day's direct sunlight. Space new plants 2 feet apart and fertilize in the spring when shoots appear and again in mid-summer just before flowering.

Plants thrive in rich soils improved regularly with generous amounts of organic matter. To maintain attractive plants throughout the growing season, deep, regular watering is essential during summer dry periods.

Mulch around plants to conserve moisture.

Healthy plants should be divided every three years, or more often if clumps become crowded, and this is a good time to rework the soil in the planting area. If plants become crowded during the growing season, thin them by removing stems from the center of the clump. The flowering period may be extended by promptly removing faded blooms.

Uses in the Garden and Landscape

Garden Phlox is a classic border plant because of its strong, upright habit and long flowering period. Locate small groups of plants at intervals in the middle and rear ranks of the sunny border. Combine plants with other late-summer-and fall-blooming wild flowers, such as Queen-of-the-Meadow, Ironweed, and Boltonia. The pink blooms of Garden Phlox mix especially well with the yellow-flowering Sunflowers and Goldenrods.

Plants are also effectively naturalized at the edge of a wooded area. Although not long lasting as a cut flower, Phlox is attractive in arrangements.

Related Species

There are many attractive native eastern species of Phlox. *P. maculata*, Wild Sweet William, also clump forming, is similar in appearance to *P. paniculata*, but is usually shorter and bears pink to lavender or white flowers earlier in the summer. *Phlox subulata*, Moss Pink, spreads rapidly to form dense mats which are covered in spring with pink to rose flowers on 2-to-4-inch stems; the plants do best in a rather dry, well-drained site. *Phlox nivalis* bears a close resemblance in habit and flower color to *Phlox subulata*, but has a more southern distribution. *Phlox divaricata*, Blue Phlox (the flowers are a light lavender, or have a bluish cast), and *Phlox stolonifera*, Creeping Phlox (usually with lavender flowers), bear flowers on 8-to-12-inch stems in late April and May and prefer a deep, fertile soil. Both occur in white flowering forms. *Phlox pilosa* is similar to *Phlox divaricata*, but usually has taller (to 20 inches) stems and pink to dark lavender or, rarely, white flowers.

Creeping Phloxes root at the nodes and are readily increased by division and stem cuttings. Clump-forming Phloxes are propagated by cuttings in the spring and by division after flowering.

Production Notes

Both stem cuttings and division are appropriate for large-scale propagation. Field-grow plants in an open, sunny plot in deep, fertile soil and irrigate regularly during the summer months. Make tip cuttings as described above, root them under mist, and pot them in 4-inch containers when cuttings are well rooted. Fertilize plants weekly during the summer months, transplant them to quart containers in the fall, and market the next spring.

Division offers larger plants for sales. Clumps can be divided every second year, potted in gallon containers in the fall, and marketed the following spring. After the plants are divided, replant one division per plant in the field plot. Select only half of the plants for division each year, leaving the remaining plants to become of sufficient size to divide the following year.

Turtleheads

Chelone lyonii
Scrophulariaceae

Duration: perennial

Blooming time: August–September

Flower color: purple

Height: 2–4 feet

Soil: rich, moist or boggy

Exposure: light shade

Description

Turtleheads produce their large interesting flowers in terminal racemes in late summer and fall. The opposite, petiolate, dark green leaves are broadly lanceolate, or lance shaped, and continuous on the stem to the base of the compact spikelike racemes. The strongly two-lipped, purple corolla, over an inch (3–4 cm) long, does, as its name implies, give the appearance of a turtle's head; the upper lip is broadly curved and notched at the apex, and the lower lip is bearded with tiny yellow hairs.

Although this species of Turtleheads is restricted in nature to the rich coves, spruce-fir forests, and open stream banks of the southern Appalachians, it is easily cultivated and in fact has naturalized as an escape from cultivation throughout the Northeast.

Fruit and Seed

The broadly oval papery capsules, arranged tightly around the stalk, are slightly less than ½ inch (1.25 cm) long and are evident on the spike while the plant

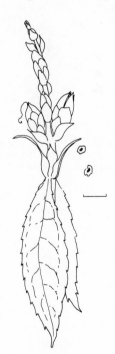

is still in flower. They turn darker shades of brown as the numerous, flattened seeds approach maturity. Individual seeds are less than ⅛ inch (3 mm) across and have a thin, light brown outer margin and a darker, teardrop-shaped center, which contains the embryo. Prolonged rainy periods during flowering reduce the effectiveness of pollinators, resulting in low seed production.

Seed Collection, Cleaning, and Storage

Like many species that flower toward the end of the growing season, such as the Lobelias, Asters, Gentians, and Seashore Mallow, Turtlehead seeds are ready for harvest at or near the first frost. Watch for the capsules to darken, remove a few and examine the seeds inside; if the centers of the flat papery seeds are dark and slightly swollen, they are mature or will probably ripen if the fruiting stalks are collected at this time. As the capsules remain intact on the stalk for several weeks after the first frost, and sometimes into late fall, there is little risk of losing them if you want to wait a few days more before collecting.

Snip the stalks below the bottom-most capsules and allow them to air-dry for a few days prior to cleaning. When the capsules are dry, break them open and shake out the seeds which are often of various sizes. However, there is no need to separate them, as the smaller seeds may also have well developed embryos. A small amount of litter,

mostly pieces of the broken capsules, may mix with seeds during cleaning and can be removed by running the seeds and litter through a sieve. Store cleaned seeds dry in a sealed, labeled container and refrigerate.

Propagation

Seed. High germination percentages result when seeds are given a moist chill for six weeks prior to sowing. When seeds are sown after dry storage, with no moist chilling, germination is typically less than 10 percent. Mix stored seeds with a small amount of damp vermiculite or whole-fiber sphagnum moss in a sealed bag and put the mixture back in the refrigerator. This moist chilling, or stratification, duplicates the natural conditions of the wet cold of winter necessary to break dormancy. To plant inside in early winter, spread the vermiculite and seed mixture evenly in the seed flat, cover lightly with the sowing medium, and water.

Seedlings are ready for transplanting to individual 3-inch containers a month after sowing. Allow roots to fill up the pot and, when the danger of frost is past, move plants to the garden. Seedlings respond favorably to weekly applications of an all-purpose fertilizer.

Alternatively, sow seeds immediately upon collection in the fall in an outdoor seedbed. These seeds will naturally receive a moist chill over the winter and should germinate promptly when the soil warms the following spring. Seedlings may be allowed

to grow on in the seedbed until they are well rooted, when they can be transplanted directly in the garden. Some thinning may be necessary in the seedbed shortly after germination.

Cuttings. Take 6-inch stem tip cuttings in June. Remove the lower leaves from the cuttings and insert at least one node in a peat moss and sand mix or use sand alone. Be certain to keep the rooting medium constantly moist, but not soggy, and mist the cuttings when leaves are dry. Cuttings will root in a higher percentage when they are placed under mist in a greenhouse, or in a rooting chamber where a high constant humidity can be maintained.

Most cuttings will be well rooted in four to five weeks and ready to be moved into containers; transplant rooted cuttings in the garden at least a month before the expected first frost, or overwinter them in containers in the cold frame or in a protected spot outside, and plant the following spring.

Division. Divide clumps when leaves first appear in the spring. As Turtleheads do not form basal rosettes of leaves but rather send up single stems a few inches apart, the soil does not need to be removed during division. With a long trowel or small spade, section off two or three stems, replant the new divisions, water thoroughly, and apply a layer of mulch, 2 to 3 inches deep, to help conserve moisture.

Cultivation

Turtleheads grow best when grown in a light, humus-rich soil kept constantly moist. Apply a mulch of rotted leaves or compost several times during the season. If a low, wet area or natural seepage is available, plan to naturalize plants there after priming the native soil with plenty of organic matter.

Given proper soil conditions, Turtleheads will thrive in a lightly shaded setting. Sunnier sites are suitable if moisture in the soil remains constant. The clumps spread rapidly, and in a matter of two to three years several dozen stems will produce an impressive display of flowers. Staking may be required if nearby plants are not strong enough to support the slender 3-to-4-foot stems.

Uses in the Garden and Landscape

Interplant Turtleheads with other moisture-loving and bog species. *Solidago patula*, a Goldenrod native to wet areas in the mountains and cool wet meadows and bogs, has arching stalks of bright yellow flowers and makes a colorful contrast with Turtleheads. *Lobelia cardinalis*, *L. siphilitica*, *Filipendula rubra*, and native fern species, especially Cinnamon, Royal, and Marsh ferns, are also appropriate companions.

Related Species

Chelone glabra, occurring in wet areas throughout the eastern United States, is similar in appearance but has white flowers. Propagation and cultivation requirements are as for *C. lyonii*.

Virgin's Bower

Clematis virginiana
Ranunculaceae

Duration: perennial

Blooming time: August

Flower color: white

Height: climbing or sprawling vine

Soil: rich, moist to average

Exposure: sun, light shade

Description

Virgin's Bower is especially evident when in flower in mid-to-late summer. Where there is ample light, such as along road banks and edges of woods, the vine produces snow white flowers in profusion as it climbs on surrounding vegetation. It is a useful plant in cultivation, whether trained to a certain confined space or allowed to roam unrestrained.

The compound leaves of three coarsely serrated leaflets, borne on long (to 4 inches) petioles, are opposite on angled stems. The numerous flowers are borne in the leaf axils; an individual flower is about 1 inch (2.5 cm) across, and has four creamy white, petallike sepals and a central cluster of white anthers and pistils.

Fruit and Seed

Two to three weeks after the brief bloom period, each pistil matures as an oval achene with its slender, brown, feathery, persistent style still attached. The cluster of tightly arranged achenes with their feathery tails makes a beautifully textured mass that remains on the vines for several weeks after the achenes are fully developed. Thus, although the vines are in flower for only one to two weeks, the fluffy seed heads extend the attractiveness of this vine late into the fall.

Seed Collection, Cleaning, and Storage

The achenes, which are actually one-seeded fruits, are dark brown and ready for collection from late August through September. Since the seed heads persist for several months, the time of collection is not critical. As achenes from only one or two clusters should fulfill your needs, you can collect without noticeably affecting the plant's appearance. It is not nec-

essary to remove the feathery styles before storing or sowing. Store the seeds dry in a sealed, labeled container and refrigerate.

Propagation

Seed. Higher germination percentages can be expected from stored seeds sown indoors or in the cold frame than from seeds sown directly in an outdoor bed upon collection. Refrigerated seeds germinate in one to two weeks and seedlings are large enough to transplant into 2- or 3-inch containers three to four weeks later. Allow roots to fill the containers and then move the plants to the garden or other desired planting area.

Cuttings. Take 4-to-5-inch stem cuttings that include two sets of leaves at any time during the growing season. Remove the lower leaves and insert the exposed node in a sandy rooting medium. Place the cuttings in a rooting chamber, where high humidity can be maintained, and expect rooted cuttings for potting in three to four weeks.

Allow the plants to remain in containers, keeping them well watered, through the season; overwinter in the cold frame or in a protected spot outside and transplant to the garden the following spring.

Cultivation

Although mature vines are aggressive in their rate of growth, first-year plants are slow to establish and will not flower until at least the second year. Plants thrive in rich soils high in organic content which are kept evenly moist.

The herbaceous or slightly woody stems of *Clematis virginiana* may be thinned or pruned to shape at any time during the growing season. Trained to climb on a support, they will eventually become top-heavy; to encourage the vines to fill out, prune the stems in the spring to within a few feet of the ground at least every fourth year and more frequently if necessary.

Establish these vines in sunny or lightly shaded settings. The shallow roots lie only a few inches below the soil, and thus require some watering during dry periods.

Uses in the Garden and Landscape

The numerous overlapping stems of Clematis can provide a dense seasonal screen when trained on fences and, when trained on a trellis or a hoop of wire mesh positioned around a tall post, the vines are effective at the rear of a deep flower border. Other practical display possibilities for Virgin's Bower are along a split-rail fence or a rock wall or sprawled over a natural rock outcropping.

The plant's tendency to spread has caused many gardeners to avoid it; one does need a restrained space, such as a wild shrub border or an arbor or fence, to really enjoy this vine. If space is available and if you are willing to spend the little time necessary to restrain Virgin's Bower, the masses of summer flowers and the later fluffy fruiting heads are very rewarding.

Vines that ramble extensively and fruit profusely are a good source of feathery seed heads, which are effective in fall harvest wreaths and winter arrangements.

Related Species

Clematis crispa, Leather Flower, is a weakly ascending vine with leathery, bluish, bell-shaped flowers 2 inches long. Its northern counterpart is *C. viorna*, which is similar in habit and has purplish flowers. Both species are less aggressive than *C. virginiana*, and both require rich moist soil.

Clematis crispa

Clematis viorna

Bottle-Gentian, Closed Gentian

Gentiana clausa
Gentianaceae

Duration: perennial

Blooming time: August–September

Flower color: blue

Height: 1–2 feet

Soil: rich, moist or wet

Exposure: filtered to full sun

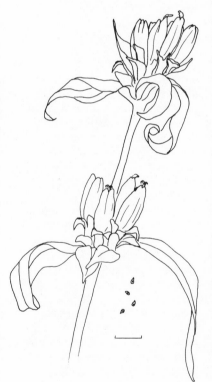

Description

The flowering of the Gentians signals the conclusion of the growing season—and their vivid blooms make a fine and fitting encore to the profusion of color of months past. They are not easy to raise, but worth the effort and are a source of pride and deep satisfaction to those who grow them. Bottle-Gentian occurs in the northern states east of the Mississippi River in meadows, on stream banks, and at woods' edge and in the upper South, where it is found on wooded slopes and stream banks in the mountains and northern piedmont.

Flowering begins in August and persists for several weeks into September and October. The terminal flower clusters are borne in axils of the upper leaves on 1-foot stems. The blue, elongate, tubular corollas are 1 inch (3–4 cm) long, opening slightly at the apex. The sessile, opposite, light green leaves are 2–4 inches (5–10 cm) long. Plants have thick fleshy roots and form large clumps with many stems from a single crown.

Fruit and Seed

The capsules, which are borne on short stalks, steadily elongate after flowering and produce many hundreds of small, oval seeds, only 1–2 millimeters long, with wings that surround the brown center. The dried corolla remains intact around the brown capsule as it matures.

Seed Collection, Cleaning, and Storage

At the Botanical Garden in central North Carolina, capsules of Gentian are collected in November after the first hard freeze when the capsules begin to open and curl back at the apex. Cut the stems just below the clusters of capsules and drop them into a bag. To clean, simply tap or gently shake out the seeds. A small amount of litter, pieces of broken capsules and dried corollas, will likely accumulate with the seed, but can be effectively removed with a sieve.

Store the seeds dry in a sealed, labeled container and refrigerate. Under these conditions Gentian seeds remain viable for at least four years.

Propagation

Seed. One enthusiastic and talented gardener from our area who has conducted propagation studies on some of the native Gentians over the past several years reports success using the following seed propagation technique.

Sow stored seeds in late spring in flats placed in the cold frame or in a protected spot outside. To assure proper drainage, use a medium consisting of two parts aged sawdust to one part coarse sand. To maintain even moisture conditions during germination, sow the seeds on a layer of milled sphagnum moss spread ¼ inch deep over the medium. Before, during, and after germination, mist the milled sphagnum regularly to keep the surface from drying out. Uniform germination should occur within two weeks.

Curiously, when seedlings were first transplanted one per pot, they all died. When two or more seedlings were transplanted in a single pot, however, they survived. Moving tender seedlings from seed flat to pot must be done with care. If the long, slender, hairlike roots are broken, the seedlings may die. When the roots reach the bottom of the flat, use a wooden stick label or spoon to gently lift a clump of several seedlings from the flat, and transplant two or more together to 3-inch containers filled with the same sawdust and sand mixture.

Keep seedlings well watered during the season and overwinter pots in the cold frame or heel them into sawdust in a protected spot outside. Move the plants to the garden the following spring and expect them to flower that fall.

Division. Divide Gentian crowns in early spring when buds appear. To avoid damage to the spreading roots, include a large ball of soil around the plant when you lift it out. The somewhat brittle crown is easily broken; each new piece should include at least one bud and several roots; replant the divisions

immediately and water thoroughly.

Cultivation

Plants thrive in well-drained organic soils. If your soil is on the heavy side, mix in a shovelful of sand or fine gravel per plant. Most Gentians also fare well in low wet areas, in a bog, or at water's edge.

The plants produce more flowers when they receive at least a half day's full sun. A setting at the edge of a wooded area that gets sun during the late-morning and afternoon hours is ideal. They can also be successfully grown in light shade; however, the plants will have looser habits.

Clumps of Gentian can remain undisturbed indefinitely; if division is necessary to produce new plants, however, plan to rework the soil to assure proper drainage. A mulch of rotted leaves or compost applied in the spring is beneficial to plants.

Uses in the Garden and Landscape

Plant the low-growing Gentians singly or in small groups in the front of the perennial border; space the plants 1½ to 2 feet apart and plant them liberally in both formal and naturalistic settings.

In sunny sites the late-bloom-

ing Maryland Golden Aster makes a good companion. In naturally moist sites Gentians combine well with Grass-of-Parnassus, *Solidago patula*, and native ferns, especially Marsh Fern (*Thelypteris palustris*) and New York Fern (*Thelypteris noveboracensis*).

Plants can be raised in large containers provided you give regular attention to watering. Gentians as cut flowers are outstanding in fall arrangements.

Related Species

The very beautiful Fringed Gentian (*G. crinita*), a biennial with fringed corolla lobes, requires a constantly moist, sunny location where a single specimen can produce as many as one hundred blooms. Start plants from seed each year to keep them in your garden; the seedlings form rosettes during the first year.

Equally striking is the Perennial Pine-Barren Gentian (*G. autumnalis*) which usually bears one bright blue flower per plant. Acid, sandy soil and full or filtered sunlight are appropriate growing conditions for this species.

Soapwort Gentian (*G. saponaria*) and Sampson's Snakeroot (*G. villosa*), which tolerate dryer conditions and have a greenish corolla striped with purple, are other perennial Bottle-Gentians worthy of cultivation.

Grass-of-Parnassus

Parnassia grandifolia
Saxifragaceae

Duration: perennial

Blooming time: September

Flower color: white

Height: 1–1½ feet

Soil: moist or wet

Exposure: sun to light shade

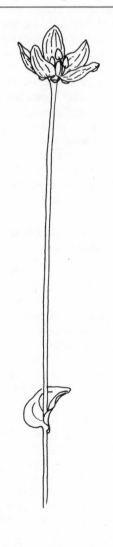

Description

These striking flowers occur infrequently throughout the southeastern United States in seepages and in wet soils characterized by the presence of limestone. The common name is derived from a plant of the same genus which grew on the slopes of Mount Parnassus in ancient Greece; the foliage, however, bears no resemblance to grass. Because of its rather exacting moisture and high pH requirements, the plant is less versatile in the garden than many of the other species discussed in this book, but if you are willing to work a bit to create the conditions that favor its establishment, or are fortunate enough to have such conditions already, *Parnassia* will reward you with an attractive foliar rosette through the growing season and beautiful blooms in September.

The shiny, light green basal leaves, borne on long petioles, are smooth, broadly oval or kidney shaped, and 2–2½ inches (5–6.25 cm) long. Clumps consist of a few to many leaves and a network of slender white roots. A smaller sessile leaf is borne just below the middle of the 1–1½ foot flowering stem, which bears a striking, solitary, open cup-shaped flower nearly 2 inches (5 cm) across. Each of the five waxy white petals is marked with seven to nine prominent green veins and has at its base a golden staminodium, or sterile stamen-like structure, deeply divided into three parts.

Fruit and Seed

During the month after the bloom period, the green, cone-shaped, four-valved capsule gradually expands. At or very near the first fall frost, the capsules begin to turn brown and split. Numerous small, angled, brownish seeds, ¹⁄₁₆ inch (1.5 mm) long, are borne on the inner surfaces of the capsule. The leaves are likely to yellow and wither in the weeks after flowering, but the fruiting stalks remain upright as the seeds develop.

Seed Collection, Cleaning, and Storage

When seeds are mature, the capsule dries out and becomes thin and papery. Collect the capsules as they turn brown or show signs of splitting. The seeds remain attached to the capsule wall for a few days after the capsule begins to split; however, you are likely to lose the seeds entirely if you wait too long.

To collect, snip off the capsules into a paper bag, then spread them over a clean, dry surface indoors to air-dry for a few days prior to cleaning. Crush the capsules open and stir the capsules and seeds loosened in handling through a sieve. To clean the seeds more thoroughly, spread seeds and litter on a sheet of paper and either fan or shake away the lighter material. Store seeds dry in a sealed, labeled container and refrigerate until time of sowing.

Propagation

Seed. Seeds can be sown upon collection in a flat or pot and placed in the cold frame or dug into a protected spot outside for overwintering and spring germination. The seeds must remain evenly moist and not be allowed to dry out after sowing; sow them on a ¼-inch-deep layer of moistened milled sphagnum spread over your standard seed mix.

Alternatively, seeds may be sown indoors in late winter or early spring, but to break their dormancy, cold stratify them for six weeks prior to sowing. This can be easily accomplished by either mixing some damp sphagnum with your stored seeds in the refrigerator or sowing the seeds as described above, then covering the flat or pot with plastic and placing it in the refrigerator for six weeks.

Allow the seedlings to remain undisturbed until the tiny rosettes have four or five leaves and well-developed roots, and then transplant them into 3-inch containers. To achieve the higher pH required by *Parnassia* amend your potting soil with agricultural lime at the rate of a quarter teaspoon or so per plant. Place young plants in a lightly shaded area and keep the soil around them moist throughout the growing season; move them into the garden in early fall. As container plants will not tolerate dry soil, keep them in a saucer and bottom-water regularly through the season.

Division. A mature plant consists of as many as a dozen closely spaced crowns. It is best to divide plants in the fall after flowering or in the spring when the rosettes of curled leaves first appear. Lift the plant from the soil and, working from the periphery of the clump, separate the individual rosettes, making sure each has as many roots attached as possible. Replant new divisions immediately and water thoroughly.

Cultivation

To assure robust, full-flowering specimens, plants must be grown in full sun in wet, boglike conditions but with the leaves high and dry, as on a hummock or decayed stump, and the roots in the cooler, constantly moist ground below. Unless your soil has a high pH, work a handful of crushed limestone into the soil at planting time and again whenever plants are taken up for division.

Space plants a foot apart and plan to divide clumps every third year or when they become crowded. Grass-of-Parnassus, which is low growing, may be shaded if taller neighboring vegetation is allowed to encroach; some weeding is essential, especially during the summer months; shadier spots produce rank foliage and weak flower stems.

Where naturally wet conditions are not available, an artificial bog may be created as suggested in the discussion of skunk cabbage.

Uses in the Garden and Landscape

Some gardeners recommend *Parnassia* for the rock garden, and where the soil is sufficiently moist, they would indeed make excellent additions. Naturalize plants in a low area of the yard where water collects or in other naturally wet, sunny spots.

Where the planting site is large enough to accommodate taller plants, work in Ironweed, Goldenrod (*Solidago patula*), Turtleheads, and Cinnamon and Royal ferns. In smaller settings combine the plant with *Lobelia cardinalis*, *L. siphilitica*, and Marsh Fern (*Thelypteris palustris*, which spreads rapidly and must be contained).

Related Species

Parnassia asarifolia and *P. caroliniana*, similar in appearance, have slightly smaller leaves and flowers and are from 8 to 12 inches tall; *P. asarifolia* has kidney-shaped leaves; *P. caroliniana*, rounded leaves. Propagation and cultivation requirements for both of these species are the same as for *P. grandifolia*.

Ironweed

Vernonia noveboracensis
Asteraceae

Duration: perennial

Blooming time: August–September

Flower color: purple

Height: to 7 feet

Soil: moist or wet

Exposure: sun

Description

The vivid purple flowers of Ironweed, perhaps the most brilliant purple of all wild flowers, are effective amid the welter of yellow blooms during the late-summer and fall months and should be included in your fall planting scheme. In nature these plants grow in wet meadows, along stream banks, and in roadside ditches throughout most of the eastern third of the United States.

Loosely branched, leafy stems arise from a single crown and can reach to 7 feet and taller. The flower heads are borne in loose or compact corymbs—flat-topped arrangements of numerous heads of disk flowers—which are usually a foot or more across. The thirty to fifty individual disk flowers of each head are bright purple with a purple pappus surrounding each small flower.

Fruit and Seed

After the blooming period, the pappus bristles may remain purple or turn a beautiful buff brown. Typically, the nutlets mature in three to four weeks. The slender, angled nutlet, approximately ⅛ inch (3 mm) long with a ¼-inch (6 mm) spreading pappus attached to the top, is slate grey when mature.

Seed Collection, Cleaning, and Storage

Nutlets can be collected in early October or later, as they usually remain intact on the receptacle for several weeks beyond the first frost. Cut through a few nutlets before collecting to determine that a white embryo has developed inside. As is common with the composites, many of the seeds never develop; thus it may be necessary to collect a large quantity to ensure that you have enough good seed for sowing. Store the dry nutlets in a sealed, labeled container and refrigerate.

Propagation

Seed. The germination percentage for Ironweed seeds is typically low; therefore, sow the seeds thickly. If you plan a winter sowing in a flat indoors or in the cold frame, allow the small, slow-growing seedlings twelve weeks

four to five weeks and may then be transplanted to 3- or 4-inch pots. When your new plants are well established in the pots, plant them in the garden or overwinter them in the pots to plant the next spring.

Cultivation

Ironweed is not particular about the soil in which it grows; a soil that remains moist or wet during the growing season, however, will produce a larger specimen. Where conditions permit, establish these plants in a wet, open, sunny site, such as a wet meadow, a roadside ditch, at water's edge, or in a bog. The sturdy stems will not require staking.

Uses in the Garden and Landscape

Place Ironweed at the rear of the sunny border close to other tall, fall-blooming species, such as the Goldenrods, New England Asters, and Frost Asters. In a shaded, naturally moist area Ironweed is effective interplanted with the Lobelias, Turtleheads, and *Solidago patula*. In a sunny, moist area Ironweed is appropriate with Bur-Marigold, Joe-Pye-Weed, and various Goldenrods. It is stunning as a cut flower, but since the leaves wilt quickly, they are best discarded before arranging.

to develop to sufficient size for permanent planting. Weekly applications of an all-purpose fertilizer will hasten growth.

You can cut the time for producing plants nearly in half by sowing stored seeds in June or July in an outdoor seed frame. Because the soil temperatures are consistently warm, germination and seedling growth are far more rapid outdoors during the growing season. Transplant seedlings to individual containers when a rosette-like cluster of three or four leaves develops and then to the garden when roots fill the pots.

Cuttings. Take stem cuttings 4–6 inches long in June or July. Remove the lower leaves and insert the cuttings in a mix of equal parts peat moss and sand and place them in a rooting chamber, where high humidity can be maintained, or under mist. Cuttings should be well rooted in

Blue Curls

Trichostema dichotomum
Lamiaceae

Duration: annual

Blooming time: August–September

Flower color: blue

Height: 1–2½ feet

Soil: average

Exposure: full sun to partial shade

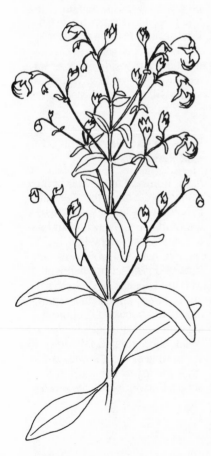

Description

Blue Curls, a native, aromatic annual that blooms in late-summer and fall, is useful in both formal and natural settings in the garden. The square, freely branched, leafy stems reach 1–2½ feet in height and develop a bushy, rounded habit by the time they flower. The small, opposite, narrowly elliptic leaves are ½–2 inches long and less than ¼ inch wide.

A single plant produces many dozens of small blue flowers, which are borne in short panicles along the stem. The short corolla tube ends in five lobes; the longest of these forms a lower lip ¼–½ inch (5–10 millimeters) long, and the remaining lobes are about ⅛ inch (2–4 millimeters) long, expanding upward.

The four long, blue stamens, which curl up out of the corolla tube and downward to the lower lip, give the plant its common name. Blue Curls occurs infrequently in sandy or rocky upland woods in many eastern states.

Fruit and Seed

A week or two after the corolla has withered and dropped, four green mericarps, or nutlets, are evident in the base of the persistent calyx. The small calyx, less than ¼ inch long, has a three-toothed lip below and a smaller two-toothed lip above; the lips turn from green to light brown and dry to a papery texture as the mericarps also darken and develop.

Many calyxes still contain the kidney-shaped mericarps, each approximately 1/16 inch (1.5 mm) long, and remain on the plant after leaves have dried and fallen, giving the plant a skeletonlike appearance.

Seed Collection, Cleaning, and Storage

Mericarps are clearly visible within the calyx; when a majority of them have darkened, pull up the entire plant and air-dry upside down for several days in a large paper bag to catch any seeds that may fall. After drying, the remainder of the seeds can be freed by placing seed stalks in a bag and shaking it vigorously.

A single plant will produce more than enough seeds for your propagation needs. Check the seeds carefully for insects and fumigate if necessary. Store seeds

224

dry in a sealed, labeled container in the refrigerator until time of sowing.

Propagation

Seed. Blue Curls typically reseeds itself, producing a carpet of seedlings in early summer where last year's plants grew. To establish plants in other areas around the garden, simply transplant the seedlings. The easiest sowing method is to sow seeds outdoors upon collection, either in a seedbed or where you want them for display the next season.

To start plants from collected seed, stratify them for four weeks prior to planting. Sow seeds in your standard sowing mix in a flat or pot, moisten, cover with plastic, and refrigerate for four weeks. Remove the flat from the refrigerator and place it in a warm, sunny spot indoors or in the cold frame and water as needed. Germination will be uniform. However, the seedlings are slow-growing and will need some extra care before they are large enough to plant out.

Cuttings. As with other fall-blooming annuals, such as Gaillardia and Bur-Marigold, rooting Blue Curls from cuttings is practical only when seed or seedlings are not available in the quantity desired.

Make stem cuttings, 2 inches long, three to four weeks after germination; remove the lower leaves and insert at least one node along the stem in a rooting medium of equal parts sand and perlite in a rooting chamber, where high humidity can be maintained. The cuttings should root rapidly, in two to three weeks, whereupon they should be transplanted directly to the garden.

Cultivation

Although tolerant of light shade, Blue Curls is larger and showier when grown in a sunny location. Mix in a shovelful of sand per plant where the soil is not freely drained. As noted above, Blue Curls self-sows freely and should be pulled up before mericarps develop unless many plants are needed for the next growing season. Given these conditions, plants are essentially maintenance-free.

Plants of Blue Curls are appropriate for areas of naturalized wild flowers, where they are best left to move about on their own. In such areas, however, it is important to break up the soil in several places each year to provide areas for these annuals to germinate and become established free from the competition of hardy and aggressive native perennials. To obtain plants with a full, rounded habit, frequent pruning is necessary.

Uses in the Garden and Landscape

Arrange plants in small groups at intervals in the first rank of the herbaceous border. Blue Curls is especially attractive when allowed to extend over the edge, softening the lines of the border, or when used liberally in the border to fill gaps left by spring and summer blooming plants.

It is also effective as an edging plant; use plants to line a path or walkway or an informal planting bed. In areas where you need an edging plant year-round, rotate Blue Curls with Blue-eyed Grass; in the fall, after Blue Curls blooms, remove plants and replant the area with sprigs of Blue-eyed Grass. The next year, when Blue-eyed Grass completes flowering and the foliage becomes leggy (about the time Blue Curls germinates) seed the area with Blue Curls or set out seedling plants.

Try Blue Curls at the base of evergreen plantings, where a dark background effectively highlights the tiny blue flowers; or combine Blue Curls with other low-growing fall-flowering natives such as Gaillardia, Meadow Beauty, and the Gentians.

Related Species

Trichostema setaceum, which closely resembles *T. dichotomum* and blooms in the fall, also requires a well-drained soil, a sunny exposure, and has similar propagation requirements.

Sunflower

Helianthus tomentosus

Asteraceae

Duration: perennial

Blooming time: August–September

Flower color: yellow

Height: to 8 feet

Soil: average, well-drained

Exposure: full sun

Description

This native short-rhizomatous sunflower is found throughout the southeastern United States in open woodlands, thickets, and meadows. The densely hairy stems may reach 8 feet in height with the lower leaves opposite and the upper ones often alternate. The ovate to lanceolate leaves, scabrous above and downy below, may be up to 8 inches long.

Flower buds, made conspicuous by several series of green involucral bracts, or phyllaries, are quite attractive and make fine additions to late-summer arrangements. Flowering heads are 2–3 inches (5–7.5 cm) across and include a mound of yellow disk flowers and an outer whorl of sterile, golden yellow ray flowers. Plants flower during August and September.

Fruit and Seed

After the ray flowers drop, the involucral bracts darken to light or medium brown, and these attractive, tawny heads may be used in dried arrangements. Nutlets are usually mature two to three weeks after flowering. The bristly bracts open steadily and remain attached for several weeks or months after the nutlets are dispersed. The triangular-shaped nutlets are deep gray at maturity and nearly ¼ inch (6.0 mm) long.

Seed Collection, Cleaning, and Storage

One problem in collecting seeds of this sunflower is that gold-finches often eat the nutlets, usually before they have completely ripened. To deter the goldfinches, secure a small piece of nylon hose, cheesecloth, or small brown paper bag around individual seed heads as soon as the flowers fade.

To determine whether nutlets are mature, remove a head and, if nutlets fall out after shaking or tapping, collect other heads of the same age. Nutlets will remain in the heads for as long as two weeks after they mature, but the heads steadily deteriorate beyond this time, so check the condition of nutlets every few days after the bracts begin to brown.

Cut the seed heads and allow them to air-dry for a few days; then place them in a bag, shake vigorously, and use a sieve to separate nutlets from the chaff. Alternatively, the heads may be broken by hand to remove the nutlets. Store nutlets dry in a sealed, labeled container and refrigerate until time of sowing.

Propagation

Seed. Unquestionably, the best time to sow sunflower seeds is mid-summer, July and August, after they have been refrigerated for nearly a year. With a summer sowing in an outdoor seedbed, excellent germination occurs in four to five days and seedlings are large enough to transplant into 3-inch pots filled with a stan-dard potting mix in three to four weeks. Young plants grow rapidly at this time of year and should be transplanted again in September to 4-inch pots and overwintered or planted directly in the garden.

Cuttings. Take stem cuttings anytime before flowering and stick them in a fast-draining me-dium—for example, one consisting of three parts sand to one part peat—in a rooting chamber; mist the leaves when they dry and keep the medium evenly moist. The cuttings are likely to rot if the rooting medium is allowed to remain soggy. When roots are an inch long, transplant cuttings into 3- or 4-inch pots, overwinter them in a protected area outside, and move plants into the garden the following spring.

Division. This is the easiest method of increase. When shoots first appear from the clump of Sunflowers in spring, take it up, shake loose some of the soil, and take large or small divisions according to how many new plants you need. Large divisions that include many shoots can be made with a shovel; smaller divisions that include one or a few shoots can be made by hand by simply separating them from the periphery of the clump. Replant and water the divisions immediately.

Cultivation

Ideally, plants should be grown in average, well-drained garden soil in an open setting in full sun. This will produce multistemmed, full-flowering specimens that make spectacular additions to the garden. Filtered sunlight or a half day's direct light, as on the edge of a wooded area, are also acceptable settings for the plants, although they are likely to have somewhat looser, rangier habits.

Fertile, well-prepared soils typi-cally produce lush growth and weaker stems, which are likely to lean or fall to the ground during a wind or rainstorm. Stake the plants if the stems begin to arch before flowering. Curb plants when they begin to encroach upon nearby plantings by remov-ing sections from the edges of the clump. Plants will of course improve their appearance by reg-ular irrigation during periods of dry weather.

Uses in the Garden and Landscape

Use Sunflowers in the sunny bor-der with Seashore Mallow, Joe-Pye-Weed, Boltonia, Swamp Milk-weed, and the Goldenrods. In display areas out of direct light, combine plants with Cardinal Flower and Great Lobelia. Sun-flowers can also be used as a seasonal screen for a fence and naturalized in dry, sunny areas.

The plants are attractive in large barrel planters provided wa-tering is regular; pinch growing tips twice during the season to create a rounded habit and more flowers. Cut Sunflowers are excel-lent in arrangements.

Related Species

Helianthus annuus, the annual parent species of many popular

Sunflower cultivars, has pale yellow ray flowers and grows to 9 feet; *H. angustifolius*, Swamp Sunflower, tolerates wet soils, has bright yellow ray flowers with purple disks, and grows to 6 feet; *H. atrorubens* grows to 5 feet and has a loose habit and attractive flowers, also with purple disks; *H. laetiflorus*, Showy Sunflower, has narrow leaves and 6-foot stems branched at their tops and tolerates dry soils.

H. tuberosus, Jerusalem Arti-

choke, produces edible tubers in fertile soils, but may become too weedy; *H. radula*, Rayless Sunflower, frequent on moist to sandy dry roadsides of the coastal plain, has flower heads of only dark maroon disk flowers that are excellent in dried arrangements. General cultivation, with some attention to specific moisture requirements, is essentially similar to that of *H. tomentosus*.

Boltonia

Boltonia asteroides
Asteraceae

Duration: perennial

Blooming time: September

Flower color: white

Height: 4–5 feet

Soil: good garden soil

Exposure: sun to light shade

Description

Boltonia occurs in moist or wet soils of the southeastern coastal plain area and is not well known among wild flower gardeners. It should become more popular, however, because it has a number of very desirable qualities: the plant is attractive, requires little attention, propagates easily, and makes an effective background for shorter plants.

At first glance this species, with its numerous flowering heads, is reminiscent of Michaelmas Daisy, prominent in many gardens during the fall months. Boltonia, however, develops a naturally rounded habit, is not as top-heavy, and bears smaller but more numerous flowers.

The sturdy stems branch freely and reach a height of 4–5 feet, and sometimes taller. The gray green, grasslike, alternate leaves are 2–6 inches (5–15 cm) long and ¾ inch (1.8 cm) wide.

The inflorescence is multibranched, bearing many individual flower heads that measure ¾ inch (1.8 cm) across. A single inflorescence, or flower head, bears twenty-five to thirty-five white ray flowers and a yellow center of many small disk flowers. At the Botanical Garden, in central North Carolina, the plant begins blooming in mid-August and concludes in mid-September.

Fruit and Seed

When the ray flowers drop, signaling the end of the bloom period, make a note to check on the condition of the seed in about two weeks. During this period the receptacle of the seed head turns from yellow to grayish and begins to expand. The receptacle is quite small and looks like nothing more than a slight swelling at the end of the stalk. The very small, flattened nutlets have a pair of awns at the apex.

Seed Collection, Cleaning, and Storage

As in many species in the Aster family, only a small percentage of the nutlets contain embryos and are viable. Break open a few receptacles and separate out the larger nutlets. With a razor blade, cut a dozen or so nutlets in half and with the aid of a hand magnifier look inside for the embryos. No doubt most of the nutlets will be empty, but if you find a few "good" nutlets then it is worth collecting more seeds. If, after examining the nutlets from several receptacles, you find no via-

ble nutlets, it would be best to plan to propagate new plants by division. Store any collected seeds dry in a sealed container and refrigerate until time of sowing.

Propagation

Seed. Sow stored seeds indoors or in the cold frame in mid-winter, allowing ten to twelve weeks before the last spring frost to produce plants large enough for permanent planting in the garden.

Cover the surface of the sowing mix completely with the nutlets (seed). As germination is typically very low, there is little danger of overcrowding in the seed flat. Transplant seedlings when three to four leaves appear on the rosette.

Since the leaves are hairy and easily trap water, the seedlings should be slightly mounded in the container to improve the drainage away from the leaves. Mounding also avoids prolonged contact between the leaves and the soil, a condition which encourages fungus growth.

A weekly application of an all-purpose fertilizer will speed seedling growth. When roots completely fill the container, and the last spring frost date is past, transplant your seedlings into the garden.

Cuttings. Take stem cuttings in June or July; cuttings should be 3 to 4 inches long. Remove the bottom three or four leaves and stick the cuttings in a rooting mix of equal parts of sand and peat moss, or pure sand, in a rooting

chamber, where high humidity can be maintained. Expect most cuttings to develop roots within four to five weeks, whereupon they can be transplanted to individual containers. Move cuttings into the garden a month or so before the expected first frost date or hold plants in containers in a protected spot outside and plant the following spring.

Division. A clump of Boltonia consists of numerous rosettes borne on short rhizomes and a mature plant may produce forty to fifty such individual rosettes. Because these plants actively produce basal foliage after they flower and during warm periods over the winter, early spring is the best time to divide clumps. Lift mature plants from the garden with a shovel and shake loose the soil. Individual rosettes pull apart easily; replant and water new divisions thoroughly.

As a single large clump yields so many new plants, plan to pot up a few of the divisions to share with other gardeners. Also, the plants do well in container culture and may be held in pots for several months. Make sure to loosen the root ball when transplanting potted specimens.

Cultivation

Plants thrive in full sun, but tolerate a lightly shaded setting. Boltonias are not very specific as to soil type in cultivation, but clumps do appear to spread faster when grown in a raised bed or in a deeply prepared planting area with plenty of organic matter

worked in. If you intend to naturalize plants in a heavy clay soil, you should improve the planting site with organic matter. Plants will of course benefit from watering during dry periods.

Space plants 1½ to 2 feet apart and, although Boltonia tends to remain strongly erect, it would be wise to stake tall plants to maintain an attractive appearance following late-summer storms. Rejuvenate large clumps by division every other year.

Uses in the Garden and Landscape

Include Boltonias in your fall color scheme. In the sunny border the mass of white flowers is a welcome contrast to the profusion of yellow during the late-summer and fall months. Their full, rounded habit is effective next to fall-blooming columnar plants, such as certain of the Goldenrods (*S. canadensis* and *S. sempervirens*, in particular) and Blazing Star. The plant also mixes well with *Rudbeckia fulgida*, Great Lobelia, and Seashore Mallow.

Interplant Boltonia in a naturalized setting with Bur-Marigold, New England Aster, and Queen-of-the-Meadow. The brilliant red Cardinal Flower is stunning against the white background of Boltonia. Use cut sprays of Boltonia as filler material in fall flower arrangements.

Production Notes

Cuttings root best under mist in the greenhouse. Overwinter potted plants in a cold frame or other protective structure and market the following spring.

If propagating by division, field-grow the plants in an open, sunny plot in loose, well-drained soil. Pot divisions into 4-inch or quart containers in early spring and market several weeks later.

Blazing Star

Liatris spicata
Asteraceae

Duration: perennial

Blooming time: September

Flower color: lavender

Height: to 6 feet

Soil: fertile, moist

Exposure: full sun

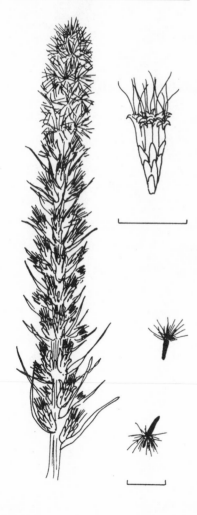

Description

In September Blazing Star becomes a center of attention in the garden. Tall (up to 6 feet) showy spikes of lavender blooms stand in bold contrast to the profusion of yellow flowers appearing at this time of year. A dense grasslike clump of narrow basal leaves arise from a tough, rounded rootstock; the crowded stem leaves are smaller toward the top of the stalk.

The flower clusters are tightly arranged spikelike against the stalk, and those at the top of the stalk open first, followed by those lower down. Unlike the heads, or inflorescences, of most of the other members of the Aster family discussed in this book, which have both disk and ray flowers, the compact heads of Blazing Star are composed of only disk flowers, which are tightly held on elongated receptacles encircled by scalelike bracts tinged with purple.

Blazing Star occurs in coastal savannas, bogs, and roadside ditches throughout the southern states.

Fruit and Seed

Following the bloom period, the plant remains essentially unchanged in appearance until after the first few autumn frosts. Protruding from the small cluster of nutlets in each seed head are the hairlike pappus bristles at first purple, then changing to grayish white. Around the first October frost, the bracts surrounding the seed heads loosen, making the fluffy pappus conspicuous. The nutlets, ¼ inch (5–8 mm) long, taper at their base and are a dark gray at maturity.

Seed Collection, Cleaning, and Storage

When the bracts loosen and the seed head expands, grasp the pappus bristles and pinch out the nutlets. Although all nutlets may be a uniform gray, not all are viable: a fully developed nutlet that contains a moist white embryo is swollen and larger than the flattened, undeveloped, and often empty inviable nutlets. As in other species of the Aster family, you may find that a majority of the nutlets are undeveloped.

Wait until the flower heads on the entire stalk have a fluffy appearance before collecting—usually mid-to-late October in our area. Bring the stalks inside in a large paper bag and let them air-dry for several days, whereupon the heads may expand further and the nutlets can be removed by simply brushing them free from the heads or by vigorously shaking the stems in the bag. Some nutlets may have to be pinched free from unopened heads.

There is no need to attempt to separate the undeveloped nutlets and smaller chaff from the good seed unless you have good seed-cleaning equipment. Store the nutlets dry in a sealed, labeled container and refrigerate.

Propagation

Seed. Try this easy sowing method: when the nutlets are ripe, merely cut the flowering stalk and lay it down in an outdoor seedbed or in the cold frame and cover with a half inch or so of soil; look for seedlings the following spring.

For indoor sowing in late winter sow stored seed heavily in late winter in a flat. Expect germination in two to three weeks and thin where necessary. As seedlings, which look like tufts of grass or onions, are slow-growing, allow them to remain in the flat until they are well rooted—probably eight to ten weeks from your sowing date—then transfer to small containers and on into the garden in early May.

In the flat, germination is hastened by a warm soil temperature (70°F); the seedlings benefit from a starter solution fertilizer, and weekly applications of an all-purpose fertilizer are helpful after the plants are moved to containers. Young plants grow rapidly when moved into the garden.

Division. In early spring before the leaf buds break is the best time to divide Blazing Star. Lift a mature clump from the garden and note the several crowns that make up the tough, woody rootstock. With a sharp knife or pruning shears, separate the crowns, replant, and water thoroughly.

Cultivation

Once established in the garden, Blazing Star demands little attention. The plant thrives in moist, fertile soils, where it develops tall, slender stems. In drier, less fertile conditions, the plants are shorter, almost stocky in appearance, but equally attractive.

A sunny setting is best. If Liatris is shaded by other tall plants, its stems will tend to twist and bend toward the light, causing the plant to lose its bold vertical character. Allow two feet between plants in the perennial border. Staking as the stems begin to lengthen will keep the flowering stems from falling during late-summer and fall storms.

The cormlike rootstocks of Blazing Star seem to be a preferred food of chipmunks, mice, and other burrowing rodents. A planting mixture of one part soil and one part sharp-edged, clean, 1-to-2-inch gravel may help keep these rodents from the plant roots.

Uses in the Garden and Landscape

Blazing Star makes a dignified addition to the formal border. It goes well with the fall-blooming Black-eyed Susans (*Rudbeckia fulgida* and *R. triloba*), Boltonia, and the Goldenrods, especially the Rough-leaved Goldenrod (*Solidago rugosa*).

With a little attention to soil improvement, Blazing Star will succeed in a rather dry garden bed and even in dry roadside, meadow, or naturalized areas. Try it in a roadside ditch interplanted with Bur-Marigold for a spectacular fall display.

The plant also makes an excellent cut flower for use in arrangements, and if cut at the beginning of its bloom, it will develop into a dried stalk of pale purple after the harvest is long past.

Related Species

A number of other native *Liatris* species occur in decidedly drier sites and are also suitable for use in the garden or for naturalizing. These include: *L. aspera* (to 6 feet), *L. graminifolia* (to 4 feet), *L. helleri* (to 4 feet), *L. regimontis* (to 4 feet), and *L. squarrosa* (to 3 feet). Propagation is essentially the same for all of these as for *L. spicata*.

Production Notes

Sow seeds in an outdoor bed in July, move seedlings into 4-inch containers by September, overwinter, and offer for sale the following spring.

If propagating by division, you will find that plants grow remarkably when field-grown in a sunny plot with light, well-drained soil. Divide clumps in early spring and put in 4-inch containers.

Ludwigia

Ludwigia bonariensis
Onagraceae

Duration: perennial

Blooming time: September

Flower color: yellow

Height: 3–6 feet

Soil: moist or wet

Exposure: full sun

Description

Beautiful yellow flowers in late August and September make Ludwigia a desirable addition to the wild garden. *Ludwigia bonariensis*, one of the showiest, has naturalized from South America into marshes and wet places throughout the southeastern states.

Mature plants produce sharply angled stems as long as 6 feet, with downy, sessile, alternate leaves that are narrowly elliptic to oblanceolate and up to 6 inches long and ½ inch wide.

The flowers are borne singly from leaf axils on slender half-inch pedicels. The four large, overlapping petals, each ½–1 inch (1.25–2.5 cm) long, are broadly ovate. The primroselike flowers and willowlike leaves account for the common name Primrose-Willow sometimes given to Ludwigia species.

Fruit and Seed

The narrow, distinctive, four-sided capsule, up to 1¼ inches (3.2 cm) long, is evident soon after the petals drop; four sepals persist at the apex of the capsule which tapers sharply toward its base. The hairy capsules develop several prominent ribs and turn from green to tan over the next three to four weeks as the seeds develop. The boxlike apex of the capsule gives the Ludwigias another common name: Seedbox. Numerous tiny yellow or reddish seeds, only 0.5–1 mm long, are produced along a central axis within the capsule.

Seed Collection, Cleaning, and Storage

Seeds shake from longitudinal slits as the ribs of the capsule separate. For seed collection the ripening capsules should be gathered just as the first ones begin to split. However, there is really no hurry because plants produce many flowers over a

long period, and capsules will be at different stages of development during the months of September and October.

Select a capsule that shows signs of darkening, split it, and examine the seeds. If they have darkened to yellow or red, collect the pods; if the seeds are still developing, move on to another capsule until you find mature seeds.

To clean, split the capsule, tap out the seeds, and let them air-dry for a few days before storing them in a sealed, labeled container in the refrigerator.

Propagation

Seed. Sown indoors or in the cold frame in late winter or early spring, seeds stored from the previous season germinate rapidly, in one to two weeks. It is vital that seedlings not be allowed to dry out; monitor the moisture condition of the soil daily or keep the seed flat in a shallow pan of water.

Transplant seedlings into individual containers when they have two leaves and roots an inch long, about four to five weeks from germination. Set plants in the permanent location in the garden when roots fill containers and danger of frost is past. Plants can usually be expected to flower the first year from seed.

Cuttings. Take tip cuttings from mature plants in early June. Remove the lower leaves and insert cuttings in a rooting medium of equal parts sand and perlite. Put the flat of cuttings in a rooting chamber, where high humidity can be maintained, and expect cuttings to be well rooted in about three weeks. (Cuttings placed under mist in the greenhouse root very rapidly and are ready to be potted in one week.) Pot rooted cuttings in your standard potting medium and when roots fill containers, locate plants in the garden.

Cultivation

Ludwigias grow best in a constantly moist soil with direct sunlight for all or most of the day. Drier or shadier conditions will produce less showy specimens.

Establish these plants in informal settings where they can sprawl and not detract from nearby plants. Ludwigias thrive in fertile soil, so incorporate generous amounts of rotted leaves and compost in the planting area.

Where light and moisture conditions are favorable, plants require little maintenance. To limit their spread into areas where they are not wanted, simply pull up stems from the edges of the stand. Stems may be cut back to ground level after flowering, or stems and capsules may be left intact—the seeds produced provide food for birds.

Uses in the Garden and Landscape

Ludwigia is a natural for the edge of a pond or pool or in a bog planting, or try plants in roadside and drainage ditches and in low, sunny areas where the soil remains moist throughout the season. For pleasant color contrasts, mix with Ironweed, Seashore Mallow, the Lobelias, the Eupatoriums, and Meadow Beauties.

Related Species

Ludwigia alternifolia, Seedbox, though not nearly as showy in flower, is common throughout the eastern United States. It is also perennial, hardier further north than *L. bonariensis*, but propagated and grown the same. The dried branches of little boxlike capsules are frequently collected for fall and winter dried arrangements. Bright orange to red foliage in the fall makes this an attractive "weed" in the wild garden.

Seashore Mallow

Kosteletskya virginica
Malvaceae

Duration: perennial

Blooming time: September

Flower color: pink

Height: 5 feet or taller

Soil: good garden soil

Exposure: full to filtered sun

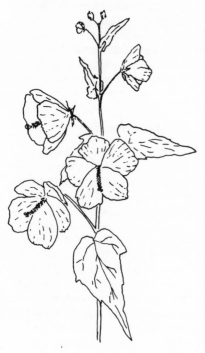

Description

Too few gardeners enjoy the delights and charms of this little-known native perennial. Blooming in late summer, its attractive pale to deep pink flowers make an engaging contrast to the swirl of yellow bloom so prominent during the final months of the growing season.

The axillary cup-shaped flowers, 3 inches (7.5 m) across, with five petals and a central column of yellow stamens, are borne toward the tips of the leafy shoots. The simple, alternate, three-to-five-lobed, gray green leaves are up to 5 inches (12.5 cm) or more long and wide. A mature plant can grow to 5 feet or more and is often much branched and angular in habit.

In the Southeast the species inhabits brackish marshes in the coastal counties, but notwithstanding its natural habitat the Seashore Mallow is an appropriate plant for gardens in colder climes, proving durable even in the Southern Appalachians. The plant closely resembles *Hibiscus militaris*, the Halberd-leaved Marsh Mallow, another member of the Mallow family.

Fruit and Seed

The bristly, broadly rounded, five-lobed, light green capsule, ¼ inch (6–8 mm) long, ¼–½ inch (8–14 mm) broad, is evident shortly after the blooms wither. Each of the five compartments of the fruit holds a single seed. As the 3/16-inch (3.5–4.5 mm) oval seeds ripen, the capsules age to

dark green and finally to brown. At collection time you will most likely notice a few holes bored into the dark brown seeds by boll weevils, which lay their eggs in the seeds.

Seed Collection, Cleaning, and Storage

Wait for the capsules (technically, schizocarps) to split open before collecting seeds; the seeds may be ready earlier, but cleaning is easier when the capsules open on their own. Snip off individual fruits as they ripen and drop them into your collection bag. Remove the seeds from the capsules immediately after collection (to minimize damage by the weevils) either by hand or by vigorously shaking the bag of collected fruits. Alternatively, cut

stalks a foot or so below the capsules and remove the seeds by beating or threshing seed into an open container.

To take care of the weevil problem put the cleaned seed in a glass or plastic container, place a 2–3 inch segment of No-Pest Strip into the container, seal, and store at room temperature in a dark, out-of-the-way place for two weeks. Then remove the strips and store seeds dry in the refrigerator. When handling No-Pest Strips, use forceps or tweezers. If you chance to touch them, wash hands in warm, soapy water immediately. Store disinfested seeds dry in a sealed, labeled container in the refrigerator.

Propagation

Seed. Seedlings are easily raised in late winter indoors or outdoors in a cold frame or seedbed. A warm soil temperature (70°F) will hasten germination. Germination typically occurs within a week and seedling growth is rapid. The seedlings should be large enough to transplant to containers within a month; six to eight weeks later the plants should be well rooted and can be moved directly into the garden. Weekly applications of a liquid all-purpose fertilizer will hasten seedling growth.

Cuttings. Tip cuttings, taken before flowering, root readily in a sand and perlite medium in a shaded cold frame or small, enclosed rooting chamber and can be potted in six weeks. Allow rooted cuttings to remain in pots over the winter and transplant them into the garden next spring.

Cultivation

Even though in nature it occurs in saline soil, Seashore Mallow performs admirably in good garden soil. The addition of a shovelful or so of sand to the soil at planting time, however, is beneficial. An exposure of a half day's full sun or more is ideal; more shade produces a rangy, less attractive plant.

The tough root system grows deep, and plants require no additional watering during periods of regular rainfall. The appearance of the plant can be improved, however, with frequent watering during drought periods, and of course the seedlings and cuttings need regular watering until established in the garden. Even first-year plants can be expected to flower modestly, and once the root system is well developed and the plant established, blooming can be profuse. If you plant Seashore Mallow among other tall fall-blooming plants, be sure to allow room for the plant's 4-foot or greater spread.

Uses in the Garden and Landscape

Use Seashore Mallow liberally in the garden. Try it in a fall planting scheme, where its alluring pink blooms will become a focal point. The Asters, Blazing Star, Boltonia, and the Goldenrods are lively companions in the perennial border. The plant is, of course, a natural choice for a sunny, wet area or at pond's edge.

Seashore Mallow is late to break dormancy—not until May do the leaves appear—so it can be safely interplanted with shallow-rooted spring- and early-summer-blooming plants. A single grouping of plants—say, at the base of a deck, next to a porch, or against an evergreen backdrop—can be spectacular. This species has an old-timey feel about it and, as Hal Bruce notes in *How to Grow Wildflowers and Wild Shrubs and Trees in Your Own Garden*, bears a resemblance to the single-flowered Hollyhock, a plant fading from use in contemporary gardens.

Production Notes

Transfer seedlings from small containers into quart pots ten to twelve weeks from sowing to accommodate the aggressive, fast-growing root system. Container culture is impractical beyond this time because of the deep-reaching root system.

Root cuttings under mist and overwinter rooted cuttings in containers and offer for sale the following spring.

Bur-Marigold, Beggar Ticks

Bidens polylepis
Asteraceae

Duration: annual

Blooming time: September

Flower color: yellow

Height: 2–6 feet

Soil: moist

Exposure: full sun to open shade

Description

The bright yellow flowers of this native annual measure nearly 3 inches across, and golden drifts of Bur-Marigold add late-summer color to roadside ditches, old fields, and sunny, wet areas.

The opposite, petiolate leaves are pinnately or bipinnately lobed or dissected and the showy flower heads are terminal on the numerous branches of the large plants. The cluster of yellow disk flowers may be ½ inch (1.25 cm) or more broad and the rich yellow ray flowers or "petals" are 1–1½ inches (2.5–4 cm) long.

Similar in appearance to some of our native *Coreopsis*, this species, which may attain a height and spread of 4 to 6 feet, has tremendous ornamental potential in the home landscape.

Fruit and Seed

As the yellow ray flowers fade and drop, the central disk gradually expands. The developing nutlets are at first light green, then turn dark brown as they mature; they are flat, tapered from base to apex, and ¼ inch (5–6 mm) long and ⅛ inch (2.5–3.5 mm) wide and often exhibit several awns, or hairlike appendages, at the apex.

Seed Collection, Cleaning, and Storage

Seeds are mature and ready for collection after the first or second October frost. Beyond that time the seed head deteriorates rapidly, and any winds or rainstorms will remove the last nutlets from the seed head. Conveniently, seeds may be harvested earlier when they are dark green as they will mature and turn brown on the cut plant within a few days after collection.

The easiest method of gathering seed is simply to cut off or pull up the entire plant—as Bur-Marigold is an annual, no harm will be done. Allow the plants to air-dry for several days; then cut the stems a foot or so below the seed heads, bunch the severed stems together, and beat the seed heads into an open container; a bucket, box, or large paper bag is fine.

Considerable chaff will be mixed with the seed in this process, and so some cleaning will be desirable and can be easily accomplished with sieves or by carefully separating the litter with a blower.

Seeds should not be stored dry because their viability will be greatly reduced or lost entirely. Thus, if seeds are to be held for a spring sowing, they must be stratified by mixing or layering the seeds in damp whole-fiber sphagnum moss in a sealed, labeled plastic or glass container, and refrigerated.

Propagation

Seed. Seeds of *Bidens* species appear to require a moist chill of at least thirty days and then a warm soil temperature in order to germinate. If these conditions are satisfied, germination is quite rapid and occurs in a high percentage. When started indoors, seeds should be sown thirty days prior to the last spring frost in your area. This will be ample time for seedlings to be removed from the seed flat and grown on in individual containers before transplanting to a seasonal planting site in the garden.

Direct sowing outdoors is also reliable, but make sure that the site in which the seeds are to be sown is naturally moist. Fall sowing outdoors, relying on nature to break dormancy is very effective for spring germination.

Cuttings. If seeds are scarce, these annuals can be increased early in the season by cuttings. Tip cuttings taken from young plants in the spring are easily rooted. Insert the cuttings in a rooting medium of equal parts peat moss and sand and mist several times during the day. The use of a small rooting chamber in which high humidity can be maintained is helpful.

Cultivation

Although tolerant of a fairly wide range of growing conditions, Bur-Marigold thrives in a sunny, moist setting. Once it has been started, you are free essentially to ignore these plants for the remainder of the growing season—until, of course, September, when this is no longer possible due to the spectacular display of flowers.

Though full sun is preferred, good flowering has been observed on plants in open shade and partial sun at a woodland edge. Bur-Marigold is one of the few native wild flowers that can be established by simply broadcasting the seeds in the desired planting site. Again, fall sowing is recommended. Once established, the plant self-sows freely and can be considered permanent in its location if the site is mowed in late fall or early spring. This annual cannot persist in competition with established grasses and other perennials.

In addition to naturalizing, single plants or small clumps can be effectively used in a garden bed or throughout a home landscape. Given ample moisture, light, and nutrients, a single plant can become quite spectacular, up to 6 feet high and 6 feet across, and bear hundreds of bright yellow flowers.

Uses in the Garden and Landscape

In addition to a sunny ditch planting, where a display of several hundred feet can be achieved with little more than a handful of seed, Bur-Marigold lends itself to many other possibilities in the garden. Massed plantings produce the most striking effects. Consider clustering plants along the edge of a wooded area or planting in such a way as to soften a more formal planting.

Bur-Marigold can also be used effectively at the rear of the perennial border or established along a path as a loose, informal seasonal hedge. If plants are established in drier sites, regular watering during the summer months will produce larger, more attractive plants. Because of its loose, spreading habit, Bur-Mari-gold is best planted in open areas where it will not interfere with other plantings.

Related Species

Bidens aristosa is nearly indistinguishable from *B. polylepis* save for slightly smaller flowers. Propagation and cultivation requirements are the same.

Production Notes

Cuttings produce roots within three days when placed under mist, and can be potted in a week's time.

Rough-leaved Goldenrod

Solidago rugosa
Asteraceae

Duration: perennial

Blooming time: September

Flower color: yellow

Height: 4 feet

Soil: average, well-drained

Exposure: full sun

Description

The Goldenrods are attractive, low-maintenance perennials that are not yet fully appreciated by American gardeners. This neglect can probably be traced to the long-standing but misplaced association of the plant with hay fever; in fact, it is not the Goldenrods but Ragweed (*Ambrosia spp.*) blooming at the same time that makes fall the hay fever season. Also, because many species of Goldenrod occur in profusion in poor soils in abandoned fields and waste places, the plant is often branded a roadside weed, further reducing its acceptance for use in the garden. Northern European gardeners, however, have long recognized the ornamental possibilities of our native American Goldenrods, using them liberally to enhance the garden in late summer and fall, and we would do well to emulate them and make better use of this durable and rewarding group.

For a three-to-four-week period in the fall the thin sprays of long, arching flowering stems of the Rough-leaved Goldenrod can only be described as spectacular. In established clumps the stalks can reach to 4 feet or more and bear many sturdy flowering branches. The numerous narrow, toothed cauline (stem) leaves are rugose (with rough surfaces) and are 4–6 inches (10–15 cm) long. The clumps, which are handsome and dense through the season, make effective foils for low-growing plants and plants with looser, more open habits, such as Fire Pink and Sundrops.

The Rough-leaved Goldenrod occurs naturally in low woods, meadows, old fields, bogs, and pine barrens throughout much of the eastern United States.

Fruit and Seed

The pale pappus bristles are evident in the fruit clusters a week or two after the flowers fade. A month later the stalks are covered with the fluffy clusters of pappus bristles and take on a grayish appearance. Like other fall-blooming composites, Goldenrods mature their numerous seeds, small triangular nutlets 1–2 millimeters long, near the first frost. The attached pappus is 3–4 millimeters long. As the seeds mature, the lower leaves begin to yellow and drop, and numerous basal rosettes, which will produce the next year's stalks, appear and continue to develop through the late-fall months.

Seed Collection, Cleaning, and Storage

In October pluck a tuft of nutlets from a seed head and examine it. If the nutlets are off-white or gray, they are mature; if they are still white, give them more time. Most nutlets will be flattened and will lack embryos; typically less than 5 percent will be thicker, fully developed, and viable. The fruits remain in the seed head for several weeks past the first frost, which allows adequate time for collecting. Indeed, a convenient collection time may be during the fall garden cleanup when the old Goldenrod stalks are removed.

To remove the nutlets from the numerous small seed heads grasp the bottom of several stalks and shake them into a large paper bag; or the nutlets may be rubbed free by hand. The seeds may be planted as soon as collected or stored dry in a sealed, labeled container in the refrigerator.

Propagation

Seed. Since germination is often very poor, sow seeds thickly in an outdoor seedbed early in the fall or sow stored seed later in a flat indoors or in the cold frame. Transplant the tiny rosettes from the flat into 3-inch pots when they have three or four leaves. When roots fill the pots and the last spring frost date is past, move plants into the garden. Allow nine to ten weeks from sowing to permanent planting.

The critical period in a seedling's development is during the week or two after transplanting from the flat or bed into individual pots. If the leaves remain in contact with the soil for extended periods, the seedling is likely to rot. As a safeguard, mound seedlings slightly in the pot so that leaves are just above the soil.

Cuttings. Take stem tip cuttings, 3–4 inches long, in May or June. Remove the lower leaves and insert cuttings into a mixture of equal parts peat moss and sand or into straight sand. Place the cuttings in a rooting chamber, misting leaves and saturating the rooting mix before they become dry.

Cuttings root best under mist in the greenhouse; however, 50 percent rooting can be expected in any situation in which humid conditions are constant. Pot rooted cuttings in 4-inch containers, and when roots have filled the pots, transplant into the garden or overwinter the plants in the cold frame or a protected spot outside for spring planting in the garden.

Division. Division of the cluster of basal rosettes, best performed in late winter, offers the easiest and most practical method of increase. Lift the entire clump, break it into pieces, and separate the rosettes. A mature plant can yield thirty to forty divisions; if you need only a few new plants, cut a section from the edge of the clump with a trowel or spade and separate the rosettes. Replant the divisions at once and water thoroughly. Divisions of flowering size may be made by simply sectioning a large clump into four or five pieces.

Cultivation

Plants grow well in almost any soil, although a loose, well-

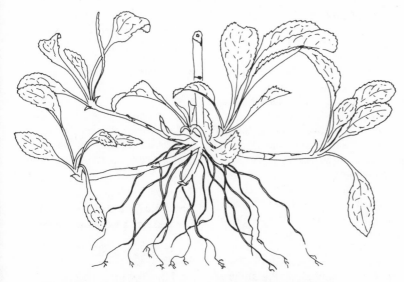

Many other Goldenrod species have application in the garden or may be naturalized in sunny areas. Seaside Goldenrod (*S. sempervirens*) produces a tight clump of narrow evergreen basal leaves and then stalks of yellow flowers in late summer. Pinch the growing tips in June for a more compact plant.

Among other species of *Solidago* suitable for cultivation are *S. patula*, which is suitable for wet areas; *S. curtisii*, which grows to 2–3 feet and does well in shade; *S. altissima, S. fistulosa,* and *S. gigantea*, common but attractive Goldenrods of roadside and field, which bear familiar arching flower stalks and form colonies via long rhizomes, making them ideal for naturalizing; *S. juncea*, which flowers as early as June and spreads by rhizomes; and *S. odora*, the leaves of which produce an anise odor when crushed.

Production Notes

Grow plants in an open, sunny field with well-drained soil. Clumps spread rapidly in these conditions and can be divided and potted early in the second season and marketed that spring.

drained medium with plenty of leaf mold and aged manure enhances growth. A thick mulch of leaves around clumps will reduce, and in many cases eliminate, the need for watering during the growing season. Plants thrive in an open, sunny exposure and develop a tight, rounded habit at flowering. A lightly shaded setting will do, but expect the plants to be looser and leggier.

Few, if any, herbaceous perennials can impede the spread of Rough-leaved Goldenrod, so space plants a good 3 feet from their nearest neighbors. If your Goldenrod plants begin to encroach upon nearby plants, curb the clumps by sectioning off their edges or plan to divide the clumps every other year. The sturdy, upright stalks will not require staking.

Uses in the Garden and Landscape

Plant Rough-leaved Goldenrod in the rear of the sunny border. Where space allows, establish plants at intervals along the border, say every fifteen feet or so. New England Aster, Halberd-leaved Marsh Mallow, Seashore Mallow, Boltonia, Ironweed, and Great Lobelia are effective companions in a border planting.

Plants are also quick to naturalize on a dry sunny bank. Where a darker background is available, such as in front of evergreen shrubs, against a fence, or at the corner of the house, plants can be established singly or in small groups. The brilliant stalks of Goldenrod used as cut flowers are outstanding in fall arrangements.

New England Aster

Aster novae-angliae
Asteraceae

Duration: perennial

Blooming time: September

Flower color: lavender, purple

Height: to 5 feet

Soil: average garden soil

Exposure: full sun

Description

Of the several hundred species of asters native to North America, the New England Aster is among the most attractive, a fact which has not eluded breeders of ornamental plants. This species is parent to a number of varieties of the familiar Michaelmas Daisy, popular in American gardens for many years.

The plant, which forms clumps with sturdy stems that can reach to 6 feet or more under favorable conditions, is found in most of the eastern United States in wet areas, such as damp thickets, meadows, and along the margins of bogs and marshes. The color of the ray flowers can vary from pale lavender to pink, rosy lilac, violet purple, deep purple, and, rarely, white; discerning gardeners can select and grow plants with the colors they desire.

The stems bear many alternate, lance-shaped leaves with clasping, auriculate, or ear-shaped, bases and branch toward the top into numerous side shoots terminating in clusters of flowering heads. A single head has forty to eighty ray flowers and a mound of yellow disk flowers. Plants flower for three weeks or more in September and October.

Fruit and Seed

The compact seed heads and the small nutlets, only a few millimeters long, are typical of other species, such as Maryland Golden Aster, the Erigerons, Boltonia, and the Goldenrods. The nutlets develop two to three weeks after the ray flowers fade and drop. The nutlets are tightly arranged on the receptacle, which forms the base of the head and which is surrounded by a series of green or purple involucral bracts, or phyllaries. As the elliptic nutlets develop and change from white to dark brown at maturity, the tan pappus bristles become more conspicuous, extending out from the head.

Seed Collection, Cleaning, and Storage

The seed heads remain intact on the plants for several weeks beyond the first frost when the seeds are fully expanded, or nearly so, and the rows of nutlets loosened within. At that time you can shake the nutlets loose or easily pluck them from the head by hand, whereas if you gathered the heads earlier, you would have to let them air-dry for several days to facilitate nutlet removal. The fall cleanup of your garden can be a good time to collect seeds of this and other fall-blooming wild flowers.

Allow the cleaned nutlets to air-dry for a few days to remove remaining moisture. You may notice insects, most commonly small worms, among the nutlets during cleaning. If so, fumigate the seeds by placing them and a small piece of No-Pest Strip in a bag or sealed container for two weeks. Store disinfested nutlets dry in a sealed, labeled container and refrigerate until sowing.

Propagation

Seed. As with many members of the Aster family, only a small portion of the nutlets will have developed embryos; so sow seeds heavily to guarantee some seedlings from your efforts. Nutlets may be sown upon collection in an outdoor seedbed, with some germination likely in the spring. Stored seeds may also be sown indoors or in the cold frame in late winter; germination should take place, albeit in a low percentage, in one to two weeks.

When rosettes have three or four leaves and roots are 1–2 inches long, transplant the seedlings into 3-inch pots and then later into the garden when roots fill the pot. Plan on an eight-to-ten-week production time from seed to permanent planting. Seedlings benefit from weekly applications of an all-purpose fertilizer.

Cuttings. Cuttings root faster and in a higher percentage when taken early in the season—late May and June—before flowering shoots develop. Take tip cuttings

6–8 inches long, remove the leaves from the lower half of the stem, and insert cuttings in a moist, well-drained rooting medium, such as one made up of equal parts sand and peat moss. Keep cuttings in a rooting chamber where high humidity can be maintained and make sure the medium remains evenly moist. Under these conditions, cuttings should be well rooted and ready to pot in four to five weeks. Hold rooted cuttings in pots through the summer and move them into the garden in early fall.

Division. Mature plants include many stems closely spaced in the clump. Division may be performed in the spring by sectioning off individual stems, with their associated roots, from the edge of the clump or by lifting the entire clump and making divisions that include one or more stems. Use a shovel or long trowel to divide the clump, although stems may often be pulled up by hand with enough roots attached to sustain the new plant. Replant and water new divisions immediately.

Cultivation

To produce robust, full-flowered specimens, grow New England Aster in full sun or in a setting that receives at least a half day's direct light, such as at the edge of a wooded area. Less light results in rangy specimens with fewer flowers. Grow plants in ordinary garden soil that is not too rich; you might simply spade over the native soil in your garden several times and then work in a moderate amount of humus.

Plants decline in vigor if the clump is too crowded so plan to divide plants every two years or as needed. For more, but smaller, blooms, pinch the growing tips of the stems in July. Mature plants definitely benefit from staking or other support, such as inserting a small branch or two in the clump. When irrigating, remember to water the plants at their bases and avoid wetting the foliage, as this will reduce mildew problems.

Uses in the Garden and Landscape

Work plants of New England Aster into your fall planting scheme. Use them singly or in small groups in the rear of the sunny border, where they combine so effectively with the native Sunflowers, Goldenrods, and Seashore Mallow. Naturalize plants in roadside ditches, road banks, and open grassy areas; a sunny site where the soil remains moist through the season is ideal. New England Asters are long lasting and beautiful in fall arrangements as cut flowers.

Related Species

Aster divaricatus has smaller, white ray flowers, grows to 2 feet, and makes a good groundcover for the shade garden. The New York Aster, *A. novi-belgii*, has the same requirements as *A. novae-angliae*, grows to 4 feet, and has beautiful but smaller blue flowers; *A. pilosus*, Frost Aster, has small white or lavender flowers, grows to 4 feet, and is effective when naturalized; *A. linariifolius*, Bristle-leaved Aster, has bluish flowers, grows to 2 feet, and works well in the rock garden.

Production Notes

Stick cuttings directly into 3-inch containers and place them under mist. Transplant rooted cuttings into quart pots later in the season, overwinter them in a protected spot in the nursery or in the cold frame, and market the following spring. For propagating by division field-grow plants in an open setting and pot divisions in early spring with a single stem in quart pots for marketing that spring or in the fall.

Maryland Golden Aster

Heterotheca mariana
Asteraceae

Duration: perennial

Blooming time: September–October

Flower color: yellow

Height: 8 inches–2 feet

Soil: well-drained

Exposure: full sun

Description

Maryland Golden Aster is found in poor clay and sandy soils throughout the southeastern United States. This drought-resistant perennial is conspicuous in September when its bright yellow flowers bloom on our roadsides. When introduced into the garden, the plant's appearance improves rather dramatically.

The numerous hairy basal leaves persist through the winter; the leafy flowering stems range from 8 inches to 2 feet tall and support dense terminal clusters of flower heads, ¾–1 inch (1.8–2.5 cm) wide which consist of yellow ray and disk flowers and look like miniature Chrysanthemum blooms. In fact, you can treat the plant in much the same manner as you would cultivated Mums—that is, beginning in June cut the stems back to encourage a bushy, more floriferous specimen. Like many native plants that endure dry, sunny conditions in nature, Maryland Golden Aster luxuriates in the garden and requires little care.

Fruit and Seed

After the flowers fade, the seed heads become noticeable as tightly woven whorls of bracts surrounding the developing nutlets. Four to five weeks after flowering the seed heads begin to expand and the tannish brown pappus bristles of the disk flower nutlets become evident; the nutlets produced by the ray flowers do not have a pappus. As the nutlets reach maturity the seed heads take on an attractive, light, fluffy appearance similar to the mature seed heads of other Aster family species, such as Asters and Goldenrods. Although only a single fruit, or nutlet, is produced by each small ray or disk flower, nutlets are numerous within the head. The nutlets turn from white to reddish brown at maturity.

Seed Collection, Cleaning, and Storage

The best time to collect seed is in October, after the first few frosts. Experience has taught that a much higher percentage of mature seed can be expected at this time. Cut the stems below the fruiting heads and air-dry them indoors for several days.

247

Clean seeds by grasping the fluffy pappus and plucking seeds (nutlets) from the receptacle; or vigorously shaking the seed heads in a paper bag may dislodge all the seeds needed. There is no need to remove the pappus. Sometimes groups of nutlets stick together when they are first removed from the receptacle, but they can be easily separated by simply rolling them between your fingers.

As is common with many species in the Aster family, less than half the nutlets will contain embryos. Undeveloped nutlets are thin and flattened; mature viable nutlets are slightly swollen and of a darker color. The task of removing bad seeds is laborious and, for our purposes, unnecessary, as they do not affect germination of the good seed. Frequently many of the good seeds have been consumed by insect predators. Store all seeds in a sealed, labeled container and refrigerate.

Propagation

Seed. To allow for a considerable percentage of bad seed in your lot, sow stored seed heavily in a flat indoors or in a cold frame in late winter or early spring. Completely cover the surface of your seed mix with seeds and cover lightly with soil. Germination will probably not be high, but should occur within a week's time. A warm soil temperature (70°F) and a well-drained medium are recommended.

Four weeks after germination, the seedlings should be large enough to pot. Add an extra measure of sand to your potting mix to ensure good drainage and do not overwater. Allow the surface of the soil to become dry between waterings; seedling leaves are densely hairy and hold moisture—which could be fatal to them if they were kept continually moist. Mounding seedlings in containers facilitates drainage of excess water so that leaves may dry quicker. Seedlings grow at a moderate rate and should be planted out soon after the last spring frost.

Division. A single mature plant produces a half dozen or more crowns borne on short stolons. In early spring take up an entire clump and separate individual rosettes by tugging them apart. Cut off approximately one-third of the foliage, plant the divisions, and water immediately.

Cultivation

Maryland Golden Aster needs an open, sunny exposure and well-drained soil. Amend heavy clay soil with a shovelful of sand per plant. Beyond this, little is required to produce healthy specimens. Space plants 1–1½ feet apart to allow the branching stems to spread as the plant approaches flowering. Lifting and dividing plants every other year and occasional watering during dry periods will produce more attractive plants.

Uses in the Garden and Landscape

Maryland Golden Aster is ideal for the front of the sunny perennial border; or use it to soften the corners in a formal border, or repeat it in small staggered groupings. It is also a good filler plant in pockets left by other plants. Try it as an edging plant along a path or establish a few plants in front of the fall-blooming Blazing Star for a colorful contrast. The plant is also a good choice for naturalizing on a dry road bank. It grows well in a large container and makes a fine cut flower for fall arrangements.

Related Species

Heterotheca subaxillaris, native to sandy soils and roadsides, also has ornamental value in the garden. This species grows to 3 feet and has yellow flowers in late summer on loosely branched stalks; *H. graminifolia* has attractive rosettes of densely pubescent silver gray grasslike foliage and loose panicles of smaller yellow flower heads in the fall. Propagation and cultivation are the same for all three species.

Part 4. Carnivorous Plants

Introduction

Plants that "eat" insects are an unusual switch in a world where anything leafy and green is usually preyed upon by an array of sucking and chewing predators. Carnivorous plants, which have evolved the capacity to catch and digest insects as supplements to the mineral nutrients they receive from the soil, are one of the wonders of the natural world. Pitcher Plants (*Sarracenia*), Sundews (*Drosera*), Butterworts (*Pinguicula*), Bladderworts (*Utricularia*), and the well-known Venus' Flytrap (*Dionaea*) are all carnivorous plants. These plants never fail to capture the imagination and interest of every new generation of hobbyists, students, and researchers.

Many people are surprised to learn that it is the leaves, and not the flowers, of carnivorous plants that catch insects. The leaves have evolved into highly modified traps for attracting, capturing, and digesting prey. These leaf traps, which are often produced throughout the growing season, usually contain some chlorophyll and thus carry on the normal food-manufacturing process of photosynthesis while they lie in wait for prey that will supplement the mineral nutrition of the plant.

Different species of carnivorous plants utilize different mechanisms, both passive and active, to capture their prey. The best example of a passive trap is the Pitcher Plant. Insects are attracted by nectar secreted at the opening of its tall, tubular leaf. If, after drinking the nectar, insects slip or crawl down into the hollow leaf, steep, narrowing walls and a lining of stiff downward-pointing hairs or small wax particles usually prevent escape. The Venus' Flytrap employs a very rapid, active trapping mechanism. Crawling and hopping ground insects suddenly find themselves encased in a lethal leafy envelope that snaps shut in the blink of an eye when they touch trigger hairs on the inside of the leaf.

In spite of the fact that there are many different genera of carnivorous plants that catch insects with their leaves, they are not all closely related to one another. They have all become carnivorous independently as a result of growing in similar habitats—typically, bogs or wetlands with acidic soil that is very low in nutrients, especially nitrogen. This is a good example of convergent evolution, whereby rather different organisms have evolved similar structures or functions in response to similar environmental pressures.

Carnivorous plants are distributed throughout North America, from frozen Alaskan peat bogs to pools and sloughs in the Florida Everglades. One reason they are seldom encountered even though they are so widely distributed is that they occur only in specialized habitats, such as bogs, savannas, swamps, and other wetlands. Sadly, these wetlands, once considered marginal or unsuitable for agriculture or development, are rapidly disappearing as they are drained for croplands, pastures, and pine plantations. Even moderate drainage can sufficiently alter a bog so that it is forever unsuitable for carnivorous plants and the host of other bog-loving plants that share their distinctive habitat.

This section contributed by Rob Gardner, curator, North Carolina Botanical Garden.

Cultivation

Carnivorous plants are not difficult to grow in the home garden if you can provide them with a small natural or artificial bog which meets their specialized horticultural requirements. The best way to understand this group of plants is to see them in the wild and to observe them first hand in the acid bogs, pond margins, savannas, seepage areas, and even roadside ditches scattered throughout the eastern United States. Carnivorous plants grow in areas with high water tables, often just a few inches below the soil surface. Plants in the garden will need a similar environment if they are to be healthy. Although there are slight variations in the growing requirements of each species, carnivorous plants all need the same basic horticultural conditions: strong sunlight, a growing medium with a low pH and an ability to hold moisture (such as commercial-grade whole-fiber sphagnum moss or a mix of equal parts peat moss and coarse vermiculite or sharp sand), and, during the growing season, a constant water supply. The peat moss and sand or vermiculite mix is especially well suited for the smaller carnivorous plants, such as Sundews, Venus' Flytraps, and Butterworts; its finer texture helps it to make better contact with the plant's root system. Both whole-fiber sphagnum moss and peat moss have low pHs and hold water much like a sponge.

Basically, carnivorous plants are sun lovers, and need at least six to eight hours of direct sunlight per day to form properly shaped leaves and develop the full coloration that makes them so attractive. The only exceptions to this are the Butterworts and the Purple Pitcher Plant (*Sarracenia purpurea*), which require lots of strong sunlight in the spring but actually benefit from partial shading from the sun the rest of the growing season.

All of the above-mentioned factors can be nicely drawn together in an artificial bog created in a sunny spot in your garden. You can use almost any kind of plastic or porcelain container, from something as modest as a plastic dishpan to an old sink or bathtub or a child's wading pool. Make three or four drainage holes about halfway up the side of the container and cover them with a piece of plastic screening. Bury the container in the ground to within a few inches of its rim or, to elevate the bog and show your plants off a bit, sink it only halfway and mound the dirt you excavated around the outside.

Next, fill the container with either whole-fiber sphagnum moss or a peat moss and sand mix. Fill the bog from a gently flowing hose and check to make sure that the drainage holes are working. If the bog has been properly prepared, the bottom half of the container should be full of water all the time and the planting medium should wick water up to plants from this reservoir.

After the planting mix settles for a few days it is time to put plants in the bog. Usually, low-growing plants are placed in the front and taller plants toward the back. Be sure to check at least once a week during dry periods to see that the water level is up to the drainage holes.

Finally, carnivorous plants need a dormant period. If your plants are growing outside, they will naturally go dormant in the fall. If your plants are in pots and are being grown under artificial lights or in a greenhouse, however, you will have to help them along. One method for handling plants in pots is to place the plants outside in the fall and bury them to the rim. If you do not have sufficient outdoor space, keep your plants inside but withhold water as the fall progresses until the planting medium is just moist. Keep the plants in this condition until you notice new leaves or flower stalks emerging in the spring, and then resume their regular watering regime. If you try to force your plants into active growth before they have had sufficient dormancy, they may rot. Many growers believe that providing this yearly period of dormancy results in more robust, floriferous plants.

An excellent reference book on the subject is Donald Schnell's *Carnivorous Plants of the United States and Canada*; also, the periodical *Carnivorous Plant Newsletter*, the official journal of the International Carnivorous Plant Society, is quite helpful. For further information on the society and its

newsletter write:
  Carnivorous Plant Society
  Fullerton Arboretum
  California State University
  Fullerton, CA 92634

Venus' Flytrap

Dionaea muscipula
Dionaeaceae

Duration: perennial

Blooming time: June

Flower color: white

Height: prostrate to 3 inches

Soil: boggy

Exposure: full sun

Description

Of all the curious plants in the world, the Venus' Flytrap must be the best known. This carnivorous plant, a low perennial often overlooked except when in bloom, can still be found growing in wet sandy ditches, savannas, and open bog margins of southeastern North Carolina and adjacent South Carolina. In May or June the plants, which grow from a short rhizome, develop a loose cluster of white flowers on a 6-to-12-inch stem. The traps, which are really highly evolved leaves, form on the end of a short expanded petiole.

The inner surfaces of the traps of some plants are a rich, dark red, while those of other plants are green. This difference is probably controlled by a genetic factor, but the amount of sunlight an individual plant receives also affects how red the leaves become. Whether a trap is red or green does not seem to affect its ability to capture ants, spiders, grasshoppers, beetles, and of course a few flies—which account for only 2 percent of the Venus' Flytrap's prey.

Fruit and Seed

The small seeds take about a month to develop in the rounded capsules and are shiny, jet black when mature. Usually several capsules are clustered together at the end of each flower stalk, often concealed in layers of the blackened, dried petals. The papery capsule splits and the seeds are dispersed soon after they are mature, so the plants must be watched carefully (or the seed heads bagged) if seeds are to be collected.

Flowers must be cross-pollinated to produce seeds. To insure proper cross-pollination in a home situation many growers simply use an open, pollen-shedding flower of one plant to dust the stigmas of all other flowering

Venus' Flytraps. This should be done daily for as long as the flowers continue to open. Seeds usually take about a month to develop and mature.

Seed Collection, Cleaning, and Storage

To collect seeds cut the flower stalk several inches below the cluster of ripe seed pods. Spread out the capsules on newspaper and allow them to air dry. The pods and stems will turn black and brittle when properly dry. Clean the seeds by putting them through a sieve or metal screen. Put the dry, clean seeds in a paper envelope, label properly, and store in the refrigerator.

Propagation

Seed. Seeds should be sown thinly in a pot or flat containing a

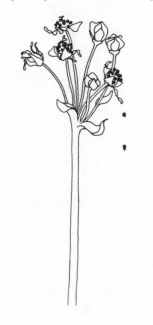

mix of one part peat to one part vermiculite. Do not cover the seeds. Place the container in a warm protected location with indirect light. Bottom water is essential, so place the seed container in a shallow tray that will allow water to reach one-fourth to one-third up the sides of the pot or flat. Germination usually occurs within thirty days, and if you have not sown them too thickly, you can leave them in their original container for several months until they are large enough for easy transplanting. Once they have germinated, the seedlings can be gradually exposed to full sun. Given normal summer temperatures, the three most important factors for germinating these seeds are protection from rain or overhead watering, a constantly damp growing medium, and sufficient sun or appropriate artificial light after germination.

Cultivation

Venus' Flytraps require six to eight hours per day of sunlight. This minimum amount of sunlight is required for the plant to survive for any length of time. A planting medium of equal parts peat moss and vermiculite or whole-fiber sphagnum moss is recommended.

The area in which Venus' Flytraps are planted should be constantly moist during the growing season. Creating an artificial bog, as suggested in the introduction to this section, is a good way to provide all the cultural requirements necessary for growing healthy Venus' Flytraps.

Uses in the Garden and Landscape

Gardeners who are interested in growing Venus' Flytraps, Pitcher Plants, Sundews, and Butterworts but do not have moist, acid, sandy spots in their gardens can easily create special environments in limited areas by using dishpans, plastic liners, fiberglass pools, or children's plastic wading pools. These containers may be sunk in the ground or earth can be mounded around the edges to help blend them into the landscape and protect them from winter conditions. To prevent plants from becoming waterlogged three or four drainage holes should be cut half way up the container.

Special Note

If you are one of those people who cannot resist the temptation to feed his Venus' Flytrap, you should remember that it takes very little to satisfy the needs of the plant. If a leaf is given something too big for it, there is a good chance it will die. If you must feed your plant, give it only very small, soft-bodied insects—a spider or an ant is a good choice. Never feed your plant hamburger, boiled egg, or anything else that comes from the kitchen. Venus' Flytraps are green plants and produce their own food by photosynthesis; hand feeding is not necessary on a routine basis. Also, once a leaf trap has closed, it takes several days for it to reopen, so do not snap the traps too often.

Sundews

Drosera species
Droseraceae

Duration: perennial	
Blooming time: April–August	
Flower color: white to pink	
Height: prostrate to 8 inches	
Soil: boggy	
Exposure: full sun	

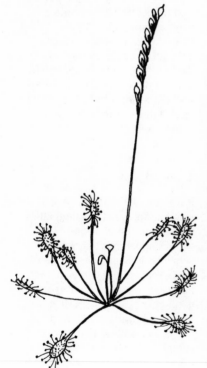

Description

The one hundred or more different species of this colorful and fascinating carnivorous plant are distributed throughout the world. There are seven species in the eastern United States: *Drosera anglica*, *D. brevifolia*, *D. capillaris*, *D. filiformis*, *D. intermedia*, *D. linearis*, and *D. rotundifolia*. All of these herbaceous plants occur in constantly moist soils and bogs.

The dozens of slender, crimson- or green-tipped filaments that stud each Sundew leaf give the plant a jewellike appearance. Each gland secretes a minuscule droplet of a clear mucilaginous substance which entraps tiny insects. As the insect struggles to escape, it stimulates nearby glands to bend slowly toward the prey and secure it even more firmly. Typical prey include mosquitoes, gnats, damselflies, and other small flying insects. Sundews usually bloom in mid-to-late summer. The slender flower stalks, 6–12 inches (15–30 cm) long, rise above a rosette of basal leaves and produce a series of small pink or white flowers. One flower opens each day and can pollinate itself upon closing in the afternoon.

Fruit and Seed

The fruit is a small green capsule that turns blackish when mature, five to seven weeks after flowering. The numerous minute seeds are black or dark grey.

Seed Collection, Cleaning, and Storage

Since the Sundew flowers over an extended period of time with one bud on the flower stalk opening each day, it has an equally extended period of seed maturation. Very often the last few flowers are still blooming as the lower capsules are mature and ready to disperse their seeds. You should collect the flowering stalk at the time that it presents the most mature capsules.

Cut the entire flower stalk off just below the lowest capsule and put it in a paper seed envelope or fold of paper. (Since the seeds are so small, many would be lost if paper bags were used to collect the seed.) Remove the stalks from the envelope and lay them out on a sheet of white paper to dry. When completely dry, most of the seeds can be shaken out of the capsules onto the sheet of paper. In some cases it may be helpful to break the capsules apart to release all of the seeds. Put the cleaned, dry seeds in a paper envelope, label it as to the collection site and date collected, and put it in the refrigerator.

Propagation

Seed. All the Sundews mentioned here can be grown from seed and can be established in an artificial or natural bog by lightly sowing seeds over the surface. This is probably best done in the fall or early spring. Once the plants are established and allowed to go to seed they usually produce new seedlings each year and need little extra attention.

Plants may also be started in pots. Fill a 3- or 4-inch plastic pot with slightly moistened mix of equal parts of peat moss and coarse vermiculite. Sow seeds thinly over the surface of the planting medium and place the pot in a tray. Fill the tray with enough water to bring the level to one-fourth to one-third up the side of the pot. The pot should always be watered from the bottom tray and never from overhead.

Germination usually occurs in from twenty to thirty days, depending on the time of year the seeds are sown. Seedlings are usually ready to transplant to the bog garden or larger display pots after two to three months. They

can either be transplanted individually or in small clumps. Sundew seedlings produce long hairlike roots that are easily damaged when transplanting, so care must be taken when transplanting them.

Cuttings. Sundews can be vegetatively propagated from leaf cuttings. This method can be useful if you have only a few plants and do not have access to seeds. Also, cuttings are an easy and dependable way of increasing your Sundews and they are much quicker and convenient than seeds. Cut fresh new leaves from the plant, choosing leaves that have not captured any insects because the presence of captured bugs can increase the danger that the leaf will decay. Fill a pot with either moistened milled sphagnum moss or peat moss, and place the leaf cuttings "face up" on this medium. They should be pinned or weighted down to insure that the entire lower leaf surface is in contact with the medium, as the leaf will not form buds if it is not touching the soil, but will curl up at the edges and die. Water the pot with water mixed with a fungicide, allow to drain thoroughly, and enclose in a plastic bag, creating the humid environment essential to the formation of buds. Place the bagged pot under fluorescent lights or in a window with strong but indirect sunlight. Plantlets, which will form in three to five weeks, can be transplanted once they have formed their own roots and are large enough to handle easily. Be sure to give newly transplanted

plantlets a chance to acclimatize in the shade before you move them to a sunnier location.

Another easy way to increase your Sundews by leaf cuttings is the water method. Sterilize thoroughly washed baby-food jars and lids with a solution of Chlorox, fill with sterilized or distilled water at room temperature, and place the leaf cuttings in the jar and seal. You can either use whole leaves or cut the leaves into pieces. Place the jar where it gets indirect sunlight or under a fluorescent light. Depending on the species of Sundew and the time of year you take the cuttings, plantlets should form in fifteen to thirty days. Again, make sure the plantlets are well formed before transplanting them. When transplanting, place the well-budded leaves on a premoistened planting medium. Gently press the plantlets into the planting medium with your finger to insure good contact with the soil. Keep new transplants in the shade for several days and very gradually introduce them to progressively stronger light.

Cultivation

Sundews require a constant supply of moisture, a growing medium with a low pH, like peat moss, and at least six to eight hours of sunlight each day. Many gardeners fulfill these requirements by creating artificial bogs in sunny spots in their gardens, as described in the introduction to this section.

Uses in the Garden and Landscape

If you have a small container bog or a natural wet area, Sundews are easy to cultivate and make an interesting addition in even the smallest area. Many gardeners grow Sundews in pots for their horticultural interest. Some growers even specialize in Sundews and have collections of dozens of different species.

Butterworts

Pinguicula species

Lentibulariaceae

Duration: perennial

Blooming time: April–May

Flower color: yellow, pink, purple, white

Height: prostrate

Soil: boggy

Exposure: full sun to partial shade

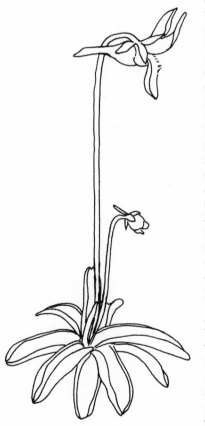

Description

Butterworts are perennial herbaceous plants with glandular, yellow green or purplish leaves in a basal rosette. Six species are native to the bogs and moist savannas of the Southeast: *Pinguicula caerulea, P. ionantha, P. lutea, P. planifolia, P. primuliflora*, and *P. pumila*. These carnivorous plants capture insects in much the same way as Sundews, but on a smaller scale. Minute glands that completely cover the upper surface of each leaf secrete droplets of sticky fluid that essentially glue small insects to the surface of the leaf. The struggling of a captured insect stimulates the glands to secrete even more sticky fluid until the insect is hopelessly stuck to the leaf. The plant then secretes digestive enzymes that dissolve the soft parts of the insect and make the minerals available to the plant. The colorful solitary flowers are held 3–10 inches (7.5–25 cm) above the leaves on slender stalks, or scapes. Depending on the species, the spring-blooming flowers can be either yellow, pink, purple, or, rarely, white.

Fruit and Seed

The fruit is a green capsule about ⅛ inch in diameter that swells slightly and gradually turns buff or brown when ripe. Mature seeds are brown or black and very small, about the same size as finely ground pepper.

Seed Collection, Cleaning, and Storage

Seeds are ready to collect when the capsule has turned brown, three to four weeks after the flower fades in the late spring. The ripe capsules can be easily broken open and the dry seeds shaken out. Store the dry seeds in a paper envelope in the refrigerator. Be sure to label the envelope as to collection site and date.

Propagation

Seed. Fill a pot with moistened peat moss, milled sphagnum moss, or a mix of one part peat moss to one part vermiculite; water the pot with a mix of water and fungicide. Sow seeds on the surface of the medium but do not cover them. Place the pot in a shallow tray of water reaching approximately one-fourth of the way up the side of the pot. Do not water from above, especially once the seeds have begun to germinate, as this will displace them. To maintain high humidity and aid germination, it is sometimes useful to put an ordinary pane of

glass or a piece of clear plastic wrap over the top of the pot. If you do cover the top of the pot, though, be careful to keep it out of direct sunlight and be on daily alert for fungal infection; treat immediately with a fungicide if any appears.

Cultivation

In general, Butterworts have the same requirements as Sundews and Venus' Flytraps: a moist area that gets full sun. Plant Butterworts on a low mound in your bog to help prevent overwatering. This method is also useful for the low or prostrate Sundews and has the added value of showing your plants off to their best advantage.

Uses in the Garden and Landscape

You can grow Butterworts if you have, or can create, a suitable sunny wet spot in your garden. They are the perfect companions for Pitcher Plants, Venus' Flytraps, and Sundews. Butterworts can also be grown in pots, much like the Sundews and the Venus' Flytraps.

Pitcher Plants

Sarracenia species
Sarraceniaceae

Duration: perennial	
Blooming time: April, May, June	
Flower color: yellow, maroon	
Height: 6 inches–3 feet	
Soil: boggy	
Exposure: sunny	

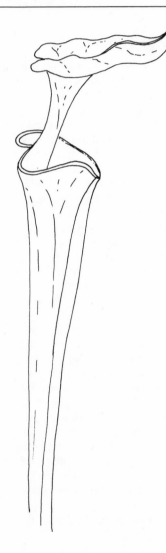

Description

The colorful, highly modified tubular leaves of the Pitcher Plants, which vary from 6 inches to 3 feet in length, enable the plant to trap insects. They range from central Canada south to central Florida and west along the Gulf Coast into eastern Texas, but are most highly concentrated in the bogs, savannas, and other wetlands of the Deep South. There you can find the Pale Pitcher Plant (*Sarracenia alata*), the Yellow Pitcher Plant (*S. flava*), the White-topped Pitcher Plant (*S. leucophylla*), the Hooded Pitcher Plant (*S. minor*), the very rare and federally protected Green Pitcher Plant (*S. oreophila*), the Parrot Pitcher Plant (*S. psittacina*), and the Sweet Pitcher Plant (*S. rubra* and other members of the *S. rubra* complex). The Purple Pitcher Plant (*S. purpurea*) is also found in much of the South, as well as throughout the Mid-Atlantic states, New England, the Great Lakes Region, and much of eastern and central Canada.

The yellow or maroon flowers of Pitcher Plants are solitary on long stalks, or scapes. These in-

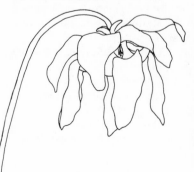

teresting flowers bloom in April or May, and although they drop their petals after seven or eight days, the rest of the interesting flower structure remains throughout the growing season as the seeds mature.

Fruit and Seed

The fruit is a green, five-chambered capsule that remains on the tall scape for the entire growing season and turns brown in the fall when ripe. The numerous, small, tear-shaped seeds are tan to brown or purplish brown when ripe.

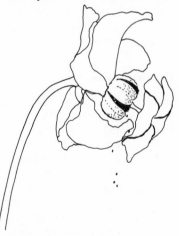

Seed Collection, Cleaning, and Storage

The best time to collect seeds is in the fall when the capsule sutures begin to crack open and the capsule starts to turn from green to greenish yellow or tan. If collected before the capsule begins to split, the seeds may not be mature, but if you wait too long, the seeds will have already been dispersed—once the capsules start to dry and crack open, all of the seeds can be dropped in a matter of days.

Cut or break off the ripe capsules and place them in a paper bag to dry out for a few days; or lay the capsules out on paper and allow them to air-dry. After they dry, break them open, sieve the seeds to remove any debris, and store them dry in a plastic bag. Label each envelope as to collection site and date and place in the refrigerator. Experience indicates that if Pitcher Plant seeds are collected fresh and stored correctly, a fairly high rate of germination may be expected for up to five years from the time of collection.

Propagation

Seed. The best medium for germinating *Sarracenia* seeds is a mix of equal parts peat and coarse vermiculite. Sterilize a 4-inch plastic pot in dilute chlorine bleach to minimize the chances of introducing diseases, rinse well, and fill to ½ inch below the rim with moistened soil mix. Water in the soil with the label-recommended strength of a fungicide (such as Benlate) and allow the soil to drain for several hours to reduce excess moisture.

Sow fresh seeds, or seeds that have been stored dry in the refrigerator, on top of this soil mix. Do not cover the seeds. It is better to sow several pots lightly rather than one pot heavily because it will be much easier to separate the seedlings once they have germinated and are ready to transplant.

Enclose the pots in a plastic bag and place in the refrigerator for sixty days. Then remove from the refrigerator, take the pots out of the plastic bag, and place in a tray of water that reaches approximately one-fourth to one-third up the side of the pot. Use distilled, deionized, or rain water if possible. Do not water pots from above because splash and washing of seeds to low spots will occur. Overhead watering is especially harmful once germination has begun because it disrupts the delicate hold that the tiny roots have on the soil.

Germination can be expected to start in from twenty to forty days after removal from the refrigerator, depending on the time of year and temperature. Bottom heat will speed the rate of germination but is not essential.

The pots of seedlings should be placed in the greenhouse or other protected place for the entire first year to give the seedlings time to get established. Do not leave seedling pots outside because splash from rain can do much damage. Transplanting to individual pots is usually done in the spring of the second growing season.

Good ventilation and monthly applications of a fungicide (Benlate) on seedlings are recommended to prevent the growth of soil fungi and damping-off of seedlings, which are common in such high-moisture conditions.

Division. The easiest way to increase your Pitcher Plants vegetatively is crown division. Over the years a healthy, mature plant will form several to many crowns. Dig up or unpot the original plant and carefully break or cut the rhizome to separate out each individual crown, being careful not to damage the roots. Replant the divisions immediately.

Cultivation

As with most other plants, the four important factors in growing Pitcher Plants are soil, sunlight, moisture, and dormancy.

Many different garden and greenhouse soil formulations have been used with success, but they all have two things in common: namely, a low pH and a good capacity for moisture retention. Although whole-fiber sphagnum moss is somewhat expensive, many growers regard it as the best growing medium, but a medium of equal parts peat moss and sharp sand or coarse vermiculite is also acceptable and less expensive.

The site you select to grow your plants must have at least six to eight hours of full sunlight each day during the growing season. Lacking adequate sunlight, Pitcher Plants will be weak, have poor color, and ultimately die. The Purple Pitcher Plant (*S. purpurea*) is the exception to this rule: it benefits from direct morning sunlight, but does well if shaded from the intense afternoon sun.

Overwatering during the growing season is never a problem with Pitcher Plants as they must have a constant supply of water. However, the plants should be 5 or 6 inches above the water table of your bog garden, and you will need to check the bog at least once a week to be sure the water level is maintained.

Pitcher Plants are especially sensitive to salts in the water supply. Over the course of time, as water is used by the plants or evaporates, these salts can accumulate and concentrate and will weaken or kill your plants. To avoid this problem be sure to "flush out" your potted plants with lots of extra water two or three times each growing season to rinse away any accumulated salts. A build-up of salts is usually indicated by a thin whitish crust that begins to accumulate on top of the growing medium. Some growers who have small collections of Pitcher Plants use rain, distilled, or deionized water to avoid the problem of dissolved salts.

Uses in the Garden and Landscape

Any sunny bog garden would be incomplete without a few clumps of Pitcher Plants. The tall, striking leaves can be seen from a distance and are guaranteed to draw visitors as quickly as they draw their insect prey.

Pitcher Plants can also be grown successfully in pots, as long as they receive their basic requirements, especially winter dormancy, as discussed above. However, Pitcher Plants are not houseplants. Because of their specialized growing requirements, especially strong light and high humidity, they are not at all suited for growing indoors unless they are in large terrariums and under extensive batteries of fluorescent lights. If you have any sunny outdoor space at all, that is the place to make a bog and grow your Pitcher Plants. (See the introduction to this section for information on constructing a bog garden.)

Part 5. Ferns

Introduction

Ferns offer a wide assortment of forms, colors, and textures for the native plant garden. Dark green fronds range in texture from the simply cut Christmas Fern to the lacy foliage of the Southern Lady Fern and the delicate leaflets of the Maidenhair Fern. Lighter green foliage of the Deciduous Southern Shield Fern and the New York Fern catch the sunlight and add contrast to the cool, dark glades of the fern garden. Fertile fronds of such ferns as the Cinnamon and Royal Ferns provide accents of color as well as interesting forms in the wild garden. Each species offers a unique combination of characteristics and landscape potential.

Most ferns are easy to grow. Many of the more common species thrive in the shady, moist, well-drained soil of the hardwood forest. Others, however, such as the Cinnamon and Royal ferns, can do well in full sun "with their feet wet," and so are suitable for accenting the edges of a pond or bog.

Sensitive Fern and Netted Chain Fern also thrive in poorly drained soil. Ebony Spleenworts prefer soil with better drainage or even the dry crannies of a stone wall. And the aggressive Bracken Fern spreads even in full sun and dry soil.

Ferns may be used in a variety of ways in the landscape. Rosettes of slow-growing, solitary types, such as Fancy Fern and Marginal Shield Fern, may be planted singly to provide a focal point. The lacy foliage of the Southern Lady Fern or the finely pointed leaves of the Silvery Glade Fern provide a contrasting backdrop for wild flowers with medium to coarse foliage. The delicate leaves of the New York Fern make a spring green groundcover in the warm months and turn a pleasing straw color in the fall and winter. A mass of Christmas Fern will deepen in hue to a rich forest green by the time the snow falls and remain green until the silver-scaled fiddleheads emerge in the spring.

This section contributed by Charlotte A. Jones-Roe, curator, North Carolina Botanical Garden.

Structures and Terms

Knowledge of a few simple terms makes it easier to study ferns. The portion of the fern which is visible above the ground is called the *frond*. The frond includes the *blade*, or leafy portion, and the leafless stalk, or *stipe*. The stem of the fern is generally called the *rhizome*. The rhizome grows horizontally on or near the surface of the soil. Roots produced by the rhizome serve to anchor the fern and absorb water and minerals from the soil, rocks, or bark on which it grows.

Unlike many familiar plants, ferns bear no flowers and produce no seed. Instead, ferns reproduce by making tiny *spores* on some or all of their leaves. Fronds which bear spores are said to be *fertile*; those leaves which bear no spores are called *sterile* fronds.

Budding fronds unroll from croziers, or *fiddleheads*, as they mature. Very few flowering plants have this characteristic, whereas almost all ferns have distinct fiddleheads.

The fronds are borne on the rhizome, and the manner in which the rhizome grows determines much about the overall form of the fern. In species such as Hay-scented Fern, the rhizome produces widely spaced single fronds. In others, the fronds are borne in clumps or even in elevated rosettes. Ferns are sometimes said to have *long-creeping* rhizomes, *short-creeping* rhizomes, or *ascending* rhizomes.

Since the fronds of most ferns are lacy and dissected, it is also useful to have a few terms to describe the degree of dissection. A few ferns have simple, uncut leaves (Adder's Tongue and Walking ferns, for example). A fern blade which is cut part of the way to the mid-vein is said to be *pinnatifid* (Netted Chain Fern and Rock Cap Fern, for example). *Pinnate*, or "once-cut," ferns are those divided into leaflets with a narrow point of attachment to the main stem (Christmas Fern and Glade Fern, for example). Ferns with divided leaflets are said to be *bipinnate* (twice-cut), or *tripinnate* (thrice-cut). Many ferns fall somewhere in between; they are described by adding *-pinnatifid* to the description. For example, a tripinnate-pinnatifid fern is one which is cut 3½ times. Such a description could well apply to a very lacy frond, such as that of a Fancy Fern.

Spores, when present, are borne in spore cases, or *sporangia*, which are located on the backs or edges of the fronds. Clusters of sporangia are known as *sori*. (One sporangial cluster is known as a *sorus*.) There may be a thin piece of tissue present called an *indusium*, which covers and protects the sorus as the spores develop. Sometimes the spore-bearing leaflets or the entire fertile frond may be reduced in size and different in color from the rest of the plant. For example, careful examination of the brown fertile frond of the Cinnamon Fern reveals a blade which is greatly reduced in size.

Life Cycle

The life cycle of ferns is somewhat different from that of flowering plants. The plant with leafy fronds which produces spores is called the *sporophyte* generation or stage. Spores released by the plant germinate to form the *gametophyte*, or sex-cell producing, generation. The gametophyte stage is a thin heart-shaped flap of green tissue called a *prothallus*. Tiny rootlike structures called *rhizoids* anchor the prothallus and help obtain water and minerals. It is on the wet surface of the prothallus that sexual fertilization and genetic mixing occur in ferns. Sperm-producing male organs called *anthe-*

ridia are located near the point or wings of the prothallus. After a rain or mist, mature sperms swim across the wet surface to the *archegonia*, or female structures, each of which encloses the fern equivalent of an egg. After fertilization, one of the eggs will divide and grow a new sporophyte, complete with roots and fronds.

Ferns may also reproduce *vegetatively*, without sexual mixing. Fragmentation and budding occur in nature and may be used by gardeners to propagate a number of identical ferns rather quickly.

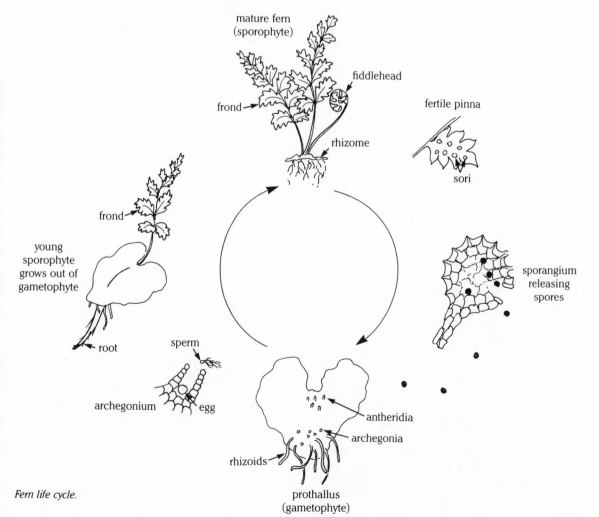

mature fern
(sporophyte)

fiddlehead

fertile pinna

frond

rhizome

sori

frond

young
sporophyte
grows out of
gametophyte

sporangium
releasing
spores

sperm

root

archegonium

egg

antheridia

archegonia

rhizoids

prothallus
(gametophyte)

Fern life cycle.

Sources of Ferns and Spores

Just as our native wild flowers have been exploited, native ferns are commonly dug from the wild and sold directly to gardeners. Some species of our native ferns are already in jeopardy in their native habitats because of this practice of wild collection, and others may become rare if they are overcollected.

Native ferns for the garden and landscape may be obtained from a variety of sources which do not deplete and jeopardize natural populations. Some of the ways of getting plants and propagation material for the native fern garden are described below, but one of the best sources is "plant rescue," the salvaging of plants from sites destined for clearing and construction. Owners and developers are often quite willing to permit gardeners to remove plants for their home landscapes. North-facing slopes, moist woods, and stream banks are most apt to yield a variety of attractive and useful species of ferns and other native plants.

Because many types of ferns take several years to grow to planting size from spores, plant rescue is an attractive alternative for obtaining these plants. To determine how much soil should be moved with each fern, dig the first plant with a large ball of earth. Then break away the soil gently to determine the shape of the rhizomes and the extent of the root system. If the plants are growing in rocky soil and the root system is damaged in transplanting, cut back at least one-third to one-half of the fronds to keep the plant from drying out. Most native fern species may be moved in fall, winter, and early spring. If plants must be transplanted in warmer months of the year, special care should be taken to trim back part of the fronds and water the newly planted ferns frequently until they establish roots. For more information on how to organize a plant rescue in your community consult the appendix section on that subject.

Spore Collection and Storage

Large numbers of ferns for the garden and landscape may be obtained by collecting fertile fronds and propagating from spores. Every species has an optimum time for spore collection, but the exact dates vary from year to year, according to local climate and weather conditions. If collected too early, spores may not be mature enough to germinate. Late in the season, spores may still remain on the fronds, but the number will be greatly reduced.

For best results collect fertile fronds when the sori are dark and just beginning to release a fine powder when tapped over white paper. In most species the ripe sori are dark brown or black. A few species are golden brown or cinnamon in color when they release their spores.

When handling several species at a time, wash hands and wipe clippers between species to help keep different types of spores separate and avoid unnecessary contamination. Clip the fertile portions of the fronds and place them in a clean paper or glassine envelope. Seal the envelope and keep it

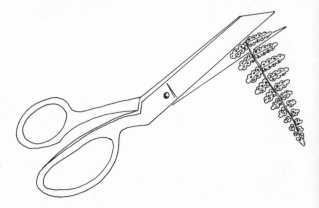

in a warm, dry place for a couple of days. (Placing the envelopes atop the shade of a small reading lamp works well.) Moderate heat and drying encourages the release of spores and retards the growth of fungus.

After the fronds are dry, separate the leaves from the spores by placing the contents of the envelope on a clean, dry sieve over clean wax paper or nonporous typing paper. Fold the paper over carefully or transfer the spores to a small glassine envelope of the type used by stamp collectors. Close the packet with tape, seal it in a dry plastic bag and refrigerate at about 40°F until the spores are to be sown.

Although spores of some species will germinate

after several years of storage, the viability of spores does decrease with time. Sow spores directly from the fertile fronds or as soon as possible for best yield. Late fall is a good time to sow spores because the gametophytes and small sporophytes may be kept inside in compact containers through the winter months and transferred outside to pots or beds the following spring or one year later. (Spore propagation requires as much as one to three years to produce ferns large enough for planting.)

Ordinarily spore collection does not harm the plants and is perfectly acceptable. Spores should not be collected, however, if the fern is so rare as to warrant legal protection as an endangered or threatened species. Any damage to the plants or removal of spores may affect the survival of the population and possibly of the species. So spores should not be collected from very rare ferns in the wild except under the supervision of state and federal plant conservation agencies. One should not, of course, collect from ferns in display collections and botanical gardens. Collection of fertile fronds is not appropriate when the appearance of the plants is important or when the ferns may be part of a research collection.

Spore Exchanges

Many botanical gardens furnish seeds and spores to their supporters and to other institutions at little or no cost. Some gardens and arboreta have a formal distribution program, and at many others the curator will assist with reasonable requests for limited quantities of spores. Lists of spores available from gardens with formal programs may usually be obtained by writing.

Other sources of spores are the spore exchanges sponsored by local and national associations for the study and protection of ferns and other native plants. The American Fern Society provides lists of spores available for exchange. The membership fee is modest, and the journal, newsletter, field trips, and spore exchange are well worth the cost. Persons interested in receiving information on the American Fern Society or lists of native plant and fern societies and native seed and spore exchanges should send a stamped, self-addressed envelope to:

North Carolina Botanical Garden, GNP
Totten Center, 457-A
University of North Carolina at Chapel Hill
Chapel Hill, NC 27514

Propagating Nurseries

While many plant dealers offer native ferns, few nurseries are actively propagating the native plants they sell. The North Carolina Botanical Garden strongly urges against purchasing wild collected plants because the practice may jeopardize the existence of rare or popular species in their natural habitats. As other growers begin to sell propagated materials, the North Carolina Botanical Garden will gladly refer customers.

Trading Spores and Divisions

One of the most common methods of obtaining ferns for the home garden and landscape is through friends and acquaintances who also grow ferns. Members of some plant societies get together regularly to trade plants. And no present will please a fern lover more than a gift of a division of a favorite fern. By exchanging plants and spores and by obtaining ferns through rescue and propagation, we can enjoy a wealth of ferns in the garden without destroying the source plants in the wild.

Propagation Methods

Spore Propagation

Fern spores may be grown on several types of media and in a variety of containers, but all of the techniques must begin by doing several things: provide a very moist (but not soggy) growing medium; raise the humidity of the surrounding air; decrease competition from competing organisms such as algae and fungi; and provide enough light and moisture at the right times to allow fertilization and growth. If the ferns are to be transplanted, the medium should be loose enough to allow moving the sporophytes without damage.

One simple method is to remove the fibrous netting from the top of a peat pellet (or jiffy pot), place it on a clean dish, and water it with distilled water. When the pellet has expanded, sow spores on top of it by gently tapping a fertile frond or sifted packet of spores. Cover the pellet with a new, clean clear plastic cocktail cup and place in indirect light. The light of an east-facing window or a fluorescent plant light is ideal. Check about once a week and add distilled water to the dish before it becomes completely dry.

After several weeks to as much as several months for some species, a green mossy haze of tiny prothallia will appear on the surface of the pellet. Remove the cup covering the pellet and mist gently with distilled water twice each week. The gametophytes must be covered with a thin film of water for fertilization to occur. Continue to mist the prothallia regularly and wait patiently for the appearance of tiny ferns. This development may take place in only a few weeks, or it may take as much as a year.

When several of these tiny ferns, or sporophytes, reach at least ¾ inch in height or have at least three fronds, transplant them carefully to a container such as a large jar or clear plastic shoe box which contains 1½ inches of moist sterile potting soil. Set the plants at the same depth and at least 2 inches apart and mist well. Seal the container with a lid or plastic film and set in indirect light. Check the container at least twice a week and mist thor-

Peat pellet or jiffy pot in dish under clear cup.

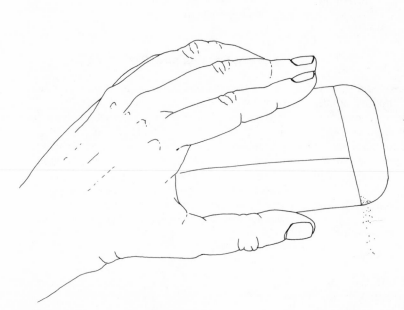

Sow spores evenly by gently tapping packet.

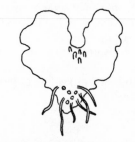

The tiny prothallus or gametophyte bears reproductive organs.

Mist gently with distilled water each week.

oughly if there is no moisture condensing at the top. Remove the lid or plastic film after two weeks or when ferns have begun to grow and produce new fiddleheads.

A second method for propagating ferns from spores is useful for production on a slightly larger scale. It requires little attention or watering during the long wait for germination and sporophytes transplant readily from the potting soil medium.

Wash hands, and cleanse a shoebox and lid, a spoon, tweezers, and a mister bottle with hot water and soap or a dilute chlorine bleach solution (nine parts water to one part bleach). Spread a 1½-inch layer of new commercial potting soil mix in the bottom of the box. Moisten but do not saturate the soil with distilled water or clean tap water.

Sprinkle spores lightly and as evenly as possible over the surface of the soil. Remove any large pieces of leaves or stems from the surface with tweezers, and mist it very lightly with distilled water or clean tap water. Finally, place a clear plastic cover over the box and label it with the species name and date.

Place the covered box in an east-facing window or under grow lights. Do not place it either in intense direct sunlight or in a dark corner.

Check for a green haze or tiny leaves (gametophytes) on the soil surface after two to three weeks, and weekly thereafter. Tap the lid occasionally so condensation will drop back onto the soil. If soil begins to appear dry and no moisture condenses, mist gently, but be careful not to wash spores to one end of the box. Be patient. Fern spores may take from one to six months or more to germinate and form visible gametophytes.

When individual gametophytes appear, open the cover and mist thoroughly, but do not saturate the soil. Replace the cover. Mist gametophytes twice a week to keep their surfaces moist and encourage fertilization and formation of the adult (sporophyte) fern stage. Watch for tiny fronds of sporophytes growing up out of gametophytes.

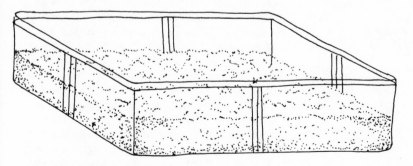

A clear plastic shoebox makes an excellent propagation case.

The young sporophyte grows out of the prothallus.

When sporophytes reach ¾ inch in height or have at least three frondlets, transplant gently to a small flat or 2-inch pots of new potting soil, taking care not to cover the crowns with soil. Cover the flat or pots with clear plastic to keep humidity high and ease the transition. Continue to mist and observe gametophytes remaining in box.

Place young sporophytes in filtered sun or shade. Remove plastic film after two weeks or when ferns have begun to grow and produce new fiddleheads. Check at least once each day and water when soil becomes dry to the touch. Do not overwater or allow the soil to become so dry that fronds wilt.

When ferns reach 3–4 inches tall, transplant them to larger pots or set in a shaded nursery bed with well-drained, humus-rich soil. Check at least twice a week to remove leaves and debris and water when dry. To encourage faster growth, apply fish emulsion at one-quarter the recommended concentration every two to four weeks from March to July. When ferns reach 6–12 inches, transplant to permanent beds or plantings.

Spore propagation takes six months to two years or more, depending on the species and conditions. Although the process is slow, it is a fascinating and inexpensive way to grow great numbers of ferns and obtain rare species without jeopardizing natural populations.

Transplant each sporophyte to a separate pot and seal in clear plastic.

Rhizome Division and Other Vegetative Methods of Fern Propagation

A much faster method of propagating ferns is by dividing their underground stems, or rhizomes. While hundreds of ferns may be obtained with a pinch of spores and great patience, many gardeners prefer to make a few new plants much more rapidly through rhizome division. Since plants made by vegetative means are genetically identical to the parent plants, division also offers the gardener or horticulturist the opportunity to select desirable characteristics.

The rhizomes of some ferns branch frequently, whereas those of others grow in a line and maintain a single, unbranching rhizome. Others creep so slowly that they seem to grow scarcely at all. The easiest ferns to divide are those which branch often and put up several clusters of fronds at once. These plants may be divided by simply cutting between the clusters of fronds with a sharp knife or shovel and digging up the smaller clump and replanting it in humus-rich soil at the same depth. Or the entire plant may be dug, cut between clumps, and replanted. When using either method, be sure to trim back at least one-third of the foliage and water plants thoroughly.

Other ferns which grow along in a single line and do not branch should be divided more carefully to make certain that the parent plant will survive. Gently remove the surface soil between the clusters and cut part of the way through the rhizome. When the fern produces a growth tip with another fiddlehead near the parent, cut the rest of the way through the rhizome at the point of the original injury. Using a trowel, gently dig up the severed section and transplant it to a similar location or a well-worked, humus-rich bed and water thoroughly. Be sure the soil is not allowed to become too dry while the division is becoming established.

Rhizomes of some ferns are quite brittle and may be cut with clippers or snapped easily with the fingers. Others are larger and tougher and must be cut with a sharp knife, pruning saw, or hacksaw. The *Osmundas* (Cinnamon, Royal, and Interrupted ferns) all produce a fibrous mass around their rhizomes which requires a sharp tool to cut.

When the center of an old *Osmunda* dies, a "fairy ring" of dozens of smaller plants frequently radiates from the empty center. To restore a specimen planting to its original condition, dig up the entire ring in late fall or very early spring before the croziers begin to unfurl. Cut the clumps apart with a saw and select the one with the largest and best-formed fiddleheads. Work up the site with organic matter and plant the selected division in the place of the original specimen. Make sure to set the plant in at a slightly elevated position for good drainage and water thoroughly. Plant the other divisions at least 3 to 4 feet apart or give them to fellow fern lovers.

One of our native ferns, *Cystopteris bulbifera*, the Bulblet Bladder Fern, has the peculiar trait of making small, scaly appendages called bulbils or bulblets on the underside of some of its fronds. These may be gathered carefully, lest they all fall off, and sown like seeds in potting soil to grow new ferns. Although the ferns grow directly from the bulblets and do not go through the gametophyte stage or fertilization, the process is still slow and may take as much as two years to grow a mature fern.

Still another vegetative method which may be of particular interest to commercial growers is the production of ferns in a sterile, artificial medium from cultured tissue of the parent plant. In this method, a portion of the fern which is actively growing is removed, cleansed, and placed on a sterile growth medium containing nutrients and growth-regulating substances in a sealed clear container. The tissue is grown under lights in a carefully controlled temperature regime, where it eventually differentiates into roots and leaves of separate plants. Detailed instructions for tissue culture propagation are beyond the scope of this text. Because the procedure allows for selection of desirable characteristics and rapid production of great numbers of plants from a small source, however, tissue culture should be considered by the serious commercial grower of ferns.

How to Use This Section

The descriptions in this section provide information about the propagation, cultivation, and landscape uses of selected ferns native to the southeastern United States. The ferns are all perennials, some deciduous and others evergreen. All are hardy throughout most of the eastern United States, except where noted in the descriptions.

The appearance and uses of fifteen native ferns are described in detail. They are presented alphabetically by scientific name. Other ferns are discussed in relation to the principal species under the heading "Special Notes" or introduced in the section "Other Ferns of Interest to Gardeners," which concludes the chapter. Native species not mentioned are rare or even in danger of extinction and should not be collected or disturbed.

The methods and recommendations are based on propagation research and cultural experience at the North Carolina Botanical Garden in Chapel Hill, North Carolina, at 35°54′ north latitude, 79°2′ west longitude and 290 feet above sea level. The exact times at which new fronds will appear in the spring and deciduous species will become dormant in the fall vary with local weather and the condition of the planting site. Dates will generally be earlier for areas further south or lower in elevation and later for areas further north or higher in elevation.

Botanical terms used to describe ferns are presented in the introductory material. For definitions of other horticultural and botanical terms, see the glossary.

Format

Names. Common and botanical names are given for each of the species. Scientific names, common names, and botanical authorities are those given with the descriptions by Murray Evans in the *Manual of the Vascular Flora of the Carolinas*. Plant family names, which end in "-aceae," are given for each of the species treated in the detailed descriptions. Family names used here follow "A New Generic Sequence for the Pteridophyte Herbarium," by J. A. Crabbe, A. C. Jermy, and J. T. Mickel in the *Fern Gazette* 11, nos. 2 and 3 (1975).

The classification of ferns has long presented problems. The internal structures and spore-producing parts of ferns are the least variable structures and those which are most often compared when grouping the ferns. New techniques, equipment, and studies have increased understanding and brought about revisions of older systems of classification. Until recently, there has been little agreement as to the relationships among the ferns. Some botanists lump all the ferns of the world into only three or four families, while others split the group into dozens of distinct families. For insight into the problems facing botanists who study, classify, and name ferns, see John Mickel's discussion "How Ferns Are Classified" in *The Home Gardener's Book of Ferns*. Although the botanical family name is extremely helpful when discussing the flowering plants, the genus (the first word of the scientific name) is generally the most inclusive level of classification of use to the fern gardener. The most widely accepted family names of ferns are included here as a matter of botanical interest and for consistency with the rest of the book.

Common names of plants vary from one region to another. To request spores or to look for more information in botanical manuals, always use the scientific name. Although scientific names are occasionally changed as new information becomes available, the scientific names are much more constant and universally understood than the common names of ferns and other plants.

Drawings. The outline drawings are provided in the margins to help the reader recognize the ferns described in the text. Additional drawings show closeups of the spore-producing portions of the fronds of selected species.

Description. This section discusses the appearance and size of the fern, the natural range of the species, and the habitat where it is commonly found.

Spore Collection. The appearance of the spore-bearing fronds at the time for collection is described. Any special techniques for the species are given.

Propagation. A summary of the general method and any special techniques for growing the fern from spores or by division are described here. For step-by-step instructions, see the section in the introduction to the fern chapter.

Cultivation. This section describes preparation of the planting site, moisture and soil requirements, and care of the ferns for best growth and appearance.

Uses in the Garden and Landscape. Native ferns are best used in informal gardens or naturalized in a woodland landscape. This section describes appropriate uses of each of the species. Special qualities of various species make some more attractive as solitary specimens and others ideal for ground covers or mass plantings. The section also mentions native wild flowers that are attractive when planted with ferns of the species decribed.

Special Notes. The final section of each of the species descriptions mentions other ferns that are closely related botanically or that have similar uses in the landscape.

Maidenhair Fern

Adiantum pedatum
Adiantaceae

Deciduous

Collect Spores: August–October

Height: 20–28 inches

Texture: very fine; tripinnate

Form: erect with trailing, fanlike foliage; fronds clustered

Soil: moist, well-drained, rich

Light: filtered sun to deep shade

Description

The Maidenhair Fern is considered by many to be the loveliest and most graceful of all the ferns. Its delicate leaflets are the texture of fine silk, and they flutter softly in the slightest breeze. Mature Maidenhairs range in height from 1 to 2 feet. Their leaflets trail from slender radiating ribs and trace a fanlike pattern like that of no other native fern in the gar-

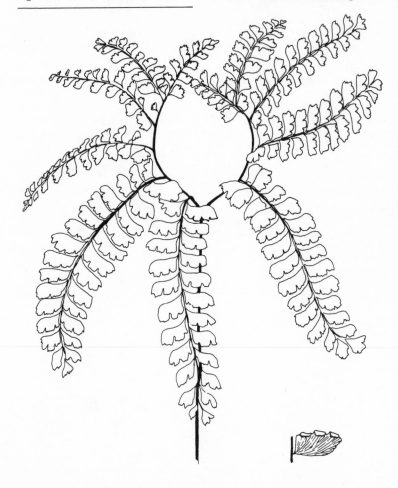

den. The fronds are light to gray green, and the glossy stems that support them are dark reddish-brown to ebony. Maidenhair ferns are found throughout much of North America. In the mountain and piedmont counties of the Southeast they thrive in the humus-rich soil of old woods and on shady slopes which are moist but well drained.

Spore Collection

Spores of Maidenhair Fern are produced on the backs of the leafllets where the edges fold under and cover the sori. As the spores ripen from mid-summer to early fall, the sori become dark brown in color and curl back to release the mature spores. For best results collect the fertile fronds when the sori are dark and the covering folds are just beginning to open. Place the fronds in an envelope for a few days and place in a warm, dry place, such as under a light.

Propagation

Spores. Sow spores on moist, sterile potting soil or peat pellet in a humid case and mist with distilled water. When gametophytes become visible, mist twice a week to promote fertilization. The young sporophytes are very delicate and sensitive to drying. To encourage a higher rate of survival, transplant sporelings to moist, sterile potting soil in a second closed case. Set the young plants at least 1 inch apart to give them a chance to grow a better root system before transplanting to uncovered pots or outdoor beds.

Rhizome Division. Division of the rhizomes of the Maidenhair Fern is best done in the late fall or early spring when the fern is dormant, but it may be done during the warm months if you are careful to water frequently. The small brittle rhizome snaps easily, or the mature plant can be cut between clusters of fronds with a sharp knife. If possible, dig up the plants and move them apart several weeks later. Each rhizome section should have at least one frond or bud and be at least 2 inches long. If the plant is not dormant, trim back all but one frond on each segment. Set each segment at least a foot apart in a bed of humus-rich soil and water in well with a fine spray.

Cultivation

This species is native to moist but well-drained slopes in the mountains and piedmont, so choose a north- or northeast-facing slope or a level area with deep soil and plenty of shade. In a residential setting, plant on the north side of the house. The site should also be well protected from the wind. One of the most pleasing features of the Maidenhair is its gentle fluttering and constant movement in light breezes, but the delicate stems cannot stand up to a harsh wind.

Uses in the Garden and Landscape

Maidenhair Ferns may be planted singly to show off their delicate fans of foliage, or they may be massed in a bed to produce a rich summer groundcover or a textured backdrop for flowering plants. The fine, translucent foliage of the Maidenhair Fern looks especially attractive when backlit or dappled with sunlight. Try planting a mass or a specimen on the uphill side of a wooded path to take advantage of this quality.

Unlike species with more rapidly growing rhizomes, Maidenhair Fern will grow to a robust specimen in a large pot. Move the pot indoors for a few days at a time to enjoy the graceful foliage in an interior setting. Be sure to mulch the pot well in winter to prevent drying and cold damage to roots and rhizomes.

The Maidenhair Fern is delicate but quite vigorous. It looks attractive in a bed with shade-loving cultivated plants as well as with wild flowers. The fine texture and flowing lines of the Maidenhair provide a visual contrast to the foliage of Jack-in-the-Pulpit or large-leaved woody plants, such as Rhododendron and Magnolia. Use this fern to please the eye and to grace any shady site in the garden.

Special Notes

The Southern Maidenhair or Venus' Hair Fern, *Adiantum capillus-veneris*, is a related species which has some of the graceful characteristics of the Maidenhair. Although the Southern Maidenhair does not share the gracefully curved rachis and fanlike appearance, its very fine, lacy foliage makes it attractive and even more delicate in appearance. This species is more common in the Deep South and coastal counties, but in a protected site it should survive even in areas with some freezing weather. Southern Maidenhair grows best in soil which is somewhat basic and very well drained. Usually smaller than the northern Maidenhair, the Southern Maidenhair is ideally suited for planting in the crevices of a rock wall or a well-drained cobble.

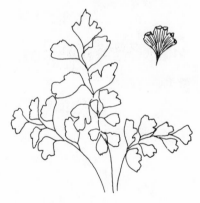

Southern Lady Fern

Athyrium asplenioides
Aspleniaceae

Deciduous

Collect Spores: June–October

Height: 12–48 inches

Texture: Very fine; bipinnate to tripinnate

Form: fronds arching and in irregular clusters

Soil: moist and rich

Light: filtered sun to deep shade

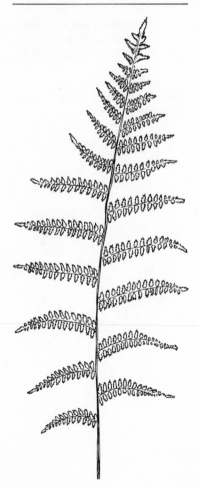

Description

The Southern Lady is a fern of lacy texture and tremendous variability. Closely related to the northern Lady Fern, *Athyrium filix-femina*, this species is found throughout the southeast in moist woods and swamp forests, especially along the banks of creeks and streams. Among the first to put up fiddleheads in the spring, it is often noticed because of its translucent wine-red stems. Nearby Southern Lady Ferns, however, may have light green stems supporting their feathery foliage. The fronds of the Southern Lady Fern may grow to 4 feet in height and 15 inches in width by the end of the growing season. Most specimens, though, are somewhat smaller. Early in the spring the foliage of the Southern Lady Fern is a delicate yellow green. The color darkens with the passing of the season to a forest green and then takes on a bronze tone before turning dark brown at the onset of winter. The short-creeping rhizome of this fern supports dense clusters of graceful fronds at irregular angles.

Spore Collection

The spores of Southern Lady Fern are produced on the backs of the fronds in linear or crescent-shaped sori which are arranged in a herringbone pattern. The best time to collect the spores is when the indusia covering the sori are beginning to open and starting to spew black spores. This may occur anytime during the growing season, from late spring to frost. Some spores may still be obtained late in the season from fronds with honey-colored sori. Place the fertile fronds in an envelope and dry under a lamp or in some other warm dry spot.

Propagation

Spores. Southern Lady Ferns are easily grown from spores. Sow the spores on moist, sterile potting soil or peat pellet in a humid case and mist with distilled water. Mist twice a week as soon as the green mosslike gametophytes become visible. Transplant small sporophytes to a humid, intermediate case to improve the rate of survival. Since the fronds of the young fern are very delicate, they should be watered carefully with a fine mist or by soaking the pots

for the first few months after planting so as to avoid splattering soil on the fronds and weighting them down.

Rhizome Division. The Southern Lady Fern is easier than most species to divide. Shake clumps gently to remove excess soil, then pull apart at natural dividing points. Cut back one-third to one-half of the foliage and set in a prepared bed. Water often during the first season. Rhizome division is best done when the fern is dormant. However, it is sometimes difficult to find the rhizome and its growth points at this time. The fern may also be divided during late fall or early spring. Take care not to bruise or break tender budding fiddleheads while separating the rhizomes.

Cultivation

This species may be planted to form a deep luxurious summer groundcover. In a moist but well-drained site, work up a bed by tilling well and mixing in composted organic matter to a depth of at least 6 inches. Set out rhizome divisions or sporelings at least 1 foot apart in a staggered but fairly uniform pattern. Mulch the bed with leaves and water gently but thoroughly until the plants establish a root system and begin to produce new fronds.

Uses in the Garden and Landscape

Southern Lady Fern is most often found in moist woods, river bottoms, and along stream banks. It is particularly well suited for use as an accent for a shaded pool or brook. Set out singly, this species takes on a distinctive, graceful form that shows off the feathery texture of its fronds. Plant Southern Lady next to rocks or boulders to soften harsh angles and contrast with the great weight of structural materials.

Special Notes

Complement the attractive wine-colored stems of the red form of the Southern Lady Fern by choosing companion plants with similar colors. Jack-in-the-Pulpit, Wild Geranium, and several of the Trilliums are good choices for planting near this species.

Glade Fern

Athyrium pycnocarpon
Aspleniaceae

Deciduous

Collect Spores: July–September

Height: 12–24 inches

Texture: fine; pinnate

Form: fronds clustered, featherlike

Soil: moist but well-drained, basic, and rich

Light: filtered sunlight

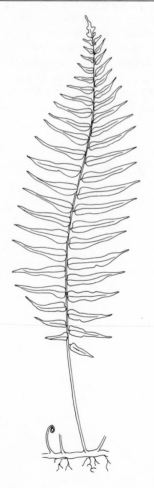

Description

The deciduous Glade Fern grows to a height of 3 to 4 feet in clusters 3 to 4 feet wide. Its tapering leaflets are pinnate, glossy, and rather soft and thin. The fertile fronds are somewhat taller and narrower than the sterile fronds, and they usually emerge later in the season. The color of the gracefully arching fronds ranges from pale green in spring to bright medium green later in the summer. In the fall the color is a russet brown before the foliage dies back completely. The rhizome of Glade Fern is of the short-creeping type and produces a dense cluster of fronds. The pinnae are simply cut, smooth on the edges, and sharply pointed at the tips. The lines of the Glade Fern are clean and simple rather than frilly and lacy like those of some ferns. Yet the appearance is still quite delicate because of the thin, flexible leaves.

Spore Collection

The sori of the Glade Fern are long and thin and arranged in diagonal ranks on the underside of the fertile fronds. Fertile fronds usually grow later in the season and tend to be more erect than the sterile fronds. Collect spores by cutting the fertile fronds when the sori turn from silver brown to dark grey and begin to split along the sides and release fine dark spores. This usually occurs in early-to-mid fall. Place fronds in an envelope and keep in a warm dry place for a few days.

Propagation

Spores. Sow the sifted spores of Glade Fern on a sterile medium. Mist thoroughly with distilled water and seal in a clear container to maintain high humidity. Set container in indirect light and mist twice a week after the gametophytes appear on the surface of the soil or pellet. The prothallia of Glade Fern are larger than those of most species, and they fertilize readily upon misting. Whereas some fern species take one to three years to mature to planting size, 3-inch Glade Ferns may be grown in approximately six months. The critical stage for this species is the transplantation from the humid propagation case (the plastic shoe box or cocktail cup) to pots or beds. Ease the transition by covering newly potted plants with plastic for a few weeks, or mist pots and beds several times daily. Be sure to keep plants out of direct sunlight.

Sow spores in late September or October and set out plants in late April or May. The best time is

just after the last frost, giving plants ample time to develop their root systems before hot weather. If fronds die back after transplanting, save them in a protected place through the winter. This species often produces new fronds after appearing to die.

Rhizome Division. Clumps of Glade Fern may be successfully divided between clusters of fronds. Divide rhizomes in cool weather if possible, or cut back more than one-third of the fronds. New fiddleheads are very tender, so avoid bruising them.

Cultivation

Glade Fern thrives in the rich soil of mature hardwood forests and forested seepage slopes of the mountains. The common name of this species refers to the small sunny openings of the forest where the Glade Fern is often found. The plant will grow in a very shady site, but it thrives in filtered sunlight if moisture is adequate.

This handsome fern is not difficult to grow even in warmer climates if given humus-rich soil and plenty of moisture. In nature, Glade Fern is found in areas with basic soil. It will grow best in garden beds with enough lime to raise the soil pH to 7 or 7.5.

Uses in the Garden and Landscape

Glade Fern is attractive planted singly, or it may be used as a deciduous groundcover. Plant Glade Fern among the rocks of a mountain garden for visual soft-ening of massive structural elements. Trim back dead fronds in early spring for a tidier appearance.

Special Notes

Interplant Glade Fern with spring wild flowers for a pleasing effect. The Phacelias are a good choice because the plants die back after flowering and so give the ferns more room to expand and grow in the summer and early autumn. Some other wild flowers which thrive in similar conditions are White Wood Aster, Wild Geranium, Cone-flower, Jack-in-the-Pulpit, and Bleeding Heart. For late-summer and early-fall bloom, plant Turtleheads among the Glade Ferns.

Silvery Glade Fern

Athyrium thelypteroides
Aspleniaceae

Deciduous

Collect Spores: July–September

Height: 24–48 inches

Texture: fine; pinnate-pinnatifid

Form: fronds in irregular clusters, arching

Soil: moist and rich, basic

Light: filtered sunlight

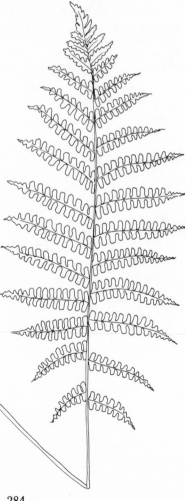

Description

Silvery Glade Fern (sometimes known as Silvery Spleenwort, even though it looks nothing like the spleenworts and is not closely related) is a moderately tall plant with soft, grey green foliage. The green of the fronds has a light yellowish tint in the spring which darkens in the summer and takes on a distinctly silvery sheen. The 2-to-4-foot fronds are erect and rather brittle and emerge in dense clusters at random angles. The rhizome of Silvery Glade Fern is of the short-creeping variety. The plant spreads at a moderate rate while maintaining a dense mass of foliage in a prepared bed.

Spore Collection

Watch for ripening spores in late summer. When the linear, silvery sori on the backs of the leaves begin to split their indusia and shed dark spores, clip the dry fertile fronds and save them in an envelope.

Propagation

Spores. Sift the spores to remove debris and sow on sterile potting mix or peat pellets in a humid case. Mist thoroughly with distilled water. After the gametophytes appear, mist twice a week until the sporophytes develop. Give the soft, delicate sporophytes at least a few weeks in a humid terrarium or clear plastic box before transplanting into outside beds or pots.

Rhizome Division. Silvery Glade Fern may be propagated rapidly by dividing the rhizomes. In late fall or very early in the spring, lift clumps of the rhizomes and gently separate them. Clip rhizomes between growth points where new clusters of fiddleheads are forming. If dividing the plants in early fall, clip back any remaining fronds. Set divisions into pots or prepared beds at least 8 to 12 inches apart for a mass effect the following year. Water in well after transplanting and do not allow the soil to become too dry during the growing season.

Cultivation

Choose a site which is moist and very well drained. Add compost and sand if necessary to improve drainage and include enough lime in the soil mix to increase the pH to 7 or 7.5 for best growth. This species does well in raised beds of soil rich in humus or in moist alluvial soil, such as that found near stream banks.

In even a mild summer drought, the fronds of this moisture-loving mountain fern may turn brown and collapse prematurely if the bed is not watered regularly. Cut back or rake away dead foliage and debris in the late winter before the delicate fiddleheads begin to emerge for improved appearance.

Uses in the Garden and Landscape

Silvery Glade Fern is attractive planted singly, but it is best used in a mass for a groundcover or backdrop for other ferns or wild flowers.

Special Notes

Because of its unusual silvery to bluish cast, Silvery Glade Fern may be used to complement plants with red or blue tones. Some plants which look good against a backdrop of this species are the Great Blue Lobelia and Bluebells and any of the white spring wild flowers of medium height.

Hay-scented Fern

Dennstaedtia punctilobula
Dennstaedtiaceae

Deciduous

Collect Spores: July–September

Height: 12–42 inches

Texture: very fine, bipinnate to bipinnate-pinnatifid

Form: single fronds in large colonies

Soil: moist but well-drained

Light: filtered sunlight to full sun

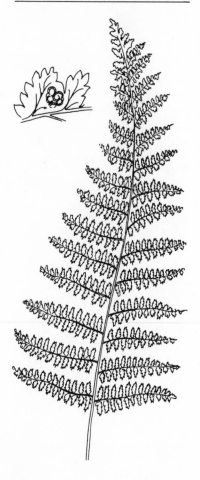

Description

Hay-scented Fern is a fast-growing fern of medium height, 2 to 3½ feet, with fronds as much as a foot wide. The plant earned its common name from the sweet scent of the dry or bruised fronds. The foliage is yellow green to medium green in color and two or more times cut, yielding a rather fine texture. The most striking thing about this fern is its soft hairy surfaces, which give it a flat, nonreflective quality compared to the glossy appearance of many other ferns. The rhizome is of the long-creeping type. It supports a single frond every few inches and will fill a prepared soil bed with a soft dense mass of foliage very rapidly.

Because this fern grows so vigorously in the Northeast and the southern Appalachian Mountains, many gardeners consider it to be an aggressive weed. Slightly south of its normal range, however, Hay-scented Fern can safely make a rich groundcover and provide new and exciting colors and textures for the landscape.

Spore Collection

In the Southeast, Hay-scented Fern seems to reproduce most commonly by spread of its rhizomes. However, fertile fronds may occasionally be found by careful examination of the backs of the fronds in mid-to-late summer. Sori of this species protrude distinctly from the surface of the frond. Collect fertile fronds when spores are being released from the sori as fine dark dust and place them in envelopes.

Propagation

Spores. Sow sifted spores on a sterile medium in a clear container. Moisten thoroughly with distilled water and seal. Be prepared to wait for several months for germination. After gametophytes appear mist twice each week to encourage fertilization and production of sporophytes. Transplant sporophytes when they are at least 2 inches tall.

Rhizome Division. Cut rhizomes between fronds about every 2 inches with a sharp knife or clippers. Set out divisions at least 6 inches apart in a well-worked bed and trim at least half of each frond.

Cultivation

In nature Hay-scented Ferns thrive in small openings in the forest which receive several hours of bright sunlight. To establish a mass planting of Hay-scented fern, choose a site near the edge of a wooded area where the plants will receive plenty of light but will still be protected from too much direct sun. Hay-scented fern dies back early if beds become too dry. For best growth and healthiest appearance, beds should be well drained but frequently moistened.

Uses in the Garden and Landscape

Hay-scented Fern is not suitable for planting in single clumps, but it makes a soft, dense ground-cover. It should be used with caution, however, particularly in the southern Appalachians and northeastern states, where it is so well adapted. Beds should be bordered with aluminum strips to prevent this aggressive fern from spreading too greatly. Avoid planting Hay-scented Fern near small, delicate herbs which cannot compete with this vigorous plant. And be sure not to plant it too close to property lines if you wish to remain on good terms with your neighbors.

Special Notes

Because Hay-scented Fern is often invasive, it is best to plant this species alone or near the base of trees and shrubs and keep it separate from beds of other ferns and wild flowers. When planted where its growth can be controlled, however, Hay-scented Fern provides a very attractive and aromatic addition to the landscape.

Several other southeastern species are thought to be "mixed blessings" by fern gardeners. The best known of these is Bracken, *Pteridium aquilinum*. This species occurs throughout the world in a wide variety of habitats. The species is tremendously variable, growing to from 1 to 4 feet in height. In our part of the world Bracken grows best in loose sandy soil and partial shade to full sun. Many people think the distinct slender fronds of the "eagle fern," as it is sometimes called, are quite attractive, but the plant is weedy and invasive and very difficult to eradicate once it is established. Bracken is not recommended for garden and landscape use, not even with metal edgings and vigilant control.

Two other ferns that grow rapidly and may be used as ground-covers in the Southeast are considered weedy farther north. New York Fern and Marsh Fern, described elsewhere, may grow a bit too well under the right conditions. However, these species have rhizomes that are not so resistant to removal as those of the Bracken, and they do make lovely underplantings and masses of foliage in our area.

Fancy Fern

Dryopteris intermedia
Aspleniaceae

Evergreen

Collect Spores: July–October

Height: 18–36 inches

Texture: very fine, bipinnate-pinnatifid to tripinnate-pinnatifid

Form: fronds clustered, vaselike and symmetrical

Soil: moist but well-drained, rich

Light: filtered sun to deep shade

Description

Fancy Fern, a member of the woodfern group, has fronds of fine, lacy foliage which form a perfect urn. At the bottom of the vase of fronds, tightly coiled fiddleheads await the next season in a tiny nest. The blade of Fancy Fern is cut three and one-half to four times, producing the characteristic frilly appearance of this species. It ranges from 1½ to 3½ feet in height with fronds as

much as 8 inches wide. The fronds are medium to forest green in color and are somewhat evergreen. Fancy fern is commonly found in the mountains, where it thrives on rocky slopes under mature hardwoods.

Spore Collection

Spores of Fancy Fern are borne on the backs of the fronds in kidney-shaped sori which are covered with indusia. Spores may be gathered when the sori become dark and the indusia open and begin to shed a fine black powder. This may occur any time from late spring until frost. Cut the fertile fronds carefully to avoid damaging remaining fronds and fiddleheads. Place in an envelope and store near a light bulb for a few days to drive out moisture. Sift to remove leaves and debris and store spores in a cool dry place.

Propagation

Spores. Fancy Ferns may be grown from spores fairly readily, but they require somewhat more time and care than some other species. Sow in a sterile medium and moisten thoroughly with distilled water. When gametophytes appear, mist twice a week and keep in a sealed, humid container. Wait patiently for the young sporophytes to develop, and then transplant them to potting soil in a humid case so that the plants may develop a greater root system before being set out.

Rhizome Division. Mature Fancy Ferns often produce secondary growth points supporting one or more fronds near the main crown. Or the mature fern may send up fronds from two crowns that are similar in size. Smaller plantlets may be cut away without disturbing the larger portion of the fern, or the entire clump may be dug up and carefully cut and separated to start several new plants. Divisions should be set in humus-enriched beds and spaced at least 2 to 3 feet apart. Prune back at least half of the fronds of the divisions, removing every other one to preserve the vaselike form of the plant.

Cultivation

Like all woodferns, Fancy Fern should be watered frequently until established, but allowed to drain and dry in between waterings. In a site with rich organic soil, shade, and good drainage, this fern requires little care. You may wish to clip dead fronds for a neater appearance.

Uses in the Garden and Landscape

The perfect vase formed by the lacy fronds of Fancy Fern is its most distinctive feature. Plant it singly or in a staggered pattern with centers at least 3 feet apart. It grows best on a rocky hillside or set in a bed enriched with organic matter. Setting plants 2 to 3 feet from a path gives a view of the new fiddleheads nested in the center of the radiating fronds. Plant Fancy Fern with other mountain plants, such as Bloodroot, Hepatica, and Bleeding Heart, which require very little sunlight and similar soil conditions.

Special Notes

Dryopteris campyloptera and *Dryopteris spinulosa* are woodferns which share many of the characteristics of *Dryopteris intermedia*. The lacy texture and symmetrical shape of these ferns are similar to those of a mature Fancy Fern. Like Fancy Fern, both of these ferns stay green well into the winter, but neither is dependably evergreen in colder regions of the country.

Evergreen Southern Shield Fern

Dryopteris ludoviciana
Aspleniaceae

Evergreen

Collect Spores: July–October

Height: 20–60 inches

Texture: medium, pinnate-pinnatifid

Form: tall arching fertile fronds over cluster of sterile fronds

Soil: very moist

Light: filtered sun to full shade

Description

The Evergreen Southern Shield Fern is native to the Deep South, where it grows in bottomlands and swamps of the coastal plain. The plant is among the largest of the southeastern ferns, with fertile fronds often growing to an impressive height of 4 to 5 feet and 8 to 10 inches across. The fronds are twice cut, dark green and leathery, and have a glossy appearance. The fertile fronds are taller than the sterile fronds and are slightly reduced in width and somewhat thicker. The rhizome of Evergreen Southern Shield Fern is slow-growing and supports dense clusters of fronds.

Spore Collection

Gather fertile fronds in mid-to-late summer, just as the indusia open and release the dark powdery spores. Some spores may still be present into the fall months. Dry fronds for a few days, sift, and store in envelopes in a plastic bag or jar in a refrigerator.

Propagation

Spores. Sow spores on sterile soil or pellets in humid cases and moisten with distilled water. When gametophytes appear, mist twice each week to promote fertilization and development of sporophytes. When transplanting young sporophytes, be sure to keep the soil medium quite moist until the plants become established.

Rhizome Division. The slow-growing rhizome of Evergreen Southern Shield Fern produces offsets or nearby clusters of fronds. Divide carefully between clusters in late fall or early spring for best results. Avoid bruising tender new fiddleheads. Set out divisions 3 to 5 feet apart for specimens; plant somewhat closer for an evergreen mass or backdrop. Water thoroughly after transplanting and often thereafter to keep the soil moist.

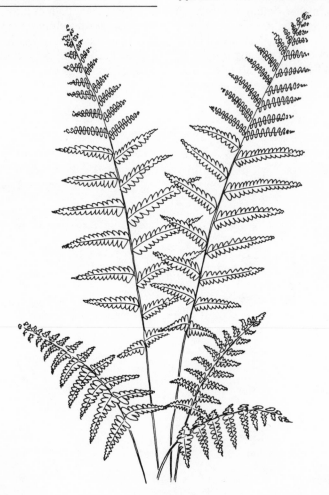

Cultivation

Evergreen Southern Shield Fern is a rugged fern which can tolerate a wide range of conditions. Filtered sunlight to deep shade is adequate for this species to thrive. Unlike most fern species, it can grow in waterlogged soil and survive occasional flooding. It is also able to withstand punishingly high temperatures in the summer months if the site has sufficient moisture.

In nature Evergreen Southern Shield Fern is often found in swamp forests, perched at the bases of Bald Cypress trees on precarious sites that may be very dry in late summer and under water at other times of the year. In the home garden it grows best in a humus-rich bed which is very moist and receives plenty of filtered sunlight. This species is quite hardy in the central piedmont areas of the Southeast, but it may not be able to tolerate the frigid winters of the Northeast and upper Midwest.

Uses in the Garden and Landscape

The Evergreen Southern Shield Fern has great value in the landscape because of its height and evergreen foliage. Use it as a specimen in a place which needs color throughout the year, or plant it in a mass as an evergreen backdrop for other ferns and wild flowers. Like most species, Evergreen Southern Shield Fern will thrive in a prepared bed. But unlike most others, this plant can survive and grow even in a low site with poor drainage.

Special Notes

A closely related and very similar fern which is more familiar to northern gardeners is the large Goldie's Woodfern, *Dryopteris goldiana*. This species lives in moist woods of cooler climates and is at the southernmost extent of its range in the southern Appalachians. Use Goldie's Fern very much like Evergreen Southern Shield Fern on moist seepage slopes and in prepared beds. For best results gardeners should plant Goldie's Woodfern as an evergreen in more northern climes and Evergreen Southern Shield Fern in the warmer Southeast. Both plants are striking in appearance and add height and winter color to the garden.

Two other species of *Dryopteris* are somewhat similar in appearance to *D. ludoviciana*. *Dryopteris celsa*, or Log Fern, is an uncommon species found occasionally in the swamps and bottomland woods of the eastern United States. It is similar in appearance to Evergreen Southern Shield Fern and Goldie's Fern, the two species from which it is thought to have been derived as a fertile hybrid. Log Fern is somewhat shorter but may be used similarly in the landscape. Interplant these three evergreen species of *Dryopteris* with wild flowers such as Turtleheads for a tall, colorful display. Other tall wild flowers to consider planting are Cardinal Flower, Ironweed, and Turk's Cap Lily.

Dryopteris cristata, Crested Shield Fern, is somewhat smaller and coarser than the species mentioned, but it too is a glossy evergreen plant with a short-creeping rhizome which grows well in moist conditions. Plant Crested Shield Fern in a shady bog garden for best results. The smaller, sterile leaves of this fern remain evergreen even in very cold climates.

Marginal Shield Fern

Dryopteris marginalis
Aspleniaceae

Evergreen

Collect Spores: June–October

Height: 18–24 inches

Texture: fine, bipinnate to bipinnate-pinnatifid

Form: fronds clustered, vaselike, symmetrical

Soil: moist, well-drained, rich

Light: filtered sun to deep shade

Description

Marginal Shield Fern has glossy evergreen fronds which are 18 to 24 inches long and as much as 10 inches wide. The fronds form a symmetrical inverted cone which is about 18 inches high and 2½ to 4 feet across. The next season's fiddleheads may be seen nestled in the center of the vase. The fronds are dissected two to two and one-half times, giving this species a texture which is fairly fine but not so lacy as that of the related Fancy Fern.

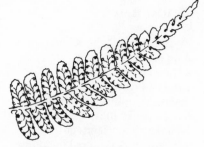

the spores when the sori swell, darken, and begin to shed black spores. This may occur anytime from early summer until frost.

Propagation

Spores. Sow spores on moist, sterile potting soil or a peat pellet in a clear, humid case. Mist with distilled water to keep humidity high enough to cause condensation. Be prepared to wait patiently for several months for the spores to germinate. Then mist gametophytes regularly with distilled water to encourage fertilization and development of sporophytes. The tiny sporophytes of Marginal Shield Fern benefit from a few weeks in a cool humid case before transplanting to an outdoor nursery.

Rhizome Division. As is true for Fancy Fern, small crowns are frequently found right next to the main rosette. After separating crowns, prune back one-third to one-half of foliage before setting out separated plants. Cut carefully to avoid bruising new fiddleheads.

Spore Collection

The species name "marginalis" refers to the location of the sori on the very edge of the pinnae, where they may be found on the underside of the fronds. Collect

Cultivation

Marginal Shield Ferns require conditions similar to those necessary for the other mountain ferns described. A rocky slope or a well-worked, humus-rich bed which is moist but well drained is ideal. It benefits from cool, shady conditions even more than some other ferns, so select a planting site that gives good protection from the sun and drying winds.

This fern grows well in containers. You can leave it outside in winter in a well-mulched two-gallon pot. Bring it indoors for brief displays or color accents during the bleak months of late winter. Repot regularly as the rhizome advances to the side of the pot to prevent the plant from becoming weakened and lopsided.

Uses in the Garden and Landscape

Because of its evergreen foliage, Marginal Shield Fern is ideal for use as a year-round feature in a rock garden or woodland landscape. Plant individual plants in uneven numbers with centers at least 3½ to 4 feet apart for a pleasing effect. Even though these ferns are evergreen, fronds are continuously being replaced. Trim back dead foliage after the flush of new growth in the spring to keep a neat appearance.

The deep forest green of the Marginal Shield Fern will complement wild flowers of almost any color, but whites and true reds and yellows nearby look especially nice. Since this species thrives in a cool site, avoid interplanting wild flowers that require a great deal of light to bloom. Foamflower, Jack-in-the-Pulpit, and Partridge Berry are a few species which are suitable.

Cinnamon Fern

Osmunda cinnamomea
Osmundaceae

Deciduous

Collect Spores: April–June

Height: 30–60 inches

Texture: medium, pinnate-pinnatifid

Form: fronds tall, arching around central fertile fronds

Soil: moist, rich

Light: filtered sun to deep shade

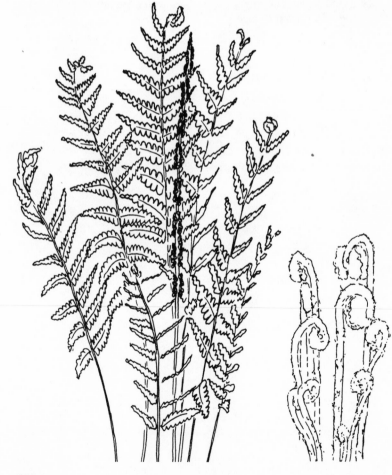

Description

Cinnamon Fern is the tall beauty of coastal swamps and moist mountain slopes of eastern North America, growing to a height of 4 feet or more. The sterile fronds are as much as a foot across and vary in color from yellow green to dark green. Hairs, which are rust to golden in color, are often found on the main rachis, at the attachment of the pinnae, and sometimes on the backs of the fronds. The fiddleheads of the Cinnamon Fern are large, 1 to 3 inches across, and covered with golden hair. They begin to grow in mid-spring and unfurl visibly each day. The fertile fronds come out early in the growing season, sometimes preceding the sterile fronds, and are quite different from them in appearance. The fertile frond is rusty green to deep cinnamon in color and waves like a plume in the center of the huge vase of sterile fronds.

Spore Collection

The rusty fertile fronds mature, release spores, and collapse early in the season. Try to harvest them as soon as the brown spores begin to fall and before the supporting stalks grow limp and wither. Some spores are still present in late summer, but the shriveled fertile fronds may be difficult to locate. It is better to collect in early summer to assure greater numbers of spores and to reduce fungal contamination.

Propagation

Spores. Sow spores on moist, sterile potting soil or peat pellet in a humid case. Take care to sift spores from fertile frond fragments and avoid dropping bits of the fertile frond on sterile potting soil or peat pellets. If portions of leaves and stems are placed on the moist medium, growth of fungi and algae often results. When gametophytes become visible, mist twice a week to promote fertilization. Transplant the young ferns when they reach 2 inches in height.

Rhizome Division. The large crowns of Cinnamon Fern may be divided to make separate plants. Since this species has a short-creeping rhizome, it is often helpful to use a sharp knife or hacksaw to cut the rhizome and the dense fibrous mass between the crowns. Trim back damaged and wilted foliage, and then cut away every third frond to help compensate for the loss of root tissue. Set plants at least 4 feet apart to show the mature plant to best advantage.

Cultivation

Cinnamon Ferns are very tolerant of different growing conditions, but they must have plenty of water. In coastal and piedmont areas, this species often grows "with its feet wet," perched on hummocks along streams and in frequently flooded bottomlands. Given adequate moisture, Cinnamon Fern can flourish in full sun as well as in dappled shade, and on a well-drained slope as well as in a swampy area.

Uses in the Garden and Landscape

This stately and versatile fern is one of the most striking for the garden and landscape. In the mountains it thrives on moist slopes and boulder fields as well as along stream banks. This species makes a strong focal point on the edge of a pond or pool, where it will generate its own fibrous hummock and reappear year after year. Use Cinnamon Fern at 6-foot intervals to give a large bed or swampy area an exotic, tropical appearance. Plant a mass of Cinnamon Ferns at 2-foot intervals to make a dense green background for late-spring and summer wild flowers, such as Cardinal Flower. Plant along the base of a high porch or rock wall to soften harsh angles and add a lush screen in the summer months. Plant a solitary Cinnamon Fern near a bend in a path or near the base of a tree to frame its interesting fiddleheads, colorful fertile plume, statuesque fronds, and generally graceful appearance.

Special Notes

Interrupted Fern, *Osmunda claytoniana*, is a related fern which is somewhat similar in form and appearance to Cinnamon Fern. Unlike Cinnamon Fern, it has no fertile spike but bears its spores on smaller brown fertile pinnules located midway down otherwise sterile fronds. This species seldom grows as tall as Cinnamon Fern and so may be more suitable for gardens where space is limited. The natural range of Interrupted Fern is more restricted than that of Cinnamon Fern, being primarily the northeastern and north central states and the cool mountainous areas of the southeastern United States. Plantings of Interrupted Fern are more apt to succeed in cooler climates; Cinnamon Fern, however, is equally at home in the mountains and in the coastal areas of the Deep South and Southeast.

Royal Fern

Osmunda regalis var. *spectabilis*
Osmundaceae

Deciduous

Collect Spores: April–June

Height: 24–60 inches

Texture: fine to medium, bipinnate

Form: fronds clustered, shrublike

Soil: moist, rich

Light: filtered sun to full sun

Description

Royal Fern offers form and texture quite different from those of any other common native fern. Its fronds are cut twice into large rounded leaflets. The resulting foliage looks at first glance like that of a member of the bean family with compound leaves. The fertile portion of the frond is borne at the tip like a plume. This species is sometimes called Flowering Fern because the golden brown fertile pinnae stand out like the inflorescence of such flowering plants as False Solomon's Seal, Queen-of-the-Prairie, and Staghorn Sumac.

Fronds of Royal Fern range in height from 2 to 5 feet and are often 18 inches or more in width. The overall form of the plant may be feathery or shrublike, depending on the maturity of the plant and the number of fronds in the crown. As the slender fiddleheads of Royal Fern unfurl in the spring, they are frequently tinted with burgundy. The emerging foliage is a delicate pink, which soon becomes green. The color of the foliage may vary from yellow green to blue green and often has a silvery cast.

Spore Collection

The fertile portion of the fronds turns from green to golden brown in early summer and soon withers and disintegrates. Watch for the spores as soon as the fertile pinnae begin to change color in late spring and clip off the tips of the fertile fronds as soon as fine, rust-colored dust begins to be released.

Propagation

Spores. Sow spores on moist sterile mix or peat pellets. Mist thoroughly with distilled water. When a green haze of gametophytes becomes visible, mist twice a week to promote fertilization and development of mature ferns. Transplant sporophytes when they become approximately 2 inches tall.

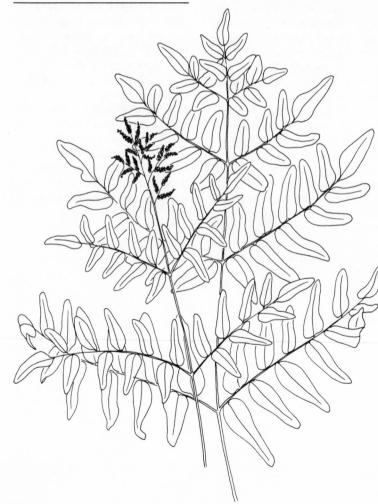

Rhizome Division. Select a dense cluster of fronds and look closely to see if more than one crown or circular cluster of fronds or fiddleheads is present. After digging the entire clump, separate crowns as much as possible by gently removing soil and tugging apart with the hands. Then sever the rhizome between the crowns and the tough surrounding fibrous roots with clippers or a sharp knife or hacksaw. Remove one-third to one-half of the fronds to compensate for root loss. Set the divided crowns in a bed with good drainage at least 3 feet apart. Water well and check moisture regularly for the first few months.

Cultivation

Like its relative the Cinnamon Fern, Royal Fern has a large geographic range and the ability to tolerate a wide variety of conditions. Royal Fern is a majestic feature from the moist slopes of the mountains to the low swamps and bottomlands of the coastal plain. This species will grow in moderate shade or full sun. Generally the plant is much more sparse in the shade, since each crown does not produce as many fronds as it might in full sun. Like Cinnamon Fern, Royal Fern can grow in full sun with its rhizome perched right at the edge of a body of water.

Uses in the Garden and Landscape

Royal Ferns are attractive planted singly, or they may be planted in masses to achieve an unusual texture. In the wild Royal Fern grows on moist mountain slopes, in very wet areas of the coastal plain, and occasionally along the floodplains of streams in the piedmont. Planted in a mass in a well-worked bed which is moist but well drained, Royal Fern will produce slender wine-colored fiddleheads followed by a dense green mass of foliage of medium texture. In late spring and early summer, the golden fertile pinnae at the tips of the fronds add interest and color.

Plant Royal Ferns with such wild flowers as Cardinal Flower or Atamasco Lily near a partially shaded pond; plant as a background for Foamflower, Twinleaf, or Bloodroot under dense deciduous shade; or set a large clump of Royal Fern so it will complement Beard Tongue, Joe-Pye-Weed, or Green-and-Gold on the edge of a wooded bed.

Rock Cap Fern

Polypodium virginianum
Polypodiaceae

Evergreen

Collect Spores: May–October

Height: 4–14 inches

Texture: fine to medium, pinnatifid

Form: fronds loosely clustered, upright or prostrate

Soil: well-drained, rich

Light: filtered sunlight

Description

Rock Cap Fern is a small evergreen fern with fronds from 4 to 14 inches high and from 1 to 4 inches wide. The blade is pinnatifid, or lobed almost all the way into the main stem. The fern is frequently found growing in a mat of moss and soil on top of rocks or limbs. The small scale and simple lines of the Rock Cap Fern make it ideal for inclusion in a rock garden or for tucking into a crevice of a stone wall.

Spore Collection

Spores of Rock Cap Fern are borne in large round sori on the underside of the tips of the taller fronds. The sori mature from mid-summer to frost, darkening from cream color to golden and then to brown. Snip off the fertile fronds when the sori become dark and begin emitting spores. Place in an envelope and store near a light bulb for a few days. After sifting the spores, store in a cool, dry place until you are ready to sow them.

Propagation

Spores. Sow on sterile soil medium or peat pellets in a humid case and mist with distilled water. When the gametophytes become visible, mist twice a week to promote fertilization. Transplant young ferns when they reach approximately 1½ inches in height.

Rhizome Division. Dig a clump of this shallow-rooted species and separate the major rhizomes gently. Use sharp clippers to cut rhizome and fibrous material so that each division has at least one or preferably two fronds or fiddleheads. Cut back each frond by half, especially if the fronds are large and the roots are scanty. Set divisions in a prepared bed or use wire or hairpins to secure the rhizomes to the growing medium. Stake fronds upright with a pencil-size piece of wood if the plant seems in danger of toppling when watered. For a rock garden or wall planting, tuck the rhizome into a small crevice with a few teaspoons of soil and water frequently until the new fiddleheads emerge.

Cultivation

The plant is very resistant to drought and can live in a dry, elevated situation once it becomes established. Water well after transplanting Rock Cap Fern and water when the soil becomes dry to the touch until the plant begins to produce new fronds.

Uses in the Garden and Landscape

The Rock Cap Fern is especially useful because of its evergreen fronds and tidy size. Plant it in rockeries, in crevices of stone walls, and along shaded walks. Plant Rock Cap Ferns on an old log or on the limb of an ancient oak, just as they are sometimes found in nature. Use this species for a miniature touch of evergreen foliage in a small planting where a large plant would be out of proportion. Or plant Rock Cap Fern in a leaf-mold-enriched bed and it will grow to its full height and support lustrous green foliage.

Special Notes

Resurrection Fern, *Polypodium polypodioides*, is a closely related species which is somewhat similar in appearance to the immature Rock Cap Fern. This species is even more able to resist severe drought. Like the Rock Cap Fern, the Resurrection Fern is frequently found on logs, tree limbs, and old stonework. When the Resurrection Fern becomes dry, it curls up and looks quite dead. After a rain the Resurrection Fern unfurls and turns green again. The lower surface of the Resurrection Fern is densely scaly, and the color of the fern is usually a drab olive. The species is often known as the Common or Gray Polypody. Although Resurrection Fern is somewhat more drought tolerant than the Rock Cap Fern, it is not as attractive or versatile. Use Resurrection Fern to add interesting detail to your rock garden, but rely on Rock Cap Fern for short evergreen foliage in the garden year-round.

Christmas Fern

Polystichum acrostichoides
Aspleniaceae

Evergreen

Collect Spores: June–October

Height: 12–30 inches

Texture: fine, pinnate

*Form: fronds clustered,
sometimes vaselike*

Soil: moist but well-drained, rich

*Light: filtered sunlight to
full shade*

Description

Christmas Fern is a robust, leathery fern which has glossy green fronds year-round. It is found on shaded slopes and in moist woods and swamps from the mountains to the coast. The fronds grow in dense clusters and range in length from less than 1 foot to more than 2 feet. The fronds are once divided into pointed pinnae, resulting in a medium to coarse texture. Silvery green fiddleheads appear in the mid-spring and add interest to gardens as they unroll to form new light green fronds.

Spore Collection

Fertile fronds are easy to spot because the pinnae at the end are reduced in size and more corrugated than those of the sterile fronds. Collect spores when the indusia turn golden brown and begin to peel back from the sori and drop a fine, rusty powder. This usually begins in mid-summer and continues late into the fall. After releasing spores the fertile tip of the frond turns dark, withers, and dies.

Propagation

Spores. Sow spores on moist, sterile potting soil or peat pellets in a clear humid case and mist with distilled water. When the new gametophytes become visible as a fine green haze, mist twice each week to promote fertilization. Transplant sporophytes when they reach 1½ inches in height.

Rhizome Division. After digging up an entire clump, tug gently and work the clusters apart as much as possible. Then clip the rhizome between the crowns with sharp pruning clippers. Avoid bruising the new fiddleheads. Set small plants at least a foot apart and plant larger divisions 2 feet on center for an even groundcover.

Cultivation

Christmas Fern will grow well almost anywhere except in full sun. To create a vigorous groundcover with this species, first prepare the soil by working in generous quantities of composted leaves or other organic matter and a nitrogen source, such as composted horse manure. Plant the ferns in an offset pattern, approximately 12 to 18 inches apart, depending on the size of the ferns. Prune back dead or damaged foliage and water well.

Throughout the winter months, the evergreen fronds will drape gracefully down a steeply sloping planting site. In early spring, as the new fiddleheads begin to unfurl, you may want to trim off the dead fronds from previous seasons for the sake of neatness. This is certainly not necessary, however. Some people also prefer to remove the brown fertile portion of the fronds for the same reason, but this takes a lot of time for a large planting.

Although it is best to move ferns in the cooler months of the year, Christmas Fern is so vigorous that it may be transplanted during any season. Cut off damaged fronds and up to one third of the foliage to help the ferns become established.

Uses in the Garden and Landscape

Because of its evergreen foliage and general vigor, Christmas Fern makes an ideal groundcover for shady areas, especially those that resemble the moist, north-facing slopes on which it is found in nature.

Christmas Fern also grows well in pots. Move pots indoors for a few days at a time or use to brighten planters during the drab winter months. This plant is excellent for perking up any outdoor displays and exhibits as well as for household decoration. Like most native ferns, however, Christmas Fern grows best outdoors and should not be left indoors for too long.

Use beds of Christmas Ferns to define portions of the yard and walkways, especially in the winter months. Plant bright wild flowers nearby, such as Green-and-Gold, Foamflower, or Indian Pink. Almost every flower looks better against a background of evergreen fern foliage.

Special Notes

The only species which is occasionally confused with Christmas Fern is a smaller pinnate evergreen fern called Ebony Spleenwort, *Asplenium platyneuron*. This species is ideal for planting in dry sites, such as rock gardens and stone walls. It is fairly common in dry rocky woods throughout the East and may easily be propagated by spores or by division. Older plants may also make new plantlets at the base of the fronds.

Deciduous Southern Shield Fern

Thelypteris kunthii
Thelypteridaceae

Deciduous

Collect Spores: July–October

Height: 22–45 inches

Texture: fine, pinnate-pinnatifid

Form: fronds in irregular clusters

Soil: moist but well-drained, rich

Light: filtered sunlight to full sun

Description

The Deciduous Southern Shield Fern is a medium-sized fern with gracefully arching fronds which are lime to medium green in color. The fronds grow to 2 ½ to 3 feet in height and 8 to 12 inches in width. The fronds reach in all directions from clusters of stalks which grow out of the rhizome at intervals. The foliage is cut 1¾ times, and each of the pinnae tapers to a point. The blade is usually triangular in shape and covered with a thin layer of soft hairs. The foliage of the species takes on a pleasing bronze cast as winter approaches.

Spore Collection

Collect fertile fronds from mid-summer to frost when sori begin to release a very fine brown powder. Place envelopes of fertile fronds near a light bulb for a few days. Store cool and dry, or sow immediately.

Propagation

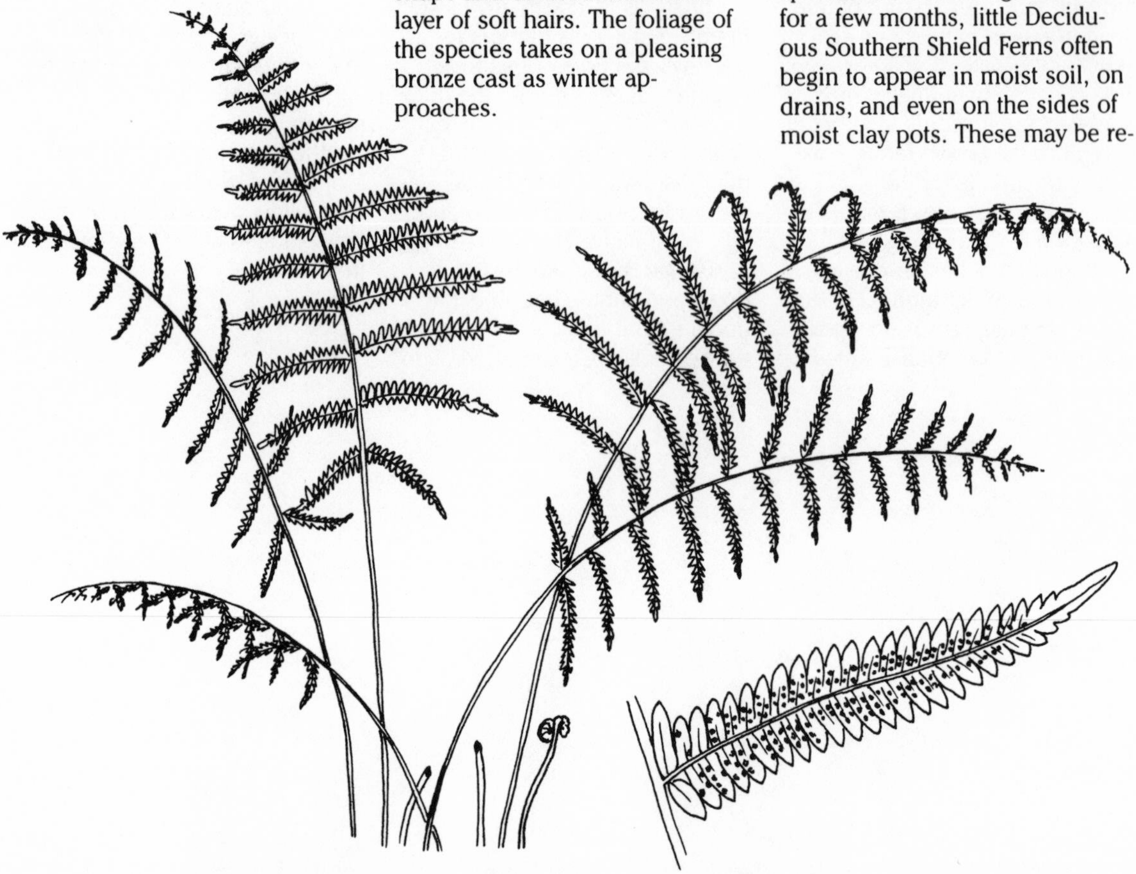

Spores. This species is the easiest of our southeastern ferns to grow from spores. If a mature specimen is left in a greenhouse for a few months, little Deciduous Southern Shield Ferns often begin to appear in moist soil, on drains, and even on the sides of moist clay pots. These may be removed carefully and transplanted to more desirable locations in spring or fall. To grow this species from spores, sow spores on moist, sterile potting soil or peat pellets in a clear, humid container. Mist thoroughly with distilled water. When gametophytes become visible, mist twice a week to promote fertilization and sporophyte development. Transplant young ferns when they reach 1 inch in height or have several fronds.

Rhizome Division. Plants are easily divided by cutting the rhizomes between clusters of fronds. Set out divisions a foot or more apart and trim back damaged foliage of this rather brittle fern.

Cultivation

Deciduous Southern Shield Fern may be killed by prolonged freezing of the ground. In warmer areas, however, this species is one of the last deciduous ferns to lose its color in the fall. It usually does not go into dormancy until it is exposed to freezing temperatures in late fall. This species is typically found on marl or in shady woods near the coast. It benefits from the addition of lime to the soil and application of a protective mulch in the winter. In areas where the ground freezes for weeks, Deciduous Southern Shield Fern should be moved into a greenhouse or sunny window for the winter.

The fronds of this species are quite brittle, so trimming may improve the appearance of the plant during the growing season. Fastidious gardeners may also wish to trim dead foliage from the previous year in early spring. Although this fern is quite vigorous and grows back rapidly after trimming, it is not aggressive or weedy in areas which have at least a little cold weather.

Uses in the Garden and Landscape

Use this plant for lush green foliage and lighter colors in the garden. Interplant this fern with Jack-in-the-Pulpit. The red fruit of the Jack in the fall provides a beautiful contrast to the green of the Deciduous Southern Shield Fern. *Thelypteris kunthii* grows very well in a large pot with good drainage. If kept in a greenhouse during the winter and brought inside occasionally, it provides springlike foliage to brighten the season.

Special Notes

A related species, *Thelypteris hexagonoptera*, the Broad Beech Fern, is more common inland and north of the range of the Deciduous Southern Shield Fern, where it occupies the well-developed soil of mature, moist hardwood forests. The triangular blade forms a lovely plane of green over the forest floor when grown in a wooded lot or in deep beds that have been enriched with composted leaves. The sori of this species are quite small; so look carefully to find the fertile fronds. Broad Beech Fern may also be propagated readily by division of the rhizomes.

New York Fern

Thelypteris noveboracensis
Thelypteridaceae

Deciduous

Collect Spores: July–September

Height: 12–24 inches

Texture: very fine, pinnate-pinnatifid

Form: fronds borne singly in large colonies

Soil: moist but well-drained, rich

Light: filtered sunlight to full sun

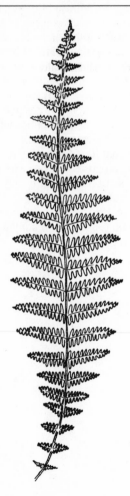

Description

New York Fern is a soft, deciduous yellow green fern which stands 12 to 24 inches high. The blade of the frond has a maximum width of about 4 inches in the middle and tapers gradually to both top and bottom. The reduced size of pinnae toward the base of the frond is characteristic of this species. The blade is cut almost twice. Although the fern is not extremely dissected, the small size of the pinnules and the thinness of the leaves give a rather fine texture and translucent quality to the foliage. Fronds of New York Fern emerge from the fast-growing rhizome singly or in small clusters, but do not form symmetrical crowns. After frost the deciduous foliage turns light tan to golden brown and is a rather attractive winter bed cover.

Spore Collection

Fertile fronds of this species look very similar to sterile ones, so it is necessary to turn fronds over and examine them carefully. Some colonies of this fern, however, seem to produce no fertile fronds and spread only vegetatively. Harvest spores when the sori turn light brown and begin to shed brown powder, usually in mid-summer or later. Save fertile fronds in envelopes and dry over a light to discourage fungus. Store cool and dry until time of sowing.

Propagation

Spores. Sow spores on moist, sterile potting soil or peat pellets in a humid case and mist with distilled water. When gametophytes become visible, mist twice a week to promote germination. Transplant or pot sporophytes when they are at least 2 inches tall.

Rhizome Division. New York Fern is one of the easiest of all ferns to propagate by dividing the rhizomes. Dig up a clump of the fern in the fall, pull rhizomes apart between clusters of fronds, and set out divisions 6 inches to 1 foot apart in well-worked beds. If divisions are made during the growing season, trim back broken fronds and cut off enough additional fronds to reduce foliage by about one-third. In either case, water well and check moisture often during the first few months. If the bed is properly prepared and receives several hours of sunlight each day, New York Fern will reproduce very rapidly and cover the area with a dense layer of soft foliage.

Cultivation

Beds should be enriched with composted organic matter and should be moist but well drained. This species naturally thrives in openings in wooded areas, so for best results, it should be planted where it will receive plenty of filtered sunlight and two or three hours of direct exposure. A planting along the northern or eastern edge of a wooded area is ideal,

but any moist, well-drained area which is partially shaded is suitable.

Uses in the Garden and Landscape

New York Fern may be used singly, but to take advantage of its fast multiplication it is best used as a groundcover.

New York Fern is sometimes aggressive and may become a pest. This species should not be planted in an area where it will overrun less vigorous species. In cool moist climates, use of aluminum edging may be advisable to help define the bed and keep the ferns in bounds. In areas which are warmer and drier, New York Fern is particularly useful because it is so easy to grow.

One of the most pleasant features of New York Fern is the translucent quality of its fronds. Plant this species in a setting where persons walking through the garden may glimpse the sun glowing through the delicate leaves and enjoy the play of shadows cast by the moving foliage.

Take advantage of the light requirement of New York Fern by planting it as a groundcover among flowering shrubs or small trees which require filtered light to some full sun. Or plant near tall vigorous wild flowers and cultivated plants which can compete with the rapidly spreading rhizomes of this fern.

Special Notes

A related species, *Thelypteris palustris*, or Marsh Fern, is somewhat similar in appearance, although the base of the blade does not taper and the frond may be twice as tall as that of the New York Fern. Marsh Fern may be grown in filtered light or even in full sun if moisture is adequate. Plant Marsh Fern along the edge of an open bog garden or in a humus-enriched bed and it will grow and multiply rapidly to form a dense mass of light green foliage.

Netted Chain Fern

Woodwardia areolata
Blechnaceae

Deciduous

Collect Spores: August–October

Height: 12–24 inches

Texture: medium, pinnatifid

Form: fronds loosely clustered, often forming colonies

Soil: moist, rich

Light: filtered sunlight

Description

Woodwardia areolata, or Netted Chain Fern, is a deciduous waxy green fern which stands 12 to 24 inches high and has fronds 4 to 8 inches wide. The sterile and fertile fronds are quite different in appearance. The sterile fronds are pinnatifid, or deeply lobed, rather than cut all the way to the rachis. The ends of the coarse lobes are rounded, and the veins in the leaf form a netted or chainlike pattern. Fertile fronds of Netted Chain Fern are as tall as the sterile fronds, but very reduced in width. As the fertile fronds ripen and turn from green to brown, the narrow erect pinnules relax and hang downward from the main stem. Close examination of the fertile frond reveals a chainlike pattern on each of the pinnae.

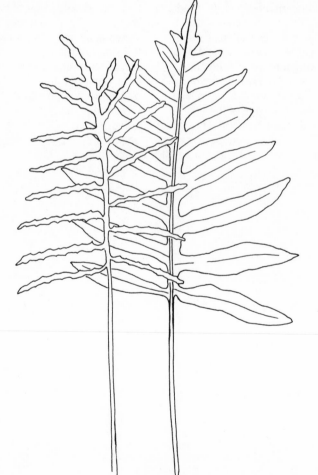

The rhizome of Netted Chain Fern is a long-creeping one which puts up one or more fronds every few inches to several feet apart.

Spore Collection

Collect fertile fronds when they turn brown and the indusia begin to open. This usually occurs in late summer or fall, but some spores may be obtained from the brown fertile fronds the following year. Place in envelopes or sow directly. Set the envelopes near a light bulb for several days to drive out moisture. Then store the spores in a cool, dry place until ready to sow.

Propagation

Spores. Sow spores on peat pellets or sterile potting soil in a clear, humid case and mist with distilled water. When gametophytes become visible, mist twice each week to promote fertilization and sporophyte development. Transplant young ferns when they are at least 1 inch in height. For best results transplant young sporophytes to a medium that is rich in composted organic matter and low in pH.

Rhizome Division. Vegetative propagation of this species is very easy. Preferably in early winter, when deciduous fronds are still visible, dig up the creeping rhizomes and clip between clusters. If transplanting before frost, be sure to prune back about one-third of the sterile fronds. Set divisions in a moist, well-worked bed or a low area, such as the floodplain of a stream.

Cultivation

The chief advantage of Netted Chain Fern is that it thrives in low areas with poor drainage where most ferns and wild flowers suffer and die. The medium-coarse green foliage of Netted Chain Fern provides a most interesting groundcover. Given a bed of rich soil and better drainage, the Netted Chain Fern will grow even larger and form attractive clusters of foliage.

Uses in the Garden and Landscape

In the fall the fertile fronds turn dark brown and provide an interesting contrast among the green sterile fronds. Other attractive plants that will grow in the same poorly drained conditions include Jack-in-the-Pulpit, Jewelweed, and Skunk Cabbage.

Special Notes

Onoclea sensibilis, Sensitive Fern, is similar in appearance to the Netted Chain Fern. Bead Fern, another common name for this species, refers to the distinctive rounded shapes on the fertile frond which protect the spores through the winter and open to release them in early spring. Although the fertile fronds of Sensitive Fern are different from those of Netted Chain Fern, the sterile fronds of these two ferns are easily mistaken for each other. Sensitive Fern, too, is suitable for sites with poor drainage. However, this species is very susceptible to drought and frost and so does not remain attractive through much of the growing season. Sensitive Ferns are eaten by many insects and often look quite chewed upon by mid-summer. Because of its sensitivity to conditions and insect pests, Sensitive Fern is not nearly as useful in the landscape as Netted Chain Fern.

Woodwardia virginica, the Virginia Chain Fern, is a fern of the same genus as the Netted Chain Fern, but requires quite different growing conditions. This fern grows best in full sunlight along moist ditches and slight depressions in the sandy soil of the coastal plain. The 2-to-3-foot fern is easy to recognize by its thick black stems which emerge singly from the fast-creeping rhizome. Spores of this plant may be found in the chain-shaped sori that trace the shape of the frond on the back side of the leaves. This fern is useful because it is one of the few native ferns which thrives in sunlight and because it takes on an attractive bronze color in the fall.

Other Native Ferns of Interest to Gardeners

No discussion of native ferns would be complete without mention of the little ferns that are capable of living in the tiniest crevices of trees, rock walls, and fences.

Among this group are the spleenworts, the most common of which is the Ebony Spleenwort, *Asplenium platyneuron*. This evergreen species has a rosette of once-pinnate sterile fronds 3–5 inches in length. In the summer the fern has fertile fronds that wave as much as a foot above the center of the plant. Ebony Spleenworts are commonly found on dry hillsides, atop rocky bluffs, and in the crevices of old stonework and walls. Planted in a rock gar-

den, the Ebony Spleenwort provides evergreen foliage among the stones. It can be propagated from spores or by division and will thrive in soil that is somewhat limed and very well drained.

A small fern of great interest and curious habit is *Asplenium rhizophyllum* (also known as *Camptosorus rhizophyllus*), the Walking Fern. This plant is not divided like a fern at all, but has long tapering leaves with uncut edges. Where a narrow leaf tip touches down on suitably moist soil or moss, first a leaf and then a new rosette of Walking Fern soon appear. This fern may be grown from the spores found in sori on the back of the widest leaves. The most difficult step is the successful transplantation of the young sporophytes to the thin soil or moss covering a rock or large boulder in the garden. One method is to fasten the plants to the moss with old-fashioned hair pins and mist them frequently until the ferns are established. For the best results, the underlying rock should be soapstone, limestone, or some other type of calcareous rock which will weather to a soil which is high in pH.

Several other native *Asplenium* species may be grown readily from spores, and each adds detail to a rock garden or stone wall. One is *Asplenium resiliens*, the Black Stem Spleenwort, which grows among fairly dry, cool calcareous rocks and can reach as much as 8–12 inches in length. This fern is somewhat similar to Ebony Spleenwort in appearance except that it is smaller, more delicate, and rather grey green in color. The rachis, or stem, of this fern is brittle and should be handled very carefully during transplantation.

Asplenium trichomanes, the Maidenhair Spleenwort, is smaller still, seldom as much as 7 inches long, and has delicate, rounded leaflets on either side of each thin black rachis. This little fern grows among rocks and in tiny cool shaded crevices throughout much of the Northern Hemisphere. To grow this fern successfully, quite a bit of moisture is essential. Choose a site such as a moist, rocky seepage, and mist frequently.

Other rare *Aspleniums*, such as the parsleylike *Asplenium ruta-muraria*, or Wall Rue, and *Asplenium montanum*, the Mountain Spleenwort, are also difficult to grow in the Southeast and are best left in their native setting.

Ebony Spleenwort

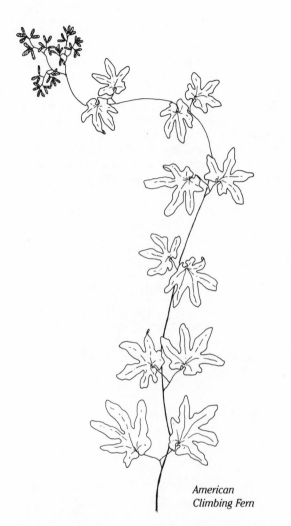

*American
Climbing Fern*

they slowly cover the surface with an unusual furry texture. Gardeners are reminded that Lipferns are rare in some states, and that the spores should be collected with great care to avoid disturbing natural populations.

A fern which will twine on a fence or cover a rock wall when planted in the soil nearby is *Lygodium palmatum*, the American Climbing Fern. The hand-shaped leaflets of this unusual fern are spaced along the vinelike rachis of the frond. Narrow fertile pinnae develop at the tip of the slender rachis if the plant receives enough sunlight. The leaflets form a densely interwoven layer which drapes over the surface of the supporting material and gives an unusual and pleasing effect. This fern is most easily grown by division of its fibrous rhizomes. The plant is deciduous and should be cut back in the fall so that the next season's foliage will not become intertwined with the dead material.

For walls and rock gardens of the coastal plain in the Deep South, Spider Brake Fern, *Pteris multifida*, is suitable for planting. This slender and unusual species is marginally hardy in areas with freezing weather, but it may persist near buildings or massive masonry walls. If a mature plant is taken into a greenhouse, Spider Brake will multiply rapidly from spores and spawn small Spider Brakes in every moist drain and corner. These sporelings may be transplanted into a rock garden or warm moist site along a stone wall.

Some small ferns that prefer moist level sites are the Grapeferns and Rattlesnake Ferns. The common names are assigned rather loosely to the numerous members of this group that are found in the Southeast. Those with fertile stalks arising from the base of the blade are generally called Rattlesnake Ferns, especially the deciduous *Botrychium virginianum*, a fern which emerges in spring and may grow to as much as 1 to 2 feet tall. The members of this group that have fertile fronds arising from near soil level are known as Grapeferns. Two Grapeferns that are common in the Southeast are the Dissected Grapefern, *Botrychium dissectum*, and the coarser Sparse-lobed Grapefern, or bronze *Botrychium biternatum*. In general the new fronds of the Grapeferns emerge in late summer and re-

Another group of small ferns which adds interest to the rock wall or garden are those known as the lipferns. *Cheilanthes lanosa*, the Hairy Lipfern, may have fronds as much as 18 inches in length. Usually, however, it is much smaller. This fern gets its common name from the dense coat of spreading reddish hairs that cover its upper and lower surfaces. Fronds of *Cheilanthes tomentosa*, the Woolly Lipfern, may grow 1 to 2 feet long, but they too are often smaller. This lipfern is covered with dense curly hairs. Both of the lipferns grow well on well-drained sites on noncalcareous rocks, where

Three other fairly small lacy ferns are readily grown from spores and add interest to the garden. *Woodsia obtusa*, the Blunt-lobed Woodsia, grows throughout the eastern United States, where it is most commonly found on shaded ledges. The plant is quite suitable as a medium-sized plant for the rock garden. *Cystopteris protrusa*, the Southern Fragile Fern, is usually found along rocky banks of woodland streams. It is suitable for adding lacy, parsleylike foliage to a rocky garden pool or water feature, or even a delicate groundcover in a cool

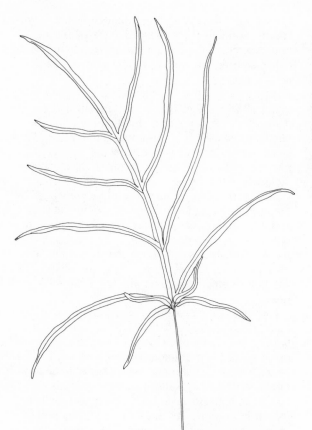

Spider Brake Fern

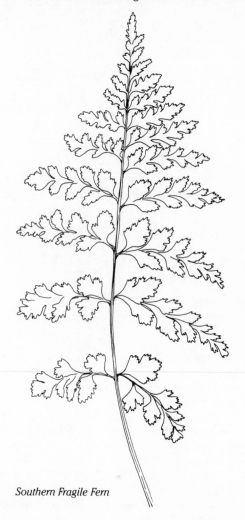

Southern Fragile Fern

main evergreen through the winter. These ferns grow in moist woods and swampy areas. Some are found on the edges of moist pastures, where their succulent fertile fronds are frequently eaten by livestock. New studies of *Botrychium* suggest that the spores of some species benefit from passing through the acid digestive tract of cattle. Unlike those of most ferns, the spores of *Botrychium* may germinate as much as 6–8 inches underground. *Botrychiums* for home gardens are best obtained by collecting them from areas where construction is imminent (see plant rescue discussion in appendix). The evergreen Grapeferns have an interesting form and add much-needed green color to the garden in winter.

310

climate. A relative, *Cystopteris bulbifera*, also grows along cool moist seepages in the mountains. Like Woodsia and the Southern Fragile Fern, this Bulblet Bladder Fern may be readily grown from spores. Unlike other fern species, the Bulblet Bladder Fern produces small green masses on the undersides of the fronds which may be picked off and planted to grow a mature plant without going through the gametophyte stage.

Another little fern which is not to be missed by the dedicated grower of native plants is the Southern Adder's Tongue, *Ophioglossum vulgatum* var. *pycnostichum*. This most unfernlike little plant has one sterile oval leaf and a taller slender fertile stalk. The plant is commonly found in moist, somewhat open areas and will grow as a specimen in a moist humus-rich bed. The plant is usually grown more as a curiosity than as a major part of the landscape.

Still another unusual fern for the garden is the Mosquito Fern, *Azolla caroliniana*, a free-floating aquatic fern of the eastern coastal plain. Mosquito Ferns multiply rapidly on the surface of a quiet pond or pool, where the fingertip-size plants provide a colorful, textured surface to all or part of the body of water. In a setting with quite a bit of light, Mosquito Fern will turn vivid reddish or burgundy in color; plants in the shade remain a dusty green. Where a pool is partially shaded, the surface is tinted with a gradient of color. This effect may be emphasized by planting a cluster of Cardinal Flower or other red flowers strategically along the edge of the pond. The Mosquito Fern is only marginally hardy in areas subject to freezing weather and snow. Gardeners in colder areas should bring some plants indoors in early fall and keep them growing in a large jar or well-lit aquarium as a starting culture for the next growing season.

Only a portion of the native fern flora is discussed in this chapter, but the species mentioned include a wide variety of sizes and textures. And of course ferns offer infinite shades of green for the landscaper's palette. With a bit of skill and imagination, the gardener may use native ferns to add great interest and beauty to the garden of native plants.

Appendix 1. How to Organize a Plant Rescue

Native plant rescue, like propagation, is a way to acquire plants for the garden without harming the environment. Each year residential and commercial development and highway construction claim more of the natural landscape. Plant rescue means going into areas destined to go under the bulldozer's blade and removing desirable plants. It is not the solution to the problem of protecting our rare species, but it does provide opportunities to salvage plants for use in the garden which would otherwise be destroyed and it is a means to preserve a few of our native plants.

Plant rescue should appeal to anyone interested in displaying native wild flowers, shrubs, and ferns. The possibility of acquiring plants of usable size is of course an attractive one. In addition, rescuing plants gives gardeners opportunities to work with native species essentially untried in the home garden. *Ruellia caroliniensis*, for instance, is a little-used perennial found in dry woods and sandy fields in the southeastern United States. It requires little care and has attractive blue flowers that bloom in summer. We first became aware of the potential of this plant for the home garden when we collected several specimens on a rescue operation and began working with the seeds and taking cuttings.

In addition to botanical institutions and home gardeners, local nurseries, garden clubs, and landscapers will find these operations valuable. For nurseries in particular they can be a source for stock plants of certain species that are generally hard to come by. For example, Green-and-Gold is an outstanding evergreen groundcover that is in considerable demand by wild flower gardeners, but sources of propagated plants are limited. Nursery operators can rescue plants, propagate them by cuttings and division, and in, say, two years' time offer attractive potted plants for sale.

The Botanical Garden has conducted a native plant rescue program for many years. The success of the program is due largely to the enthusiastic efforts of Garden volunteers. Interested persons are usually quick to respond to the need for plant rescue in the community as a means to save and utilize threatened native plants. Although a plant rescue can be carried out by a group or an individual, a successful rescue involves proper organization, best achieved by establishing a network of cooperating individuals. The following ideas should prove helpful as you organize your rescue operation.

1. Compile a list of individuals and organizations in your area interested in participating in a local rescue. Determine the kinds of native plants they could use—evergreen shrubs, shade-loving wild flowers, ferns, and so forth.

2. Find out about potential rescue sites in your area. Individuals who are in positions to know about local development plans can be invaluable here.

3. When you have targeted a likely site, get written permission from the owner, developer, or holding agency to scout and later remove plants from the site. Most owners are glad to comply once they understand the reasons for the rescue activity. If the owner has any doubts, make it clear that he or she is not legally responsible for anything that may occur during a rescue but is simply allowing your group to enter and remove plants from the site. It is important to have a copy of the permission form, signed by the owner or contractor, in hand during the rescue. (Refer to the sample permission form below.) Be certain that someone in your group knows exactly the boundaries of the site within which you can remove plants.

4. Scout the site before digging plants. Ideally, you should try to engage a local botanist to identify the species on the site and an experienced native plant gardener to assess their application in the garden. They can supply information before the dig that will enable rescuers to prepare for the types of incoming plants. Scouts can also tag desirable plants on the site and estimate their numbers.

5. Notify diggers when written permission is secured and the site is deemed worthy of rescue. You would want to let each participant know such details as the time and place to meet, car pool arrangements, tools and equipment needed, proper clothing, plants on the site and their numbers, and a rain date.

6. Prepare for the rescue. When participants know ahead of time the plants they wish to rescue and reestablish in their gardens, they can make proper preparations at home. These may include

preparing a new planting bed or making a small nursery area close to a water source where plants can be tended immediately after a rescue.

7. Dig. Make sure everyone knows the boundaries of the site and where they may and may not remove plants. Demonstrate the proper methods for digging the different plants on the site. Woody material will need to be pruned back by two-thirds before removal.

8. Set out rescued wild flowers and ferns in permanent plantings or heel them in in holding beds of loose soil or sawdust as soon as possible.

9. Moisten the plants and beds thoroughly and mist foliage frequently until the root systems recover. Extra care at this critical time will prevent plant loss and keep specimens looking healthy.

10. Thank the landowners or developers for their permission and assistance. Everyone appreciates this courtesy, and some developers are more likely to invite you to conduct plant rescues in the future.

```
                    LETTER OF PERMISSION
                            TO
                   DIG AND REMOVE PLANTS


_____ has/have permission to search for, dig,
(name of individual or group)
and remove native plants at the _____ site

located at _____

_____

which will soon be cleared or developed.

Expected date of clearing or construction: _____

Restrictions: _____

_____

_____

I understand that the plants dug will be used in the

_____

_____ Garden or in other appropriate public

and private gardens.


                         Signature _____ Date _____

                         Title (if other than land owner): _____

                         Address: _____

                                  _____

                                  _____

                         Phone: _____

_____ Please send an inventory of the plants collected to the address above.
```

Appendix 2. Calendar of Blooming Dates

These blooming dates are based on eight years of data collected at the North Carolina Botanical Garden, located in Chapel Hill, North Carolina. Although blooming dates will vary from area to area, this chart will give you an idea of the duration of bloom of a particular species and indicate what other species can be expected to be blooming at the same time. This information is especially useful in planning a perennial bed.

Scientific Name	Common Name	Feb.	Mar.	Apr.	May	Jun.	Jul.	Aug.	Sep.	Oct.
Symplocarpus foetidus	Skunk Cabbage	■	■							
Erythronium americanum	Trout Lily		■							
Sanguinaria canadensis	Bloodroot		■	■						
Jeffersonia diphylla	Twinleaf			■						
Dentaria diphylla	Toothwort			■						
Gelsemium sempervirens	Yellow Jessamine			■						
Chrysogonum virginianum	Green-and-Gold			■	■	■	■	■	■	■
Mertensia virginica	Bluebells			■						
Viola pedata	Bird-foot Violet			■						
Trillium grandiflorum	Great White Trillium			■						
Aquilegia canadensis	Columbine			■	■					
Tiarella cordifolia	Foamflower			■	■					
Dicentra eximia	Bleeding Heart			■	■	■	■	■	■	
Iris cristata	Crested Dwarf Iris			■						
Phacelia bipinnatifida	Phacelia			■						
Amsonia tabernaemontana	Blue Star			■						
Erigeron pulchellus	Robin's Plantain			■	■					
Asarum canadense	Deciduous Wild Ginger			■	■					
Arisaema triphyllum	Jack-in-the-Pulpit			■	■					
Geranium maculatum	Wild Geranium			■	■					
Zephyranthes atamasco	Atamasco Lily				■					
Pinguicula lutea *	Butterwort				■					
Sedum ternatum	Stonecrop				■					
Coreopsis auriculata	Coreopsis				■					
Sarracenia flava *	Pitcher Plants				■					
Baptisia pendula	White Wild Indigo				■					
Diphylleia cymosa	Umbrella-Leaf				■					
Potentilla tridentata	Wine-Leaf Cinquefoil				■					
Anisostichus capreolata	Cross Vine				■					
Sisyrinchium angustifolium	Blue-eyed Grass				■					
Tradescantia virginiana	Spiderwort				■	■	■			
Heuchera americana	Alumroot				■	■				
Penstemon smallii	Beard Tongue				■	■				
Chrysanthemum leucanthemum	Ox-eye Daisy				■	■	■			
Lysimachia nummularia	Moneywort					■				
Thermopsis villosa	Carolina Bush Pea				■	■				
Oenothera tetragona	Sundrops				■	■				
Silene virginica	Fire Pink				■	■				
Verbascum blattaria	Moth Mullein				■	■				
Hydrophyllum virginianum	Waterleaf				■					
Opuntia compressa	Prickly Pear					■				
Rudbeckia hirta	Black-eyed Susan					■	■			
Asclepias tuberosa	Butterfly Weed					■	■	■		
Daucus carota	Queen Anne's Lace					■	■	■		
Stokesia laevis	Stokes' Aster					■	■			
Achillea millefolium	Yarrow					■	■			
Gaillardia pulchella	Gaillardia					■	■	■		
Dionaea muscipula *	Venus' Fly Trap					■	■			
Monarda didyma	Bee-balm					■	■			
Echinacea purpurea	Purple Cone-flower					■	■	■		
Campsis radicans	Trumpet Vine					■	■			
Filipendula rubra	Queen-of-the-Prairie					■	■			
Ruellia caroliniensis	Ruellia					■	■			
Eryngium yuccifolium	Button Snakeroot					■	■			
Pycnanthemum incanum	Mountain Mint					■	■			
Lilium superbum	Turk's-Cap Lily						■			
Passiflora incarnata	Passion Flower						■	■		
Rhexia mariana var purpurea	Meadow-Beauty						■	■		

Scientific Name	Common Name	Feb.	Mar.	Apr.	May	Jun.	Jul.	Aug.	Sep.	Oct.
Allium cernuum	Nodding Onion						█			
Hibiscus moscheutos	Rose Mallow						█	█		
Eupatorium fistulosum	Joe-Pye-Weed							█	█	
Lobelia cardinalis	Cardinal Flower							█	█	
Phlox paniculata	Garden Phlox							█	█	
Chelone lyonii	Turtleheads							█	█	
Clematis virginiana	Virgin's Bower							█		
Drosera intermedia	Sundew							█	█	
Gentiana clausa	Bottle-Gentian							█	█	
Parnassia grandifolia	Grass-of-Parnassus							█	█	
Vernonia noveboracensis	Ironweed							█		
Trichostema dichotomum	Blue Curls							█	█	
Helianthus tomentosus	Sunflower							█	█	
Boltonia asteroides	Boltonia							█	█	
Liatris spicata	Blazing Star							█	█	
Ludwigia bonariensis	Ludwigia							█	█	
Kosteletskya virginica	Seashore Mallow								█	
Bidens polylepis	Bur-Marigold								█	
Solidago rugosa	Rough-leaved Goldenrod								█	█
Aster novae-angliae	New England Aster								█	█
Heterotheca mariana	Maryland Golden Aster								█	█

* Carnivorous Plants

Appendix 3. Production Timetable

This reference chart is directed to commerical nursery operators and growers interested in producing wild flowers on a large scale. The information provided here has been extracted from the species descriptions, which should be referred to for explicit methods and handling techniques.

Species	Seed					Cuttings		Division
	Storage	Pretreatment	Time Sown	Location Sown	Total Production Time	Time Taken	Weeks to Potted	Time of Year
Symplocarpus foetidus	siuc	—	siuc–fall	shaded outdoor seedbed	2 yrs	—	—	fall
Erythronium americanum	siuc	—	siuc–late spring	shaded outdoor seedbed	3–4 yrs	—	—	early summer
Sanguinaria canadensis	siuc	—	siuc–late spring	shaded outdoor seedbed	2 yrs	—	—	fall
Jeffersonia diphylla	siuc	—	siuc–late spring	shaded outdoor seedbed	4–5 yrs	—	—	fall
Dentaria diphylla	siuc	—	siuc–late spring	shaded outdoor seedbed	3–4 yrs	—	—	summer
Gelsemium sempervirens	dry	—	spring	outdoor seedbed	8–12 wks	summer	5–6	anytime
Chrysogonum virginianum	dry	—	late winter	gh or cf	8–10 wks	spring–fall	4–6	fall
Mertensia virginica	siuc	—	siuc–spring	outdoor seedbed	3 yrs	—	—	late spring
Viola pedata	siuc	—	siuc–spring	outdoor in container	1 yr	late spring	3–4	late winter
Trillium grandiflorum	siuc	—	siuc summer	shaded outdoor seedbed	3–4 yrs	—	—	summer
Aquilegia canadensis	dry	stratify 3–4 weeks	late winter	gh or cf	6–7 wks	—	—	fall
Tiarella cordifolia	dry	—	late winter	gh or cf	12–14 wks	—	—	fall
Dicentra eximia	siuc	—	siuc spring–fall	shaded outdoor seedbed	1 yr	—	—	fall
Iris cristata	siuc	—	siuc summer	outdoor seedbed	1–2 yrs	—	—	fall
Phacelia bipinnatifida	dry	—	late winter	gh or cf	8–10 wks	—	—	—
Amsonia tabernaemontana	dry	scarify and soak overnight in H$_2$O	late winter	gh or cf	8–10 wks	spring	3–4	fall
Erigeron pulchellus	siuc	—	siuc late spring	outdoor seedbed	1 yr	—	—	summer
Asarum canadense	siuc	—	siuc late spring	shaded outdoor seedbed	2 yrs	summer	4–5	fall
Arisaema triphyllum	siuc	—	siuc fall	shaded outdoor seedbed	3 yrs	—	—	—
Geranium maculatum	siuc	—	siuc late spring	shaded outdoor seedbed	2 yrs	—	—	fall
Zephyranthes atamasco	dry	—	late winter	gh or cf	2–3 yrs	—	—	late summer
Sedum ternatum	dry	—	late winter	gh or cf	10–12 wks	anytime	2	anytime
Coreopsis auriculata	dry	—	late winter	gh or cf	8–10 wks	—	—	fall
Baptisia pendula	dry	soak overnight in hot H$_2$O	late winter	gh or cf	8–10 wks	—	—	fall
Diphylleia cymosa	siuc	—	siuc	shaded outdoor seedbed	2 yrs	—	—	—
Potentilla tridentata	dry	stratify for 6 weeks	late winter	gh or cf	1 yr	anytime	4–5	fall
Anisostichus capreolata	dry	—	late winter–early spring	gh or cf	1 yr	summer	4–6	anytime
Sisyrinchium angustifolium	dry	—	summer	cf or seedbed	8–10 wks	—	—	early spring
Tradescantia virginiana	siuc	—	siuc summer	outdoor seedbed	4–6 wks	spring–fall	3	fall
Heuchera americana	dry	—	early spring	gh or cf	6–8 wks	—	—	spring or fall
Penstemon smallii	siuc	—	siuc–summer	outdoor seedbed	8–10 mos	early summer	5–6	fall or early spring
Chrysanthemum leucanthemum	dry	—	late winter	gh or cf	12 wks	late spring	4–6	fall or spring

Species	Seed					Cuttings		Division
	Storage	Pretreatment	Time Sown	Location Sown	Total Production Time	Time Taken	Weeks to Potted	Time of Year
Lysimachia nummularia	siuc	—	siuc late summer	outdoor seedbed	1 yr	spring–fall	3	anytime
Thermopsis villosa	dry	soak overnight in hot H$_2$O	late winter	gh or cf	8–10 wks	—	—	fall
Oenothera tetragona	dry	—	late winter	gh or cf	8–10 wks	summer	2–3	fall
Silene virginica	dry	stratify for 3 weeks	late winter	gh or cf	8–10 wks	summer	4–5	fall
Verbascum blattaria	dry	—	late winter	gh or cf	8 wks	—	—	—
Hydrophyllum canadense	siuc	—	siuc late summer	shaded outdoor seedbed	2 yrs	—	—	fall
Opuntia compressa	siuc	—	siuc	outdoor seedbed	2 yrs	anytime	3–4	spring or fall
Rudbeckia hirta	dry	—	late winter	gh or cf	8–10 wks	—	—	late winter–early spring
Asclepias tuberosa	dry	—	late winter	gh or cf	8–10 wks	late spring	6	—
Daucus carota	dry	—	summer	outdoor seedbed	4–6 wks	—	—	—
Stokesia laevis	dry	—	late winter	gh or cf	8–10 wks	—	—	spring or fall
Achillea millefolium	dry	—	late winter	gh or cf	6–8 wks	—	—	early spring
Gaillardia pulchella	dry	—	late winter	gh or cf	8 wks	early summer	2–3	—
Monarda didyma	dry	—	winter	gh or cf	10–12 wks	summer	4–5	early spring
Echinacea purpurea	dry	stratify for 4 weeks	late winter	gh or cf	8–10 wks	—	—	fall
Campsis radicans	siuc	—	siuc–fall	outdoor seedbed	6 mos	early summer	3–4	fall
Filipendula rubra	siuc	—	siuc–summer	outdoor seedbed	1 yr	—	—	spring or fall
Ruellia caroliniensis	dry	—	late winter	gh or cf	8 wks	summer	4–5	—
Eryngium yuccifolium	siuc	—	siuc	outdoor seedbed	6–8 mos	—	—	fall
Pycnanthemum incanum	dry	—	late winter	gh or cf	14 wks	early summer	3	fall or spring
Lilium superbum	moist	stratify for 12 weeks	late winter	indoors	4–5 yrs	—	—	fall
Passiflora incarnata	siuc	—	siuc–fall	outdoor seedbed	6 mos	early summer	3–4	anytime
Rhexia mariana u. purpurea	dry	—	late winter	cf or gh	8–10 wks	summer	3–4	fall
Allium cernuum	dry	—	early summer	outdoor seedbed	1 yr	—	—	fall
Hibiscus moscheutos	dry	—	late winter	gh or cf	8–10 wks	summer	3–4	—
Eupatorium fistulosum	dry	—	late winter	gh or cf	8–10 wks	—	—	fall
Lobelia cardinalis	dry	—	late winter	gh or cf	14–16 wks	summer	4–6	fall or spring
Phlox paniculata	dry	stratify for 4 weeks	late winter	gh or cf	8–10 wks	late spring–early summer	4–5	fall
Chelone lyonii	dry	stratify for 6 weeks	winter	gh or cf	8 wks	—	4–5	spring
Clematis virginiana	dry	—	late winter	gh or cf	8 wks	spring–fall	3–4	—
Gentiana clausa	dry	—	spring	cf	1 yr	—	—	spring
Parnassia grandifolia	siuc	—	siuc fall	cf	1 yr	—	—	fall or spring
Vernonia noveboracensis	dry	—	summer	outdoor seedbed	9 mos	summer	4–5	—
Trichostema dichotomum	dry	stratify for 4 weeks	late winter–spring	gh or cf	8–10 wks	—	—	—
Helianthus tomentosus	dry	—	summer	outdoor seedbed	6–8 wks	summer	4–5	spring
Boltonia asteroides	dry	—	winter	gh or cf	10–12 wks	summer	4–5	spring
Liatris spicata	dry	—	late winter	gh or cf	1 yr	—	—	early spring
Ludwigia bonariensis	dry	—	late winter–early spring	gh or cf	6–8 wks	early summer	3	—
Kosteletskya virginica	dry	—	late winter	gh or cf	10–12 wks	summer	6	—
Bidens polylepis	dry	stratify for 4 weeks	late winter	gh or cf	10 wks	spring	1	—
Solidago rugosa	dry	—	spring	gh or cf	8–10 wks	early summer	3–4	late winter
Aster novae-angliae	dry	—	late winter	gh or cf	8–10 wks	early summer	4–5	spring
Heterotheca mariana	dry	—	late winter	gh or cf	10–12 wks	—	—	spring

key: siuc = sown immediately upon collection; gh = greenhouse; cf = cold frame.

Appendix 4. Guide to Recommended Literature

Wild Flowers

Aiken, George D. *Pioneering with Wild Flowers*. Englewood Cliffs, N.J.: Prentice-Hall, 1968. Propagation techniques and habitat descriptions for selected North American wild flowers.

Bailey, Liberty H. *The Nursery Manual*. New York: Macmillan, 1967. Propagation techniques of herbaceous and woody plants.

Birdseye, Clarence and Eleanor G. *Growing Woodland Plants*. New York: Dover, 1972. How to grow approximately two hundred eastern woodland wild flowers; how to prepare a woods garden.

Brooklyn Botanic Garden. *Gardening with Native Plants*. Plants and Gardens, vol. 18, no. l. Brooklyn: Brooklyn Botanic Garden, 1964. Native plant cultivation and propagation techniques. Literature review.

Bruce, Hal. *How to Grow Wildflowers and Wild Shrubs and Trees in Your Own Garden*. New York: Knopf, 1976. The author encourages an appreciation for plants as they occur in nature through vivid description and offers much information on how to raise them at home.

Crocket, James Underwood, and the editors of Time-Life Books. *Perennials*. Alexandria, Va.: Time-Life Encyclopedia of Gardening, 1972. Practical information on how to establish, care for, and propagate perennials and biennials. Includes an "encyclopedia" of plants, each entry with detailed instructions on how to cultivate and propagate.

Curtis, Will C. *Propagation of Wild Flowers*. Framingham, Mass.: New England Wild Flower Society. Basic propagation techniques, specific treatments for selected species.

Everett, Thomas H. *The New York Botanical Garden Illustrated Encyclopedia of Horticulture*. 10 vols. New York: Garland, 1980. A comprehensive description and evaluation of horticulture as it is practiced in the United States and Canada. Emphasis on the "how-to" aspects of gardening. Considerable information on eastern wild flowers.

Foster, H. Lincoln. *Rock Gardening*. New York: Crown, 1968. How to create a rock garden; includes information on how to cultivate and propagate many wild flowers.

Free, Montague. *Plant Propagation in Pictures*. Garden City, N.Y.: American Garden Guild, and Doubleday, 1957. Excellent nontechnical guide to increasing plants at home.

Hartmann, Hudson T., and Dale E. Kester. *Plant Propagation Principles and Practices*. 3rd edition. Englewood Cliffs, N.J.: Prentice-Hall, 1975. Standard technical reference covering all aspects of propagation.

Hebb, Robert S. *Low Maintenance Perennials*. New York: Quadrangle, 1975. Includes some wild flowers and many hardy named varieties and how to care for them.

Hunt, William Lanier. *Southern Gardens, Southern Gardening*. Durham, N.C.: Duke University Press, 1982. A historical and highly informative look at gardening in the southern states; arranged by months, the book includes practical propagation and cultivation techniques for many native plants; covers 150 topics.

Janick, Jules. *Horticultural Science*. San Francisco: W. H. Freeman, 1972. Technical reference covering many aspects of horticulture.

Justice, William S., and C. Ritchie Bell. *Wild Flowers of North Carolina*. Chapel Hill: University of North Carolina Press, 1968. Nontechnical identification of selected wild flowers, trees, shrubs, and vines of North Carolina and surrounding areas; 400 color photographs.

Kaufman, Peter B.; T. Lawrence Mellichamp; Janice Glimn-Lacy; and J. Donald Lacroix. *Practical Botany*. Reston, Va.: Reston, 1983. Botany and its relation to horticulture; useful chapters on soils, cloning plants, landscaping, pest control, and growing plants in controlled environments.

Niering, William A., and Nancy C. Olmstead, *Field Guide to North American Wildflowers*. Audubon Society. New York: Knopf, 1979. Nontechnical identification guide featuring colored photographs; includes description, habitat, and range.

North Carolina Wild Flower Preservation Society. *North Carolina Native Plant Propagation Handbook*. Chapel Hill: n.p., 1977. A practical guide for propagation and cultivation of selected eastern wild flowers based on experiences of society members.

Penn, Cordelia. *Landscaping with Native Plants.* Winston-Salem: Blair, 1982. Includes helpful checklists covering the habitat and range for selected eastern wild flowers of woodland and field as well as for recommended native trees, shrubs, and vines. Plot plans for country and suburban lots.

Peterson, R. T., and M. McKenny. *A Field Guide to Wildflowers.* Boston: Houghton Mifflin, 1968. Peterson Field Guide Series. Nontechnical identification guide to northeastern and north central U.S. wild flowers; drawings, descriptions, and ranges.

Radford, A. E., H. E. Ahles, and C. R. Bell. *Manual of the Vascular Flora of the Carolinas.* Chapel Hill: University of North Carolina Press, 1968. Technical reference with keys and taxonomic descriptions of ferns, fern allies, and flowering species native to North and South Carolina.

Rickett, Harold William. *Botany for Gardeners.* New York: Macmillan, 1957. The principles of botany applied to gardening.

————. *Wild Flowers of the United States: The Southeastern States.* Vol. 2. New York: McGraw-Hill, 1967. Color photographs, descriptions, ranges, habitats, general blooming dates.

Rock, Harold W. *Prairie Propagation Handbook.* 6th edition. Hales Corners, Wis.: Wehr Nature Center, 1981. Suggested propagation methods and seed harvest dates for prairie species, many of which occur in the eastern United States.

Steffek, Edwin F. *The New Wild Flowers and How to Grow Them.* Portland, Ore.: Timber Press, 1983. Enlarged edition of a standard wild flower propagation reference. Over 560 plants included.

Taylor, Kathryn S., and Stephen F. Hamblin. *Handbook of Wild Flower Cultivation.* New York: Macmillan, 1963. Treats eastern wild flowers and features lists of plants by cultural requirements.

Wells, B. W. *The Natural Gardens of North Carolina.* Chapel Hill: University of North Carolina Press, 1967 (orig. pub. 1933). General description of vegetation types, keys by flower color, emphasis on understanding relation of plant to its habitat.

Wilson, Helen Van Pelt. *Perennials Preferred.* New York: M. Barrows, 1945. How to build a perennial border; descriptive accounts of perennials for each season; cultural indexes.

Wilson, William H. W. *Landscaping with Wild-Flowers and Native Plants.* San Francisco: Ortho Books, 1984. How to design and plant native plant gardens; sources of native plants and seed. How to propagate native plants.

Woodward, Carol H., and Harold William Rickett. *Common Wild Flowers of the Northeastern United States.* Woodbury, N.Y.: Barron's, 1979. Color photographs and descriptions of wild flowers found within 50 miles of New York City.

Yepsen, Roger B., Jr. *Organic Plant Protection.* Emmaus, Pa.: Rodale, 1976. Comprehensive reference on controlling insects and diseases in the garden.

Carnivorous Plants

Lerner, Carol. *Pitcher Plants: The Elegant Insect Traps.* New York: Morrow, 1983. Author-illustrator Carol Lerner examines many of the fascinating aspects of Pitcher Plants in this well-illustrated book.

Pietropaola, James and Patricia. *The World of Carnivorous Plants.* Shortsville, N.Y.: R. J. Stoneridge, 1974. Good cultural information.

Schnell, Donald E. *Carnivorous Plants of the United States and Canada.* Winston-Salem, N.C.: Blair, 1976. The standard reference for North American carnivorous plants. Useful range maps. Good information on growing carnivorous plants.

Slack, Adrian. *Carnivorous Plants.* Cambridge: MIT Press, 1980. Discusses carnivorous plants throughout the world. Beautiful photographs.

The *Carnivorous Plant Newsletter* is the quarterly publication of the International Carnivorous Plant Society. It contains articles, reviews, cultural information, and plant sources and offers a seed exchange for members.

Ferns

Brooklyn Botanic Garden. *Handbook of Ferns.* Special printing of Plants and Gardens, vol. 25, no. 1, #59. Brooklyn, N.Y.: Brooklyn Botanic Garden, 1983. Collection of articles on growing and using northeastern and exotic ferns in the home, greenhouse, and landscape.

Cobb, Boughton. *A Field Guide to the Ferns and Their Related Families.* Peterson Field Guide Series. Boston: Houghton Mifflin, 1963. Good reference for the layman; covers most eastern species.

Dean, Blanche E. *Ferns of Alabama.* Southern University Press, 1969. Describes several southern species not well treated elsewhere.

Evans, Murray. Pteridophyta in Radford et al., *Manual of the Vascular Flora of the Carolinas.* Chapel Hill: University of North Carolina Press, 1968. The only technical reference with keys and descriptions for all ferns and fern allies native to North Carolina and South Carolina.

Fernald, M. L. *Gray's Manual of Botany.* New York: American Book Company, 1950. Technical reference with keys and descriptions for vascular plants of the central and northeastern U.S. and adjacent Canada.

Foster, F. Gordon. *Ferns to Know and Grow.* New edition. Portland, Ore.: Timber Press, 1984. Excellent descriptions and cultural instructions for many species.

Gleason, Henry A., ed. *The New Britton and Brown Illustrated Flora.* Lancaster, Pa: Lancaster Press, 1952. Technical reference includes keys and descriptions for many eastern fern species.

Hallowell, Anne C., and Barbara G. Hallowell. *Fern Finder: A Guide to Native Ferns of Northeastern and Central North America.* Berkeley: Nature Study Guild, 1981. Pocket-size picture key to ferns of piedmont, mountains, and much of northeastern and central U.S.; understandable for the novice but complete enough to be useful to advanced students. Does not include coastal plain species.

Mickel, John T. *How to Know the Ferns and Fern Allies.* Dubuque, Iowa: William C. Brown, 1979. The definitive guide for North American ferns and fern allies. Keys, illustrations, descriptions, and cultural tips. Best reference available; by the curator of ferns at the New York Botanical Garden.

_____, with Evelyn Fiore. *The Home Gardener's Book of Ferns.* New York: Holt, Rinehart, and Winston, 1979. Guide to cultivation, propagation, and appreciation of ferns of the world.

Parsons, F. T. *How to Know the Ferns: A Guide to the Names, Haunts, and Habits of Our Common Ferns.* New York: Dover, 1961. Useful reference includes habitat information.

Perl, Philip. *Ferns.* Alexandria, Va.: Time-Life Encyclopedia of Gardening, 1977. Species descriptions, detailed cultural information. Thoroughly illustrated.

Shaver, Jesse M. *Ferns of the Eastern Central States with Special Reference to Tennessee.* New York: Dover, 1954. Descriptions, illustrations, and general information. Particularly useful for the lime-loving species of the South.

Wherry, Edgar T. *The Fern Guide: Northeastern and Midland United States and Adjacent Canada.* Philadelphia: Morris Arboretum/Doubleday, 1961. Useful reference for areas covered.

_____. *The Southern Fern Guide: Southeastern and South-Midland United States.* Bronx, N.Y.: New York Botanical Garden, 1961. Descriptions, illustrations, and cultural information for southern species.

The *American Fern Journal* is a quarterly technical publication of research on pteridophytes. The *Fiddlehead Forum* is a bimonthly newsletter which includes information for the fern grower and fancier as well as for botanists. Both are sent to members of the American Fern Society.

Glossary and Plant Physiology

Achene. A small, hard, dry, thin-walled, one-seeded, indehiscent fruit.

Acuminate. Tapering to a point.

Annual. A plant whose life cycle is completed in one year.

Anther. The part of the stamen that produces pollen.

Anthesis. The time of flowering.

Areole. A small pit or cavity.

Aril. An enlarged outgrowth on the seed.

Auriculate. Shaped like an ear.

Awn. A bristly appendage on some plants.

Axil. The angle formed between a stem and the upper surface of a leaf.

Axis. The stem of a plant.

Basal. Growing from the base of a stem.

Biennial. A plant whose life cycle is completed in two years or seasons.

Bipinnate. With multiple leaflets arranged in a featherlike manner on opposite sides of the stalk.

Bract. A reduced leaf, particularly one subtending a flower, or inflorescence, as the involucral bracts in the Aster family.

Bulb. A short underground stem surrounded by fleshy leaves or scales.

Calyx. The outer part of a flower, the sepals, usually green.

Carpel. One member of a compound pistil; a simple pistil.

Cauline. Growing on the stem.

Compound. Composed of two or more similar parts; used especially of leaves.

Corm. A bulblike, underground, reproductive structure.

Corolla. The petals of a flower, usually colored.

Corymb. A flat-topped, indeterminate inflorescence, the outer flowers opening first.

Cyme. A broad, determinate inflorescence, the central flowers opening first.

Deadhead. To remove the blooms after flowering.

Dehisce. To split apart and discharge seeds.

Dentate. Having toothlike projections.

Elaiosome. A fleshy, protein-rich "food patch" on some seeds or fruits that is attractive to ants and thus aids dispersal.

Ellipsoidal. Widest at or about the middle; margins are symmetrically curved, being narrowed to relatively rounded ends.

Epicalyx. A whorl of bracts outside the calyx.

Follicle. A dry, single-celled, many-seeded fruit that dehisces along a single suture.

Frond. The leaf of a fern, usually having many divisions.

Fruit. The mature ovary of a seed plant.

Germinate. To sprout.

Globose. Globe-shaped.

Glochid. A barbed hair or bristle.

Herbaceous. Having little or no woody tissue.

Indehiscent. Remaining closed at maturity.

Inflorescence. The flowering part of a plant.

Involucre. A collection of bracts surrounding a single flower or collection of flowers.

Lanceolate. Wider at the base, longer than wide, shaped like a lance, and tapering to a point.

Leaflet. One of the divisions of a compound leaf; also a small or young leaf.

Legume. A dry, single-celled fruit which dehisces along two sutures.

Locule. Compartment or cavity of an ovary, anther, or fruit.

Mericarp. The individual separated carpel of a schizocarp; resembling an achene.

Midrib. The central vein of a leaf.

Naturalize. To cause a plant to become established as if native.

Nutlet. A small nut or hard mericarp.

Oblanceolate. Inversely lanceolate.

Offset. A short sideshoot arising from the base of a plant; also a small bulb arising from the base of another bulb.

Ovate. Egg-shaped.

Palmate. Shaped like a hand with spread fingers.

Panicle. An inflorescence, the flowers growing in branching clusters.

Pappus. An appendage of the ovary which functions in dispersal of the fruit.

Pedicel. A plant stalk supporting a flower or fruit.

Peduncle. The stalk of a flower or cluster of flowers.

Perennial. A plant whose life cycle lasts for three or more seasons.

Petaloid. Like a petal, and usually showy.

Petiole. The stem supporting a leaf blade.

Phyllary. One of the bracts under the flower head of a plant, especially in Asteraceae.

Pinnate. With single leaflets arranged in a featherlike manner on opposite sides of the stalk.

Pistil. The female reproductive parts of a flower; the stigma, style, and ovary collectively.

Pollen. The microspore grains of a seed plant, usually appearing as a fine dust.

Pollination. The transfer of pollen from the anther of the stamen to the stigma of the pistil.

Raceme. An elongated, indeterminate inflorescence, the flowers opening in succession toward the apex.

Receptacle. The apex of the floral stalk bearing flowers.

Reniform. Kidney-shaped.

Rhizome. A horizontal, underground stem, usually rooting at the nodes; different from a true root in that it bears buds, nodes, and even scalelike leaves.

Rosette. A cluster of leaves radiating from a central point, usually close to the earth.

Salverform. Having a slender tube which expands abruptly.

Scape. The leafless stem of a flower.

Schizocarp. A fruit that splits between carpels into one-seeded portions.

Sepal. The outer, sterile, leaflike parts of a flower.

Sessile. Having no stalk.

Simple. Composed of a single part; having no subdivisions.

Spadix. A floral spike with a fleshy axis, usually enclosed in a spathe.

Spathe. A sheathing bract or leaf enclosing an inflorescence, especially a spadix.

Stamen. The pollen-bearing organ of a seed plant.

Stigma. The part of the pistil that receives the pollen.

Stolon. A horizontal branch from the base of a plant; a runner.

Stratify. To store seeds by placing them in layers of moisture-holding media.

Sucker. A shoot from the root or lower part of a stem.

Suture. A seam or line of dehiscence, as on a fruit.

Trifoliate. Having three leaves.

Tuber. A fleshy, enlarged portion of a rhizome or stolon having only vestigial scales.

Umbel. An inflorescence with pedicels or peduncles, or both, arising from a common point.

Urceolate. Urn-shaped.

Valves. The units into which a capsule divides when dehiscing.

Venation. The arrangement or system of veins.

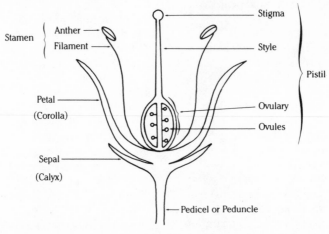

A diagrammatic section showing the parts of a typical flower

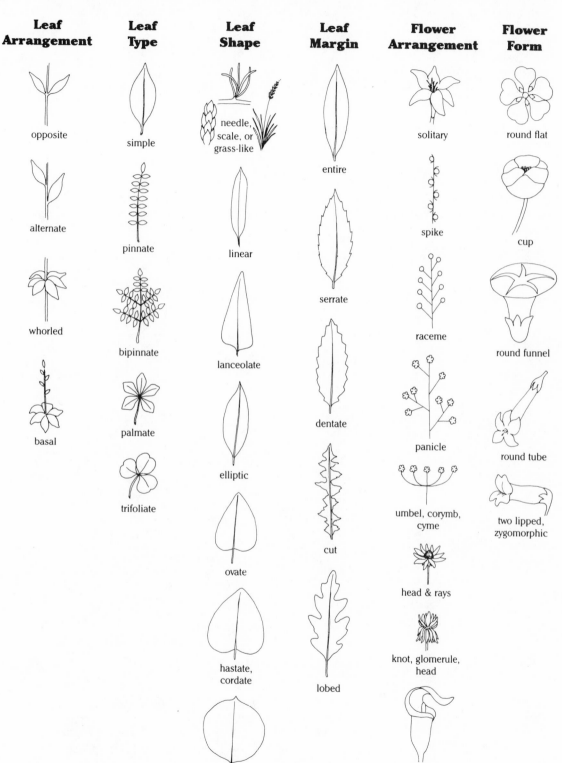

Leaf Arrangement
opposite
alternate
whorled
basal

Leaf Type
simple
pinnate
bipinnate
palmate
trifoliate

Leaf Shape
needle, scale, or grass-like
linear
lanceolate
elliptic
ovate
hastate, cordate
round

Leaf Margin
entire
serrate
dentate
cut
lobed

Flower Arrangement
solitary
spike
raceme
panicle
umbel, corymb, cyme
head & rays
knot, glomerule, head
spathe

Flower Form
round flat
cup
round funnel
round tube
two lipped, zygomorphic

Index

Page references in bold type indicate principal discussion of species.